COMPARING LAW

The enterprise of comparative law is familiar, yet its conceptual whereabouts remain somewhat obscure. *Comparing Law: Comparative Law as Reconstruction of Collective Commitments* reconstructs comparative law scholarship into a systematic account of comparative law as an autonomous academic discipline. The point of that discipline is neither to harmonize world law, nor to emphasize its cultural diversity, but rather to understand each legal system on its own terms. As the proposed reconstruction exercise involves bridging comparative law and contemporary legal theory, it shows how comparative law and legal theory both stand to benefit from being exposed to the other. At a time when many courses are adding a transnational perspective, Valcke offers a more theoretical, broadened and refreshed view of comparative law.

Professor Valcke is Full Professor, Faculty of Law at the University of Toronto. She has taught, lectured and published on comparative law, comparative law theory and legal theory worldwide, including in such journals as *Nomos*, *The American Journal of Comparative Law*, *Harvard Journal of Law and Public Policy*, *Yale Journal of International Law*, *European Review of Private Law* and *Canadian Journal of Law and Jurisprudence*. Her work on English and French contract law, in particular, was recently cited as 'illuminating' by the British House of Lords. An elected member of the International Academy of Comparative Law, she has acted as National Reporter for Canada to the Congress of the Academy.

ASCL STUDIES IN COMPARATIVE LAW

ASCL *Studies in Comparative Law* is designed to broaden theoretical and practical knowledge of the world's many legal systems. With more than sixty years' experience, the American Society of Comparative Law have been leaders in the study and analysis of comparative law. By promoting the investigation of legal problems in a comparative light, whether theoretical or empirical, as essential to the advancement of legal science, they provide an essential service to legal practitioners and those seeking reform of the law. This book series will extend these aims to the publication of monographs and comparative studies of specific legal problems.

The series has two general editors. Mortimer Sellers is Regents Professor of the University System of Maryland and Director of the Baltimore Center for International and Comparative Law. He is an Associate Member of the International Academy of Comparative Law. Vivian Curran is Distinguished Professor of Law at the University of Pittsburgh School of Law.

Comparing Law

COMPARATIVE LAW AS RECONSTRUCTION OF COLLECTIVE COMMITMENTS

CATHERINE VALCKE

University of Toronto

CAMBRIDGE
UNIVERSITY PRESS

CAMBRIDGE
UNIVERSITY PRESS

University Printing House, Cambridge CB2 8BS, United Kingdom

One Liberty Plaza, 20th Floor, New York, NY 10006, USA

477 Williamstown Road, Port Melbourne, VIC 3207, Australia

314–321, 3rd Floor, Plot 3, Splendor Forum, Jasola District Centre, New Delhi – 110025, India

79 Anson Road, #06-04/06, Singapore 079906

Cambridge University Press is part of the University of Cambridge.

It furthers the University's mission by disseminating knowledge in the pursuit of education, learning, and research at the highest international levels of excellence.

www.cambridge.org
Information on this title: www.cambridge.org/9781108470063
DOI: 10.1017/9781108555852

First published 2018

Printed in the United States of America by Sheridan Books, Inc.

A catalogue record for this publication is available from the British Library.

Library of Congress Cataloging-in-Publication Data

NAMES: Valcke, Catherine, author.
TITLE: Comparing law : comparative law as reconstruction of collective
    commitments / Catherine Valcke, University of Toronto.
DESCRIPTION: Cambridge [UK] ; New York, NY : Cambridge University Press,
    [2018] | Includes bibliographical references and index.
IDENTIFIERS: LCCN 2018012841 | ISBN 9781108470063 (hardback : alk. paper) |
    ISBN 9781108455176 (pbk. : alk. paper)
SUBJECTS: LCSH: Comparative law.
CLASSIFICATION: LCC K583 .V35 2018 | DDC 340/.2 — dc23 LC record available at
    https://lccn.loc.gov/2018012841

ISBN 978-1-108-47006-3 Hardback
ISBN 978-1-108-45517-6 Paperback

Pour Charlotte, Matthew, Benjamin et Arthur

Contents

Acknowledgements

This book is the product of long years of reflection fuelled by the insightful work of many fellow comparative lawyers. Prominent among them are Léontin-Jean Constantinesco, Helge Dedek, William Ewald, Patrick Glenn, Jacco Husa, Mitchel Lasser, Robert Leckey, Pierre Legrand, Ralf Michaels, Étienne Picard, Adrian Popovici, Geoffrey Samuel, William Twining, Mark Van Hoecke and James Whitman.

Several sections began as journal articles or chapters in edited collections. Chapters 1 and 2 rework and expand on material from Comparative Law as Comparative Jurisprudence: The Comparability of Legal Systems, which appeared in 52 *American Journal of Comparative Law* (2004). Chapter 3 draws on Le système de droit en droit comparé : Réflexions sur l'épistémologie d'une définition, published in *Comparer les droits, résolument* (Pierre Legrand, ed., 2009). Some of the ideas advanced in Comparative Law and Legal Diversity: Theorising about the Edges of Law V *Transnational Legal Theory* (2014), coauthored with Matthew Grellette, are revisited in Chapter 4, the second section of which substantially reprints Legal Traditions or Legal Systems? in *Sustainable Diversity in Law. Essays in Memory of H. Patrick Glenn* (Helge Dedek and William Twining, eds., forthcoming 2018). Finally, Chapter 5 reworks material that appeared in both Three Functions of Function in Comparative Law (*The Method and Culture of Comparative Law: Essays in Honour of Mark Van Hoecke* (Maurice Adams and Dirk Heirbaut, eds., 2014)), coauthored with Matthew Grellette, and Reflections on Comparative Law Methodology: Getting Inside Contract Law (*Practice and Theory in Comparative Law* (Maurice Adams and Jacco Bomhoff, eds., 2012)).

Heartfelt thanks go to the many friends and colleagues who kindly reviewed preliminary chapter drafts – Jacco Bomhoff, Alan Brudner, Bruce Chapman, Abraham

Drassinower, David Dyzenhaus, Pierre Gorisse, Matthew Grellette, Karen Knop, Charlotte Lemieux, Ralf Michaels, Arthur Ripstein, Fred Schauer, Arnold Weinrib and the two anonymous Cambridge University Press external reviewers – as well as to my University of Toronto colleagues who attended the Faculty Workshops at which I presented some of this work. Their comments proved invaluable for polishing, adjusting, revisiting or altogether scrapping some of my thoughts; their generosity, exacting intellectual standards and all around sage advice testified yet again to the exceptionally collegial and invigorating quality of the professional environment in which I have had the privilege to evolve since my first days as an academic.

I am also grateful to Maurice Adams, Jacco Bomhoff, Dirk Heirbaut, Jorge Fabra and Maksymillian Del Mar for giving me the opportunity to present preliminary work at conferences and workshops skillfully organized by them in exotic venues. I also owe a debt of gratitude to Haley Goldfarb, Stefan Jovic, Maryam Shahid and Sinziana Tugulea for their diligent research assistance, and to Sergey Lobachev for his highly professional indexing. The research and writing of this book were greatly facilitated by the collegial and highly effective institutional support of the University of Toronto Faculty of Law. The unrelenting support of my past and present deans Robert Sharpe, Ron Daniels, Mayo Moran and Edward Iacobucci, the quiet responsiveness and sustained efficiency of Sufei Xu and the other members of our library personnel, and the patient technical assistance of May Seto, were invaluable; as was the financial assistance of the Social Sciences and Humanities Research Council of Canada. My thanks also to the owners and staff of the EM Café and Starbucks Monkland in Montreal, who cheerfully welcomed my laptopping presence for months on end for little more than just one teabag sale daily. Finally, I want to thank John Berger and the members of the CUP boards for believing in the project, and Danielle Menz, Catherine Smith and Llinos Edwards for seeing it through.

My biggest of all debts however are to Charlotte, Matthew, Benjamin and Arthur, who made it so hard yet also profoundly worth it.

Prologue

The 'Malaise' of Comparative Law

The enterprise of comparative law is familiar yet its conceptual whereabouts remain somewhat obscure. The purpose of this book is to reconstruct extant comparative law scholarship into a systematic account of comparative law as an autonomous academic discipline. The object of that discipline is neither to harmonize world law, nor to emphasize its cultural diversity, two opposite aims often advanced for comparative law, but to understand each legal system on its own terms. The specificity of each system indeed is uniquely elucidated in and through its contrast with the others. Moreover, the reconstruction exercise proposed involves bridging comparative law and contemporary legal theory insofar as it makes explicit fundamental assumptions about the nature of law that are currently implicit in comparative law scholarship. As such, it would also serve to show how comparative law and legal theory both stand to benefit from being exposed to the other.

The historical and abiding importance of comparative legal studies is well established.[1] For as long as there have been states, judges and legislators have looked to the law of other states for inspiration in the making and application of their own law. Comparative law has also played a central role in the harmonization

---

[1] An elaborate typology of the various historical and contemporary uses of comparative law can be found in Günter Frankenberg, Critical Comparisons: Re-thinking Comparative Law, 26 HARV. INT'L L. J. 411 (1985). See also: Rudolf B. Schlesinger, The Past and Future of Comparative Law, 43 AM. J. COMP. L. 477 (1995); MICHAEL BOGDAN, COMPARATIVE LAW 18 (1994); Ferdinand F. Stone, The End to Be Served by Comparative Law, 25 TUL. L. REV. 325 (1951); George A. Bermann, The Discipline of Comparative Law in the United States, 51 REVUE INTERNATIONALE DE DROIT COMPARÉ [R. I. D. C.] 1041, 1042 (1999) (Fr.); Hein Kötz, Comparative Law in Germany Today, 51 R. I. D. C. 753, 761–66 (1999); David J. Gerber, System Dynamics: Toward a Language of Comparative Law, 46 AM. J. COMP. L. 719, 720–21 (1998); Mathias Reimann, The Progress and Failure of Comparative Law in the Second Half of the Twentieth Century, 50 AM. J. COMP. L. 671 (2002); MATHIAS SIEMS, COMPARATIVE LAW 2–5 (2014); COMPARING COMPARATIVE LAW (Samantha Besson et al. eds., 2017).

and unification of domestic law within federated states, as well as between states involved in punctual or long-term cross-border joint ventures. The contribution of comparative law at the international level has been similarly significant. As private international law seeks to coordinate the domestic law of the world's nations or trans-national law more generally, it cannot but involve heavy doses of comparative legal knowledge. As for public international law, it has always tapped more or less directly into "the law of the civilized nations."[2] On the academic front, comparative law has long been drawn upon for the purpose of supporting or refuting philosophical, economic, sociological, anthropological and other theories about law,[3] as it indeed offers an invaluable "reservoir of institutional alternatives not merely theoretical but actually tested by legal history."[4]

The interest in comparative law moreover has risen to unprecedented levels over the last decades.[5] The dramatic increase in cross-border activity attending the rise of globalization has led to the creation of a plethora of transnational institutions and partnerships that are both the outcome and the source of considerable comparative legal work, in fields as diverse as trade, finance, crime control, civil responsibility, human rights, environmental protection and intellectual property. Countless comparative legal studies have been produced in the context of such historic political events as German reunification and European unification, as well as in connection with the numerous development initiatives led by the World Bank. Comparative law scholars have likewise been central players in the latest waves of constitutional,

---

[2]   Statute of the International Court of Justice, June 26, 1945, art. 38 (1)(c), 59 Stat. 1055, T.S. No. 993, reprinted in 3 Bevans 1179.

[3]   In legal philosophy, similarities and differences in the world's legal systems have respectively been advanced as evidence for (e.g. James Gordley, Is Comparative Law a Distinct Discipline?, 46 AM. J. COMP. L. 607 (1998); TOWARDS UNIVERSAL LAW – TRENDS IN NATIONAL EUROPEAN AND INTERNATIONAL LAWMAKING (Nils Jareborg ed., 1995); R. SALEILLES, CONCEPTION ET OBJET DE LA SCIENCE JURIDIQUE DU DROIT COMPARÉ, 173, vol. I (1905–07); GIORGIO DEL VECCHIO, HUMANITÉ ET UNITÉ DU DROIT: ESSAIS DE PHILOSOPHIE JURIDIQUE (1963)) and against (e.g. Nora V. Demleitner, Combating Legal Ethnocentrism: Comparative Law Sets Boundaries, 31 ARIZ. ST. L. J. 737 (1999); Vivian Grosswald Curran, Dealing in Difference: Comparative Law's Potential for Broadening Legal Perspectives, 46 AM. J. COMP. L. 657, 661, 663, 666–67 (1998); Richard L. Abel, Law as Lag: Inertia as a Social Theory of Law, 80 MICH. L. REV. 785 (1982)) universalistic theories about the nature of law.

[4]   UGO MATTEI, COMPARATIVE LAW AND ECONOMICS ix (1997).

[5]   GLOBAL MODERNITIES (Mike Featherstone, Scott Lash & Roland Robertson eds., 1995); VOLKMAR GESSNER & ALI CEM BUDAK, EMERGING LEGAL CERTAINTY: EMPIRICAL STUDIES ON THE GLOBALIZATION OF LAW (1998); William Twining, Globalization and Comparative Law, 6 MAASTRICHT J. EUR. & COMP. L. 217 (1999); COMPARATIVE LAW IN THE 21ST CENTURY (Andrew Harding & Esin Örücü eds., 2002); Horatia Muir Watt, Globalization and Comparative Law, in THE OXFORD HANDBOOK OF COMPARATIVE LAW 579 (Mathias Reimann & Reinhard Zimmermann eds., 2006). The political importance of comparative law however may have been declining: Reinhard Zimmermann, Comparative Law and the Europeanization of Private Law, in Reimann & Zimmermann eds., ibid., 539, 577–78; Mathias Siems, The End of Comparative Law, 2 J. COMP. L. 133, 137 (2007); Ralf Michaels, Comparative Law by Numbers? Legal Origins Thesis, Doing Business Reports and the Silence of Traditional Comparative Law, 57 AM. J. COMP. L. 765, 777–78 (2009).

private law and criminal justice reforms in Asian, African and Latin American countries.

Recent trends in legal education confirm the rising prominence of comparative law in all aspects of domestic, transnational and international legal reform.[6] Whereas the law school curriculum traditionally contained nothing but domestic law courses, foreign and comparative law offerings are now standard fare. Even domestic law courses, moreover, are commonly being taught from a comparative perspective. Transnational student and faculty recruitment and exchanges are proliferating rapidly, as are comparative and foreign law mooting, journals and internships; most faculty research, regardless of the field, now draws on foreign law to some extent.

The voluminous comparative law literature accumulated to date however remains highly fragmented, and its theoretical foundations and overall scholarly purpose(s) at times difficult to ascertain. A cursory examination of that literature confirms that the issues for investigation, the jurisdictions and representative materials identified, and the comparison criteria are often selected haphazardly or based on factors of convenience (linguistic abilities, availability of documents, domains of expertise, etc.), fuelling enduring questions as to the scientific value of the whole enterprise.[7] The very status of comparative law as an academic discipline indeed is periodically called into question.[8] In particular, it has been said that comparative law scholarship

---

[6]   See generally: Catherine Valcke, Global Law Teaching, 54 J. LEG. EDUC. 160 (2004); THE LAW SCHOOL – GLOBAL ISSUES, LOCAL QUESTIONS (Fiona Cownie ed., 1999); Mary C. Daly, The Ethical Implications of the Globalization of the Legal Profession: A Challenge to the Teaching of Professional Responsibility in the Twenty-First Century, 21 FORDHAM INT'L L. J. 1239 (1998); ANTHONY O'DONNELL & RICHARD JOHNSTONE, DEVELOPING A CROSS-CULTURAL LAW CURRICULUM (1997); Alberto Bernabe-Riefkohl, Tomorrow's Law Schools: Globalization and Legal Education, 32 SAN DIEGO L. REV. 137 (1995).

[7]   Jaro Mayda, Some Critical Reflections on Contemporary Comparative Law, 39 *Revista Jurídica de la Universidad de Puerto Rico* 431 (1970); ALAN WATSON, LEGAL TRANSPLANTS: AN APPROACH TO COMPARATIVE LAW, 10–16 (2nd ed. 1993); William Ewald, Comparative Jurisprudence (I): What Was It Like to Try a Rat?, 143 U. PA. L. REV. 1898, 1961–90 (1994–95); John Henry Merryman, Comparative Law Scholarship, 21 HASTINGS INT'L & COMP. L. REV. 771 (1998); Étienne Picard, L'état du droit comparé en France, en 1999, 4 R. I. D. C. 885, 888–89 (1999); Bermann, *supra* note 1, at 1044 ("virtually all recent assessments of the discipline in the legal literature find it wanting in basic ways. Even discounting for the fact that academic literature is always more likely to bear witness to dissatisfactions than satisfactions, the assessments are conspicuously negative."); GEOFFREY SAMUEL, AN INTRODUCTION TO COMPARATIVE LAW THEORY AND METHOD 15 (2014) ("a tradition ... that can at best be described as theoretically weak and at worst startlingly trivial"). These traditional critiques admittedly may lack traction against more recent streams of comparative law scholarship as the 'legal origins' literature (surveyed in Legal Origin Symposium 57 AM. J. COMP. L. (2009)), whose analytic frameworks and overall purposes are, by all accounts, carefully articulated. Whether such recent streams might not be better slotted within comparative economics/comparative sociology than within comparative law however remains an open question.

[8]   Otta Kahn-Freund, Comparative Law as an Academic Subject, 82 L. Q. REV. 40, 41 (1966); Arthur T. Von Mehren, An Academic Tradition for Comparative Law?, 19 AM. J. COMP. L. 624 (1971); Basil Markesinis, Comparative Law – A Subject in Search of an Audience, 53 MOD. L. REV. 1 (1990); Nora V. Demleitner, Challenge, Opportunity and Risk: An Era of Change in Comparative Law, 46

is bereft of the usual hallmarks of a discipline proper, viz. some measure of consensus on analytic premises and overall direction, a somewhat constant and transparent methodology, a pool of problems, designated criteria and parameters with which to test hypotheses and control for scholarship quality, etc. As a discipline, comparative law hence would in fact be deeply 'malaised':[9] far from a somewhat unified "scholarly tradition susceptible of transmission to succeeding generations" and a "shared foundation on which each can build,"[10] it would amount to no more than "a chance to satisfy idle curiosity,"[11] the product of "a blind eye to everything but surfaces,"[12] on par with "stamp collecting, accounting, and baseball statistic hoarding."[13]

Reactions to this indictment vary widely. Some have seen in it a welcome impetus for fresh and broadened reflection on the object and nature of comparative law, in time leading to the elaboration of new conceptual foundations, if not a shift towards altogether new directions.[14] In that spirit, a wave of literature has emerged which offers theoretical reflections on the main process issues facing comparative lawyers, viz. whether to compare entire legal systems ('macro comparisons') or only some of their components ('micro comparisons'); whether to focus on cross-jurisdictional similarities or differences; what legal materials to investigate in each jurisdiction and from what perspective; how to delineate and select relevant legal systems; and so on.[15] A few scholars have even undertaken to construct more systematic models

---

AM. *J.* OF COMP. *L.* 647 (1998); Reimann, *supra* note 1; Gordley, *supra* note 3; SIEMS, *supra* note 1, at 5–6; SAMUEL, *supra* note 7, at 8–10; JAAKKO HUSA, A NEW INTRODUCTION TO COMPARATIVE LAW 1–2 (2015); GÜNTER FRANKENBERG, COMPARATIVE LAW AS CRITIQUE 9–13 (2016) (questioning the notion of 'discipline' altogether).

[9] Frankenberg, *supra* note 1, at 624ff; WATSON, *supra* note 7; Ewald, *supra* note 7; Vivian Grosswald Curran, Law and the Legal Origins Thesis: "[N]on scholae sed vitae discimus", 57 AM. *J.* COMP. *L.* 863 (2009) (referring to comparative law's "existential angst", at 863); Harding & Örücü, *supra* note 5, at xii ("a sense of mid-life crisis").

[10] Von Mehren, *supra* note 8, at 624.

[11] Walter J. Kamba, Comparative Law: A Theoretical Framework, 23 INT'L & COMP. *L. Q.* 485, 489 (1974).

[12] Lawrence M. Friedman, Some Thoughts on Comparative Legal Culture, *in* COMPARATIVE AND PRIVATE INTERNATIONAL LAW: ESSAYS IN HONOR OF JOHN HENRY MERRYMAN ON HIS SEVENTIETH BIRTHDAY 49 (John Henry Merryman & David S. Clark eds., 1990).

[13] Ewald, *supra* note 7, at 1961.

[14] E.g.: Hubert Izdebski, Le rôle du droit dans les sociétés contemporaines: essai d'une approche sociologique du droit comparé, 3 R. I. D. C. 563 (1988); Jonathan Hill, Comparative Law, Law Reform and Legal Theory, 9 OXF. *J.* LEG. STUD. 101 (1989); Pierre Legrand, Comparative Legal Studies and Commitment to Theory, 58 MOD. *L.* REV. 262 (1995); Geoffrey Samuel, Comparative Law and Jurisprudence, 47 INT. & COMP. *L.* QUART. 817 (1998); Mark Van Hoecke & Mark Warrington, Legal Cultures, Legal Paradigms and Legal Doctrine: Towards a New Model for Comparative Law, 47 INT'L & COMP. *L. Q.* 495, 495–97 (1998); Twining, *supra* note 5, at 217; Lawrence Rosen, Beyond Compare, *in* COMPARATIVE LEGAL STUDIES: TRADITIONS AND TRANSITIONS 493 (Pierre Legrand & Roderick Munday eds., 2003); Mark Van Hoecke, Deep Level Comparative Law, *in* EPISTEMOLOGY AND METHODOLOGY OF COMPARATIVE LAW 65 (Mark Van Hoecke ed., 2004); Annelise Riles, Comparative Law and Socio-Legal Studies, in Reimann & Zimmermann eds., *supra* note 5, 775; Frankenberg, *supra* note 1.

[15] E.g.: SAMUEL, *supra* note 7; Harding & Örücü, *supra* note 5; Legrand & Munday, *supra* note 14; THEMES IN COMPARATIVE LAW (Peter Birks & Arianna Pretto eds., 2004); EPISTEMOLOGY AND METHODOLOGY OF COMPARATIVE LAW (Mark Van Hoecke ed., 2004); Reimann & Zimmermann eds., *supra* note 5;

for comparative law – 'legal transplants,'[16] 'legal formants,'[17] 'comparative jurisprudence,'[18] 'legal cultures'[19] – based on their respective conceptions of its ultimate purpose. Importantly, while these scholars obviously disagree as to said purpose, they
are all agreed that comparative law must be redesigned from the top down – from
a priori reflection on what comparative law *should* look like, come what may of the
existing stock of scholarship.[20]

Others are much less concerned by the malaise indictment. In their view, the
fragmentation and apparent theoretical randomness of extant scholarship only
serves to confirm what should have been suspected all along, namely, that comparative law never was, or even aspired to be, a discipline proper, structured around a

---

COMPARER LES DROITS, RÉSOLUMENT (Pierre Legrand ed., 2009); THEORISING THE GLOBAL LEGAL ORDER
(Andrew Halpin & Volker Roeben eds., 2009); PRACTICE AND THEORY IN COMPARATIVE LAW (Maurice
Adams & Jacco Bomhoff eds., 2012); METHODOLOGIES OF LEGAL RESEARCH: WHICH KIND OF METHOD
FOR WHAT KIND OF DISCIPLINE? (Mark Van Hoecke ed., 2011); METHODS OF COMPARATIVE LAW (Pier
Giuseppe Monateri ed., 2012).

[16] WATSON, *supra* note 7 (comparative law as legal history, aimed at tracking the evolution of legal rules
across time and territory). For critical discussions: William B. Ewald, The American Revolution and
the Evolution of Law, 42 AM. J. COMP. L. SUPP. 1701 (1994); Pierre Legrand, The Impossibility of
'Legal Transplants', 4 MAASTRICHT J. EUR. & COMP. L. 111 (1997); Yves Dezalay & Bryant Garth, The
Import and Export of Law and Legal Institutions: International Strategies in National Palace Wars, *in*
ADAPTING LEGAL CULTURES 241 (David Nelken & Johannes Feest eds., 2001); William Twining, Social
Science and Diffusion of Law, 32 J. L. & SOC. 203 (2005); JEDIDIAH J. KRONCKE, THE FUTILITY OF LAW
AND DEVELOPMENT: CHINA AND THE DANGERS OF EXPORTING AMERICAN LAW (2016).

[17] Rodolfo Sacco, Legal Formants: A Dynamic Approach to Comparative Law (Installment I of II), 39
AM. J. COMP. L. 1 (Part I), 343 (Part II) (1991) (comparative law as study in legal function, investigating
all factors causally impacting court decisions). See likewise: ERNST RABEL, THE CONFLICT OF LAWS:
A COMPARATIVE STUDY, vol. I (2nd ed. 1945). For critical discussions: Michele Graziadei, The
Functionalist Heritage, *in* Legrand & Munday eds. 100, *supra* note 14; Geoffrey Samuel, Dépasser
le fonctionalisme, *in* Legrand ed., *supra* note 15, at 409; Ralf Michaels, The Functional Method of
Comparative Law, *in* Reimann & Zimmermann eds., *supra* note 5, at 339; RICHARD HYLAND, GIFTS:
A STUDY IN COMPARATIVE LAW 63–98, 112 (2009).

[18] Ewald, *supra* note 16 (comparative law as comparison of forms of legal reasoning). For critical
discussions: James Q. Whitman, The neo-Romantic Turn, *in* Legrand & Munday eds. 312, esp. 334–
36, 343–44; James Gordley, *Comparative Law and Legal History, in* Reimann & Zimmermann eds.
753, *supra* note 5, at 765–66.

[19] PIERRE LEGRAND, FRAGMENTS ON LAW-AS-CULTURE (1999); LAWRENCE M. FRIEDMAN, THE LEGAL
SYSTEM: A SOCIAL SCIENCE PERSPECTIVE (1975); BERNHARD GROβFELD, MACHT UND OHNMACHT
DER RECHTSVERGLEICHUNG (THE STRENGTH AND WEAKNESS OF COMPARATIVE LAW) (Tony Weir trans.,
1990); COMPARATIVE LEGAL CULTURES (Csaba Varga ed., 1992); COMPARING LEGAL CULTURES (David
Nelken ed., 1997); LAWRENCE ROSEN, LAW AS CULTURE: AN INVITATION (2006); JOHN BELL, FRENCH
LEGAL CULTURES (2001); Van Hoecke & Warrington, *supra* note 14; Riles, *supra* note 14, at 796–
99; HUSA, *supra* note 8; SIEMS, *supra* note 1; FRANKENBERG, *supra* note 8; MITCHEL DE S.-O.-L'E.
LASSER, JUDICIAL DELIBERATIONS: A COMPARATIVE ANALYSIS OF JUDICIAL TRANSPARENCY AND LEGITIMACY
(2005); Sherally Munshi, *Comparative Law and Decolonizing Critique* (August 24, 2017): https://
ssrn.com/abstract=3025595. For critical discussions: William Ewald, The Jurisprudential Approach
to Comparative Law: A Field Guide to "Rats", 46 AM. J. COMP. L. 701 (1998); Alan Watson, Legal
Transplants and European Private Law, 4.4 ELECTRONIC J. COMP. L. (2000) (www.ejcl.org/44/art44-2.
html); Ruth Sefton-Green, Compare and Contrast: Monstre à deux têtes, 54 R.I.D.C. 85 (2002).

[20] E.g., Ewald, *supra* note 7, at 1975–90, esp. 1990; WATSON, *supra* note 7, at 10–16.

single overall purpose. Rather, it was always meant to be just a method – extending the scope of investigation beyond the domestic realm – that could be tailored to a variety of extraneous disciplinary purposes, be they economic, philosophical, anthropological or any other.[21] The existing scholarship would thus be not so much devoid of scholarly purpose as informed by a variety of competing purposes, none of which need be specifically legal.[22] In the view of this second group of observers, then, the real malaise lies not in the failure to find a single unifying conception for comparative law but in the persistent search for one that does not exist. And the best strategy forward in fact would be to proceed from the ground up: the multiple purposes underlying the current stock of scholarship first need to be exposed and sorted out in order for the true scientific value of that scholarship (and of comparative law as a whole) to eventually come to light.

As I see it, the malaise of comparative law, if any, boils down to a bifurcation overload. That is, on each of the process issues listed above, legal comparatists tend to divide into two camps, as if these issues indeed were either/or questions.[23] On whether to privilege macro or micro comparisons, the 'legal family'[24] treatises and more recent 'legal origins'[25] scholarship side with the first whereas the notorious 'common core'[26] projects and the 'legal transplant'[27] literature side with the second.

---

[21] HAROLD C. GUTTERIDGE, COMPARATIVE LAW: AN INTRODUCTION TO THE COMPARATIVE METHOD OF LEGAL STUDY AND RESEARCH 2 (2nd ed. 1949) ("its employment should not be hampered by confining it to specified categories"); PETER DE CRUZ, A MODERN APPROACH TO COMPARATIVE LAW 3 (1993) ("a method of study"); RUDOLF B. SCHLESINGER ET AL., COMPARATIVE LAW: CASES, TEXT, MATERIALS 2 (6th ed. 1998) ("primarily a method, a way of looking at legal problems, legal institutions, and entire legal systems"); John C. Reitz, How to Do Comparative Law, 46 AM. J. COMP. L. 617, 625 (1998) (an "appendage of social science"); William P. Alford, On the Limits of "Grand Theory" in Comparative Law, 61 WASH. L. REV. 945 (1986); Joachim Zekoll, Kant and Comparative Law—Some Reflections on a Reform Effort, 70 TUL. L. REV. 2719, 2736 (1996); Mads Andenas & Duncan Fairgrieve, Intent on Making Mischief: Seven Ways of Using Comparative Law, in Monateri ed., *supra* note 15, at 25.

[22] See the debate over whether 'comparative law' (singular) would be best renamed 'comparative legal studies' (plural): SIEMS, *supra* note 1, at 5–6; FRANKENBERG, *supra* note 8, at 11; HUSA, *supra* note 8, at 17.

[23] See Samuel's list of what he rightly describes as the 'methodological dichotomies' of the comparative law literature: SAMUEL, *supra* note 7, at 4.

[24] See generally: KONRAD ZWEIGERT & HEIN KÖTZ, AN INTRODUCTION TO COMPARATIVE LAW (Tony Weir trans., 3rd ed. 1998); Jaakko Husa, Classification of Legal Families Today – Is it Time for a Memorial Hymn?, 56 R.I.D.C. 11 (2004), esp. 14–16; LÉONTIN-JEAN CONSTANTINESCO, TRAITÉ DE DROIT COMPARÉ, vol. I, p. 154, note 161 (1972); Esin Örücü, Family Trees for Legal Systems: Towards a Contemporary Approach, Epistemology and Methodology of Comparative Law, in EPISTEMOLOGY AND METHODOLOGY OF COMPARATIVE LAW 359, 361 (Mark Van Hoecke ed., 2004); Mariana Pargendler, The Rise and Decline of Legal Families 60 AMERICAN JOURNAL OF COMPARATIVE LAW 1043 (2012).

[25] *Legal Origin Symposium, supra* note 7.

[26] E.g., INTERNATIONAL INSTITUTE FOR THE UNIFICATION OF PRIVATE LAW, THE UNIDROIT PRINCIPLES (2004); FORMATION OF CONTRACTS: A STUDY OF THE COMMON CORE OF LEGAL SYSTEMS (Rudolf B. Schlesinger & Pierre G. Bonassies eds., 1968); INTERNATIONAL ENCYCLOPEDIA OF COMPARATIVE LAW (André Tunc ed., 1983) (17 volumes covering 150 states); THE COMMON CORE OF EUROPEAN PRIVATE LAW (Mauro Bussani & Uggo Mattei eds., 2003).

[27] *Supra* note 16.

On whether to emphasize similarities or differences, the common core projects and some legal family treatises ostensibly fall under the first whereas the 'legal formants'[28] and 'legal cultures'[29] literatures resolutely align with the second. Concerning the materials for investigation, the common core projects and the legal transplant literature target the 'law in books' while the legal formants and legal cultures literatures centre on the 'law in action.' On the issue of perspective, the 'comparative jurisprudence'[30] scholarship and legal culture literature militate for an internal, participant ('expressivist,' 'hermeneutic' or 'constructivist') outlook on foreign law, in contrast with the legal transplants, legal formants and legal origins scholars, who favour an external, observer ('functionalist,' 'causal' or 'cognitivist') standpoint. Concerning the legal systems to be canvassed, any one legal transplant project typically limits itself to a small number of somewhat analogous legal systems,[31] whereas the legal culture literature and some legal family treatises reach more broadly, in fact encompassing systems that are as widely dissimilar as possible.[32] And whereas the new wave of 'legal pluralists' advocate a loose, strictly epistemic conception of legal systems, mainstream comparatists seem to want to hang on to the Westphalian, territorial conception.[33]

The bifurcation moreover persists, I would suggest, as we move from the groundwork of comparative law to the more theoretical scholarship, for the latter itself splits, as explained, into two streams respectively propounding a top-down and a bottom-up approach.[34] And zooming out further still, so as to capture the groundwork and theoretical scholarship at once, we notice that these likewise are quite neatly demarcated from one another: as legal comparatists tend to be either field workers ('doing it') or theorists ('talking about it')[35] – few are both – the groundwork typically is, as indicated, largely *a*-theoretical whereas the theoretical scholarship in contrast comes across as *strictly* theoretical, i.e. detached from any field work.

If that diagnosis of the malaise of comparative law is sound, the key to reconstructing it into an autonomous discipline arguably lies in some kind of synthesis. It indeed seems odd that legal comparatists should have to choose between

---

[28] *Supra* note 17.
[29] *Supra* note 19.
[30] *Supra* note 18.
[31] WATSON, *supra* note 7, at 5.
[32] E.g. COMPARATIVE LEGAL STUDIES IN ASIA (Penelope Nicholson & Sarah Biddulph eds., 2008).
[33] See generally: John Griffiths, What is Legal Pluralism? 24 J. LEG. PLURALISM & UNOFFICIAL LAW 1 (1986); Gunther Teubner, The Two Faces of Janus: Rethinking Legal Pluralism, 13 CARDOZO L. REV. 1443 (1992); BOAVENTURA DE SOUSA SANTOS, TOWARD A NEW COMMON SENSE (1995); BRIAN Z. TAMANAHA, A GENERAL JURISPRUDENCE OF LAW AND SOCIETY (2001); WILLIAM TWINING, GLOBALISATION AND LEGAL THEORY (2000); EMMANUEL MELISSARIS, UBIQUITOUS LAW: LEGAL THEORY AND THE SPACE FOR LEGAL PLURALISM (2009).
[34] *Supra*, text accompanying notes 20, 21 and 22.
[35] HUSA, *supra* note 8, at 18–19. Likewise: Maurice Adams & Jacco Bomhoff, Comparing Law: Practice and Theory, *in* Adams & Bomhoff eds. *supra* note 15, at 1; SAMUEL, *supra* note 7, at 19–20.

cross-system similarities and differences: insofar as these are just counterparts of one another, one would expect comparative law to attend to both. After all, the very process of comparison is possible only as between objects that are distinct *yet also* somewhat alike.[36] And it likewise is difficult to see what might prevent comparatists from engaging with the foreign 'law in books' *as well as* the foreign 'law in action,' given that each arguably shines light on the other. Similarly, one would be hard pressed to think of a comparative law project that would be best conducted *exclusively* from an internal or external perspective. With law being a practice, a rich understanding of it presumably requires looking, at least to some extent, to what the participants aim to express through it. But this does not preclude also examining its actual impact on the ground, since concerns about that impact typically motivate legal actors. What the law expresses indeed most likely is somewhat related to how it functions, and conversely. To be sure, from the moment the scope of study widens beyond just one national legal practice, an external perspective simply becomes unavoidable. Comparison presupposes the possibility of viewing the objects compared side by side, which presumably requires standing outside them all. If anything, then, comparing legal systems seems to call for some kind of a *mix* of internal and external perspectives. This in turn might suggest that the best conceptualization of such systems would correspondingly comprise a material *and* an epistemic dimension. Finally, why wouldn't investigating a small number of very similar, or a large number of very dissimilar, legal systems be *equally* legitimate comparative law projects? Could it not be that some pointed legal issues are best explored through the (micro) comparisons of otherwise similar legal systems while larger questions call for more broadly scoped (macro) comparisons? If that is the case, wouldn't any self-respecting discipline of comparative law have to offer guidance on micro and macro projects alike?

Similar remarks come to mind concerning the debate over the proper way to proceed to rebuild comparative law, moreover. While a heavy dose of the conceptual rebuilding proposed by the 'fresh start' scholars does seem both inevitable and desirable, such rebuilding could hardly proceed without any regard to what already exists. For one, an analytic framework that might account for the work produced to date as well as guide future research clearly would, all else being equal, prove superior to one that does only the latter. And whereas reflection from first principles might achieve the latter, it would likely fail to account for the existing scholarship. Conversely, a purely inductive method might work descriptively but would likely do little on a prescriptive level. Admittedly, while it is theoretically possible that what has come to be accepted as 'comparative law scholarship' in fact is, as the most virulent critics have claimed, so theoretically random as to be altogether undeserving of that label, that is unlikely. More likely, comparative lawyers have been struggling along on a somewhat instinctive basis, at times perhaps even losing track of where

---

[36] Sefton-Green, *supra* note 19.

they were going, but without for that matter running completely off course. If so, their work is bound to be of at least *some* relevance to any purported theory 'of comparative law.' In this respect, it is worth noting that whereas scholars and practitioners form distinct groups in domestic law, in comparative law (as in legal history, legal philosophy, etc.) these groups are in fact one and the same: the practice of comparative law *is* its scholarship.[37] As a result, to ignore the scholarship here would effectively amount to ignoring the only practice that exists. The deductive/inductive split running through the current debate over the reconstruction of comparative law hence seems no more warranted than the divisions pervading the comparative groundwork.[38]

This book aims to bridge these various divisions by offering a comprehensive account of comparative law that distils and merges the strengths on each of their two sides. It aims to show, in particular, that it is possible to view extant comparative law scholarship as simultaneously and coherently attending (even if only implicitly) to legal similarities *and* differences, to the 'law in books' *and* the 'law in action,' to the material *and* epistemic dimensions of legal systems, as housing narrow- *and* broad-scoped, and micro *and* macro, projects alike, as calling for a mix of internal *and* external perspectives, as speaking to both past *and* future research, etc.

Such an account first involves going back to basics and revisiting the 'law' in 'comparative law.' That is, before reflecting on the ins and outs of '*comparative* law,' it might prove useful to firm up what is here meant by 'law.'[39] Relatively little work has been done that tries to connect, in any systematic fashion, the theoretical work on comparative law with existing theories about law in general.[40] That is puzzling, to say the least, given that any theory of 'comparative law' cannot but presuppose a particular theory of 'law.' What is more, greater reflection on the 'law' underneath 'comparative law' might prove pointedly helpful for the purpose of resolving the divisions afflicting the latter. For it may be that these divisions denote an inadequate (perhaps just incomplete or conflicted) theorization of law. A thoroughly hybrid conception of law, one that would smoothly merge apparently antithetical

---

[37] Neil Walker makes a similar point with respect to global law: NEIL WALKER, INTIMATIONS OF GLOBAL LAW 148–49 (2015). But see: BASIL MARKESINIS, ENGAGING WITH FOREIGN LAW (2009), esp. 28ff ("*(d) The Practitioner Comparatist: An Untapped Gold Mine*").

[38] For a suggestion that comparative law indeed involves a form of practical wisdom (Aristotelian *prudentia*), defying clear theory/practice dichotomization, see: HUSA, *supra* note 14.

[39] See however: Ralf Michaels, A Fuller Concept of Law Beyond the State? Thoughts on Lon Fuller's Contributions to the Jurisprudence of Transnational Dispute Resolution—A Reply to Thomas Schultz, 2 J. INT. DISPUTE SETTLEMENT 417 (2011) (suggesting that 'law' and 'comparative law' need not rest on the same theoretic foundations).

[40] See however: John Bell, Comparative Law and Legal Theory, *in* PRESCRIPTIVE FORMALITY AND NORMATIVE RATIONALITY IN MODERN LEGAL SYSTEMS 19 (Werner Krawietz, Neil MacCormick & Georg Henrik von Wright eds., 1994); Ewald, *supra* note 7; SAMUEL, *supra* note 7, at 121–51; JACCO BOMHOFF, BALANCING CONSTITUTIONAL RIGHTS: THE ORIGINS AND MEANINGS OF POSTWAR LEGAL DISCOURSE (2013); Whitman, *supra* note 18; Michaels, *supra* note 39.

dimensions, presumably would open the door to a conception of comparative law that would likewise prove unified rather than bifurcated.[41] If so, one path to unifying comparative law would lie in legal theory pure and simple. Thus, whereas comparative legal knowledge as mentioned has long contributed to legal theory, the time may have come for legal theory to return the favour.

The book accordingly opens with a particular, hybrid conception of law. Drawing on the Aristotelian intellectual tradition pursued through the Enlightenment and German idealism in particular, this approach, which I call 'law as collective commitment,' conceptualizes law as a social practice that both reflects and constitutes a community's commitment to governing itself in accordance with certain shared ideals. As a *practice* embodying *ideals*, law as collective commitment combines a material and an ideal dimension, very much in line with Kant and Hegel's teachings, and with such later accounts of law as those penned by Lon Fuller, Ronald Dworkin, Neil MacCormick, Jeremy Waldron, Nigel Simmonds and Gerald Postema.

Chapter 1 first analyzes law in terms of six formal features – effectiveness, argumentativeness, coherence, publicness, formality and normativity – all of which are shown to derive from the central notion of 'collective commitment,' and its attendant premises: citizen equality and citizen-official reciprocity. Thereafter, in Part II, these six features are synthesized into what will hopefully prove a smooth blend of material and ideal. The argument there proceeds through the contrasting of law as collective commitment with two antithetical legal ideal-types, constructed for the occasion, viz. the 'natural law ideal-type,' on one hand, and the 'positivist ideal-type,' on the other. Whereas the natural law and positivist ideal-types indeed respectively are ideal and material through and through, I argue that law as collective commitment in contrast is a truly hybrid, ideal cum material, conception.

The remaining chapters aim to establish that the corresponding hybrid conception of comparative law – comparative law as comparison of the collective commitments underlying the world's legal systems – transcends, or even pre-empts, the various divides described above. Chapter 2 considers the extent to which law as conceptualized in Chapter 1 is amenable to comparison. More specifically, I there argue that the hybridity of law as collective commitment is the key to legal systems possessing the combination of distinctness and commonality required for their 'meaningful comparison,' by which I mean a comparison holding the potential of yielding new knowledge about either or both of the systems compared and/or legal systems in general. Whereas under radical natural law, legal systems exhibit commonality but insufficient distinctness, and conversely boast distinctness but insufficient commonality under radical positivism, they are adequately distinct *and*

---

[41] In the same vein, Adler and Pouliot describe, in the field of international relations, their central notion of 'community of practice' as "[o]vercoming dichotomies in social theory": Emanuel Adler & Vincent Pouliot, International Practices: Introduction and Framework, *in INTERNATIONAL PRACTICES* 3, 12 (Emanuel Adler & Vincent Pouliot eds., 2011).

common under law as collective commitment. Chapter 3 takes on the epistemological issue of the proper perspective from which to engage foreign legal systems, and aims to show that while comparative law as comparative collective commitment entails that outsiders contribute valuable insights to the local understanding of legal systems, such contributions necessarily proceed from a movement of back and forth between the foreign (external) and local (internal) perspectives on the understanding in question. On the issue of the proper delineation of legal systems, Chapter 4 first argues that comparative law as comparative collective commitment motions to a largely internal, self-defining, conception of the legal system as epistemic community yet one that remains externally anchored in material considerations of time and space (territory, jurisdiction, coercion, etc.), which combination causes legal systems to be structured much like bee swarms. We thereafter stand back to consider how these swarm-like structures interact in the global universe, which causes us to engage with the legal pluralism debate as to whether non-state entities can qualify as 'legal systems' proper. Finally, Chapter 5 offers a methodology for comparing legal systems that operationalizes the ideal/material analytic framework laid out in the previous chapters insofar as it too oscillates between internal and external, expressivism and functionalism, similar and different, micro and macro. In the way of epilogue, the concluding chapter sums up the account of comparative law as comparative collective commitments and outlines that, against critics' predictions, comparative law so conceived meets the requirements of an autonomous academic discipline.

The argumentative strategy deployed throughout these chapters likewise harbours synthetic aspirations insofar as it combines a deductive and an inductive method. At the same time as I here reflect on the ideas inherent in 'comparison' and comparison in 'law' from the top down, I aim to show that these ideas are to some extent implicit in the comparative law scholarship produced to date. In particular, I aim to show that that scholarship already contains the various possible conceptual justifications for overcoming the above divisions. Given this combined top-down and ground-up approach, comparative law as comparative collective commitments here is not so much 'constructed' as 'reconstructed' from existing materials.

This reconstruction arguably carries important theoretical and practical implications. From a theoretical standpoint, it promises a most effective response to the malaise critics given that, if comparative law can be 'cured' merely by making explicit what is implicitly present in it, it actually is in much better shape than they have claimed. A successful reconstruction would serve to establish that comparative law is not theoretically *empty* so much as theoretically *non-explicit* – not so much *flawed* as *non-understood*. From a practical standpoint, it would serve to provide guidance to all who engage in comparative legal studies in the pursuit of a specifically legal purpose. It would also entail that the general call for legal comparatists to reflect more deeply on the theoretical whereabouts of their work must be somewhat qualified, as theorization would then have to be a collective rather than individual aspiration. That is, explicit theory clearly is an invaluable source of guidance, and as it falls to the (collective) discipline of comparative law to provide that guidance, it also falls to it to articulate the theory. But it may be that not every comparatist needs to be involved in theory formulation. If good comparative law theory can be implicit, it simply follows that not *every* comparatist needs to fully articulate, or even grasp or care to grasp, the theoretical commitments underlying their work.[42]

Finally, there is yet another purpose to this book, and that is to contribute to legal theory. As mentioned, whereas comparative law has long serviced legal theory, the reverse has yet to happen in any serious and systematic way. Had legal theorists cared to cross over into the comparative realm, they might have realized that their theories carry less than full traction against at least some of law's many dimensions. Legal philosophers have focused on a possible universal dimension (a moral ideal, an institutional structure, a social function, etc.) and in comparison have neglected the many differences between legal systems. Legal anthropologists and sociologists in contrast have paid great attention to the political, economic or cultural specifics of legal systems while tending to discount what these systems might have in common. Legal historians have followed the movement of legal rules through time and territory, noting patterns of convergence and divergence, but have typically abstained from commenting on the larger significance of these patterns for our understanding of law and legal systems. And so on. It is my hope that the account of comparative law developed in the coming chapters might help these various theorists to break free from such insularity. Because to compare entails seeing the similar *and* the different – any form of legal comparison cannot but engage the commonality as well as the specificity of law. Insofar as law is recognized as being at least to some extent dynamic, a proper understanding of legal similarities and differences necessarily involves tracking these over time and across territories, and conversely. Comparative law thus cannot but shed light on the interaction of a number of legal dimensions that generally tend to be examined independently of one another.

Most immediately, of course, should it be established that the working conception of law used here succeeds at accounting for an entire area of legal studies that had hitherto withstood theorization, that fact alone might cause legal theorists to contemplate the possibility that that conception might ultimately be right, rather than just plausible.

---

[42] Zweigert & Kötz, *supra* note 24, at 33; Adrian Popovici, Droit comparé et enseignement du droit – Aperçu de l'enseignement, au Québec, du droit comparé, et de l'enseignement comparatif du droit, 36 Revue Juridique Thémis [*R. J. T.*] 803, 807–08 (2002). Of course, insofar as theory and practice indeed might be symbiotically interconnected, in that good scholarship would be based in good theory yet good theory would itself feed on good scholarship, anyone producing good scholarship in a sense necessarily contributes, at least implicitly, to theory building.

DETAILED DESCRIPTION OF CHAPTER CONTENTS

Part I of Chapter 1 analyzes law as collective commitments in terms of six formal features – effectiveness, argumentativeness, coherence, publicness, formality and normativity – all of which indeed can be derived from the central notions of commitment and citizen equality. Whereas all human institutions are to some extent intentional, the product of deliberation, law is more than just 'intention' insofar as it is amenable to systematic collective enforcement: law making pertains not just to contemplating or wishing for a certain state of affairs but also to committing to deploying the means to realize that state of affairs, to make it *effective*. The second of law's essential features is its argumentative quality, it being an exchange of *reasons*, a *justificatory* debate. If law is a commitment, an enforceable intention, the officials have an obligation both to support their enforcement decisions with arguments that the citizens can accept as valid and to debate with them what those arguments might be. Law as collective commitment further specifies, moreover, that the arguments being exchanged must be *coherent* as well as *public*. Legal arguments must be coherent in the sense of being both comprehensible and not inconsistent with one another; they must be public in the sense of being transparent and reflecting the commitments of the entire community rather than the private aspirations of some or even all of its individual members. The fifth feature is *formality* (or 'institutionality'): as the tangible manifestation of law's intentionality, institutional markers make it possible for all to see and debate what are and are not the community's collective commitments – to rope off the 'legal' from the 'non-legal,' as it were. The sixth and final feature is normativity – law embodying *ideals*, some of which are peculiar to particular communities while others are common to them all. Because these contingent and non-contingent ideals indeed are 'ideals,' law is bound always to remain aspirational to some extent: it motions to a state of affairs that *ex hypothesi* never can be fully realized. Part II draws on German idealism to bring these six features together, into what will aim to be a smooth synthesis of material and ideal. The argument here proceeds through a systematic contrast of law as commitment with radical natural law on one hand, and radical positivism on the other.

Chapter 2 opens with a reflection on comparability and meaningful comparison. As not all comparisons are meaningful, the requirements for meaningful comparison are expectedly more stringent than those for mere comparability. It is contended that in order for any two entities to be comparable, they must be distinct yet also connected, with the intensity of that connection being unimportant: so long as the entities are connected *in some way*, they are comparable. A particular degree of connectedness however is necessary for the comparison to be meaningful in addition to just possible. I describe as 'meaningful' any comparison the outcome of which is not fully determinable from the outset, and argue that where the entities are connected either too thickly or too thinly, the comparison, though technically possible, cannot be meaningful in that sense. It is concluded that for legal systems to be amenable to meaningful comparison it must be possible to conceptualize them as entities that are both (1) distinct and (2) adequately connected. The rest of the chapter is devoted to arguing that such conceptualization is unavailable under either of the natural law or positivist ideal-types laid out in Chapter 1, whereas it is available under our hybrid conception of law as collective commitment. That argument takes the form of an incursion into system theory, which teaches that systems come in different varieties, only some of which, I argue, meet our two requirements. The legal systems of natural law correspond to what system theorists call 'synthetic systems,' which fail to meet the distinctness requirement (Part II), whereas the legal systems of positivism, as 'cybernetic organic systems,' fail to meet the connectedness requirement (Part III). In contrast, the legal systems of law as collective commitment, as 'autopoietic organic systems,' are here shown to meet both requirements (Part IV). It therefore seems that of these three conceptions, only law as collective commitment allows for the possibility of meaningful legal comparison.

Chapter 3 takes on every comparatist's main epistemological dilemma: whether to investigate foreign law from an external (cognitivist) or internal (constructivist) perspective, or some combination thereof. Part I briefly recounts the history of that debate in the humanities in general, with particular emphasis on the philosophy of history. Part II transposes the debate onto the study of law, suggesting that the natural law and positivism ideal-types both motion to an external perspective whereas law as collective commitment mandates an unequivocal internal perspective – the legal actors' own. Two classic objections to adopting an internal perspective in law are thereafter reviewed. According to the 'heterogeneity objection,' the deep and insuperable disagreement among legal actors as to how their law should be interpreted suggests that there is no single 'internal' view of it that can be identified as somehow superior to any other. As for the 'subjectivity objection,' it provides that whichever views the actors hold of their law are necessarily subjective, and hence devoid of normative weight. It is suggested that the heterogeneity objection simply misses the mark as it mistakes the internal perspective, an essentially interpretive attitude, for a matter of empirical determination. With respect to the subjectivity objection, it is submitted that a certain form of actor subjectivity is both inevitable and necessary given that collective debate ultimately arises from subjective disagreement. As for the less desirable, opportunistic forms of actor subjectivity, these are somewhat mitigated by law's publicness requirement, which contributes to filtering out individual positions not justifiable in terms of collective legal ideals. Part III moves the analysis to the comparative context, wherein the individual seeking an internal understanding of one body of law is already acquainted with another. The standard objection against that move (the 'home bias objection') charges that one cannot possibly understand two bodies of law on the inside, as the cultural lenses attending the first will necessarily colour the understanding of the second, which latter understanding accordingly cannot but differ from that of the local actors. It is argued in response that while an outsider's understanding of the law does differ from the local understanding, both can nonetheless be described as internal. Under comparative law as comparative collective commitments, comparative lawyers indeed are, like the local actors, full participants in the reconstruction of the local law, though their way of proceeding (constant in-and-out movement) and the character of their contribution (comparative) are markedly different. Most importantly, comparative lawyers differ from local lawyers in that they reconstruct several bodies of local law (however many they are comparing) at once while also participating in the construction of the discipline of comparative law.

The discussion of Chapter 3 naturally raises the question of the proper delineation of legal systems: if all who participate in law's reconstruction are to be considered legal actors proper, where do legal systems begin and end? This is the question addressed in Chapter 4, which more specifically looks to the identification of the spatial, temporal and demographic contours of legal systems as the objects of analysis under comparative law as comparative collective commitments. Here again comparatists face the dilemma of whether to proceed externally, by just adopting the traditional Westphalian mapping of legal systems as territory-based nation states, or else internally, by accepting as 'legal system' whatever is locally determined as such. Harking back to Chapter 3, Part I of Chapter 4 advocates an internal delineation of legal systems. As 'autopoietic organic systems' (Chapter 2), the legal systems of comparative law as comparative collective commitments are largely *self*-defining. After all, the legal actors' own treatment of boundary issues is as revealing of their collective commitments as is their treatment of any other legal issue. Legal systems on that account accordingly are fuzzy and fickle. They are fuzzy in that their elements belong to them not categorically but as a matter of degree; they are fickle in that they change constantly, along with the legal materials that constitute them. They purportedly take on a diversity of geographic configurations – some encompassing more than one state (the Commonwealth, Europe) or less than one (provincial law, municipal law); others qualifying as such despite being demographically or thematically, rather than territorially, defined (law applicable exclusively to certain groups of citizens or certain types of transactions) or despite combining an array of legal traditions within the same territory (the so-called 'mixed jurisdictions'). They also are temporally relative, as confirmed by the reports from colonial history concerning the challenges in pinpointing precisely when legal systems come in and out of existence. Finally, it seems that they can clash and/or intersect with one another, as when judges from different jurisdictions invoke the same body of authorities or when judges from the same jurisdiction invoke authorities from different jurisdictions. At the same time, the internal delineation of legal systems does not (*contra* some legal pluralist claims) result in their being severed from any kind of material anchors. As Part II aims to show, a strictly ideal delineation of legal systems is neither conceptually workable nor consonant with practice. On the conceptual front, it is recalled that our base definition of law as collective commitment (effectiveness, argumentativeness, coherence, publicness, formality and normativity) places firm if minimal a priori limits on what can qualify as a legal system for present purposes. In particular, that definition insures that the legal systems of comparative law as comparative collective commitments, however elusive their contours, retain a clear institutional focus. They accordingly possess a persistent measure of tangibility, in particular some kind of temporal relevance and connection to territory, as is pointedly confirmed in practice, through the debates surrounding forum and applicable law determinations in private international law.

Chapter 5 crystallizes the discussion of the previous chapters into a proposed tripartite methodology for comparative legal studies, sequentially addressing the start-up, reconstruction and overall comparison stages of the comparative process. Part I discusses the choice of topic and legal systems, and the identification of the relevant materials in each system. The challenge at this early stage is to secure an appropriate '*tertium comparationis*,' or neutral vantage point from which to enter the various systems, one that will avoid rigging the analysis in favour of one of them. As legal labels ('contract,' 'contract law,' 'private law') are not standardized across systems, they offer notoriously poor entry points. Accordingly, many comparatists have instead resorted to problem-based legal research, wherein the various materials identified for comparison are not those earmarked with particular labels so much as those typically deployed to respond to particular problems. The requisite 'effectiveness' of law under the present account entails that such functionalistic research method ought to be available under comparative law as comparative collective commitments, which method is consequently endorsed and defended. Part II recounts the process by which the materials gathered are thereafter analyzed and interpreted through micro comparisons. Functionalism is of little use at this stage, as it only speaks to law's function and is hence ill-equipped to explain *why* legal systems have historically deployed different means to resolve similar social problems. Comparative lawyers are therefore advised to turn to a hermeneutic approach, which in contrast zooms in on such differences. Whereas it is often claimed that cross-system variations are best explained by reference to non-legal (cultural, historical, economic, etc.) factors, legal hermeneutics aim to make sense of each set of materials on its own terms, each set being tentatively reconstructed into a distinct coherent discourse. As such reconstruction exercise necessarily involves relating the various materials to one another and to the set's peculiar grammar and ideals, such grammar and ideals – the systems' respective collective commitments – are bound to come to light. Part III discusses the immediately ensuing question of the extent to which (if at all) legal systems meaningful on their own yet perhaps no other terms, thus potentially incommensurable, can possibly be compared among themselves in the context of macro comparisons. It is there argued that, contrary to received wisdom, it does not follow from comparisons necessarily involving an external perspective (whence all the entities can be gleaned at once – Chapter 2) that the standards used in those comparisons must likewise be externally determined. Drawing on the economic literature on proportionality, which distinguishes comparability from commensurability, I suggest that it is possible to compare (externally) the extent to which various legal systems have lived up to their respectively incommensurable (internal) commitments. While such proportional (rather than cardinal) comparisons clearly are comparisons proper, they do not encroach, and if anything might serve to preserve and reinforce, the internal integrity of the systems involved. Particular attention is here drawn to the 'legal family' and 'legal origins' literatures, both of which have been accused of comparing legal systems as against externally imposed criteria, thus contributing to conveying ultimately distorted understandings of these systems.

The book closes with an Epilogue outlining that my proposed account of comparative law meets the standard requirements for an autonomous academic discipline. That is, comparative law as comparative collective commitments boasts a distinct area of knowledge and inferential purpose, a transparent process, a pre-established methodological framework and a priori uncertain conclusions. At least, comparative law so conceptualized fares, by these standards, as well as any other well-established such discipline. The chapter closes with some general remarks on the upshot of our discussion for legal theory.

1

Law

INTRODUCTION

I here lay out the particular conception of law – law as collective commitment – on which the upcoming account of comparative law is based. On that conception, law is a particular kind of human institution, namely, that through which a community expresses its commitment to certain ideals. More specifically, it is *an argumentative social practice that both reflects and constitutes a community's commitment to governing itself in accordance with certain ideals*.[1]

That conception might clearly be less than adequate for purposes other than the present. It might prove too thin, thus over-inclusive, from the perspective of legal philosophy, which typically seeks to give as complete an account as possible of the essential nature of law.[2] It might conversely be too thick, under-inclusive, for the purpose of, say, such strictly semantic exercise as exposing all possible intelligible

---

[1]   This conception draws on the work of several contemporary legal theorists, among whom are Ronald Dworkin (*Law's Empire* (1986)); Neil MacCormick (*Institutions of Law: An Essay in Legal Theory* (2007) [hereinafter MacCormick, *Institutions of Law*]; *Rhetoric and the Rule of Law: A Theory of Legal Reasoning* (2005) [hereinafter MacCormick, *Rhetoric and the Rule of Law*]); Nigel Simmonds (*Law as Moral Idea* (2007)); Gerald Postema (Law's Ethos: Reflections on a Public Practice of Illegality, 90 *Boston U. L. Rev.* 101 (2010); Law's Rule: Reflexivity, Mutual Accountability, and the Rule of Law, *in* Bentham's Theory of Law and Public Opinion (Xiaobo Zhai & Michael Quinn eds., 2014) [hereinafter Postema, *Law's Rule*]; Law's System: The Necessity of System in Common Law, *New Zealand L. Rev.* 69 (2014) [hereinafter Postema, *Law's System*]); Jeremy Waldron (The Concept and the Rule of Law, 43 *Georgia L. Rev.* 1 (2008)); Lon Fuller (*The Morality of Law* (1969); *Anatomy of the Law* (1976)) and Hans Kelsen (*Pure Theory of Law* (Max Knight trans., 1967)).
[2]   Perhaps most conspicuous in this respect is the absence of any reference to 'fairness,' 'justice,' 'equity,' 'morality' or other equivalent, and to the likes of 'rules,' 'principles,' and 'standards.' Many legal philosophers presumably would insist that some such notions ought to appear in a sound definition of law, however bare. We will however see below (in Chapter 2) that including them here would be superfluous and in fact unduly constraining.

uses of the word 'law'.[3] But my present purpose merely is to present an appropriate analytic basis on which to build the upcoming account of comparative law. 'Law as collective commitment' accordingly is here offered as no more than a *working* or *nominal* conception, specifically tailored to our immediate comparative concern, not a *real* conception, "embod[ying] an ontological claim."[4] As such, it specifies only the features speaking directly to said concern and remains provisional, i.e. amenable to whatever refinement would make it a better support for our account of comparative law. At the same time, no conception (nominal or real) admittedly can afford to be completely at odds with the foundational notions it calls into play. I will therefore attempt, as we move along, to underscore the general resonance of law as collective commitments by showing how the various features cohere with one another, carry inherent normative appeal and match legal practice.

Part I analyzes law as collective commitment in terms of six essential features – effectiveness, argumentativeness, coherence, publicness, formality and normativity. Part II aims to show that the combination of these features accounts for what will prove a most important quality of law as collective commitment in the chapters to come, namely, its being at once ideal and material.

I. 'LAW AS COLLECTIVE COMMITMENT'

As its designation suggests, law as collective commitment is structured around the notion of commitment, which indeed serves to interconnect and justify its six core features. The first of these is effectiveness. Law being institutional entails it being conscious, wilful, intentional, the product of rational reflection and a deliberate creation of the human intellect. But it is not just any kind of intention. It is intention that is particularly reliable insofar as it is realized through collective *enforcement*: law making pertains not just to contemplating or wishing for a certain state of affairs but also to committing to deploying the means to make that state of affairs happen.

The second core feature of law under law as collective commitment is its argumentative quality, its being an exchange of reasons, a justificatory debate. It indeed follows from law being a commitment, enforceable intention, that the officials have an obligation both to support their enforcement decisions with arguments that the

---

3 On the appropriateness of conceptual analysis in different contexts, see: FREDERICK SCHAUER, THE FORCE OF LAW section 3.5 (2015); Waldron, *supra* note 1, at 36–40.
4 Kenneth I. Winston, The Ideal Element in a Definition of Law, 5 LAW & PHIL. 89, 101 (1986). In the same vein: William Ewald, Comparative Jurisprudence (I): What Was It Like to Try a Rat?, 143 U. PA. L. REV. 1889, 1950–51 (1995) ("[we need] a conception of law that makes no claim to serve any purpose beyond those of comparative law"); William Twining's critique of Neil MacCormick's definition of law as "inappropriate for the comparative lawyer" (William Twining, Institutions of Law From a Global Perspective, *in* LAW AS INSTITUTIONAL NORMATIVE ORDER 20, 22 (Maksymillian Del Mar & Zenon Bankowski eds., 2010) at 17 and 187 respectively, further discussed *infra*, Chapter 2, note 16).

citizens can accept as valid and to debate with them what those arguments might be. Since law as collective commitment further specifies that the arguments being exchanged must be coherent as well as public, moreover, these qualities here appear as respectively third and fourth features. Legal arguments must be coherent both in the sense of being comprehensible and in the sense of not clashing with one another; they must be public both in the sense of being transparent and in the sense of reflecting the commitments of the entire community rather than the private aspirations of individual community members.

The fifth feature is formality. As the tangible manifestation of law's intentionality, formality makes it possible for all to see and debate what are and are not the community's collective commitments – to rope off the 'legal' from the 'non-legal', as it were. The sixth and final feature is normativity – law embodying *ideals*, some of which are peculiar to particular communities while others run across them all. Because these contingent and non-contingent ideals indeed are 'ideals,' law is bound always to remain aspirational to some extent: it aims at a state of affairs that *ex hypothesi* can never be fully realized. This first Part discusses in more detail each of these six features, their interconnection through the central notion of commitment and correspondence with legal practice, and their significance for the chapters to come.

i. *Effectiveness*

Like all human institutions – religious and moral traditions, social conventions, art, culture, politics – law is a product of the intellect. If only as such, it is deliberate, planned, wilful, the result of conscious thought. Any form of intellectual production indeed involves a measure of intentionality. One often hears of the rules of etiquette, for example, that they *aim* or were *meant* to achieve such and such purpose. Works of art likewise are commonly described in terms of the artist's *intention* or *vision*. And religious rituals are recognized as having been established *with a view* to, say, supplying a concrete support for spirituality. Such purposive language underscores the intentionality inherent in all human institutions, law included.

Legal intentionality is particular, however, in that it comes with the potential of collective coercive enforcement. As Max Weber famously noted, law stands out from other human institutions in that it insures that people generally comply with it, if necessary through the deployment of sanctions that are collectively determined and administered.[5] Insofar as religious and social rituals are enforced only through

---

[5] MAX WEBER, ECONOMY AND SOCIETY: AN OUTLINE OF INTERPRETIVE SOCIOLOGY VOL I 29ff (Guenther Roth & Claus Wittich eds., 1978). Likewise: Waldron, *supra* note 1, at 41 ("a way in which a community takes public control of the conditions of its collective life"). For a recent reiteration of this point in the context of comparative law, see: Stefan Vogenauer, Sources of Law and Legal Method in Comparative Law, *in* THE OXFORD HANDBOOK OF COMPARATIVE LAW 869, 870 (Mathias Reimann & Reinhard Zimmerman eds., 2008). The relation of coercion to compliance (coerced or voluntary) has been the object of much debate. See generally: SCHAUER, *supra* note 3, citing e.g. MATTHEW

spontaneous social sanctions, privately initiated by the individuals immediately affected, rather than systematic public sanctions, administered in the name of the entire community – moral condemnation, relationship termination, trading bans, social ostracism – they would evince an intentionality different from legal intentionality. While it can be said that the rules of etiquette, for example, in a sense 'mandate' that knives be held in the right hand, nothing more than private scorn or a drought of dinner invitations ensues where knives are held in the left hand. Quite simply, if holding knives in the right hand were a legal rule, collective force would be deployed to insure that people generally comply with it. As Fred Schauer puts it, law is distinctive in that it *"makes* us do things we do not want to do."[6]

Effectiveness relates to law being intentional in two ways. The first is rather mechanistic, instrumental. To say that law is effective is to say that it has tangible and potentially weighty consequences on people's lives – that it *matters*. If only for that reason, the law makers generally take care to 'get it right' – they make sure, or at least have good reasons to make sure, that whatever consequences befall the citizens as a result of the law they make are called for. Law's effectiveness thus is a cause, in a mechanistic sense, of its being intentional: greater deliberation goes into the making of law than into the making of any other institution because law makers are attuned to the fact that law materially affects people's lives in a way that other institutions do not.

But effectiveness also relates to law's intentionality in a more significant, for inherently expressive rather than just instrumental, way. Law being destined to enforcement entails that all generally can rely on its provisions actually materializing – that law is *reliable* in a way that other institutions are not.[7] When a state decides to enshrine freedom of expression into its constitution, it thereby signals that violations of that freedom will henceforth be amenable to forcible redress. When it legislates to ban smoking, it likewise indicates that public coercion is being enlisted to enforce that ban. When it orders, through a judge, that a particular contract be performed, it affirms that the designated means will be taken to insure that performance actually

---

H. KRAMER, *IN DEFENSE OF LEGAL POSITIVISM: LAW WITHOUT TRIMMINGS* (1999); Grant Lamond, Coercion and the Nature of Law, 7 LEGAL THEORY 35 (2001); Dan Priel, Sanction and Obligation in Hart's Theory of Law, 21 RATIO JURIS 404 (2008); Nicos Stavropolous, The Relevance of Coercion: Some Preliminaries, 22 RATIO JURIS 339 (2009). It has been argued in particular that whereas Weber reduces compliance to coercion, and hence conceptualizes law as essentially coercive, coercion in fact is just "an addendum, an additional security … a practical necessity in a world in which some people … will not voluntarily respect the rights instituted by positive law." NEIL MACCORMICK, *LEGAL RIGHT AND SOCIAL DEMOCRACY: ESSAYS IN LEGAL AND POLITICAL PHILOSOPHY* 240 (1982). See likewise: H. L. A. HART, *THE CONCEPT OF LAW* (1961); LESLIE GREEN, *THE AUTHORITY OF THE STATE* 75 (1988); SCOTT J. SHAPIRO, *LEGALITY* (2011); Postema, *Law's Rule, supra* note 1, at 7–8.

[6] SCHAUER, *supra* note 3, at 1 (my italics).

[7] SIMMONDS, *supra* note 1, at 143; FRIEDRICH A. HAYEK, *THE CONSTITUTION OF LIBERTY* 156–57 (1960) ("The law tells [the individual] what facts he may count on and thereby extends the range within which he can predict the consequences of his actions.").

take place. Thus, while there is no guarantee that every violation will in fact be detected and sanctioned, a commitment is made to deploy the means for doing so.[8]

Legal intentionality hence simultaneously operates on two distinct levels: it contemplates a certain desired prospect (free expression, a smoke-free society, contract honouring) *as well as* the means that may have to be deployed for that prospect to materialize (collective force). And precisely because it includes the latter, it is more than just regular intention: unlike, say, the popular morality of a community, "[i]ts law belongs to it not just passively, because its members hold certain views about what is right or wrong, but as a matter of active commitment, because its officials have taken decisions that commit the community to the rights and duties that make up law." [9] In much the same way that a contractual statement of intention is made reliable by the prospect of enforcement attached to it,[10] legal intention writ large is intention *meant to be relied upon*; it is a promise, an actual *commitment*.[11]

Effectiveness comes into play most prominently in Chapter 4, which deals with the proper delineation of legal systems. We will see there that although the coercion required for legal effectiveness need not come from the state as a matter of principle, in the current Westphalian context, only state enforced law can give rise to 'legal systems' proper on the present account.

ii. *Argumentativeness*

Crucially for our purposes, it follows from law being a commitment in that sense that reasons, arguments and justifications form a key part of it.[12] This is because, as I explain below, when officials commit to enforcing the laws through collective

---

[8] "[Law] is not the mere idea of right or rights ... it is the realization of this idea. In this condition, individual right-bearers *enjoy* their rights, not in the sense that the rights are always or necessarily respected, but rather in the sense that practices and institutions needed for effective claiming of the rights and recourse against infringements of the rights exist." Postema, *Law's Rule, supra* note 1, at 11 (discussing Kant's *rechtlicher Zustand*).

[9] DWORKIN, *supra* note 1, at 97. See also: ARTHUR RIPSTEIN , FORCE AND FREEDOM 99, 108–109 (2009) (distinguishing commitment, or 'choice,' from 'mere wish'); Postema, *Law's Rule, supra* note 1, at 13 ("not merely a faith in the idea and efficacy of the rule of law, but rather a shared commitment among officials and citizens to make it work").

[10] Commitment admittedly may be much more than just an inducement to reliance. On the significance of promises and promising in general, see e.g.: Joseph Raz, Promises and Obligations, *in* LAW, MORALITY AND SOCIETY: ESSAYS IN HONOUR OF H.L.A. HART 210 (P. M. S. Hacker & Joseph Raz eds., 1977); PATRICK S. ATIYAH, PROMISES, MORALS AND LAW (1981); MACCORMICK, *supra* note 5, 'Voluntary Obligations' at pp. 190ff; THOMAS M. SCANLON, WHAT WE OWE TO EACH OTHER Chap 7 (1998); STEPHEN DARWALL, THE SECOND-PERSON STANDPOINT 194ff (2006).

[11] See Weber's distinction between an "ethics of commitment" and an "ethics of responsibility": MAX WEBER, THE VOCATION LECTURES 92 (David Owen & Tracy B. Strong eds., Rodney Livingstone trans., 2004).

[12] See generally: MACCORMICK, RHETORIC AND THE RULE OF LAW, *supra* note 1. David Enoch, Reason-Giving and the Law, *in* OXFORD STUDIES IN THE PHILOSOPHY OF LAW VOLUME I, at 1–38 (Leslie Green & Brian Leiter eds., 2011).

force, they arguably also commit (1) to justifying such enforcement with arguments that the citizens can accept as valid; and (2) to having the citizens participate in the determination of what ought to count as such arguments. If this is so, law can properly be described as argumentative through and through: as an exchange of (legal) arguments among officials and citizens as to the "canon of acceptable arguments,"[13] that is, what ought to count as valid legal arguments in the community.

Inherent in the notion of commitment indeed is a particular kind of rapport to the other. That there be at least two parties involved – one issuing the commitment and another receiving it – clearly is the first requirement of a commitment.[14] But the notion of commitment further specifies the kind of rapport that is to be had between these two parties. It follows from a commitment being meant to be relied upon that its recipient should be able to govern his or her affairs under the assumption that it will materialize regardless of what happens in fact.[15] This in turn suggests that the recipient should be regarded as being at least generally in charge of governing those affairs – as 'self-governing.' The same can be said of the committing party, moreover, for the act of committing itself supposes a power to commit, which in turn supposes agency and self-governance. The act of committing hence serves to affirm the committing party's capacity for self-governance at the same time as it serves to recognize the same capacity in the receiving party.[16] Commitment accordingly entails a reciprocal rapport of equality with the other, one whereby the committing and receiving parties are recognized as equals by virtue of their shared capacity for self-governance.[17]

Once it is recognized that the individuals governed by the law are (equal) self-governing agents, it is just a few short steps to concluding that (1) the enforcement of that law must be supported with arguments that these individuals can accept as valid, and that (2) these individuals moreover must participate in the determination of what arguments those are. To recognize you as the master of yourself is to recognize that you cannot be coerced to do something that you would not otherwise freely choose to do unless there are good reasons – reasons that *you* would consider

---

[13] Anthony M. Honoré, Legal Reasoning in Rome and Today, 4 CAMBRIDGE L. REV 58 (1973).

[14] Even a commitment 'to oneself,' to the extent that such commitments are at all possible, arguably entails conceptually splitting the self into a committing and a receiving end.

[15] See Niklas Luhmann's description (NIKLAS LUHMANN, LAW AS A SOCIAL SYSTEM 94 (Fatima Kastner et al. eds., Klaus Ziegart trans., 2009) of the function of law as "stabilizing normative expectations": "Normativity only determines that certain expectations can be maintained, even when faced with disappointment." Luhmann's account is further detailed below, in Chapter 4.

[16] This account of commitment as reciprocity is typically Kantian. See: RIPSTEIN, *supra* note 9, at 108, 120.

[17] This explains why the oracle, in Weber's description of oracular adjudication, can dispense with giving reasons: as he is speaking in God's name, whereas his interlocutors are mere mortals, his statements are naturally authoritative upon them. See: ANTHONY T. KRONMAN, MAX WEBER 82–83 (1983). Waldron (*supra* note 1, at 30–31) offers a variation on the same theme: human laws and legal orders need to be justified precisely because they, unlike divine laws, are contingent ("could be otherwise").

good – for doing so.[18] As it is *your* capacity for self-governance that is at stake, it is
only natural that you would need to accept as valid the reasons given for curtailing
that capacity.[19]

That requirement moreover would not be met merely through your having
once recognized as valid the reasons originally offered for *enacting* the law now
being enforced on you. For, any good reasons there may be to enact a general law,
a law governing an entire community, do not automatically carry over to justify the
enforcement of that law in particular cases. As Aristotle explained, the application
of rules in particular cases is not a self-evident operation, determined by logic, but
rather a matter of judgment, involving other kinds of human sensibilities. As such,
it calls for justifications independent from those supporting the rule itself: whatever
good reasons there may have been given to enact the law in the first place, once that
law is being enforced against you through specific court proceedings, fresh reasons
must be given which you can accept as valid for *that* specific purpose.[20]

To recognize you as the master of yourself moreover also entails having you participate in the determination of what reasons those are. Because that determination
proceeds, as we just saw, through judgment rather than logic, it is a matter about
which reasonable people can disagree.[21] If so, how could it legitimately be left to the
judgment of the officials alone? To recognize you as a self-governing equal is to recognize *both* that you cannot be coerced without arguments that you would accept as
valid *and* that your judgment as to what should count as such arguments is worthy
of consideration, with the result that, if the officials have a say in the matter, so
should you.[22] So where public force is exerted against you for reasons that you think
are invalid, you should at the very least be allowed to voice the reasons that make
you think so. You would then be entitled to a response from the officials, wherein

---

[18] For fuller accounts of law as justification for collective coercion, see: DWORKIN, *supra* note 1, esp.
108–13; SIMMONDS, *supra* note 1, esp. 2; David Dyzenhaus, Deliberative Constitutionalism Through
the Lens of the Administrative State *in Cambridge Handbook of Deliberative Constitutionalism* 15
(Ron Levy *et al.* eds., forthcoming 2018). The idea of law as justified coercion of course ultimately
goes back to Kant and Rousseau.

[19] SIMMONDS, *supra* note 1, at 136. As Stanley Cavell noted in the context of artistic interpretation, these
need not be arguments that you *in fact* accept as valid: it is enough that, were they discussed with you,
you would have no good reason to reject them. STANLEY CAVELL, MUST WE MEAN WHAT WE SAY?
chap. 8 (1969). This admittedly begs the question of what might qualify as a 'good' such reason. That
question is taken up in Chapter 1, Part I, sections iii–v, *infra*.

[20] Gerald J. Postema, A Similibus ad Similia: Analogical Thinking in Law, *in* COMMON LAW THEORY 102,
120 (Douglas E. Edlin ed., 2007).

[21] Building on Kant, Hannah Arendt explained that judgment indeed sits somewhere between universal
truth and individual preferences. Judgments accordingly are not right or wrong, true or untrue but
rather valid or invalid, persuasive or not, which form of assessment is altogether unavailable with
respect to individual preferences. HANNAH ARENDT, Crisis in Culture, *in* BETWEEN PAST AND FUTURE
(1961). Likewise: ERNEST J. WEINRIB, THE IDEA OF PRIVATE LAW 13 (1995); Postema, *supra* note 20, at
114; GEORG WILHELM FRIEDRICH HEGEL, PHILOSOPHY OF RIGHT §214 (1967).

[22] For Kant and for Arendt, judgment by definition involves a claim of agreement upon others: see
Arendt, *supra* note 21 at 221.

they would either accept your arguments or state their reasons for rejecting them, to which you again would be entitled to respond in the same way, and so on until the pool of reasonable arguments is exhausted on both sides.[23] That interactive process is the natural corollary of recognizing you as a self-governing agent:

> To argue is necessarily to presuppose the recognition of all speaking beings as discussion partners with equal rights; it is to commit oneself to recognizing all the possible claims by members of the communicative community that can be justified by reasonable arguments; and it is to force oneself to ground one's own claims upon others only on arguments of the same kind.[24]

What is more, as the arguments advanced on each side presumably get better with each round – 'better' in the sense of moving closer and closer to what the whole community, and hence you as well, can regard as valid coercion-justifying arguments – this process would serve to yield a gradually clearer understanding, on the part of all concerned, of what such arguments ought to look like: judges would gradually acquire a better sense of what kind of arguments ought to determine the outcome of cases, which legislators would then account for in producing new legal materials, which in turn would become the basis for renewed, improved arguments, which the citizens again would get to debate and incrementally cause to shift, and so on.[25] In that sense, what ought to be regarded as valid legal arguments in any given community would come to be determined through an ongoing collective argumentation process – what has been referred to as "a collaborative articulation of shared purposes,"[26] "a collective fabric of justification"[27] – whose participants include officials and citizens alike.[28]

---

[23] Postema, *Law's Rule, supra* note 1, at 7 ("[the citizen] is authorized to demand both an explanation and a reckoning, a narrative and reasons or arguments connecting the act to relevant standards that could provide warrant and grounds for the act. [The citizen] also has standing to assess the explanation and reckoning and to utter a judgement of the action in light of the assessment of them."); Waldron, *supra* note 1, at 8 ("a mode of governance that allows people a voice, a way of intervening on their own behalf in confrontations with power."); Bernard Williams, Realism and Moralism, *in* IN THE BEGINNING WAS THE DEED: REALISM AND MORALISM IN POLITICAL ARGUMENT 5 (Geoffrey Hawthorn ed., 2005) ("[The state] has to be able to offer a justification of its power *to each subject*." Emphasis in original.).

[24] KARL-OTTO APEL, *SUR LE PROBLÈME D'UNE FONDATION RATIONNELLE DE L'ÉTHIQUE À L'ÂGE DE LA SCIENCE: L'A PRIORI DE LA COMMUNAUTÉ COMMUNICATIONNELLE ET LES FONDEMENTS DE L'ÉTHIQUE* 94, 124–26 (R. Lellouche & I. Mittmann trans., 1987) (my translation).

[25] "[L]aw perhaps *begins* with an array of established practices that are 'half understood' and 'indistinct'; but it may then attain a degree of reflective self-awareness whereby the participants deepen their understanding of the values served by their practice, and strive to crystalize and refine the practice so as to serve those values more fully." SIMMONDS, *supra* note 1, at 8.

[26] Lon L. Fuller, Human Purpose and Natural Law, 3 NATURAL LAW FORUM 68 (1958).

[27] RICHARD HYLAND, *Gifts: A STUDY IN COMPARATIVE LAW* 106 (2009).

[28] DWORKIN, *supra* note 1, at 14–15. See likewise: CHRISTIAN ATIAS, *ÉPISTÉMOLOGIE JURIDIQUE* (1985).

I would suggest that the legal process is everywhere structured in this way, at least to some extent.[29] In all jurisdictions on record, the parties and officials involved in court proceedings (or their equivalent)[30] are expected to adduce arguments in support of their respective positions as well as respond to the arguments presented by the other parties.[31] In all jurisdictions also, the position that ultimately emerges as victorious, and that accordingly makes it to the enforcement stage, is that deemed supported by the best legal arguments, which victorious position nonetheless remains defeasible in subsequent rounds, should new contenders be found to be supported by even better arguments.[32] Also in all jurisdictions, finally, official law makers take account of the outcome of judicial proceedings in renewing the pool of materials upon which legal arguments are based and said proceedings accordingly are determined. And out of this process indeed gradually emerges an increasingly finer sense of what constitutes good legal arguments in each community[33] – law 'working itself pure,'[34] as we say. Legal practice thus seems to confirm that law is argumentative through and through, that it is a *self-reflective* collective argument, an argument among officials and citizens *as to what should count as valid such arguments*. In the

---

[29] Other comparatists have come to the same conclusions, e.g. Jacco Bomhoff, Comparing Legal Argument, *in* PRACTICE AND THEORY IN COMPARATIVE LAW 4, 5 (Maurice Adams & Jacco Bomhoff eds., 2012); HAROLD J. BERMAN, LAW AND REVOLUTION: THE FORMATION OF THE WESTERN LEGAL TRADITION 8 (1984); MARTIN SHAPIRO, COURTS: A COMPARATIVE AND POLITICAL ANALYSIS 1–64 (1981) (describing the triadic adjudicative structure as prototypical).

[30] 'Courts' here is meant to refer, more generally, to "institutions that apply norms and directives established in the name of the whole society to individual cases, that settle disputes about the application of those norms, and that do so through the medium of hearings." Waldron, *supra* note 1, at 29. See also: Lon L. Fuller, The Forms and Limits of Adjudication, 92 HARV. L. REV. 353, 363–81 (1978).

[31] "The mode of presentation may vary, but the existence of such an opportunity does not." Waldron, *supra* note 1, at 23.

[32] Whereas a civilian reader might object that such an adjudication-centered account of law is far more representative of the common law than the civil law, I would counter that the justification imperative is as strong in the latter though perhaps discharged differently: whereas the reasons for enforcement appear primarily in the body of judicial decisions at common law, they are typically found in the scholarship at civil law. See: Serge Gaudet, La doctrine et le Code civil du Québec, *in* LE NOUVEAU CODE CIVIL: INTERPRÉTATION ET APPLICATION 223 (1992); HYLAND, *supra* note 27, at 105, 122.

[33] WEINRIB, *supra* note 21, at 15 ("The law's aggregate of specific determinations does not permanently freeze the intelligibility of law to their contours. Being an exhibition of human intelligence rather than divine omniscience ... law includes a self-critical dimension that manifests itself in overrulings, dissents, juristic commentary, and other indicia of controversy."); James Whitman, The Neo-Romantic Turn, *in* COMPARATIVE LEGAL STUDIES: TRADITIONS AND TRANSITIONS 312, 340 (Pierre Legrand & Roderick Munday eds., 2003). ("To articulate legal *Vorverstandnis* is, however, to alter its nature, since it is inevitably to subject it to the process of articulate normative critique. What has been *expressed*, in the law, must inevitably be debated and defended."); SIMMONDS, *supra* note 1, at 159 ("Perhaps legal thought is at bottom a continuous reflection upon the possibility of realizing (and so fully comprehending) its own guiding ideals.").

[34] In Niklas Luhmann's words: "[law] achiev[ing its own] *independent reduction of complexity.*" LUHMANN, *supra* note 15, at 88 (original emphasis). See also at 94.

words of others, it is an "understanding of understanding,"[35] "an image of itself,"[36] "a reflection on its own intelligibity,"[37] "a quest of itself."[38] And legal arguments accordingly provide the raw material for the textual reconstruction exercise described in Chapter 5.

Now the same reason that serves to justify the citizens' entitlement to be given valid arguments, and to debate those arguments, also serves to constrain what it is that they can and cannot accept as valid such arguments. If respect for the citizens' individual agency is the reason that valid arguments must be given to them, they in turn must accept as valid any and all arguments consistent with that agency (and conversely reject any and all arguments inconsistent with it), quite apart from how they might otherwise feel about them. More specifically, they must, as I try to show next, accept any and all arguments meeting the two requirements of 'coherence' and 'publicness' (and reject any and all arguments falling short of them).

iii. *Coherence*

Coherence is here posited as the first criterion for valid legal arguments in any community:[39] quite apart from the substance of the various arguments put forward by the officials to justify public coercion, the more coherent those arguments are among themselves, the more likely it is that they will qualify as valid, all else being equal.[40]

This follows naturally from law being an intellectual product, a product of conscious design. If law is consciously designed so as to express certain commitments, it is also consciously designed so as to express those commitments in the most coherent way possible. For any form of communication by definition aspires to being as coherent as possible. The opposite would simply be illogical: to aspire to communicate incoherently would be to aspire to communicate so as not to be understood, hence to aspire both to communicate and not to communicate. In sum, if law is the

---

[35] CLIFFORD GEERTZ, *LOCAL KNOWLEDGE: FURTHER ESSAYS IN INTERPRETIVE ANTHROPOLOGY* 5 (2000).

[36] John Henry Merryman, Letter to the Editor, Civil Law Tradition, 35 AM. J. COMP. L. 438, 441 (1987) ("To understand a [legal system] you have to know ... what its image of itself is.").

[37] WEINRIB, *supra* note 21, at 14 ("law is an exhibition of intelligence that operates through reflection on its own intelligibility.").

[38] LON L. FULLER, *THE LAW IN QUEST OF ITSELF* (1940).

[39] Postema, *Law's System*, *supra* note 1 at 70, 88. See *contra*: H. Patrick Glenn, Legal Traditions and Legal Traditions, 2 J. COMP. L. 69, 71–72 (2007) (suggesting that coherence is a feature of Western law only).

[40] 'Coherence' should not be confused with mere 'consistency.' Whereas the latter "is satisfied by non-contradiction" (e.g., FULLER, *supra* note 1, at 65–70), the former is "a matter of [norms] 'making sense' by being rationally related as a set, instrumentally or intrinsically, to the realization of some common value or values." MACCORMICK, *RHETORIC AND THE RULE OF LAW*, *supra* note 1, at 190, 193. Likewise: Waldron, *supra* note 1, at 34: "we should interpret [legal norms] so that the point of one does not defeat the point of another." Postema, *Law's System*, *supra* note 1, at 91: "Law not only aspires to present itself as publicly intelligible but it demands this of itself because it is necessary for it to perform its fundamental task of normative guidance."

product of rational thought, it is necessarily governed by the same imperatives as govern reason itself, and avoidance of internal contradiction is one such imperative.[41]

The coherence imperative moreover also follows from recognizing the citizens as self-governing agents. We saw above that for the citizens to self-govern, they need to be able to rely on law's commitments actually materializing. Before one can even begin to assess the likelihood of materialization of any commitment, however, there must be a certain understanding of what is being committed to. And it is not possible to understand what is being committed to where the commitment is incoherent – where it is simultaneously committed to X and non-X. It therefore is imperative, if the citizens' entitlement to self-governance is to be taken seriously, that the reasons invoked to curtail that entitlement be as coherent as possible.

More fundamentally, however, the coherence imperative reflects the *equality* of the citizens as self-governing agents. We saw above that if law indeed is a commitment, it entails a rapport of equality between the officials and the citizens as respectively issuing and receiving parties of that commitment. But law is not just a two-party commitment; it is a collective commitment, the commitment of an entire community to itself. The rapport of equality inherent in it therefore applies, not just between the citizens and the officials, but also across citizens. As all are parties to this collective commitment, it is their collective equality – their equality as against one another – that is being recognized through it.[42] And if all are equal in this way, it is imperative that the various arguments put forward to justify curtailing individual self-governance in particular situations be consistent across situations. Thus, whereas recognizing the citizens as self-governing agents entails curtailing their self-governance only where there are good reasons to do so, recognizing them as *equal* agents entails that the good reasons given to different citizens be coherent among themselves.

In actual fact, legal materials admittedly often seem to defy this coherence imperative.[43] Constitutions, statutes and regulations are regularly drafted in response to a multitude of divergent if not conflicting moral and social concerns. Judicial and administrative proceedings yield different rulings in cases that appear similar, and similar rulings in cases that appear different. Those faced with having to interpret these materials moreover seem destined never to be able to reach any kind of lasting consensus. As the array of arguments available to support any one legal position

---

[41] On this point more generally, see: DIETER HENRICH, THE UNITY OF REASON: ESSAYS IN KANT'S PHILOSOPHY (Richard Velkley ed., 1994).

[42] Coherence "means equality before the law ... in the more consequential sense that government must govern under a set of principles in principle applicable to all." RONALD DWORKIN, JUSTICE IN ROBES 176 (2006).

[43] See generally: ANDREI MARMOR, POSITIVE LAW AND OBJECTIVE VALUES 69 (2001); James Gordley, Comparative Law and Legal History, in THE OXFORD HANDBOOK OF COMPARATIVE LAW, *supra* note 5, at 753, 761ff.

consequently is extremely wide, it is at times difficult to resist the conclusion that just about anything goes. And many observers indeed have so concluded.[44]

The coherence imperative is nonetheless palpable, as many have pointed out, in the *way that legal actors handle* those materials.[45] It has been suggested that the 'non-transparent' way in which courts typically perform their law-making function bears witness to this imperative: when courts purport to 'discover' rather than create the law that they apply in any given case, they do so with a view to emphasizing and fostering legal continuity.[46] Their arguments to that effect may be more or less persuasive, but the mere fact that they bother to put them forward confirms the importance that they attach to that value. If only as a normative matter, then, "[t] he law may not be a seamless web; but the [citizen] is entitled to ask [that it be] treat[ed ...] as if it were."[47]

More generally, it seems clear that any kind of legal argument proceeds on the assumption that contradictions among the various materials governing the same question are to be overcome. Submissions before courts, judicial decisions, legislative debates and enactments, and law school examination answers all proceed on the basis that wherever distinct rules appear to yield contradictory legal outcomes, the legal materials must be reinterpreted so that one of the following contradictionfree conclusions obtains: either the two rules admittedly are irreconcilable but one does not apply to the case at hand and hence can be disregarded, or else is a bad rule and thus to be eliminated; or the two rules in fact can be reconciled in support of one of the contradictory outcomes, leaving the other, unsupported outcome, to be discarded. Different interpretations of the legal landscape are being put forward depending on which of these conclusions is being sought, and the interpretation

[44] Most prominent among them of course are the legal realists, whose most significant contribution perhaps was to uncover the nest of contradictions embodied in legal materials. See, e.g.: Karl Llewellyn, Remarks on the Theory of Appellate Decision and the Rules or Canons About How Statutes Are To Be Construed, 3 VAND. L. REV. 395 (1950).

[45] See e.g.: MACCORMICK, *RHETORIC AND THE RULE OF LAW, supra* note 1, at 134 ("[Legal actors] reinterpret phenomena as parts of a coherent and well-ordered whole"); Vittorio Villa, Neil MacCormick's Legal Positivism, *in* MAKSYMILIAN DEL MAR & ZENON BANKOWSKI eds., *Law as Institutional Normative Order* 45, 53 (2009) ("[legal actors] rationally reconstruct ... what would otherwise be the 'multiform chaos' of legal experience, imposing an order on it."); SIMMONDS, *supra* note 1, at 13; HYLAND, *supra* note 27, at 105–106. Probably the most famous account of the legal process as interpretation however remains that put forward in: RONALD DWORKIN, *TAKING RIGHTS SERIOUSLY* chap. 4 (1977).

[46] Waldron, *supra* note 1, at 29, 35. Waldron refers to the same idea as "systematicity" or "the cumulative character of law" (Waldron, *supra* at 32); Dworkin, as "integrity" (DWORKIN, *supra* note 1, at 165–66).

[47] DWORKIN, *supra* note 45, at 116. See also: MACCORMICK, *RHETORIC AND THE RULE OF LAW, supra* note 1, at 54 (arguing for full self-coherence "as a governing ideal for legal reasoning and legal interpretation," not as "representing actual legal systems as though they already had or will ever acquire this character"); Postema, *Law's System, supra* note 1, at 74 ("Theoretical consistency, stability, and internal coherence are important aims, but they can only be approximated."); WEINRIB, *supra* note 21, at 13 ("coherence is an aspiration, not a permanent or inevitable achievement."). Weinrib's own concept of coherence however is thicker than the present criterion as it motions to a particular form of justice (Aristotelian corrective justice).

deemed most convincing in any given case again is determined largely (though not exclusively)[48] by appeal to coherence: all else being equal, the more unified the interpretation, the better. This process arguably reveals that while legal actors may and clearly do disagree as to *how* the various pertinent materials are to fit together, they are at least agreed that those materials *are to be made* to fit together – much like players engaged in the construction of a jigsaw puzzle may debate how to assemble the various pieces yet agree that those pieces are to be assembled into an overall coherent picture. This at any rate would explain that the coherence imperative might commonly be described as "the fetish of municipal lawyers,"[49] despite legal materials in fact often clashing with one another.

Coherence hence is a first criterion for assessing the validity of legal arguments in any community. While the various communities will continue to debate what should count as valid coercion-justifying arguments within their realm, one term of that debate seems well settled across communities: legal materials are to be viewed as somehow holding together and the arguments most consistent among themselves accordingly are, all else equal, to be considered most convincing. We will see in Chapter 5 how this coherence criterion plays out in the comparative context, where a number of jigsaw puzzles are being assembled in tandem.

iv. *Publicness*

The second criterion for assessing the validity of legal arguments in any community is publicness. Valid legal arguments must be public in the sense, first, of being transparent and open to public scrutiny. This first sense (perhaps best captured through the slightly different term of 'publicity') is implicit in the discussion of section ii above: legal arguments must necessarily be disclosed if only because no one can govern their affairs in reliance upon, let alone respond to and debate, arguments that are unknown to them. The transparency requirement thus flows, again, from respect for the citizens' individual agency. The discussion of section iii moreover revealed that said transparency must be intellectual as well as physical: if the arguments given are incoherent, the fact that they are physically disclosed will do little to help the citizens understand them, and understanding remains the ultimate objective here. The citizens' self-governance thus requires that the arguments be transparent both physically and intellectually.[50] The discussion of section iii also revealed, finally, that transparency (physical and intellectual) is also necessary for all to be in a

---

[48] In section iv, we see that there is at least one other criterion for assessing the validity of legal interpretations, namely, 'publicness.'

[49] Rodolfo Sacco, Legal Formants: A Dynamic Approach to Comparative Law (Installment I of II), 39 AM. J. COMP. L. 1, 24 (1991). See also: Günter Frankenberg, Critical Comparisons: Re-thinking Comparative Law, 26 HARV. INT'L L. J. 411 (1985).

[50] They must be "publicly knowable," in Weinrib's words. WEINRIB, *supra* note 21, at 108.

position to see and verify that the same set of internally coherent arguments is used across citizens, i.e. that all citizens are being treated equally.[51]

But there is another sense in which valid legal arguments must be 'public.' Suppose that an official issues an order to kill all rabbits on a certain territory, stating as the only reason for that order that she abhors rabbits. If only intuitively, it seems clear that that is not a reason that the citizens should accept as valid despite it being fully disclosed, perfectly coherent and perhaps even genuine (the judge truly abhorring rabbits). The citizens could legitimately reject that reason, I would suggest, because it does not qualify as a 'public reason' in the sense coined by John Rawls.[52] That is, it is a person-specific reason, one grounded in the personal tastes of the official acting as a private party, rather than one offered by her in her official capacity, as representative for the community. A reason qualifying as 'public' in the Rawlsian sense thus is a reason that, quite apart from it being publicly disclosed, transcends private interests and holds across the entire community.[53] It is a reason that directly pertains to the community per se, distinguished from its particular member(s).[54]

Importantly for my purposes, it would make no difference, under the Rawlsian conception, whether and how widely the official's dislike of rabbits is shared among the citizens. Even if *all* citizens happened to share that dislike and would in fact love to see the rabbits in question exterminated, the official's reason would not qualify as 'public' any more than it does where only the official feels that way. It would still be a 'person-specific' reason insofar as it would still be grounded in private interests. Only, it would now be specific to more than just one person: it would be specific to many a citizen, all considered in their capacity as private persons. Just increasing the number of private persons to whom a reason is specific will not make that reason

---

[51] This refers to Kant's "formal attribute of publicness" whereby "all actions affecting the rights of other human beings are wrong if their maxim is not compatible with their being made public." IMMANUEL KANT, PERPETUAL PEACE (1795), reprinted in KANT'S POLITICAL WRITINGS 125–26 (Hans Reis ed., 1991).

[52] JOHN RAWLS, THE LAW OF PEOPLES: WITH "THE IDEA OF PUBLIC REASON" REVISITED esp. 54ff (4th ed. 2002) (1993).

[53] Hart, for one, indeed seemed to reduce publicness to a matter of broad information dissemination, possibly achievable through other means: "no society could support the number of officials necessary to secure that every member of the society was officially and separately informed of every act which he was required to do." (HART, *supra* note 5, at 21.) See likewise: JULES COLEMAN, THE PRACTICE OF PRINCIPLE 206–207 (2001). Waldron (*supra* note 1, at 26) rightly retorts that "publicity ... is not just a matter of pragmatic administrative convenience ... It embodies a fundamental point about the way in which the systems we call 'legal systems' operate. They operate by using, rather than suppressing and short-circuiting, the responsible agency of ordinary human individuals."

[54] Publicness thus "draws attention to the personal self-effacement of those who participate in [its] elucidation ... What matters is the law as something to be understood, not the lawyer or scholar or judge as a freelancing intellectual adventurer." WEINRIB, *supra* note 21, at 15. See also: BENJAMIN N. CARDOZO, THE NATURE OF THE JUDICIAL PROCESS 71 (1998) (1921); Aharon Barak, Foreword: A Judge on Judging, 116 HARV. L. REV. 18, 51 (2002); Jeremy Waldron, The Concept and the Rule of Law, 43 GA L. REV. 1, 20 (2012); Benedict Kingsbury, The Concept of 'Law' in Global Administrative Law, 20 EUR. J. INT'L L. 23, 31 (2009).

'public,' in other words. That is to say that valid legal reasons are reasons that the citizens *in their capacity as community members* ought to accept as valid, quite apart from how they feel about those reasons *in their private capacity*. A qualitative shift indeed is needed whereby private interests are altogether transcended rather than just aggregated.

Rawls (like Kant)[55] finds the requisite qualitative shift in the central tenet of the present definition, namely, in the notion of commitment.[56] If all citizens had somehow *agreed* that they would collectively aim to exterminate rabbits, then that agreement would provide the requisite 'public' basis for the official to order rabbit killings. That basis would qualify as 'public' insofar as it would relate to a collective agreement, an institution created by and through the citizens coming together as rational community members precisely for the purpose of transcending their potentially different private views on the matter. Privately, the citizens indeed might have had very different reasons to join in the collective agreement. Some might have decided to join because, like the official, they simply dislike rabbits. But others might have done so for, say, health, environmental, or economic reasons – because they thought a rabbit-free world would somehow be healthier, more environmentally friendly, or more efficient. Yet others might actually be quite fond of rabbits yet joined the agreement for the sake of social harmony, in order to keep their peers happy. Others still, not caring one way or the other about rabbits, might have joined only for log-rolling reasons, in the hope that the rabbit-haters might return the favour in future policy debates about which they feel more strongly. But beyond these widely differing reasons, there is one that necessarily applies across all citizens: as in the context of any agreement, each of the parties here agreed *because* the others did. That reciprocal bond, the *fact* of their mutual agreement, is what ties the citizens together over and above their widely differing (private) views about the *substance* of that agreement.[57]

'Public' is here meant, then, in the Rawlsian sense of that which can be ascribed to the community *as community* – to the community conceptualized as an entity altogether separate from (the sum of) its individual members[58] – for the simple

---

[55] See Rawls' (RAWLS, *supra* note 52, at 56, note 71) reference to Kant's *Doctrine of Right*.
[56] Ibid.
[57] "The conception of justice by which we live is then a conception we endorse, not for the different reasons we may each discover, and not simply for reasons we happen to share, but instead for reasons that count for us because we can affirm them together ... each of us affirming them in light of the fact that others affirm them too." Charles Larmore, Public Reason, *in* 368 THE CAMBRIDGE COMPANION TO RAWLS (Samuel Freeman ed., 2003). Dworkin describes the same idea through a distinction between 'concurrent' and 'conventional' morality: "A community displays a concurrent morality when its members are agreed in asserting the same, or much the same normative rule, but they do not count the fact of that agreement as an essential part of their grounds for asserting that rule. It displays a conventional morality when they do." DWORKIN, *supra* note 45, at 53.
[58] KARL POPPER, *OBJECTIVE KNOWLEDGE: AN EVOLUTIONARY APPROACH* 159 (1972) ("[Law is] man-made and, in a very clear sense, superhuman at the same time. It transcends its makers"); Waldron, *supra* note 1, at 31 ("norms that purport to stand in the name of the whole society and to address matters of concern to the society as such").

reason that it was collectively agreed that it would. And transparency accordingly comes into play not just as an end in itself but also for the purpose of enabling all to see and verify that the coercion-justifying arguments put forward by the officials indeed are 'public' in that sense, in addition to being consistently applied across citizens (the coherence requirement) – that they cohere, that is, not just internally, but also with the community's commitments so defined.

The next question concerns the identification of such 'public' commitments: how are we to determine what commitments can properly be ascribed to entire communities? In particular, how do such collective agreements come about? How and when do they lapse (if at all)? What are their exact contours and content? And so on. Although we discuss these and other similar questions in some detail in Chapter 4, some general remarks are in order now. The first is that, as suggested by our discussion thus far, these are questions that it will ultimately fall to the law makers in each community to determine: a collective agreement will be taken to arise when, to last as long as, and to cover and contain whatever the law makers say it does. As we just saw, moreover, only those of the law makers' relevant declarations as are made in their 'official' rather than private capacity count in this respect. The drafters of low-cost housing legislation, the judge sanctioning freedom of expression violations, the prosecutor refraining from charging compassionate crime perpetrators clearly consider affordable housing, freedom of expression and indulgence towards compassionate crime perpetrators to be among the community's commitments, quite apart from how they personally feel about those issues. Such judgments on their part should be considered compelling if only because they are particularly well positioned to assess what does and does not appear among the community's commitments. But as their title suggests (and the above discussion of *Argumentativeness* confirmed), the law makers are more than just knowledgeable observers of the community: as its official representatives, they actually speak in its name. The mere fact that they would *claim* certain commitments as the community's own therefore actually contributes to making it so.[59] Official claims as to the community's commitments to some extent are necessarily constitutive as well as declarative of those values, in other words.

This in turn begs the question of who should count as an 'official representative' of the community, as someone capable of making 'official claims' in its name. It must firstly be pointed out that law making indeed is an *office* – hence to be conferred upon or withdrawn from its holders following certain designated requirements and procedures – not an inherent quality of any particular person(s).[60] It can therefore be held by many persons simultaneously, as well as passed on from one set of person(s)

---

[59] Neil Walker describes this as 'intimation': "the very act or practice of intimating ... law is intended to contribute to the realization of the 'project'." NEIL WALKER, INTIMATIONS OF GLOBAL LAW 149 (2015). This point is unpacked below, in Chapter 3, Part I (contrasting 'cognitivism' and 'constructivism').

[60] MIRJAN R. DAMAŠKA, THE FACES OF JUSTICE AND STATE AUTHORITY: A COMPARATIVE APPROACH TO THE LEGAL PROCESS (1986).

to another sequentially. It can also be taken on or put on hold temporarily, as when judges step into court to adjudicate cases or step out of court to comment on matters they feel strongly about on a personal level. The fact that judicial and extra-judicial pronouncements typically attract very different treatments[61] arguably bears out this "schism [lying] between office and its occupant."[62]

But the foregoing discussion also confirms that even just regular citizens can in certain circumstances act like law makers: insofar as they partake in the argumentative process that serves to determine what should count as valid legal arguments in the community (*Argumentativeness* above), and insofar as only arguments that reflect commitments of the community will qualify as valid such arguments (*Publicness* above), the citizens clearly contribute to the formation of those commitments – they qualify as 'law makers' in some sense, despite perhaps not being *political* representatives of the community.[63] This is the idea of the 'self-legislating' citizen, most famously extolled in Rousseau's writings:

> [W]hen the people as a whole makes rules for the people as a whole, it is dealing only with itself; and if any relationship emerges, it is between the entire body seen from one perspective and the same entire body seen from another, without any division whatever. Here the matter concerning which rule is made is as general as the will which makes it. And this is the kind of act which I call a law.[64]

In section v, we investigate the means used by communities to designate the particular procedures, requirements and so on that will qualify as 'law making' for their purposes, the particular circumstances in which even just regular citizens can properly be considered 'law makers.'

v. *Formality*

Formality is the means by which communities designate certain institutions and their output as peculiarly 'legal,' as respectively 'law-making institutions' and 'legal

---

[61] "[We are] interested in how legal actors explain what they are doing when they are acting as legal actors. The relevant evidence of this understanding is found in judicial reports, parliamentary debates, and lawyers' arguments in courts—rather than, say, in judges or legislators' personal diaries or in psychological assessments of their motives." STEPHEN A. SMITH, CONTRACT THEORY 14 (2004).

[62] DAMAŠKA, *supra* note 60, at 19.

[63] As per Fuller's pillar notion of official-citizen reciprocity (*supra* note 1) and Postema's idea of "network of mutual accountability" (Postema, *supra* note 1, at 17–18), both of which echo Kant (Kant, *supra* note 51, at 323): "no one can bind another to something without also being subject to a law by which he in turn can be bound in the same way by the other."

[64] JEAN JACQUES ROUSSEAU, THE SOCIAL CONTRACT 81–82 (Maurice Cranston trans., 1968) (1762). See likewise: JÜRGEN HABERMAS, BETWEEN FACTS AND NORMS: CONTRIBUTIONS TO A DISCOURSE THEORY OF LAW AND DEMOCRACY 120 (1996) ("The idea of self-legislation *by* citizens ... requires that those subject to law as its addressees can at the same time understand themselves as authors of the law"); DARWALL, *supra* note 10; DWORKIN, *supra* note 45, at 186–205.

materials.' In the same way that individual actors use formalities to delineate the
domain of their private contracts, communities use them to earmark what should
count as their distinctively legal venues. In private contracting, only those of the
actors' subjective aspirations, biases, interests, etc. as make it into their designated
formal contract and are enforceable as such count as the 'law of the parties.' Likewise
with respect to communities, only those of the community members' aspirations as
have properly been processed through the community's formally designated legal
norm-making/enforcing mechanisms count as the 'law of the community.'[65]

As formality accordingly attaches to law only indirectly, via its process or 'pedigree' rather than substance, law is 'content-neutral' – just as positivist legal scholars
have long insisted.[66] It is a well-established fact that legal norms properly so-called
come in a wide variety of different contents – moral, historical, economic and so
on – which variety moreover can be observed both within and across jurisdictions.[67]
As the term 'formality' itself suggests, then, formality is (or at least is here taken to
be) just the tangible manifestation of legal intention, the particular mark that serves
to imprint certain institutions and their materials as 'legal' regardless of content.

Importantly for my purposes, while this formal designation often is accomplished
explicitly, explicit designation is in fact neither necessary nor sufficient. It not being
necessary is shown, again, through the analogy with private contracting. Where the
parties' agreement is not embodied in a formal contract, the courts simply take it
upon themselves to reconstruct from the context what the parties have implicitly
designated as the repository for their contractual intention. Likewise in the collective context, whereas some communities are endowed with written constitutions
that explicitly designate what should count as their formal law-making institutions,
not all constitutions are written. Where constitutions are unwritten, as in England,
it is nonetheless possible to identify formal legal channels by looking to what is

[65] Niklas Luhmann describes the two phases of this process as "informational openness" and "normative
closure": while the legal process is initially open to a limitless diversity of factors and points of view, it will
result in only a limited number of them actually becoming ('normatively relevant') law. NIKLAS LUHMANN,
A SOCIOLOGICAL THEORY OF LAW 174–83 (1985). See also: GUNTHER TEUBNER, LAW AS AN AUTOPOIETIC
SYSTEM esp. chap. 3 (1993); Hubert Rottleuthner, Les métaphores biologiques dans la pensée juridique,
31 ARCH. PHIL. DROIT 215 (1986). As has been pointed out (e.g. MICHAEL VAN DE KERCHOVE & François
Ost, LEGAL SYSTEM BETWEEN ORDER AND DISORDER 5–6 (1994)), Luhmann here is merely restating in
abstract terms what many legal positivists, in particular Hart and Kelsen, have described in more concrete,
legal terms. Luhmann's work is prominent in the discussion of Chapters 2 and 4.

[66] Hart refers instead to "content-independence." H. L. A. HART, ESSAYS ON BENTHAM: JURISPRUDENCE AND
POLITICAL THEORY 262–66 (1982). See also: THOMAS HOBBES, LEVIATHAN chap. 26 (1651); KELSEN,
supra note 1. While Dworkin departs from positivism in important ways, he similarly describes legal
rules as rules that "can be identified and distinguished by specific criteria, by tests having to do not
with their content but with their *pedigree* or the manner in which they were adopted or developed."
DWORKIN, *supra* note 45, at 17. (Emphasis in original.)

[67] At least under the present conception of 'inclusive' (versus 'exclusive') positivism, which distinction is
discussed in, e.g. JULES COLEMAN, THE PRACTICE OF PRINCIPLE: IN DEFENCE OF A PRAGMATIST APPROACH
TO LEGAL THEORY (1994), 'Postscript.'

de facto accepted as such. That is, it is possible to draw from the fact that English lawyers have traditionally treated Acts of Parliament as binding that Parliament is a formal legal channel for England.

Other instances of implicit, practice-induced formal designations include the treatments of scholarly writings in civil law jurisdictions, of elder's pronouncements in aboriginal law, of policy arguments in certain common law jurisdictions, and of certain norms of international law and transnational 'soft' law. It indeed is through practice that scholars have come to be regarded as a quasi-formal source of legal authority in many civil law jurisdictions. While it clearly is the case that scholarly writings are regularly invoked in the course of formal legal arguments *because* they are recognized as quasi-authoritative, the reverse arguably is also true: scholarly writings are recognized as quasi-authoritative (and their authors, correspondingly, as a quasi-formal source of law) at least in part *because* these writings are regularly so invoked. In some cases, in fact, such recognition obtains *in spite of* explicit and formal admonitions to the contrary.[68] Likewise with circles of elders in aboriginal communities: the fact that the oral rulings issued by these circles were accepted as authoritative in their respective communities long before they were (in some cases) expressly so recognized, allows for the conclusion that such circles ought to count as their communities' formal legal channels independently of explicit recognition. And with respect to policy arguments: whereas such arguments are at times expressly authorized by the legislator, it is largely through practice that they came to be recognized as formal legal arguments in certain common law jurisdictions. Though once dismissed out of hand by the judges (and hence altogether ignored by the lawyers), they gradually came into use, to the point where it arguably is now unquestionable that they have entered the realm of valid legal arguments.[69] As for norms of international law and transnational 'soft' law, finally, it has similarly been argued that insofar as 'communities of practice' might in fact have congealed around certain such norms, these areas might indeed qualify as 'legal,' despite international institutions typically lacking the debating and implementation capacity usually associated with formal legal institutions.[70]

But the most extreme case of implicit formal legal institution perhaps remains that of a dictator who would have usurped its extensive law-making powers through what would have been formally illegitimate means at the time. Although the supposed

---

[68] See, e.g., Napoleon's burning of doctrinal commentaries on his code.

[69] John C. Reitz, How to Do Comparative Law, 46 AM. J. OF COMP. L. 617, 625, 629 (1998) (discussing the integration of policy arguments in US law). See generally: PIERRE LAROUCHE & PÉTER CSERNE, NATIONAL LEGAL SYSTEMS AND GLOBALIZATION: NEW ROLE, CONTINUED RELEVANCE 99ff (2013).

[70] JUTTA BRUNNEE & STEPHEN J. TOOPE, LEGITIMACY AND LEGALITY IN INTERNATIONAL LAW: AN INTERACTIONAL ACCOUNT 8 (2010); Jutta Brunnee & Stephen J. Toope, Interactional International Law and the Practice of Legality, in INTERNATIONAL PRACTICES 108 (Emanuel Adler & Vincent Pouliot eds., 2011). The border problems caused by these various communities' overlapping on a same territory – 'legal pluralism' – is taken up in Chapter 4, Part III, section ii.

"schism between the office and the person of its occupant"[71] is admittedly rather small in such a case, it may still be possible to view the dictator as 'legal official' for the community, at least insofar as that individual might de facto come to act like one, i.e. be so treated by the community.[72] On an intuitive level, it seems at least plausible that, as Hart and other positivists took pains to demonstrate,[73] even a community that is forced to obey dictatorial orders might recognize those orders as 'law,' and their author as 'law maker.' It may do so begrudgingly, even resentfully, complaining that the orders are unwise, 'morally bad,'[74] or even 'wicked.'[75] Nonetheless, so long as the population does in fact conform, and up until the time it in fact rebels,[76] the orders in question arguably count as 'law' – even if such law is possibly 'unwise,' 'morally bad' or 'wicked.' From the standpoint of Rawlsian 'publicness,' it indeed may be possible to infer from the community's general obedience that it generally *agrees* – or at least does not *dis*agree, which may perhaps be enough – that the orders qualify as 'laws' (at least where disobedience is reasonably possible).[77] If even illegitimate dictators can properly be viewed as formal legal officials, explicit designations of formality clearly are not absolutely necessary.

Nor are such designations sufficient, moreover. It is a commonplace that law not applied is simply not law, and legal history indeed is replete with examples of rules or institutions that, though once explicitly enacted as law, come to lose their formal legal status through lack of use in legal practice. We saw above the reasons why that might be. As it is an essential feature of law that it at least call for enforcement, formality ultimately is meant to designate *that which is to be enforced.* Where the designation is not followed with actual enforcement, however, the most that can be said of the designated material is that it had the potential of becoming law, but that potential never materialized: it remained intention 'writ in water,' as contracts textbooks like to remind us. As explicit designation accordingly is neither necessary nor sufficient, reducing the formally legal to what has been explicitly designated such would be both under- and over-exclusive.

---

[71] See *supra*, text accompanying note 60.
[72] Some admittedly fall short of even that low standard. For an argument that Nazi Germany is one example of a regime that failed to even 'act' like a legal one, see: Waldron, *supra* note 1, at 18.
[73] HART, *supra* note 5; JEREMY BENTHAM, A FRAGMENT ON GOVERNMENT (J. H. Burns & H. L. A. Hart, eds., 1977); JOHN AUSTIN, LECTURES ON JURISPRUDENCE (Robert Campbell ed., 5th ed. 1885) (1863).
[74] H. L. A. HART, POSITIVISM AND THE SEPARATION BETWEEN LAW AND MORALS (1968), *reprinted in* ESSAYS IN JURISPRUDENCE AND PHILOSOPHY 53 (1983).
[75] DAVID DYZENHAUS, HARD CASES IN WICKED LEGAL SYSTEMS: PATHOLOGIES OF LEGALITY 233 (2010).
[76] By 'rebellion' is meant actual revolution, not mere civil disobedience, for it arguably is possible to construe civil disobedience as conduct aimed at disavowing the substance of the law while recognizing its authority (Catherine Valcke, Civil Disobedience and the Rule of Law: A Lockean Insight, *in* THE RULE OF LAW – NOMOS XXXVI, 45 (Ian Shapiro ed., 1994)).
[77] See generally: PERCY HERBERT PARTRIDGE, CONSENT AND CONSENSUS (1971). But see David Hume's famous objection: DAVID HUME, ESSAYS: MORAL, POLITICAL, AND LITERARY 475 (Eugene F. Miller ed., 1985) (1742).

In sum, although law is here conceptualized formalistically – as 'official law,' 'lawyers' law' or 'the internal legal culture,' as some have derogatorily described it[78] – it should not for that matter be confused with the 'law in books.'[79] If anything, the present account better fits the contrasting label of 'law in action' (and possibly also that of 'law in minds,'[80] as we will see below). For 'formal legal venue' is here taken to encompass all that is de facto treated as such by the community (legislative assemblies, court proceedings, official legal correspondence, lawyer-mediated settlements or contractual negotiations, etc.), and 'formal law' correspondingly captures all arguments, materials, rhetorical strategies, etc. that it is considered acceptable to deploy in such venues, as determined from their being de facto regularly so deployed. Precisely because formal legal arguments feed into decisions that are amenable to actual enforcement, they can be taken to reflect a willingness on the part of their authors to be held accountable for them, to stand in public judgment of their force and validity as against community standards. They can be taken to reflect – that is, a considered judgment as to what are or should be – the community's commitments in a way that informal arguments cannot. Any form of normativity ('soft law' included) that emerges from 'formal decision-making institutions' in this loose sense and is 'systematically and collectively enforced' in some way thus may potentially[81] qualify as 'law' on the present account. Whether it in fact does or not would depend on the above *effectiveness* caveat, i.e. whether 'systematic and collective enforcement' can only come from a state proper, discussed in Chapter 4.

The second, 'publicness' requirement for valid legal arguments, discussed above can accordingly be restated as follows: valid legal arguments are 'public' not just in the sense of being physically and intellectually transparent but also in that of being reflective of commitments of the whole community, *as determined from their being de facto accepted as such in formal legal settings, in settings that spawn decisions amenable to collective enforcement.* And the arguments used in the reconstruction exercise described in Chapter 5 indeed all are 'public' (and 'formal') in that sense.

vi. *Normativity*

As the conception of the citizens as self-governing agents in many ways is an ideal conception, so is the conception of law here laid out. It indeed emerges from

---

[78] LAWRENCE M. FRIEDMAN, *LAW AND SOCIETY: AN INTRODUCTION* Chap 7 (1977).

[79] Roscoe Pound, Law in Books and Law in Action, 44 AM. L. REV. 12 (1910). See, e.g. ('official law' being equated with the 'law in books'): Mitchel Lasser, The Question of Understanding, *in* COMPARATIVE LEGAL STUDIES, *supra* note 33, at 197, 208.

[80] Ewald, *supra* note 4, at 2111; William Ewald, The Jurisprudential Approach to Comparative Law: A Field Guide to 'Rats', 46 AM. J. COMP. L. 701, 705 (1998).

[81] See however the discussion of the extent to which, if at all, non-state law meets this last criterion, *infra* Chapter 4, Part III.

the discussion thus far that law is here conceived as a community's ideal self-representation – a community's representation of itself as it wishes it were or hopes to become. A community that enshrines freedom of expression in its constitution – that commits to protecting freedom of expression – clearly is a community that *aspires* to its citizens becoming free to express themselves. One enacting smoking bans clearly *aims* to become smoke-free. One that sanctions contractual breaches clearly *values* contractual performance. Precisely because (formal) laws are actually enforced, they can be regarded as reflecting a serious collective attachment to the ideals they embody.

Like the other five essential features described above, law's normative dimension is arguably also palpable in legal practice. Any form of legal interpretation to some extent involves reaching to the ideals underlying the rules being interpreted.[82] To interpret law as we saw is to reconstruct legal materials into coherent stories. And to do this necessarily involves appealing to the ideals that motivated the enactment of those materials in the first place.[83] The different interpretations of the legal landscape put forward in legal proceedings indeed reflect different understandings of the 'legislative intention' or 'judicial meaning' underlying the rules. We saw above that the determination of which of those interpretations counts as 'best' involves appealing to internal coherence – that the most coherent interpretation would, all else equal, be considered most convincing in all jurisdictions. The discussion of section v revealed that the nature of the ideals put forward as underlying the rules also plays a role in that determination: among various possible coherent interpretations, that which best coheres with the community's stock of formally designated legal ideals will win out over the others.[84]

---

[82] Fuller makes this point in his famous response to Hart: Lon L. Fuller, Positivism and Fidelity to Law: A Reply to Professor Hart, 71 *HARV. L. REV.* 632, 661–69 (1958).

[83] "Such pictures [of what judges ought to do] are actualities quite as much as the materials of legal precepts or doctrines upon which or with which they work." Nathan R. Pound, The Call for a Realistic Jurisprudence, 44 *HARV. L. REV.* 700 (1931). See also: John Finnis' 'focal meaning' (JOHN FINNIS, *NATURAL LAW AND NATURAL RIGHTS* 12–18 (1980)); Ronald Dworkin's notion of 'interpretive concepts' (DWORKIN, *supra* note 1, at 48–68); MACCORMICK, *INSTITUTIONS OF LAW*, *supra* note 1, at 293–98; SIMMONDS, *supra* note 1, at 14.

[84] While the above two-part test for the validity of legal arguments might appear to match Dworkin's 'fit' *cum* 'value' test (DWORKIN, *supra* note 45, esp. 106–107; THE PRACTICE OF INTEGRITY, ACTA JURIDICA 1, 15–16 (François du Bois ed., 2004)), the two tests arguably are slightly different. The above 'coherence' standard refers to both the intelligibility of legal arguments and their consistent application across citizens whereas the 'publicness' standard refers to their concordance with the community's formal legal ideals. In Dworkin, in contrast, "fit" refers to the correspondence of legal arguments with the rest of the community's legal materials (arguably covering both our 'coherence' and 'publicness' standards) and "value" designates "political morality" (*ibid.*), i.e. moral values that *lie altogether outside law*. (But see his concession, discussed below (note 88), that different groups, such as families, can have different "institutional moralities": RONALD DWORKIN, *JUSTICE FOR HEDGEHOGS* 408 (2011).) As discussed in Chapter 2, adding the latter requirement would result in a definition of law that is too constraining for our purposes.

The above discussion also revealed that legal ideals are of two kinds.[85] Whereas some impose themselves upon the law makers in all communities merely by virtue of their being *legal* ideals and accordingly are cross-community constants: 'non-contingent' legal ideals (also known as 'peremptory'[86] or 'exclusionary')[87] – others are determinable by the law makers and hence potentially variable across communities: 'contingent' legal ideals. Effectiveness, argumentativeness, coherence, publicness and formality are here postulated as the minimal set of formal conditions for the realization of law. As such, they are non-contingent legal ideals: law that would never be materially enforced would, as discussed, fail to represent a true commitment and thus to even qualify as 'law' under the present conception, as would 'law' that would be entirely devoid of any kind of debating and reason-giving, or that would be content to remain internally contradictory or steadfastly at odds with the community's public ideals. These formal requisites however are amenable to taking on a wide variety of contents. That is, they can materialize into different contingent legal ideals in different communities.[88] The above examples of freedom of expression, a smoke- or rabbit-free society, affordable housing, contract honouring, etc. are just a few examples of such contingent legal ideals.

Likewise contingent is the *degree* of effectiveness, argumentativeness, coherence, publicness and formality that is being sought in any given community, even though these qualities being *minimally* sought indeed are non-contingent. With respect to effectiveness, for example, communities may differ on how often and how consistently any given rule needs to be enforced in order to retain its status as legal rule. They may likewise differ on the relative weight to be ascribed to coherence and publicness in selecting 'best' interpretations of their legal materials. Whereas some communities may pursue internal coherence for its own sake, others might focus on promoting a particular substantive ideal and let coherence emerge only incidentally, as the inevitable by-product of long-repeated adherence to a same ideal.[89] Yet all communities must aspire to achieving at least *some measure* of effectiveness, coherence and publicness in order for their law to qualify as such. The distinction between contingent and non-contingent legal ideals can therefore be summed up by saying that whereas not all communities might choose to legally commit to, say, protecting freedom of expression, those that do necessarily also commit to doing so

---

[85] Many authors have drawn a similar distinction. See, e.g., CLAUS-WILHELM CANARIS, SYSTEMDENKEN UND SYSTEMBEGRIFF IN DER JURISPRUDENZ ENTWICKELT AM BESPIEL DES DEUTSCHEN PRIVATRECHTS 20, 49 (1969); Waldron, *supra* note 1, at 45ff.

[86] HART, *supra* note 5, at 252–54.

[87] JOSEPH RAZ, PRACTICAL REASONS AND NORMS (1975).

[88] "[I]t is possible to take as our starting point the core idea of the rule of law, understood as a middle-level political value, capable of being defended in a number of different ways from different ideological perspectives, and at least committed to, but not necessarily restricted to, a relatively 'thin' conception of the rule of law." Postema, *Law's Rule, supra* note 1, at 11.

[89] Logic indeed teaches that all rules rationally derived from one and the same referent necessarily are consistent with one another.

in a way that is at least somewhat effective, argumentative, coherent, public and formal.

Quite aside from their being contingent or not, however, these indeed being *ideals* (or such equivalents as 'values,' 'purposes,' 'aspirations' and so on) suggests that they naturally will always remain what no legal system can achieve perfectly.[90] Ideals inform and guide practice; they are that towards which the practice must move in order to improve itself yet by definition will never attain. If it did, any further guiding – the very *raison d'être* of ideals – would become impossible, for no guiding can take place where the guided and the guiding reference sit in exactly the same place. The material world is bound always to remain but an imperfect reflection of its ideal counterpart, and legal ideals in that respect are no different from any other kinds of ideals. Perfect congruence between legal commitment and legal enforcement hence is bound to remain unachievable precisely because they are ideal and material, respectively.

And few if any observers indeed would claim that some law somewhere has fully satisfied all of the objectives it had set for itself (freedom of expression, affordable housing, contractual performance) in the requisite law-like (effective, argumentative, coherent and public) fashion, to the point where it could no longer be improved. To the contrary, scholarly discussions of the material and ideal dimensions of law tend to focus on the distance, more than any possible congruence, between them. It is common knowledge among contracts scholars, for example, that whereas donative intent was traditionally supposed to fulfill the *causa* requirement of a valid contract under French law, French courts systematically acted as if it did not. Comparatists moreover have shown that a plethora of similar examples can be found in all legal fields and jurisdictions.[91] It thus seems quite clear that in all legal systems, some kind of rift lies between what the officials *do* and what they *say* they do – the 'enforcement' versus 'commitment' dimensions of law (also dubbed 'official action' versus 'declared rule,'[92] 'law in action' versus 'law in books,'[93] 'practice' versus 'folklore'[94] or 'mythology'[95] of law, legal 'machinery' versus 'meaning,'[96] 'norms' versus 'facts,'[97] 'towers' versus 'trenches,'[98] or simply 'practice' versus 'theory'). The extent of that rift again varies

---

[90] "Instead of saying that nothing is law unless it promotes the public good, we might say that nothing is law unless it *purports* to promote the public good." Waldron, *supra* note 1, at 32. (Emphasis in original.) See also: FULLER, *supra* note 1, at 41, 45; MACCORMICK, INSTITUTIONS OF LAW, *supra* note 1, at 297, 298–302.

[91] See, e.g.: Sacco, *supra* note 49; Vogenauer, *supra* note 5.

[92] FULLER, *supra* note 1, at 209.

[93] Pound, *supra* note 79.

[94] John Henry Merrymann, The Italian Style III: Interpretation, 18 STAN. L. REV. 583, 585ff (1966).

[95] Pierre Legrand, European Legal Systems are not Converging, 45 INT'L & COMP. L. Q. 52, 61 (1996).

[96] CLIFFORD GEERTZ, LOCAL KNOWLEDGE: FURTHER ESSAYS IN INTERPRETIVE ANTHROPOLOGY 232 (2000).

[97] Helge Dedek, From Norms to Facts: The Realization of Rights in Common and Civil Private Law, 56 MCGILL L. J. 77 (2010).

[98] Annelise Riles, Comparative Law and Socio-Legal Studies, *in* THE OXFORD HANDBOOK OF COMPARATIVE LAW, *supra* note 5, at 775, 784, 807.

from system to system depending inter alia on the nature of the political regime. It can be expected to be greatest in tyrannical regimes, where the 'law' being deployed is sometimes so thin as to be appropriately derided as mere 'pretence,' a 'sham,' a 'charade,' a 'travesty,' but it is nonetheless present to some extent in all regimes.

Theory-practice rifts naturally represent a most serious challenge from the standpoint of the third of our non-contingent legal ideals – coherence. For that ideal mandates not just that each of legal theory and legal practice be internally coherent, but also that they be congruent *with* one another. Lon Fuller went as far as to suggest that such congruence might be the most important feature of legality.[99] A legal system whose practice would be completely at odds with its theory would indeed be fundamentally flawed even though the practice and the theory taken alone might prove flawlessly coherent internally.

Again, though, this in no way undermines the above claim that coherence can reasonably be viewed as an inherent feature of law. It rather serves to confirm that coherence defines law normatively more than descriptively – that it is a value, an ideal to which law aspires, more than an actual fact about it. Insofar as legal actors treat, or even just publicly claim to treat, theory-practice clashes like they do any other kind of legal contradictions – as ills to be cured – it can safely be asserted that law seeks theory-practice coherence as much as it does any other kind of coherence.[100] And it seems that legal actors do so treat such clashes.[101] The solutions they put forward admittedly differ from jurisdiction to jurisdiction – in some, there may be a tendency to force the practice into line with the theory whereas in others, the tendency might conversely be to rework the theory so as to fit the practice[102] – but in all of them, the clashes clearly are considered troubling, problems to be remedied. Even in the tyrannical regimes just mentioned, where law in many ways may qualify as just 'a sham,' the sheer fact that the tyrants persist in *pretending* that their actions accord with a relatively unified (as well as effective, reason-supported and public) set of rules, while being fully aware that none will be fooled, arguably testifies to the pull exerted by those ideals on just about any law maker.[103] At the very least, it shows

---

99 FULLER, *supra* note 1, at 209–11. In communities where such discongruence is particularly blatant, it is given a special name (e.g. Keith S. Rosenn, Brazil's Legal Culture: The *Jeito* Revisited, 1 FLA. INT'L L. J. 1 (1984), discussed in Reitz, *supra* note 69, at 630).

100 "It is, in fact, one of the fundamental working assumptions of my methodology that the multiple discourses within a legal system are not likely to be considered irreconcilable by those who deploy them." Lasser, *supra* note 79, at 229. Lasser justifies that assumption on the basis that "[within a same legal system, [n]one of [the] professionals can afford to be ... radically incomprehensible to, the other professionals in the field. Each ... seeks, at least to some extent, to be heard, understood and followed by her professional addressees." (Lasser, *supra*).

101 Bomhoff, *supra* note 29.

102 For an argument that French law tends to follow the first model, whereas English law tends to follow the second, see: Catherine Valcke, Comparative History and the Internal View of French, German, and English Private Law, 19 CAN. J. L. & JURIS. 133 (2006).

103 See: SIMMONDS, *supra* note 1, at 63: "[The wicked legal] regime's adherence to law as its chosen instrument of governance may ... be explicable only by certain moral commitments, or by the

that even the most tyrannical among them recognizes that collective force *should* (ideally) be deployed only in accordance with such sets of rules. Here again, then, it is the response of the legal actors more than the actual state of the law that is significant, which response serves to confirm that theory-practice congruence (like other sorts of coherence, and like effectiveness, reason-giving, and publicness, as well as any contingent legal ideal) is first and foremost *aspirational*.[104]

The particular ideal of theory-practice congruence is taken up in Chapter 5, in the determination of what materials are to be considered representative of a community's legal commitments, which among them can be meaningfully compared, and by what standards.

This first Part aimed to show that the six central features of our working definition of law cohere with legal practice as well as with one another insofar as it is possible to interconnect them through the central notion of commitment as enforceable intention. Though I also attempted to justify that definition on the basis of a particular, moral conception of individuals as equally free – which may boast the definition's normative appeal for some readers – it must be noted that that justification is not necessary for the upcoming argument about comparative law.[105] All that needs to be accepted in order to be able to proceed to the next step in the argument is that law everywhere does in fact tend towards effectiveness, argumentativeness, coherence, publicness, formality and normativity in the way described; the further questions of *why* that may be, and *whether* it should be that way can safely be left to legal theorists to debate.[106] That law everywhere in fact plausibly fits the above description is all that the reader needs to accept for now.

hypocritical desire to hide behind such apparent moral commitments." Luhmann, *supra* note 15, at 110: "Even in these extreme cases ... there is a normal state of dependency on the regular administration of justice" (discussing Germany under the Third Reich). See also: GREEN, *supra* note 5, at 75; MATTHEW H. KRAMER, *IN DEFENSE OF LEGAL POSITIVISM* 238 (1999); FULLER, *supra* note 1, at 41, 45.

[104] Law indeed is commonly described in terms of a 'tendency' or 'aspiration' to systematization, coherence, etc. E.g., Postema, *supra* note 20, at 127; VAN DE KERCHOVE & OST, *supra* note 65, at 7; WEINRIB, *supra* note 21, at 13; CANARIS, *supra* note 85, at 16–17.

[105] Whereas Lon Fuller describes these features as constitutive of "the inner morality of law" (FULLER, *supra* note 1) (likewise: Evan Fox-Decent, Is the Rule of Law Really Indifferent to Human Rights?, 27 *LAW & PHIL.* 533, 549, note 33 (2008); Waldron, *supra* note 1, at 39–40 ("Legal systems ... engage the consciousness and agency of their subjects in ways that starkly distinguish them from other forms of rule.")), Joseph Raz takes the view that they merely are to law what sharpness is to knives, i.e. preconditions for efficacy (JOSEPH RAZ, *THE AUTHORITY OF LAW* 225–26 (1983)). Yet other justifications – based in economic efficiency, for example – may also be possible.

[106] The central point of contention among legal theorists indeed arguably has pertained not so much to describing *how* law is as a matter of fact as to determining *why* it is that way, and *whether* it should so be. Whereas natural lawyers have traditionally insisted that the behaviour of legal actors reflects law's grounding in some higher, universal legal morality, critical legal scholars have more recently derided the same behaviour as a smokescreen for ideology, encouraging the actors to come clean and take ownership of their ideological agenda. (See, e.g., Felix S. Cohen, Transcendental Nonsense and the

II. AN IDEALIST/MATERIALIST CONCEPTION

I here propose to show that the combination of the six features just described accounts for law as collective commitment being a hybrid idealist/materialist conception.[107] To that end, I contrast law as collective commitment with natural law and positivism, here respectively cast as the idealist and materialist ideal-types of legal theory. That demonstration is key to our upcoming account of comparative law insofar, as the next chapter aims to establish, as the very comparability of law hinges on such hybridity.

But first a word of warning. As natural law and positivism are here used, indeed reconstructed, into categorical and antithetical ideal-types,[108] specifically designed for the purpose of outlining the contrast with law as collective commitment, it may well be that they fail to capture the views of actual scholars.[109] It bears emphasizing, though, that the fact that it may not be possible to identify even a single author actually endorsing all of the features of either of these two types would not affect the validity of the present argument (although not finding a single author endorsing *any* of these features clearly might). In this spirit, I first describe each of the naturalist and positivist ideal-types in turn, and thereafter argue that law as collective commitment partakes of both yet is reducible to neither.

i. *Natural Law as Idealist Ideal-Type*

Under a radical naturalist conception, law is first and foremost its ideal dimension. It is a set of rules developed through rational deduction from first principles postulated

---

Functional Approach, 35 COLUM. L. REV. 809 (1935).) But the two groups arguably do not disagree as to *how lawyers act in fact.*

[107] See likewise Adler and Pouliot's description (Emanuel Adler & Vincent Pouliot, International Practices: Introduction and Framework, *in* INTERNATIONAL PRACTICES, *supra* note 70, at 8), in the field of international relations, of 'practice' as "weav[ing] together the *discursive and material* worlds"; "[m]ediating between the material and meaningful" (at 10); "breaking the Cartesian dualism between materials and ideas" (at 12). (Emphasis in original.)

[108] "The ideal-type is a mental image obtained, not through generalization of traits that are common to all the individuals, but through utopian rationalization. One gathers traits that are more or less scattered here and there, one underlines, one exaggerates: finally, one substitutes a coherent and rational whole for the confusion of the real." JACQUES GROSCLAUDE, PRÉFACE À LA SOCIOLOGIE DU DROIT DE MAX WEBER 16 (2007) (my translation). On ideal-types generally, see DIRK KÄSLER, MAX WEBER: AN INTRODUCTION TO HIS LIFE AND WORK 180–84 (1988).

[109] The above naturalistic ideal-type, in particular, draws for the most part on seventeenth and eighteenth centuries Rationalism and only to a limited extent on the 'earlier natural lawyers,' based on Aristotle and Thomas Aquinas (e.g. Chapter 2, text accompanying notes 20ff, below), the latter being in fact closer to the view defended here. For the difference between the earlier and later rationalists, see: James Gordley, The Universalist Heritage, *in* COMPARATIVE LEGAL STUDIES: TRADITIONS AND TRANSITIONS, *supra* note 33, at 31).

as universally true, temporally and spatially, much like physics.[110] Only, the first principles of law, unlike those of physics, are moral ideals. They are abstract ideals of juridical morality, the segment of morality pertaining to juridical matters. As any kind of moral ideals, they are 'pure' – free of the imperfections that plague the material world – and hence naturally subservient to logic, in much the same way that Leibniz, Condillac and Condorcet, among others, supposed philosophy to be. Like logic itself, then, the first principles of the Law of Nature, and all rules properly derived from them, necessarily are orderly, coherent, unequivocal, immutable. These rules and principles moreover are discoverable by humans, as humans are themselves naturally endowed with rationality, and the successive generations of natural law scholars – from the Stoics and Cicero, to Aquinas and the Rationalists of the Enlightenment, and on to Montesquieu and Blackstone – indeed made it their mission to do just that.[111]

These scholars however did not, for that matter, deny that law also comprises a material dimension. They fully recognized that the Law of Nature needs to be posited in the form of concrete rules (legislation), applied in particular situations (adjudication), and at times even coercively enforced (execution), lest it be doomed to practical irrelevance. But they regarded the material dimension of the Law of Nature as incidental rather than essential, thus as categorically distinct from and secondary to its ideal dimension. So much can be gleaned, I would suggest, from these scholars' substantive and institutional leanings alike.

On the substantive front, it is common knowledge that the great natural lawyers focused the bulk of their attention on areas of substantive law, private law in particular, and in comparison largely neglected procedural and evidentiary subjects – 'adjectival' law, as they tellingly designated it themselves.[112] One reason for this[113] arguably is that they indeed considered that whereas substantive law is directly informed by the Law of Nature, and hence logic-driven and perfectible, procedural and evidentiary matters in contrast involve a variety of contingent (social, political, historical, etc.) human factors, causing them to be, conversely, impervi-

[110] Jeremy Waldron, Foreign Law and the Modern Ius Gentium, 119 HARVARD LAW REVIEW 129, para. 10 (analogizing the law of nations to "the established body of scientific findings").

[111] Other prominent figures are e.g. Hugo Grotius (HUGO GROTIUS, DE IURE BELLI AC PACIS (1625)), Pufendorf (SAMUEL VON PUFENDORF, DE IURE NATURAE ET GENTIUM (1672)), Thomas Aquinas (SUMMA THEOLOGICA (Anton E. Pegis ed., 1945) (1486)), and John Selden (OPERA OMNIA (David Wilkins ed., 1726)). For a concise yet effective overview, see: Richard Wollheim, Natural Law, in THE ENCYCLOPEDIA OF PHILOSOPHY, vol. 5–6, 450 (Paul Edwards ed., 1967).

[112] This clearly is true only of the 'later rationalists,' not the "earlier natural lawyers," as Gordley calls them (Gordley, *supra* note 109, at 31), as Aristotle, for one, devoted much attention to the adjudicative process (see above, text accompanying note 20).

[113] Another likely is chronological: as such issues tend to relate more or less directly to the administration of the State, they did not congeal into recognizable areas of law until after the high days of natural law had passed. However, as there clearly were procedural and evidentiary issues to analyze long before these came to form recognizable areas of law, chronology alone cannot be the whole explanation.

ous to logic and non-perfectible.[114] In their view, then, procedural and evidentiary matters simply did not qualify as 'legal' issues proper; they might be of interest to historians, sociologists, anthropologists and other observers of human vagaries, but not to legal scholars properly so-called.

On the institutional front, the natural lawyers' distinctly dismissive treatment of law's material dimension arguably is reflected in their dichotomizing the legislative and adjudicative functions, and concentrating their attention on the former. Their own work tracked that of legislators in that it aimed to translate the Law of Nature into a network of rules sufficiently dense and concrete to cover any and all fact scenarios ever to come up before a judge. Judges would accordingly be left with the (somewhat menial) task of applying the rules to the facts at hand, which they would ideally discharge in a strictly mechanical, almost unreflective manner.[115] To the extent that judges are required to deploy any skills at all, the natural lawyers thought, those indeed would be psychological and/or ethical rather than intellectual skills – perceptiveness, intuition, sensitivity, meticulousness, integrity and the like, not reasoning skills as such. The real legal work in other words took place at the legislative, not the adjudicative level, in their view. They of course recognized that cases sometimes arise, which no legislator or scholar, in their limited, human foresight, could have anticipated: while the Law of Nature by definition is gapless, as we saw, its human formulation is not. In such cases, the judges admittedly would have to assume a legislative role, that is, they would have to engage in the requisite deciphering/formulating of the Law of Nature and fill in the missing rules. But while the natural lawyers conceded that the legislative function could be discharged by different classes of legal actors in different circumstances – usually by legislators and scholars, but occasionally also by judges – they insisted on treating that function as strictly distinct from, and legally superior to, the adjudicative one.

This is confirmed by the fact that in their own formulations of the Law of Nature, the natural lawyers pay little if any attention to judicial materials. This they do arguably for the same reason as caused them to prefer substantive over procedural law, namely, because the judicial process involves heavy doses of human judgment. After all, how could the outcome of a process fraught with human contingency bear on intellectual matters exclusively determined through universal logic? Precisely because they viewed legislation and adjudication as radically distinct, then, the natural lawyers thought it possible and in fact desirable that these tasks be carried out completely independently from one another: in the same way that judges ought to

---

[114] We saw that that is indeed the case with respect to adjudication (see *supra* text accompanying note 21), and the same can be said of the other aspects of legal implementation – arrest, prosecution, private litigation, sentencing, execution orders, pardon, etc. – all of which are likewise replete with contingent, human determinations.

[115] See Montesquieu's famous depiction of judges as "but the mouths that pronounce the words of the law, inanimate beings devoid of any power to temper its force or rigor." CHARLES-LOUIS DE MONTESQUIEU, DE L'ESPRIT DES LOIS; LES GRANDS THÈMES, bk. 11, chap. 6 at 178 (1970) (1748). (My translation.)

refrain from revisiting the legislative soundness of the rules they are given to apply, legislators and scholars ought not let themselves be distracted by the various judicial applications of the rules they are called upon to formulate.

As it turns out, however, they attached only marginally greater significance to legislative materials. While this may seem surprising given their respective treatments of legislation and adjudication just described, it is fully consistent with their particular conception of legislation and their treatment of the material dimension of law more generally. Legislation, let us not forget, is not law 'making' so much as law 'formulating', for the natural lawyers. Law being no other than the (ideal) Law of Nature, it indeed necessarily pre-exists its human formulation; it is *made* by the ultimate law maker (whether God or Nature), and only *formulated* by human legislators.[116] And legislative materials accordingly are just records of past such formulation attempts: they provide useful examples of possible formulations but are not otherwise significant. In the words of John Austin, they have 'locutionary,' not 'illocutionary' value, which is to say that they have no value beyond the truth-value of their particular content.[117] Insofar as such materials are authoritative at all, their authority indeed is derivative rather than inherent; it is derived from the (in contrast inherent) authority of the moral ideals they embody.[118]

This in turn suggests that materials that in fact fail to properly reflect juridical ideals – 'defective' legislative materials – are altogether *un*-authoritative, at least for the purpose of subsequent legislative attempts.[119] While judges as we saw are not at liberty to pass judgment on the soundness of legislative materials, and hence have no choice but to simply apply the rules given to them regardless of any possible such defects, legislating agents (whose first allegiance is to the higher Law) in contrast are free, and indeed have a duty to ignore defective legislative materials and rely instead on "whatever is found acceptable by *recta ratio* or *sana ratio*."[120] (Note the legislative/adjudicative divide surfacing here again.) Though legislative defects are in principle detectable through sustained reflection alone (presumably conducted by individuals more intelligent and/or more careful than the materials' original drafters), they more often than not reveal themselves through inconsistencies: if a proper formulation of the Law of Nature is necessarily internally coherent, the presence of any form of internal incoherence ought to be regarded as an indication that the

---

[116] In Locke's view (JOHN LOCKE, *TWO TREATISES OF GOVERNMENT* 87–89 (Peter Laslett ed., 1960) (1690), for example, the State's only role is the practical one of interpreting (and sanctioning) the rights that individuals already possessed in the state of nature.

[117] J. L. AUSTIN, *HOW TO DO THINGS WITH WORDS* (1962).

[118] "An appeal to authority—to requirements imposed by authority—is an *alternative* to an appeal to reasons—to requirements based on reasons for acting." DAVID GAUTHIER, *PRACTICAL REASONING* 139 (1963). (Emphasis in original.)

[119] "[C]onformity to natural law is the criterion not merely of a just law but of law itself." Wollheim, *supra* note 111, at 452; "lawmakers should aim at natural law and inasmuch as they deviate from it, what they enact falls short of the character of true law." Waldron, *supra* note 110, at para. 14.

[120] *Ibid.*

formulation at hand is to some extent defective. (Internal coherence we see here is, for the natural lawyers, not so much an end in itself as a natural consequence of the law having been properly formulated.) Whether tested through internal incoherence or otherwise however,[121] the moral soundness of legislative materials ultimately is, under a strict naturalist conception, fully determinative of these materials' relevance for the purpose of subsequent legislative attempts. Much like judicial materials, then, extant legislative materials constrain legislating agents no more than do hypothetical fact scenarios for philosophers engaged in moral investigations.[122]

Under the naturalistic ideal-type, in sum, as only the ideal, moral dimension of law qualifies as essentially legal, law is not fundamentally different from morality and in fact just a species of it. In the words of one observer, natural law theory "blurs the issue traditionally ... referred to as that of sin and crime ... it is never quite clear whether natural law is a criterion of just action or of just law."[123] And legal analysis corollarily is just an exercise in *ratio scripta*, one that essentially proceeds in the very same way as any kind of moral inquiry.

ii. *Positivism as Materialist Ideal-Type*

Like natural law, positivism draws a categorical distinction between the ideal and material dimensions of law. Also like natural law, it structures these dimensions hierarchically, as essential and incidental. But positivism has the hierarchy reversed from what it is under natural law: the material is the essential dimension whereas the ideal is the incidental.

An extreme positivist conception indeed all but ignores the ideal dimension of law and focuses primarily on its material aspects. As Joseph Raz wrote, under positivism, "a jurisprudential theory is acceptable only if its tests for identifying the content of law and determining its existence depend exclusively on facts of human behaviour capable of being described in value-neutral terms and applied without resort to moral arguments."[124] And the various constitutive elements of law under positivism indeed are all essentially material. From the outset, law is defined as whatever is

---

[121] Internal coherence cannot be the only criterion for moral soundness, here. For it does not follow from the fact that proper formulations of the Law of Nature are necessarily consistent that invalid ones are necessarily inconsistent. Formulations that accordingly might be improper yet internally consistent clearly would need to be unmasked through other means.

[122] While some natural lawyers did attempt to distil the universal law from common elements in a variety of existing legal instruments (e.g. the early Roman jurists whose writings were compiled in Justinian's *Digest*), I would argue that they nonetheless tended, on the whole, to view these instruments in the way just described, i.e. as a useful source of illustrations rather than as inherently compelling.

[123] Wollheim, *supra* note 111, at 453. Owen Fiss similarly does not deny this, but rather claims that it is precisely because law is one and the same with morality (as 'justice') that it is distinct from economics and politics. See: Owen M. Fiss, *The Autonomy of Law*, 26 YALE J. INT'L. L. 517 (2001).

[124] RAZ, *supra* note 105, at 39–40. See also: COLEMAN, *supra* note 53, at 153 ("[S]ocial facts are the grounds of the criteria of legality").

produced by a particular set of institutions, in accordance with a particular procedure, both of which have been coined 'law making' by a penultimate legal official, him/herself largely determined through such material factors as 'enforcement power' and 'habit of obedience.'[125] In some accounts, the penultimate official is replaced with a penultimate norm – a Grundnorm, Rule of Recognition, or other equivalent – which admittedly seems to introduce a certain measure of ideality into this otherwise thoroughly material backdrop. Even then, however, said norm tends to be defined in material terms – as whatever is de facto treated as such by the community[126] or a significant segment thereof[127] – or else acknowledged as at least somewhat transcendental but then said to lie, for that reason alone, altogether outside law:[128] as a transcendental matter, it essentially belongs to the moral, not legal realm, about which positivism, as a strictly *legal* theory, has little if anything to say. The integrity of positivism as an essentially material, sociological conception of law hence ends up being preserved under either of the penultimate official or penultimate norm scenario.

Nonetheless, in the same way that the natural lawyers do not completely dismiss law's material dimension, the positivists do not completely dismiss its ideal dimension. As the debate over the nature of the penultimate legal norm indicates, they recognize that there may well be such things as juridical moral ideals, a segment of morality specifically related to juridical matters, which moreover might inform law making across time and space. For moral judgments about the law (distinguishing 'right' from 'wrong' law) would otherwise be impossible yet positivists have not hesitated to pass such judgments themselves.[129] Even so, they have always maintained – like the natural lawyers with respect to legal materials – that while juridical ideals indeed are 'juridical' in the sense of bearing on legal matters, they themselves are not 'legal' per se. They are not 'legal' for the simple reason that they do not bear on any of what the positivists regard as real 'legal' questions, namely, such factual questions as concern the institutional validity of law or its application in particular circumstances.[130] Under positivism, legal analysis indeed essentially involves applying valid legal rules to particular facts in a "technically confined way,"[131] that is, independently from any normative judgments that might otherwise be passed concerning these rules' substantive quality (the so-called 'separability thesis'). While

---

[125] See *supra* text accompanying notes 71–76.

[126] See, e.g.: HOBBES, *supra* note 66; JEREMY BENTHAM, OF LAWS IN GENERAL (1970); JOHN AUSTIN, THE PROVINCE OF JURISPRUDENCE DETERMINED 193–94 (1995).

[127] For Hart, it is the practice of the community's officials that is significant in this respect: HART, *supra* note 5, at 50ff.

[128] HANS KELSEN, GENERAL THEORY OF LAW AND STATE 286ff, 193–221 (1961).

[129] See, e.g., Hart's famous assertion, against Fuller, that precisely because morality is strictly distinct from law, it is possible for law to qualify as such despite being morally reprehensible. HART, *supra* note 74.

[130] *Ibid.*; KELSEN, *supra* note 128, at 353.

[131] HART, *supra* note 5, at 266.

the positivists do not deny the existence of juridical ideals, then, they insist that any such ideals, and the judgments they inform, are only incidentally legal, and as such, ultimately external to law proper.

As might be expected, the positivists' substantive and institutional leanings accordingly are the exact opposites of those of the natural lawyers. On the substantive front, we saw that positivist scholars have traditionally displayed towards the substance of legal materials the same indifference that natural lawyers harboured towards issues of pedigree and validity.[132] On the institutional front, while the positivists endorse the naturalist dichotomy between legislation and adjudication, they consider the latter, not the former, to be legal proper. If legal analysis as they say centres on the application of valid legal rules, said analysis logically cannot begin until some such rules are in place. The legislators must necessarily produce the rules, that is, before the judges can apply them.[133] The judges accordingly are the ones discharging the truly 'legal' function (applying the rules) whereas the legislators in contrast play a role that is essentially political and *pre*-legal (creating the rules to be applied). In effect, legislators do no more than create the conditions under which the real legal work – the judges' – can take place.

Moreover, as the positivists evidently reject the naturalistic distinction between making and formulating law (if law is but its human formulation, to formulate law *is* to make it), they likewise reject the view of legal materials as merely illustrative. If human law is all the law there is, that law clearly is constraining per se. It has 'illocutionary' rather than 'locutionary' value[134] and accordingly is inherently as well as absolutely determinative of legal analysis.[135] Judges therefore are fully bound by human law, not so much because they have no say in its production (as under the naturalist conception) as because there simply is nothing else qualifying as 'legal' for them to go on.[136] Legislators in contrast are always free to enact new law, even such

---

[132] See the authors cited *supra* note 66. Perhaps most notable in this respect is Joseph Raz's account of the legal system, in which issues of content are altogether ignored: "[a]nalytical jurists ... have paid little attention to the problem of content, and as we have chosen to develop our systematic conclusions largely through the critical examination of previous theories it will be convenient to disregard it almost completely." (JOSEPH RAZ, THE CONCEPT OF A LEGAL SYSTEM: AN INTRODUCTION TO THE THEORY OF LEGAL SYSTEMS 2 (1970).) Some positivists have nonetheless allowed some minimal content to come into play in their definition of law: Marshall Cohen, Law, Morality and Purpose, 10 VILLANOVA L. REV. 640, 648 (1965); HART, *supra* note 5, at 202.

[133] We will see below (text accompanying notes 141) that, as was the case under natural law (text following note 115), judges can sometimes play a legislative role. The relevant distinction, here as there, is between the legislative and adjudication functions, quite apart from who happens to discharge them.

[134] AUSTIN, *supra* note 117.

[135] "[Under naturalism, a norm is binding] because it has a certain content, that is, because it is logically deducible from a presupposed basic norm, [whereas under positivism, a norm is binding] because it is created in a certain way ... Therefore any kind of content might be law." KELSEN, *supra* note 128, at 198.

[136] 'Human law' here includes law made by legislators or by judges taking on a legislative role, as just indicated (*supra* note 133).

as might contradict the existing one: as they are operating altogether outside law in the pre-legal, political sphere, there cannot be any *legal* constraints operating on them.[137] They may well be answerable to such things as juridical moral ideals, as we saw,[138] but these again would be moral, not legal constraints proper. From a strictly legal perspective, then, legislators act unconstrained, and their enactments are inescapable. (And internal coherence in turn is just one particular ideal that legislators may or may not choose to promote.[139])

Just like the natural lawyers, however, the positivists acknowledge that legal materials 'run out' and that judges hence are at times faced with cases not covered by extant materials. Cases of lawlessness in fact are far more problematic for the positivists than for the naturalists as it then is law itself, not just its human formulation, that runs out, under their account. At this point emerges the positivists' famous dichotomy between so-called 'easy' and 'hard' cases – cases in which materials respectively are or are not readily available for application.[140] Whereas under the naturalist conception a gap in legal materials merely means that these materials and the juridical ideals informing them must be bypassed, the same gap under the positivist conception is tantamount to definitive lawlessness – a legal void. The positivists' essentially material conception indeed allows for only two possibilities: either there is law or there is not. And where there is no law, judges have no choice but to take on a legislative role and make new law, as they do under natural law. Only, whereas under natural law the judges thereby take on a properly legal role, under positivism they in fact lower themselves to a (legally) non-essential, merely pre-legal role: just like legislators, they then act entirely unconstrained, with full discretion to endorse or reject whatever ideals they wish.[141]

---

[137] "In these conditions, ... the legislator being juridically free to decide everything, is constrained only by the *political* control of the body politic." Étienne Picard, Le droit comparé est-il du droit?, 1 ANN. INST. MICHEL VILLEY 173, 190 (2009) (my translation; italics in original). And at 191: "[Under] legiscentrism, law can only be judged as against morals, politics, philosophy, religion, beliefs—and nowadays economics—which evidently are not themselves law."

[138] They may be operating under some sort of written or unwritten constitution or penultimate legal rule, but the same analysis would then apply to said penultimate rule: see text accompanying notes 126–128.

[139] Where newly enacted law contradicts earlier law, it is usually assumed that the legislator intended the new law to replace the earlier one. One however could theoretically imagine a case where the legislator explicitly denies this and declares that the two laws instead are both to be valid despite their mutual contradiction. I would suggest that, under a pure positivist conception, both laws indeed ought to be regarded as simultaneously valid (despite the confusion inevitably ensuing) in such a case. To the same effect, see: ANDREI MARMOR, POSITIVE LAW AND OBJECTIVE VALUES 69 (2001), but see Kelsen's claim (KELSEN, *supra* note 128, at 267) that, on his positivist account, "[a] 'norm contrary to a norm' is a self-contradiction ... it would not be a legal norm at all."

[140] See Hart's famous debate with Dworkin, on this point: HART, *supra* note 74, at 121ff; DWORKIN, *supra* note 45, at 81. In French law, likewise, see the *doctrine de l'acte clair*, whereby only unclear statutes need to be interpreted before they are applied. (Vogenauer, *supra* note 5, at 889.)

[141] See HART at 131. See also: KELSEN, *supra* note 128, at 353 ("But the judge too creates law, and he too is relatively free in this function ... So far as in applying the law a cognitive activity of the law-applying

In short, where the natural lawyers view law as abstract, universal, static, and right or wrong, the positivists view it as concrete, contingent, dynamic, and valid or invalid. Under the naturalist conception we saw that law is abstract, universal, static, and right or wrong because it is geometrically derived from (similarly abstract, universal, static, and right or wrong) moral principles; its human formulation of course is concrete, contingent, dynamic, and valid or invalid, but its content is not. Under the positivist conception, in contrast, law being but its human formulation necessarily is concrete, contingent, dynamic, and valid or invalid through and through: it boasts whatever content and form were fancied by the individual law makers. Law under the positivist ideal-type in that sense is but social fact, and legal analysis but sociological investigation.

iii. *Law as Collective Commitment as Natural Law/Positivism Hybrid*

It is clear from the description of law as collective commitment given in Part I that that conception combines ideal and material elements. The very notion of 'commitment' – or 'intention,' 'will,' 'desire' and the like – after all "sits upon the cusp between what is and what ought to be."[142] What bears emphasizing here is the extent to which these sets of elements are truly combined rather than merely juxtaposed: they are neither categorically distinct nor hierarchically structured, but in fact equally important and mutually dependent. As a result, neither can be conceptualized independently from the other.

Their mutual dependence is crucial here. If the ideal and material elements were merely juxtaposed, law as collective commitment would amount to a composite of natural law and positivism rather than an altogether distinct hybrid conception. That is to say, if law as collective commitment were made of one part morality and one part social fact, tightly compartmentalized from one another, it would constitute not so much one (unified) distinct theory as two (separate) theories, respectively indistinguishable from morality and social fact. But if the ideal and material parts instead are mutually dependent, they naturally join to form just one whole, the peculiarity of which resides precisely in its being ideal through and through *as well as* material through and through. The distinctness of law as collective commitment would then lie in its operating a smooth synthesis of the naturalist and positivist ideal-types, thus partaking of both while being reducible to neither.

Synthesizing the ideal and the material of course was a central project of German idealism, itself building on Aristotelian rhetorics and its Enlightenment revival, and in this respect law as collective commitment does fit within that intellectual

organ can take place, beyond the necessary ascertainment of the frame, within which the act to be performed is to be kept, it is not cognition of positive law, but of other norms that may flow here into the process of law-creation—such as norms of morals, of justice."); RAZ, *supra* note 105, at 59, 113, 197 (describing the judges' actions as "deliberative" rather than properly "executive").

[142] SIMMONDS, *supra* note 1, at 114.

tradition. In the same way that Kant and Hegel conceptualized the state as *actualized* Idea,[143] law as collective commitment portrays law as intention that materializes in a number of ways. The first is through its formal quality. As *collective* intention, intention that runs across and ties many individuals, legal intention necessarily is externalized in some way, for intention that is not externalized cannot possibly be attributed to more than a single individual. Formalization as we saw is the means by which legal intention is publicly marked off from other intentions as that to which the whole community commits.[144] Such formalization moreover was also described as largely *implicit*, in that it ultimately emerges from legal practice. That only serves to confirm that it is but the actual embodiment – the material *alter ego* – of legal intention.

We also saw that legal enforcement ('effectiveness,' as we called it) is essential to legal practice arising in the first place, and it too arguably reflects the materialization of legal intention. Consider the claim that legal sanctions subsume all other sanctions – that, where a legal violation also constitutes a moral and/or social violation, the legal sanction is not just one of several kinds of sanctions that it is appropriate to cumulatively impose on the violator but rather one that encompasses and substitutes for all others taken together.[145] Under that claim, the imposition of the legal sanction causes the violator to be redeemed legally, for sure, but also socially and morally. So where breaching a contract might qualify as socially and/or morally reprehensible, in addition to being illegal, the imposition of the appropriate legal sanction arguably serves to cure the moral, social and legal dimensions of the breach all at once. That claim entails, I would suggest, that legal enforcement *stands for* the legal commitment actually materializing: the reason that no moral or social debt survives past the discharge of the legal debt is precisely that discharging the legal debt effectively serves to undo the whole violation and hence reinstate the ideal prospect contemplated in the law. Once the world has been returned to its ideal, pre-violation state, it is as if the violation had never taken place – the freedom to express oneself never was infringed; the prohibited smoking never took place; the contract was voluntarily performed – and all possible causes for reprobation – legal, moral, social or otherwise – have simply vanished. If so, legal enforcement can be seen as the material equivalent of legal commitment.[146]

---

[143] IMMANUEL KANT, *DOCTRINE OF RIGHT: PART 1 OF THE METAPHYSICS OF MORALS* §45 (Mary J. Gregor, ed. 1991) (1797); HEGEL, *supra* note 21, at 155–60.

[144] See *supra* Part I, section v.

[145] DORI KIMEL, *FROM PROMISE TO CONTRACT: TOWARDS A LIBERAL THEORY OF CONTRACT* 57–87 (2005). Kimel here follows Immanuel Kant's line of argument as described in Simone Goyard-Fabre, Kant et l'idée pure du droit, 26 ARCH. PHIL. DROIT 133, 141 (1981). See also Hans Kelsen's argument as to why an individual cannot be simultaneously bound in law and morals with respect to one and the same issue: "no viewpoint exists from which both morals and law may simultaneously be regarded as valid normative orders. No one can serve two masters." Hans Kelsen, *A PURE THEORY OF LAW*, 329 (Max Knight trans., 1945).

[146] "[T]he essence of law's *Sollen* is at bottom to become one with its *Sein* since there is law only where it is effective: law's deonticity disappears where the facts do not confirm law's aspirations." Picard, *supra* note 137, at 197 (my translation).

But the special contribution of German idealism – Hegel's writings in particular[147] – was to show that the connection of the Idea to its material embodiment is not just one way. That is, while the material embodiment clearly is determined by the Idea – since an embodiment necessarily is the embodiment *of* (an otherwise bodiless) something – it also is the case that the Idea in turn is to some extent determined by the embodiment, for it cannot possibly *exist* as sheer, disembodied Idea. Thus, while the material embodiment cannot be conceptualized in abstraction from the Idea, neither can the Idea be conceptualized in abstraction from its material embodiment: the existence of each fully depends, symmetrically and dialogically, on the existence of the other.

Likewise with law as collective commitment. To say that formality is the material manifestation of legal intention is not to say that formality is mere evidence of an intention that exists independently of it. If legal intention is determined by agreement of the entire community, and formality is the means through which such agreements can emerge, formality does not just *mark* a collective agreement, it also, and thereby, *constitutes* it.[148] It is the means through which a plurality of different individuals *actually join and create* an agreement; it *is* their agreement in just the same way that, in private contracting, the formal contract *is* the parties' contract. Legal intention hence depends on formality for its existence in much the same way that formality in turn depends on legal intention. Such mutuality is also inherent in legal practice, or implicit formalization (somewhat paradoxically, *informal* formalization), moreover. We saw that what is to count as the community's formal legal intention is what is de facto treated as such in practice. We also saw that, corollarily, explicit designations of formality not followed in practice are ineffective, and that what is in practice treated as the community's formal law thereby becomes so despite the absence of explicit declarations to that effect, or even against explicit declarations to the contrary. Clearly, then, practice is as much a determinant of the community's formal law as it is determined by it: "[o]ur understanding of [law's] nature is deepened by the experience of its pursuit."[149]

The same is true of legal enforcement. The prospect of enforcement is what causes legal intention to be reliable, thus to qualify as a commitment proper. Legal intention that would never be enforced would be unlikely to generate a practice as it would simply be unreliable, and as such would simply not qualify as legal intention to begin with. The above discussion of legal sanctions subsuming all other forms of

---

[147] See, e.g.: HEGEL, *supra* note 21, at §§142, 212. More generally: CHARLES TAYLOR, HEGEL 13–29 (1975); HANS-GEORG GADAMER, TRUTH AND METHOD esp. 315 (Joel Weinsheimer & Donald G. Marshall, trans., 2nd ed. 2004).

[148] What Neil Walker calls "intimation"; WALKER, *supra* note 59.

[149] SIMMONDS, *supra* note 1, at 158. See likewise Adler and Pouliot's description (Adler & Pouliot, *supra* note 107, at 9) of 'practice' as "a socially meaningful pattern of action which … simultaneously embodies, reifies and acts out background knowledge and discourse in and on the material world."

sanctions clearly shows legal sanctions as relating to legal intention as simultaneously cause and effect: legal intention there qualifies as committal *because* it is made effective and it in turn is made effective *because* it is committal.

That dialogic relation likewise is palpable in our treatment of legal coherence, wherein neither of the actual fragmentation or ideal unity of legal materials (and of the views individual legal actors have of them) is prior to or prevalent over the other. We saw that under the natural law ideal-type, all attention is focused on the materials' ideal state of perfect coherence (and the actors' ideal state of perfect agreement) whereas all attention conversely is concentrated on the materials' actual state, however incoherent (and the actors' actual views, however discordant), under the positivist ideal-type. In contrast, law as collective commitment conceptualizes law as necessarily involving both. Seeing that law on that account amounts to arguments per se, it entails the possibility of moving between actual and ideal states, which states can respectively be seen as dissatisfactory and satisfactory only in one another's light. It also entails that the actors disagree as to the nature of the ideal state and the process by which it can be reached, as arguments arise only in the face of disagreement. As one legal theorist puts it, "disagreement [is] not just ... a jurisprudential puzzlement or pathology, but ... a distinctive aspect of legal practice."[150]

The seamless interplay of actual and ideal under law as collective commitment manifests itself at the level of the legal process in a number of ways. It first shows through the impossibility of dichotomizing law making from law applying. We saw that legal analysis on that account focuses neither exclusively on ideals nor exclusively on materials but in fact seeks to reconcile the two in the context of particular cases.[151] For legal ideals and materials alike are devoid of meaning – at least *legal* meaning – when taken in isolation from the other: the materials make sense only in the light of their underlying ideals, which in turn become meaningful only when pressed through concrete circumstances, that likewise take on legal relevance only when related to the materials, and so on.[152] As legal analysis hence necessarily entails

---

[150] Waldron, *supra* note 1, at 50. See also: DWORKIN, *supra* note 1, at 20–23; Finnis, *supra* note 83, at 270 (1980) ("the state of affairs in which a legal system is legally in good shape."). *Contra* HART, *supra* note 5, at 135, for whom arguments are just an undesirable side effect of law's imperfection ("the life of the law consists to a very large extent in the guidance both of officials and private individuals by determinate rules.")

[151] See *supra* the text accompanying note 84, Part I, section vi.

[152] "Law reproduces the cycle of water, which falls as rain to feed the earth, from which it evaporates to form clouds, before falling back down again as rain." LÉONTIN-JEAN CONSTANTINESCO, *TRAITÉ DE DROIT COMPARÉ, VOL. II: LA MÉTHODE COMPARATIVE* 218 (1974) (my translation). Even in highly specific legal rules, the meaning of the various words used arguably cannot be known with any degree of certainty until they have been applied to a number of different contexts. While these words admittedly have a linguistic (or 'dictionary') meaning prior to their application, their proper 'legal' meaning remains to be disclosed. To the extent that legal actors may at times feel like they 'understand' certain statutes from the time of enactment, I would suggest they are either mistaken – they are relying on their linguistic, not legal understanding – or that understanding, while properly legal, comes from past

a cyclical movement between facts and ideals, it can indeed be said that to make law is to apply it, and to apply it is to make it, under law as collective commitment.

This is confirmed by the fact that the roles of the various legal actors do not differ nearly as much under that conception as they do under the naturalist or positivist ideal-types. Whereas natural law and positivism both associate legislators with ideals (on one hand) and judges with facts (on the other), and differ only as to which of these tasks qualifies as properly legal, law as collective commitment has all legal actors engaging one way or another in the same, ideals-*cum*-facts, legal task proper. All actors, that is, argue over the best interpretation to give to the law – over the best way to synthesize its ideal and material elements.[153] Legislators admittedly make general rules whereas judges translate those rules into concrete rulings. But when making new rules, the legislators aim to make them consistent with their best reconstruction of the whole legal system, which judges likewise do with their rulings, albeit in specific settings. As for regular citizens, it was suggested that they at times act like official law makers precisely because they too are constantly putting forward new and better arguments as to the proper way to interpret the system's ideals/materials.[154] Each of the legislative, adjudicative and litigating function[155] being ultimately fundamentally argumentative/interpretive, under law as collective commitment, no clear line can be drawn between making and applying law.

Another unsustainable distinction accordingly is that between 'easy' and 'hard' cases. The interpretive exercise clearly will be more or less arduous depending on the circumstances: where the facts of a particular situation fall squarely within some enacted rules that moreover seem to mesh well with long accepted legal ideals, the 'right' interpretation is more obvious, less polemical, than where existing rules seem irrelevant, ambiguous and/or normatively questionable. There is therefore a sense in which cases can be described as 'easi*er*' or 'hard*er*.' But there is no sense in which they can be dichotomized as categorically 'easy' or categorically 'hard.' There cannot be categorically 'easy' cases insofar as even the easiest of cases beget some measure of judgment and interpretation;[156] there cannot be categorically 'hard' ones insofar as even the hardest among them offer at least room for argument. That is to say, as law essentially *is* arguments under law as collective commitment, there can never be a complete absence of law; law simply *cannot* 'run out' in the way it

---

experience with similar materials: "it is our familiarity with the practice that gives us access to an understanding of the ideal." SIMMONDS, *supra* note 1, at 11.

[153] "Interpretation folds back into the practice, altering its shape, and the new shape encourages further interpretation, so the practice changes dramatically, though each step in the progress [*sic*?] is interpretive of what the last achieved." DWORKIN, *supra* note 1, at 48. Gerald Postema describes this process as one of ongoing "disturbance of the equilibrium state of a dynamic system." Postema, *Law's System, supra* note 1 at 80.

[154] See *supra* Part I, section iv, text accompanying notes 63–64.

[155] Insofar as scholars (see *supra*, text preceding note 68) and other legal actors might be regarded as contributing to those functions, they clearly would be included here.

[156] See *supra* Part I, section ii, text accompanying note 21.

necessarily does under natural law and positivism.[157] And there accordingly are no moments at which judges need to stop being judges and hop into a legislative role: in easier and harder cases alike, they reach their conclusions through fundamentally the same argumentative/interpretive process.

Finally, it also follows from the ideal/material merger within law as collective commitment that legal materials are neither essentially irrelevant nor absolutely authoritative. While legal materials indeed embody legal ideals, we saw that that embodiment in turn serves to form and transform said ideals. Legal materials therefore carry greater significance than mere formulations of independently existing and independently authoritative ideals (*contra* natural law). Their formal status confers them greater weight than can be ascribed to informal discussions or writings about the law, and they in fact channel the legal discourse in a way that the latter discussions and writings do not. Yet they are not, for that matter, absolutely authoritative (*contra* positivism), for they are not the word of some omnipotent and definitive law maker(s). While the various legal actors do 'make' (rather than just 'formulate') law, they do so under certain constraints, namely, the five non-contingent ideals of effectiveness, argumentativeness, coherence, publicness and formality.[158] That is, they create, from scratch, a material support for a set of ideals, some of which already exist, but as ideals only. (As one such ideal, coherence accordingly is not just a beneficial side effect of apt law making: it is a legal virtue to be sought per se (*contra* natural law) yet one that all law makers actually are legally constrained to seek (consistently with positivism).)

What is more, as no one group of actors (legislators, judges, litigants) has the monopoly on such (constrained) law making, their word is always provisional rather than final: it stands only until modified through subsequent (re)interpretations. At most, then, legal materials can be described as endowed with 'special' authority, with authority greater than what would otherwise flow from just the substantive soundness of their prescriptions. As others have described it, the formal status of legal materials has the effect of creating a 'presumption' in their favour, a 'second order' reason, which can nonetheless be overcome by strong 'first order' reasons,[159]

---

[157] Although the easy/hard case divide as we saw is more pronounced under positivism than under natural law, the legal process remains fundamentally binary under both. While the realm of ontological possibilities admittedly is limited to two under positivism – law/no law – whereas it extends to three under natural law – non-defective legal materials/defective legal materials/no legal materials – the realm of possible institutional responses is limited to two under both conceptions. Under both natural law and positivism, that is, 'easy' cases are those covered by existing legal materials (whether defective or not, under natural law) and judges hence ought to just apply them, whereas 'hard' cases are those not covered by existing materials and judges accordingly have to make new ones.

[158] See *supra* Part I, section vi, text accompanying notes 86–87. See likewise Hegel's suggestion that the law-making power of States is constrained, not by other States, but by law's own ideas: HEGEL, *supra* note 21, at §§257–58.

[159] Stephen R. Perry, Second-Order Reasons, Uncertainty and Legal Theory, 62 S. CAL. L. REV. 913, esp. 967ff (1989), arguing *contra* Raz (RAZ, *supra* note 87, at 195–97; JOSEPH RAZ, THE MORALITY OF

i.e. the effect of conferring them 'illocutionary' *as well as* 'locutionary' value.[160] And although the intensity of this presumption/second order reason need not be specified here, it can be ventured that it is not determinable a priori but rather varies across jurisdictions, institutional kinds and perhaps even subject areas.[161]

In sum, whereas natural law tends to portray law as categorically abstract, universal, static, and right or wrong, and positivism conversely describes it as concrete, contingent, dynamic, and valid or invalid, law as collective commitment in contrast shows it to be universal *and* contingent, abstract *and* concrete, static *and* dynamic and possibly right *and* invalid, or wrong *and* valid. It is universal as well as contingent insofar as it is a (contingent) human creation yet one framed by a number of (universal) ideals that, contrary to positivist claims, indeed are inherently legal. It accordingly also is static as well as dynamic: it is produced through a (dynamic) human process that nonetheless remains anchored in said (static) inherent ideals. Precisely because legal ideals and legal materials alike are inherent legal, moreover, it is possible for law – at least nascent law[162] – to be both wrong and valid, or both right and invalid: legal materials that clash with legal ideals can be criticized as (legally, not just morally) wrong despite being valid from a strict procedural standpoint,[163] and a procedural defect might likewise suffice to 'invalidate' normatively irreproachable materials. The above account of legal analysis also shows law to be both abstract and concrete, finally. The intimate connection between facts and ideals suggests that law clearly can aspire to becoming, simultaneously and without contradiction, a more accurate representation of (abstract) juridical ideals *and* one better tailored to (concrete) circumstances. Quite simply, an accurate representation of legal ideals *necessarily is* one that is tailored to circumstances, and vice versa.

Under law as collective commitment, then, while law clearly partakes of morality and social fact alike, it remains fundamentally distinct from both; and legal analysis, as it aims to mediate and in fact synthesize the ideal and the material,

---

FREEDOM 28–31 (1986)), who considers such 'second order' reasons to be 'exclusionary', i.e. reasons that substitute for, and hence are unassailable by, 'first order' reasons. Dworkin's 'relaxed doctrine of precedent' (DWORKIN, *supra* note 1, at 25) conveys the same idea.

[160] AUSTIN, *supra* note 117.

[161] Perry, *supra* note 159.

[162] Insofar as the defective (whether 'wrong' or invalid) legal materials would nonetheless come to be endorsed in practice, said defect can be expected to fade over time. With respect to invalid materials, the mere fact that they are endorsed in practice would suffice to 'validate' them from a strict process standpoint, whereas 'wrong' materials would gradually come to be made 'right,' to align with legal ideals, through interpretation as it is here conceived.

[163] For example, former US President George Bush's special military tribunal for prosecuting suspected terrorists might qualify as wrong, insofar as it is inconsistent with the rest of the due process-inspired US legal system, while nonetheless constituting valid US law, insofar as it was adopted through the right procedure and institutional channels. For other examples of legal institutions clashing with 'system imperatives,' see: Lynn M. LoPucki, The Systems Approach to Law, 82 CORNELL L. REV. 479, 493 (1996–1997); Lynn M. LoPucki, Legal Culture, Legal Strategy, and the Law in Lawyers' Heads, 90 N. W. U. L. REV. 1498, 1526, n. 139 (1996).

correspondingly steers clear of both pure moral investigation (*contra* natural law) and pure social investigation (*contra* positivism).

CONCLUSION

The purpose of this chapter was to lay out the conception of law as collective commitment grounding the upcoming account of comparative law. Under that conception, law is a social practice that is both reflective and constitutive of a community's commitment to governing itself in accordance with certain collectively shared ideals. As it hence is thoroughly ideal and material, law as collective commitment is a hybrid yet unified third conception, one altogether distinct from natural law and positivism alike.

Although law as collective commitment was here presented as just a working conception, efforts were made to show that it holds intuitive appeal from both explanatory and normative perspectives. On the explanatory level, I suggested that it sits well with common legal experience. On the normative level, I tried to show that it is – if not necessarily grounded in – at least fully consistent with the moral agency of individuals.

The larger part of that conception's appeal however has yet to be revealed, as it naturally lies with the conception's success or failure in accounting for comparative law. A first step in that direction involves us moving from law as unitary to law as plural – from 'law' to 'legal systems' – given that anything comparative calls into play a plurality of entities. To this we now turn.

2

Legal Systems

Our discussion thus far has evoked law as a unitary concept. Yet for there to be *comparative* law, it must be possible to conceptualize law as a plurality of entities,[1] which entities moreover must be amenable to mutual comparison. In this chapter we accordingly move from law as unitary to law as plural – from 'law' to 'legal systems' – and examine the circumstances under which such systems can be compared to one another. We will see, in particular, that all entities that can properly qualify as 'legal systems' under law as collective commitment indeed are amenable to meaningful mutual comparison.

Part I opens with a reflection on comparability and meaningful comparison. As not all comparisons are meaningful, it is reasonable to think that the requirements for meaningful comparison are more stringent than those for mere comparability. I suggest that in order for any two entities to be comparable, they must be distinct yet also interconnected. The intensity of that interconnection does not matter, however: so long as the entities are interconnected *in some way*, they are comparable. A particular degree of interconnectedness in contrast is necessary for the comparison to be meaningful in addition to just possible. I describe as 'meaningful' any comparison that can yield new knowledge about the objects compared and/or their common kind, and argue that where the entities are interconnected either too thickly or too thinly, the comparison, though technically possible, cannot be meaningful in that sense. I conclude that in order for legal systems to be amenable to meaningful comparison, it must be possible to conceptualize them as entities that are both (1) distinct and (2) *adequately* interconnected.

---

[1] "[C]omparison excludes the presence of a singular law" (Pierre Legrand, Au lieu de soi, *in* 11 COMPARER LES DROITS, RÉSOLUMENT 25 (Pierre Legrand ed., 2009); "the universal and the comparative ... cannot possibly share one and the same space" (Geoffrey Samuel, *Dépasser le fonctionalisme, in ibid.*, at 405, 408.) (my translations).

I thereafter argue that such a conceptualization of legal systems is unavailable under either of the natural law or positivist ideal-types laid out in the last chapter, whereas it is available under the hybrid conception proposed here – law as collective commitment. That argument takes the form of an incursion into the branch of sociology known as 'system theory,' which teaches that 'systems' come in different varieties, only some of which, we will see, meet both of the above requirements for meaningful comparability. The legal systems of natural law correspond to what system theorists call 'synthetic systems,' and accordingly fail to meet the first, distinctness requirement (Part II), whereas the legal systems of positivism, as 'cybernetic organic systems,' fail to meet the second, connectedness requirement (Part III). In contrast, the legal systems of law as collective commitment, as 'autopoietic organic systems,' meet both requirements (Part IV). I conclude that, of these three conceptions, only law as collective commitment allows for the possibility of meaningful legal comparison.

I. COMPARISON REQUIRES DISTINCTNESS AND CONNECTEDNESS

By its very nature, comparison involves joining things while at the same time preserving their integrity as distinct things.[2] A condition for the possibility of comparison accordingly is the presence of a plurality of distinct yet joinable things.

Despite the old saying, apples and oranges are comparable, at least in some ways. While distinct *qua* apples and oranges, they can be related to one another *qua* fruit. As apples and oranges, their distinctness is absolute and a bar to comparison – they cannot be compared (so goes the saying).[3] As fruit, however, their distinctness is only relative: it is possible to bring together apples and oranges, subsume them for an instant under the more abstract genus 'fruit,' and compare them in terms of colour, sweetness and ripening time, for example, without for that matter undermining their distinctness as apples and oranges. It is because apples and oranges are, simultaneously and without contradiction, distinct *and* connected ('self' *and* 'other')[4] that comparing them is in fact possible. Conversely, the act of comparing them entails

---

[2] "bringing together with a peer, with that which is *prima facie* equal, ... equals which are presumed to endure, throughout and beyond the process of com-paring." H. Patrick Glenn, Com-paring, *in* COMPARATIVE LAW: A HANDBOOK 91, 92 (Esin Örücü & David Nelken eds., 2007). See generally: Christopher McCrudden, What Does It Mean to Compare, and What Should It Mean? in COMPARING COMPARATIVE LAW (Samantha Besson *et al.* eds., 2017).

[3] As Lukas Heckendorn Urscheler indicated, the equivalent Romanian saying – "grandmothers and machine guns" (http://en.wikipedia.org/wiki/Apples_and_oranges) – may be more effective in this regard.

[4] Vivian Grosswald Curran, Dealing in Difference: Comparative Law's Potential for Broadening Legal Perspectives, 46 AM. J. COMP. L. 657 (1998); Pierre Legrand, Sur l'analyse différentielle des juriscultures, 4 REV. INT. DR. COMP. 1053 (1999), discussing MONDER KILANI, L'INVENTION DE L'AUTRE (1994) ("the other 'I' existing as unexplored virtuality of the self").

and confirms that they can be simultaneously conceptualized connectedly, as 'fruit,' and distinctly, as 'apples/oranges.'

The aspect of being 'simultaneous and without contradiction' is crucial here. Apples and oranges are comparable because they are 'apple/orange' through and through while also being 'fruit' through and through. If they instead were made of one part 'apple/orange' and one part 'fruit,' juxtaposed and independent from one another, apples and oranges would not be mutually comparable entities. They would, to begin with, lack the internal unity needed to even qualify as 'entities': they would be two-part sets, not 'entities' proper (in just the same way that, if law as collective commitment were one part ideal and one part material rather than one part ideal/material, it would not be a truly hybrid, third conception from natural law and positivism[5]). In addition, they would not be mutually comparable as neither of their two parts taken independently would be so, albeit for opposite reasons: the respective 'apple/orange' parts would not be comparable because they would lack connectedness, whereas the respective 'fruit' parts would not be comparable because they would lack distinctness. Comparability in sum requires that the distinctness and connectedness dimensions be interwoven, not merely plunked side by side, within each of the entities for comparison. Each of these requirements will now be discussed further.

i. *'Distinctness'*

It is important not to confuse 'distinctness' with 'difference.' I would suggest that distinctness goes to structure whereas difference goes to substance.[6] In order to be comparable, apples and oranges need to be (structurally) distinct, quite apart from whether they might also be (substantively) different. Clones of a same apple are examples of entities that are comparable because they qualify as distinct despite being identical in substance. Difference and sameness in other words are potential conclusions, not possibility conditions, of the comparative process: it is possible to proceed with the comparison so long as there are distinct entities to compare, regardless of whether these entities turn out to be similar or different. There may of course be other problems with comparing entities that are too similar or too different in substance. Comparing clones of a same apple may be trivial, thus entirely uninteresting; comparing entities as radically different as, say, apples and toasters may be silly, or too difficult. But both these comparisons are nonetheless technically possible. From the standpoint of strict comparability, distinctness matters, while difference does not.

---

[5] See *supra*, Chapter 1, Part II, section iii.
[6] *Contra*: Étienne Picard, L'état du droit comparé en France en 1999, 4 *R.I.D.C.* 885, 902 (1999) and Legrand, *supra* note 4, both of whom seemingly view distinctness and difference as interchangeable.

In fact, there is a sense in which the distinctness requirement motions to sameness rather than difference. For when we say that entities need to be distinct in order to be comparable, we more specifically mean that they need to be structurally distinct *as well as substantively indistinguishable* – at least from the outset. Before the act of comparison, that is, the apples and oranges are just generic iterations of 'fruitness,' equally lacking in individuating features. They of course regain their peculiar apple-ness and orangeness as soon as the comparison begins, for their respective contents – colours, sugar contents, ripening times, etc. – then gradually come to appear. The point is, however, that that differentiation process necessarily takes place as against a backdrop of sameness: apples and oranges must first be conceptualized as generic 'fruit' – as "peers ... *prima facie* equal for purposes of consideration"[7] – in order to thereafter be seen for what they really are: differentiated 'apples' and 'oranges.' For any two entities to be comparable, then, it must be possible to conceptualize them, at least initially, as structurally distinct as well as substantively indistinguishable, for equally contentless.[8]

ii. *'Connectedness'*

But comparability also requires, as indicated, a certain measure of interconnectedness. We saw that apples and oranges are comparable because they share the concept of fruitness. There are, however, many other concepts linking apples and oranges. Both are 'plants,' and indeed comparable as such, not in terms of ripening times or sweetness (as not all plants ripen and/or contain sugar), but certainly in terms of, say, lifespans and soil/light requirements (as all plants have particular lifespans and soil/light requirements). They likewise are both 'organisms,' thus comparable in terms of carbon content, nutritional needs, reproductive means, etc. Yet another concept linking apples and oranges is that of 'things,' evoking such features as weight, size, hardness, usage, etc.

These various concepts of course vary in thickness. As they are subsets of one another (all 'fruit' also are 'plants,' 'organisms' and 'things'; 'plants' also are 'organisms' and 'things'; 'organisms' also are 'things'), they thin out as we move up in abstraction. Fruitness is the thickest, as it contains all the specifications pertaining to fruit, in addition to those pertaining to plants, organisms and things, whereas thing-ness is the thinnest, containing only the specifications of things (i.e. none of those

---

[7] Glenn, *supra* note 2, at 92; Mireille Delmas-Marty, Le pluralisme ordonné et les interactions entre ensembles juridiques, 14 REC. DALLOZ 951, 952 (2006) ("des ensembles normatifs non hiérarchisés entre eux ... de même niveau"); Béatrice Jaluzot, Cartographier les droits, *in* MÉLANGES EN L'HONNEUR DE CAMILLE JAUFFRET-SPINOSI 679, 691 ("les ordres juridiques sont mis sur un plan unique qui non seulement permet la comparaison, mais aussi induit une égalité entre eux").

[8] The implications of this for the infamous *praesumptio similitudinis* of comparative law is discussed below, in Chapter 5.

pertaining to fruit, plants or organisms).[9] And the connection between apples and oranges accordingly is tightest where these are conceptualized as fruit, and loosest where they are conceptualized as things.

It of course follows that the pool of comparable entities proportionally increases in size and diversity as we move up from fruit to things. Where apples are conceptualized as fruit, they are comparable, not just to oranges, but also to raspberries, pineapple and walnuts, since all these qualify as fruit. The game might then be titled 'comparative fruitness,' and all that can reasonably be regarded as 'fruit' accordingly is included. Where apples are instead conceptualized as plants, the game changes to 'comparative plantness,' and apples hence can be compared to all other plants: oranges, raspberries, pineapple and walnuts for sure, but also palm trees and petunias. As organisms – 'comparative organismness' – apples are comparable to all of the above, as well as to bacteria and kangaroos. As things – 'comparative thingness' – they are comparable to walnuts, petunias and kangaroos as well as toasters and airplanes. The connection among the entities under comparative thingness clearly is much looser than that under comparative fruitness, and it may be that, as a result, one or the other of these two games is more interesting or valuable. Yet both qualify as *comparative* games: from a strict comparability standpoint, toasters and airplanes are just as good as oranges insofar as it is possible conceptually to link, even if very

---

[9] There in fact is room for thickness variations comparison even within the concept of fruitness, as that cluster concept can be defined by appeal to a variety of features that themselves differ in thickness. Fruitness comparison will be thicker, for example, where it is defined in terms of sweetness and ripening time than where it is defined in terms of colourfulness and ripeness. Sweetness and ripening time indeed call into play particular metrics, whereas the metrics for colourfulness and ripeness remain to be specified. To define fruit in terms of sweetness and ripening time supposes not just that all fruit are sweet and take time to ripen, but also that all fruit are reducible to a common sweetness measure (sugar units per overall weight) and a common ripening time measure (hours, days, weeks) – that they in other words are *commensurable* in those respects ("incommensurable basically conveys that we have no measure, or no common measure, for something." Giovanni Sartori, Comparing and Miscomparing, 3 *J. Theor. Pol.* 243, 252 (1991)). In contrast, to define fruit in terms of colourfulness and ripeness supposes that all fruit indeed are colourful and ripen, but it says nothing as to how these qualities are to be measured in each, thus allowing for the possibility that different measuring methods be used for different fruit. So, while all fruit are colourful, the colourfulness of strawberries is to be measured against a standard of redness whereas that of oranges is to be measured against a standard of orangeness. Likewise, while all fruit ripen, ripeness may be measured through different means (colour, growth time, texture, ease of severing fruit from stem) for different fruit. In sum, commensurable entities are, all else being equal, more thickly interconnected than incommensurable ones. Yet, as argued in the text, entities need not be interconnected to the point of commensurability in order to be comparable (see generally: Bruce Chapman, Preference, Pluralism, and Proportionality, 60 *U. Tor. L. J.* 177, 191 (2010)) – contrary to what most comparative law scholars appear to assume (e.g.: Nils Jansen, Comparative Law and Comparative Legal Knowledge, *in* THE OXFORD HANDBOOK OF COMPARATIVE LAW 305 (Mathias Reimann & Reinhard Zimmermann eds., 2006); Ralf Michaels, Comparative Law by Numbers? Legal Origins Thesis, Doing Business Reports, and the Silence of Traditional Comparative Law, 57 AM. J. COMP. L. 765, 785 (2009).). The distinction comparability and commensurability is central to the argument presented in Chapter 5.

thinly, apples and airplanes/toasters. Comparability runs out, then, only where the possibility of a common conceptual basis between the entities also runs out.[10]

iii. *From Comparability to Meaningful Comparison*

As the last comment makes clear, comparability is not the same as meaningful comparison, and while the tightness of the entities' interconnection as just explained does not matter for the first, it arguably matters for the second. While it may not be possible (if at all desirable) to pinpoint a priori what particular degree of interconnection is adequate for the purpose of meaningful comparison, it is possible to specify minimal thresholds of tightness and looseness below which any comparison cannot but be entirely meaningless.

Meaningfulness is a variable concept, and particular comparisons indeed can be meaningful in different ways and to different extents in different contexts. Comparing apples with oranges may be most informative in some contexts, but comparing them with airplanes or toasters may be better in others. Where the aim is to learn about the ripening process, for example, the comparison might profitably be limited to apples and other fruit, perhaps even just particular kinds of fruit. But where the aim instead is medicinal or nutritional, it might make sense to extend the scope of the comparison to include bacteria and kangaroos. And in the context of thermodynamic/aerodynamic studies, it may well be that it is best to compare apples with airplanes/toasters than with oranges. Limiting the comparison to tightly connected entities clearly is best in some contexts, then, but extending it to cover a wider pool of more loosely connected, and thus also more diversified, entities has its advantages as well. All in all, it seems very difficult if at all possible to specify from the outset a degree of entity connectedness that would be optimal across comparative contexts and purposes.

Yet it arguably is possible to identify thresholds of connectedness beyond which the comparison would be altogether meaningless. In the above example, we move up in abstraction from fruitness to thingness, showing how the latter's lower degree of specification allows for the class of comparable entities to be correspondingly larger and more diversified. But suppose we move down from fruitness, towards a concept that is more, not less, fully specified. We could select appleness as our connecting concept, with the result that the class of comparable entities would then shrink to just various kinds of apples. We could go even further and specify one particular kind, thereby limiting the comparison to individual specimens of that one kind. And both types of comparisons – 'comparative appleness'/'comparative Macintoshness' – could conceivably prove meaningful in the right context.

---

[10] See, for example, Andrew Halpin's criticism of Wittgenstein for using the word "game" in the singular whereas "every distinct usage of the term would require its own concept to explain it." Andrew Halpin, Conceptual Collisions, 2 JURIS. 507, 521 (2011).

But that specification process can be pressed too far. Suppose we specify our connecting concept so fully that none but one individual apple qualifies. At that point, the only comparison that remains possible is that of comparing that one individual apple to itself (or, equivalently, clones of that apple). Such comparison however cannot but be pointless, as its conclusion would necessarily be obvious from the start: the criterion for selecting the apples for comparison being that they be one and the same, the conclusion of that comparison has to be that ... they are the same. Because the outcome of the comparison is fully determined from the moment the entities for comparison have been identified, there simply is nothing left for the comparative act proper to tell us that we did not already know.

Likewise where the entities are interconnected too thinly. Suppose we undertake to compare an apple with, say, love. Such a comparison is technically possible – 'an apple is an object whereas love is a feeling' – and might indeed yield such dubiously lyrical conclusions as 'an apple is cold and hard whereas love is warm and fuzzy.'[11] But it teaches us little if anything that we did not already know about apples and love at the moment of selecting them as objects of comparison. From the moment we undertake to compare such radically different entities as apples and love, we know that the conclusion will indeed be one of just radical difference.

In contrast, there is much to be learned from actually proceeding with a comparison of apples and oranges. Contrasting their different ripening times and sugar contents, for example, can help us understand their respective ripening processes, as well as the ripening process of fruit more generally. That is so precisely because apples and oranges are interconnected neither too thickly nor too thinly: though they clearly are distinct *sorts* of fruit, as *fruit* they both ripen, hold sugar, etc. By 'meaningful' comparison, then, I mean any comparison that can yield new knowledge about the objects being compared and/or their common kind, as obtains where the entities are interconnected neither too thickly (an identical apple) nor too thinly (apples and love).[12]

iv. *Meaningful Comparison in Law*

Legal systems are the apples and oranges of legal comparison. Every comparative law project (at least, as traditionally understood) involves comparing particular

---

[11] "A talented but chronically depressed person may have to choose between suicide and accomplishment. And the two values, freedom from pain and accomplishment, are so far removed from one another that they are scarcely easy to compare. But, despite that, they come nowhere near strict incomparability. We can and do compare pain and accomplishment." James Griffin, *Well-Being — Its Meaning, Measurement and Moral Importance* 80 (1986).

[12] "If two entities are similar ... in all their characteristics, then they are the same entity – and that is that. If, on the other hand, two entities are different in every respect, then their comparison is nonsensical – and that is again that. The comparisons in which we engage are thus the ones between entities whose attributes are in part shared (similar) and in part non-shared (and thus, we say, incomparable)." Sartori, *supra* note 9.

aspects, features and elements of two or more legal systems. Where a botanist might want to compare the colour and sweetness of apples and oranges, a comparative lawyer would want to compare particular rules or groups of rules, specific institutions, modes of reasoning and/or argumentation of, say, Japanese and US law: Japanese and US law are to the comparative lawyer what apples and oranges are to the botanist. Legal systems accordingly are the entities that must exhibit distinctness and adequate interconnectedness if legal comparison is going to be meaningful.

As with botanical comparisons, moreover, it would be very difficult to specify at the outset a degree of legal system interconnectedness that could be considered optimal across comparative contexts and purposes. If one lesson can be drawn from the comparative law scholarship produced to date, it is that different comparative law projects call for different degrees of system connectedness.[13] Comparative studies of pointed legal issues commonly cover a limited number of legal systems (at most three) that are quite tightly connected to one another (e.g. English, US and Canadian law, German and French law, Japanese and Chinese law), whereas the number and diversity of systems covered rises significantly in the context of the 'common core projects'[14] (e.g. all European legal systems). 'Legal family' taxonomies,[15] finally, typically include as large a number and diversity of systems as is logistically possible (e.g. all world legal systems).

In each case, the pool of legal systems surveyed is adequate given the purpose pursued. Where one seeks to understand the role of *causa* in contract, for example, it makes sense to focus on systems that tend to converge on all but that one issue – on systems that hence stand quite close together. Comparing systems that differ, not just on *causa*, but on other components of contract would clearly be helpful for understanding contract but perhaps less so for understanding the particular role of *causa* as against that of the other components. Where the purpose instead is, as in many common core projects, to harmonize legal systems, it makes sense to include as many legal systems as are harmonizable – that are sufficiently interconnected to be harmonized without generating too much confusion and internal distortion. And where the aim is to survey and classify all that can reasonably be considered 'legal

[13] "It is difficult to speak generally of how the comparatist should limit his field of inquiry, since it all depends on the precise topic of his research." KONRAD ZWEIGERT & HEIN KÖETZ, AN INTRODUCTION TO COMPARATIVE LAW 39 (Tony Weir trans., 3rd ed. 1998); "It is not possible to proceed very far on the basis of macro-constructs, and when needed they have to be rejected and replaced with more detailed data." Jaako Husa, The False Dichotomy between Theory and Practice: Lessons from Comparative Law, in RECHTSWISSENSCHAFT ALS JURISTISCHEDOKTRIN 105, 116–17 (2009).

[14] E.g. INTERNATIONAL INSTITUTE FOR THE UNIFICATION OF PRIVATE LAW, THE UNIDROIT PRINCIPLES (2004); FORMATION OF CONTRACTS: A STUDY OF THE COMMON CORE OF LEGAL SYSTEMS, vol. 1 (Rudolf B. Schlesinger ed., 1968); INTERNATIONAL ENCYCLOPEDIA OF COMPARATIVE LAW (Andre Tunc ed., 1983) (17 volumes covering 150 states); THE COMMON CORE OF EUROPEAN PRIVATE LAW (Mauro Bussani & Ugo Mattei eds., 2001). I give a brief overview of such projects in the Prologue, note 26.

[15] See *supra* Prologue, note 24.

systems,' the pool must naturally be as large as it can be, perhaps including even such 'borderline' legal systems as religious and/or ethnic communities, though this will inevitably result in the pooled systems being interconnected in the thinnest way. Here again, then, different levels of entity connectedness will be adequate for different comparative projects, with the result that it would be inadvisable to posit from the outset a level that would be ideal across projects.

Importantly, as the discipline that encompasses all such projects, comparative law should refrain from specifying even the set of necessary and sufficient conditions applicable to each. Its task is rather to delineate the outer bounds of 'meaningful legal comparison,' and allow for the full range of possibilities falling within those bounds. That is to say, comparative law should do no more than weed out comparative projects that do not qualify as 'meaningful legal comparisons,' either because they are not properly 'legal,' or else because they are not properly 'meaningful.' To illustrate, although comparing French law to, say, English politics may be a meaningful comparative exercise, it may not qualify as an exercise in 'comparative *law*' insofar as one of the two entities compared (here, the second) arguably cannot plausibly be considered a 'legal' system. Comparing French law and English politics, that is, is not 'comparative law' so much as 'comparative social institutions,' 'comparative social organization,' or something along those lines – 'comparative plantness' rather than 'comparative fruitness.' If only for the purpose of weeding out non-legal comparisons, then, comparative law needs to lay out a particular conception of 'law' and the 'legal.' But that conception as just explained must weed out more than just non-legal comparisons; it must also weed out comparisons that, while perhaps 'legal,' are not 'meaningful' in the sense articulated above. It must also weed out, that is, any and all comparisons the conclusions of which are fully pre-determined and hence contribute no new knowledge about the objects compared – any and all comparisons tantamount to comparing a same apple to itself, or else an apple to love.

Meanwhile, as that conception must otherwise allow for the full range of comparisons that do qualify as 'legal' and 'meaningful,' it ought to include *no further* requirements than are strictly necessary to achieve that dual weeding function.[16]

---

[16] Brian Tamanaha proceeds the same way, pruning away from Hart's conception of law all that is not strictly necessary and hence unduly restrictive of what might qualify as 'law' in a globalized world: Brian Tamanaha, A General Jurisprudence of Law and Society (2001), esp. at xii, 139–40, 159–61, 207. (The present account however differs from Tamanaha's on both the starting point – a Fullerian rather than Hartian conception – and on what can be pruned away, 'effectiveness' being here retained (*ibid.* at 143–48).) See likewise William Twining's apt critique of Neil MacCormick's account of law as "inappropriate for a comparative lawyer," on the basis that it includes references to "shared 'universal' basic values," which in fact need not be posited a priori: William Twining, Institutions of Law from a Global Perspective: Standpoint, Pluralism and Non-State Law, *in* Law as Institutional Normative Order 17, 22 (Maksymillian Del Mar & Zenon Bankowski eds., 2010, 2009) ("There may or may not be some shared 'universal' basic values, but that is a matter for external juristic inquiry and interpretation, not bare assertion."). MacCormick's response (Concluding for Institutionalism, *in* Law as Institutional Normative Order, *supra*, at 187, 200) confirms that his purpose is primarily

For, to specify any additional requirements would necessarily result in some mean-ingful legal comparisons being excluded from the outset. For example, a conception of law that would be so bare as to allow for the inclusion of certain religious and/ or ethnic communities alongside the more traditional national systems would nec-essarily admit into the pool, say, Western legal systems, yet the reverse is not true: a conception thin enough to let in all Western systems may still be too thick to let in non-traditional/non-Western systems. Comparative law accordingly ought to specify *ex ante* no more than the barest possible conception of 'legal system,' leaving it to individual comparative lawyers to supplement it *ex post* – perhaps to the point of excluding all but Western (or European, or even just the French and German) legal systems – for the purpose of any given project.[17] It therefore is possible to say from the outset that insofar as comparative law aims to capture all meaningful legal comparisons, it requires *the thinnest possible conception of legal systems that is none-theless sufficiently thick to weed out non-legal or non-meaningful legal comparisons.*

I want to suggest that law as collective commitment is just such a conception. In the last chapter, law as collective commitment was presented as a bare-bone, minimal conception, one so thin as to capture all that can plausibly be regarded as 'legal.' That conception's six constitutive features (effectiveness, argumentativeness, coherence, publicness, formality and normativity) indeed are formal features, thus amenable to widely variable contents.[18] What is more, these formal features are as few as can be, given that they represent all and only that which will prove necessary for the purpose of enabling the comparative process elaborated in the coming chap-ters. Particularly noteworthy in this respect is the exclusion of any kind of reference to notions of 'justice,' 'fairness' or the like.[19] We saw that, as a result, even such non-conventional regimes as religious or aboriginal law, and such 'wicked' systems

---

philosophical – uncovering the truth about law – rather than comparative – elaborating a basis upon which to account for comparative law. See more generally: WILLIAM TWINING, GENERAL JURISPRUDENCE: UNDERSTANDING LAW FROM A GLOBAL PERSPECTIVE 116–21 (2009).

[17] Many have claimed in contrast that comparative law ought to be *ex ante* limited to comparing legal systems with similar levels of development (ZWEIGERT & KÖETZ, *supra* note 13, at 9; PETER DE CRUZ, A MODERN APPROACH TO COMPARATIVE LAW 7 (1993); HAROLD COOKE GUTTERIDGE, COMPARATIVE LAW 2, at 73 (2nd ed., 1949); Clive M. Schmithoff, The Science of Comparative Law, 7 CAMBRIDGE L. J. 94, 96 (1939)) or political ideologies (Rodolfo Sacco, Legal Formants: A Dynamic Approach to Comparative Law (Installment I of II), 39 AM. J. COMP. L. 1, 7 (1991) – capitalist and socialist legal systems may be too far apart to bear comparison).

[18] Like Ewald's "law as jurisprudence," then, law as collective commitments "imposes no substantive restrictions on the content of the ideas studied [which accordingly] can be ideas about economics, or about sociology, or about witchcraft and magic" (William Ewald, The Jurisprudential Approach to Comparative Law: A Field Guide to 'Rats', 46 AM. J. COMP. L. 701, 705 (1998)).

[19] It thus seems right to say that, whereas "in most societies the concept of law is bound up with normative questions about justice, ... *this* link ... is [in the context of the present enterprise] a purely contingent one." Ewald, *ibid.* at 705. Likewise: "The notion of just and unjust is infinitely variable and changing, but the feeling of just and unjust is a permanent feature of human nature." LÉON DUGUIT, TRAITÉ DE DROIT CONSTITUTIONNEL VOL. 1, at 50, quoted in L. Valcke, La problématique juridique de G. Del Vecchio, 23 SCIENCES ET ESPRIT 201, 213 (1971) (my translation).

as apartheid or Nazi law, indeed might potentially qualify as 'law,' under law as collective commitment. Perhaps that account could prove so thin as to even allow for altogether "distinct conceptions of law ... [dictating] no single answer, even in principle, to the question, 'What is law?'"[20]

In addition, law as collective commitments is, as we see next, sufficiently thick to weed out legal comparisons that are non-meaningful. I there press further the contrast with the natural law and positivist ideal-types undertaken in the last chapter with a view to demonstrating that, unlike either of these ideal-types, law as collective commitment conceptualizes legal systems as entities that are distinct yet sufficiently interconnected to allow for meaningful comparison. More specifically, I aim to show that legal systems lack the requisite distinctness under natural law, whereas they lack the requisite connectedness under positivism, and that they in contrast lack neither under law as collective commitment. As a result, whereas comparing legal systems is, under natural law, tantamount to comparing an identical apple with itself and, under positivism, tantamount to comparing an apple with love, it is much like comparing apples and oranges, under law as collective commitment. If so, law as collective commitment, while being extremely thin, indeed would nonetheless prove sufficiently thick to weed out comparisons that are non-legal and/or non-meaningful.

II. LEGAL SYSTEMS UNDER NATURAL LAW

Although natural law allows for conceptualizing law as a 'system' – the ideal system of the Law of Nature – that system necessarily is singular rather than plural. We will see that while that system is divisible into many subsystems, and in turn just one of many systems constituting human knowledge as a whole, it is not itself replicable into multiple iterations. What are commonly known as the world's 'legal systems' at first sight seem to be many and distinct, but these systems in fact are, under our idealized natural law conception, of a kind that is highly unstable, with the result that they quickly unravel into the sum of their parts, i.e. into just one, enlarged pool of rules.

On a natural law conception, law undoubtedly qualifies as a 'system'[21] in the generic sense of "a unified, self-contained whole."[22] It is a 'whole,' the various

---

[20] William Ewald, Comparative Jurisprudence (I): What Was It Like to Try a Rat?, 143 U. PA. L. REV. 1898, 1950–51 (1994–95). See also: R. David, The Different Conceptions of the Law, *in* 2 INTERNATIONAL ENCYCLOPEDIA OF COMPARATIVE LAW 3 (Ulrich Drobning *et al.* eds., 1981); William Twining, Globalization and Legal Theory: Some Local Implications, 49 CUR. LEG. PROB. 1, 21, 36–39 (1996); William Twining, Mapping Law, 50 NORTHERN IRELAND LEG. Q. 12 (1999).

[21] On the many uses and abuses of the word "system," see: Jean Combacau, Le droit international: bric-à-brac ou système?, 31 ARCH. DE PHIL. DU DROIT 85 (1986). As the present argument is not semantic, nothing turns on the use of the particular term "system." Any equivalent term – "order," "regime," "family" – accordingly might have done here.

[22] DICTIONNAIRE ENCYCLOPÉDIQUE DE THÉORIE ET DE SOCIOLOGIE DU DROIT, at 596 (ANDRÉ-JEAN ARNAUD ET AL. EDS., 2nd ed. 1993). (My translation.)

components of which are related to one another, not just a 'set,' wherein the components are merely juxtaposed.[23] We did see that, on the natural lawyers' account, legal rules and principles are interconnected insofar as all are logically derived from the same core of first principles, and law accordingly can be rationalized into a single, internally unified conceptual structure – precisely those scholars' life-long project.[24] *Conceptual* unity hence is what ties the law into a 'system,' under natural law.

System theorists however warn us that systems come in different kinds, only one of which is at play here.[25] Whereas 'synthetic systems' purport to represent an external reality *as it is*, 'mathematical systems' aim instead to remodel reality into a conceptually purified, ultra-rational version of itself. In contrast to both of these, finally, 'organic systems' are geared to producing an altogether new reality.[26] Synthetic systems accordingly presuppose a correspondence theory of truth, whereas mathematical systems can instead be described as supposing an internal coherence theory of truth[27] or as favouring internal coherence over truth.[28] As for organic systems, they might be best described as allowing for a variety of different truths. Since the natural lawyers aimed to do no more than reproduce the Law of Nature, to which they clearly ascribed the status of reality (if of a moral kind), their various reproductions fall squarely in the first category, that of synthetic systems.[29]

Synthetic systems however are problematic here, for they by definition defy plurality, at least the sort of plurality required for the kind of comparisons that interest us, namely, *inter-system* comparisons. A single synthetic system certainly can be *internally* plural: as a rational structure, it naturally divides into a number of (similarly rational yet smaller) substructures, whose respective positions are likewise determined rationally, by reference to the position of the other substructures. The natural lawyers clearly considered that the Law of Nature logically divides into public and private law, the latter in turn dividing into contract, tort and property law, for example (though they argued endlessly over the nature and exact location of these divisions). Synthetic systems also allow for a form of meta-plurality, moreover, plurality

[23] MICHEL VAN DE KERCHOVE & FRANCOIS OST, LEGAL SYSTEM BETWEEN ORDER AND DISORDER 5–6 (1994); H. L. A. HART, THE CONCEPT OF LAW 234 (2nd ed. 1994).
[24] See *supra*, Chapter 1, Part II, section i.
[25] Christophe Grzegorczyk, Évaluation critique du paradigme systémique dans la science du droit, 31 ARCH. DE PHIL. DU DROIT 281 (1986). See generally: ERVIN LASZLO, INTRODUCTION TO SYSTEMS PHILOSOPHY (1972); GERALD M. WEINBERG, AN INTRODUCTION TO GENERAL SYSTEMS THINKING (1972); C. WEST CHURCHMAN, THE SYSTEMS APPROACH (1979); PAUL S. LICKER, FUNDAMENTALS OF SYSTEMS ANALYSIS (1987); MICHAEL L. GIBSON & CARY T. HUGHES, SYSTEMS ANALYSIS AND DESIGN (1994).
[26] Grzegorczyk's classification (see Grzegorczyk, *supra* note 25) arguably tracks Kenneth Bailey's similarly tripartite classification ("conceptual/pattern," "abstract" and "physical" systems). KENNETH D. BAILEY, SOCIOLOGY AND THE NEW SYSTEMS THEORY 47–57 (1994).
[27] See Grzegorczyk, *supra* note 25, at 283.
[28] René Sève, Système et Code, 31 ARCH. DE PHIL. DU DROIT 77, 78 (1986). Heidegger and the German Pandectists are prime examples of thinkers falling in this last category. *Ibid.* at 77–80.
[29] The question of the extent to which a moral reality can, like a material object, be merely described, as opposed to actively constructed, is discussed below, in Chapter 3.

in the sense of distinct systems representing distinct realities. The legal system being a representation of juridical morality indeed does not preclude the possibility of other kinds of systems representing other areas of morality, or other realities beyond moral ones. And the natural lawyers did in fact consider law to be just one of many rational systems – biology, philosophy, economics, etc. – that together constitute the (similarly rational yet larger) super-structure of human knowledge writ large.

However, even if it were the case that legal domains and/or academic disciplines might somehow meet the above two requirements for meaningful comparison,[30] the resulting kinds of comparisons – contract/tort comparisons; law/biology comparisons – simply would not fit what we (and the natural lawyers) typically take 'comparative law' to be about. Comparisons among legal domains are not system–system so much as subsystem–subsystem comparisons.[31] They are comparisons *in* law, not comparisons *of* law – an integral part of legal reasoning plain and simple. As for comparisons of law with other disciplines, although they clearly are comparisons *of* law, they are comparisons of law *with something else*, whereas as we saw both of the compared entities need to qualify as 'legal' in order for the comparison to fit within comparative law as we know it.

What we need, then, is plurality that is neither internal (legal domain to legal domain) nor meta- (law to philosophy or economics) but rather of a sort that would allow for comparisons of law *with itself*: legal-system-to-legal-system comparisons. Yet synthetic systems bar that sort of plurality for the same reason that they allow for internal and meta-plurality. They allow for internal and meta-plurality only insofar as, in both cases, the various subsystems are not competing to synthesize one and the same reality but rather target distinct realities, or distinct sectors of a same reality.[32] Torts, contracts and property are typically seen, certainly by the natural lawyers,[33]

---

[30] With respect to the first requirement, though torts and contracts presumably can be regarded "presumptively equal" legal domains, legal domains may not be sufficiently independent from one another to qualify as self-standing entities, given their strong conceptual interdependence on the naturalist account. With respect to the second requirement, they would qualify as requisitely "connected" only if "legal domain" could be considered an archetypal concept, which is debatable. While it is possible to say of legal domains that they are more or less orderly, dense or complicated, for example, it is an open question whether orderliness, density and simplicity are essential characteristics of legal domains. These same qualifications apply equally with respect to biology and philosophy as "academic disciplines."

[31] See Arnaud's distinction between "legal systems" and "legal domains," ARNAUD, *supra* note 22, at 596. For a fuller discussion, see *infra* Chapter 4, Part III, section i.

[32] Known in the legal pluralism literature as "weak pluralism": John Griffiths, What Is Legal Pluralism?, 24 J. OF LEGAL PLURALISM 1 (1986). Whereas "weak" pluralism connotes the peaceful, for parallel, cohabitation of different normative regimes within a same centralized structure, "strong" pluralism in contrast entails the superimposition, and hence competition, of different normative regimes upon one and the same territory, whether defined territorially, conceptually, demographically or any other way: *ibid.* at 39. For a fuller discussion of weak vs. strong pluralism, see *infra* Chapter 4, Part III.

[33] Under a functionalistic, law and economics conception, they can in contrast be viewed as conceptually merged: Guido Calabresi & A. Douglas Melamed, Property Rules, Liability Rules, and Inalienability: One View of the Cathedral, 85 *HARV. L. REV.* 1089 (1972).

as covering respectively different conceptual territories, as are law, biology and economics. The orderly coexistence of all subsystems within one and the same larger intellectual structure is possible, on the synthetic account, only insofar as each subsystem is ascribed a separate territory. So long as the territories' boundaries can be precisely established, there is to be no encroachment, no intersection, no intersubsystem conflict – the subsystems are 'co-possible.' The problem is, comparative law typically involves comparing systems that the natural lawyers viewed as covering *the same* conceptual territory: contract law to contract law, admittedly located on different *geographical* territories, but ultimately determined as against the same *conceptual* referent, namely, the one and only Law of Nature. Now such synthetic systems cannot, as we see next, be conceptualized as 'structurally distinct and prima facie equal' entities as per our first requirement for meaningful comparison.

To the extent that synthetic systems aimed at a same referent can be plural at all, they would have to be so as distinct *approximations* of that referent. However, approximations by definition always are to some extent defective (since a non-defective, perfect approximation would necessarily be indistinguishable from the referent). It therefore has to be the case that for any two distinct approximations of the same referent, one is superior to the other.[34] There is no moment at which distinct approximations of a same referent are "peers ... *prima facie* equal for purposes of consideration."[35] They are rather presumed *un*equal (inferior or superior) from the outset: as these are *competing* approximations, and competitions are meant to be won by only one (to be sure, not all) competitor, they necessarily presuppose competitor *in*equality.

I would suggest that this is fully consistent with the natural lawyers' view of legal systems and what it means to compare them. These scholars did view world legal systems as distinct, competing and indeed prima facie unequal renditions of the Law of Nature.[36] They considered that as these renditions are the work of humans, they cannot but be somewhat imperfect, and any and all differences between them must necessarily be explainable in terms of such imperfections. Had all legal systems been perfect renditions of the same moral law, they would be exactly the same; their being in fact different hence was taken to confirm that at most one of them is perfect and all others are imperfect. Difference in other words "is perceived as an indication that there must be something conceptually wrong."[37] What is more, the fact that

---

[34] They could perhaps be equally defective – equidistant from the referent – but that would effectively amount to their being one and the same, as distance from the referent is the only relevant criterion for assessing approximations as such. In any event, it is unclear how one would go about determining, let alone comparing, the respective degrees of moral defectiveness of legal systems, and even if it could be done, such comparisons simply would not fit what we typically consider comparative law to be about (as per below in the text).

[35] See *supra* text accompanying note 7.

[36] See *supra* Chapter 1, Part II, section i.

[37] Nikolas Roos, NICE Dreams and Realities of European Private Law, *in* EPISTEMOLOGY AND METHODOLOGY OF COMPARATIVE LAW 197, 217 (*Mark Van Hoecke ed.*, 2004).

the imperfect systems in turn differ among themselves was taken to mean no more than that these systems are imperfect to different degrees.[38] So upon observing, say, that civil law and common law systems use different, inquisitorial and adversarial procedures, the natural lawyers would automatically assume that one of these procedures must be morally superior to the other: either the inquisitorial and adversarial procedures reflect two different principles, only one of which is morally justifiable, or they are rooted in the same morally justifiable principle, but something went amiss in the deduction process on one side or the other. (Or else these are altogether morally indifferent, 'coordination' or 'adjectival law' procedures, but which then do not qualify as 'legal proper' in their view, as explained below.[39]) Alternatively, both procedures might be morally unjustifiable, but one presumably less so than the other, with the result that it ought to be possible to identify the better one, tinker with it – excise some parts, add new ones – and ultimately bring it into line with the Law of Nature.

Importantly, the presumptive inequality of synthetic systems approximating a same referent causes them to be highly unstable systems.[40] Recall that these are conceptual systems, whose various components are unified only insofar as all can be intellectually traced to the same referent. This suggests that any kind of defect in a system – any kind of divergence from the referent – effectively causes the unity of the whole system to be disrupted, and the system itself in due course to unravel into just a large mass of disparate components. Now, as *all* such systems (except perhaps one) are to some extent defective and unstable in that way, it is system plurality in general that is here dissolving into component plurality, and that ends up being unsustainable from the outset. Indeed, the only entities left in this picture ultimately are, on the one hand, the referent system and, on the other hand, indistinguishable masses of disparate components. Which leaves possible only two forms of comparison, namely, referent–referent and component–component comparisons. (A third, technically possible form – referent–component comparisons – would not be one involving 'prima facie equal' entities.)

This is borne out by the kind of comparative law scholarship favoured by the natural lawyers, of which the various 'common core' projects are perhaps the best illustration.[41] Legal rules from different jurisdictions are there gathered with a view

---

[38] James Gordley, The Universalist Heritage, *in* COMPARATIVE LEGAL STUDIES: TRADITIONS AND TRANSITIONS 31 (Pierre Legrand & Roderick Munday eds., 2003).

[39] If so, they admittedly might qualify as presumptively equal and comparable precisely because they are *not* "legal" proper, as per *infra*, text accompanying notes 46–48.

[40] Otto Pfersmann makes this point in: Otto Pfersmann, Le droit comparé comme interprétation et comme théorie du droit, R.I.D.C. 275, 277 (2001) ("Either these systems are on an equal footing and neither is subordinated to another and there is plurality or else they are not and we are then back to a case of unity." My translation.).

[41] See the projects listed *supra* note 14. Even the projects ostensibly directed at strictly practical harmonization objectives (e.g. the European unification project: Bussani & Mattei, *supra* note

to discovering (and eventually harmonizing) the way these jurisdictions handle a common set of problems. As the rules are uprooted from their respective systems of origin and reclassified thematically, the systems themselves quickly wither from sight, resurfacing only incidentally wherever some backdrop is needed against which to understand the rules.[42] In the end, there really is just one legal system – the referent system – alongside a vast assortment of rules with which to reconstruct it. As the rules' parent systems – the approximating systems – are nowhere to be seen, the only possible form of comparison (beside the obviously pointless one of the referent to itself) in fact is rule–rule comparison.[43] This moreover is fully consistent with the natural lawyers' more general account of comparative law as being only extensionally different from law *simpliciter*: if legal systems are just assortments of rules with which to reconstruct the Law of Nature, many such systems admittedly is better than one insofar as the pool of relevant data is correspondingly enlarged, but the analytical and methodological frameworks remain essentially the same.[44]

Yet, as even the natural lawyers themselves recognize, that account of legal systems and comparative law (and hence the very conception of law as a synthetic system) is problematic on at least two counts. The first is that it flies in the face of traditional comparative law scholarship, which has focused on systems rather than rules, and has taken system differences seriously.[45] This of course need not trouble natural lawyers insofar as their account of comparative law, like their account of law, is an *ideal* account, one that accordingly may or may not be met in practice. But they

---

14) are premised on at least the *possibility* of harmonization, and accordingly exhibit some kind of naturalistic/universalistic inclination.

[42] "[The result is] the atomization of juridical orders, which disappear as global entities. When giving importance merely to the multitude of solution-types, one ends up forgetting what constitutes the structure of juridical orders as well as their specificity." LÉONTIN-JEAN CONSTANTINESCO, TRAITÉ DE DROIT COMPARÉ, VOL. III "LA SCIENCE DES DROITS COMPARÉS" 72 (1983) (my translation). Gordley indeed asserts that, in final analysis, there really are no such things as 'legal *systems*' proper (James Gordley, Comparative Law and Legal History, in THE OXFORD HANDBOOK OF COMPARATIVE LAW, *supra* note 9, at 754, 761).

[43] See THE ENFORCEABILITY OF PROMISES IN EUROPEAN CONTRACT LAW (James Gordley ed., 2001), "Case 12: Promises to take less than was agreed," 267–78, wherein the final summary of the solutions reached in the ten jurisdictions surveyed is preceded by succinct descriptions of the rules deployed to that effect in each jurisdiction. These descriptions, written in language accessible to outsiders, touch on the rest of the respective legal systems only insofar as that is felt necessary for outsiders to make sense of the rules themselves.

[44] E.g. James Gordley, Is Comparative Law a Distinct Discipline?, 46 AM. J. COMP. L. 607, 608–613 (1998) (asserting that all legal jurisdictions share a common body of juridical principles, set of intellectual foundations and form of reasoning, and that the task of the comparatist accordingly is limited to assessing which of the various legal rules in presence best reflect this common body of principle); Hessel E. Yntema, Comparative Legal Research: Some Remarks on "Looking Out of the Cave", 54 MICH. L. REV. 899, 901 (1972) (equating "comparative law" with "legal science").

[45] "[Under the rationalist approach] either the differences would not matter or they would be the result of some error in logical deduction. Yet, if comparative law has taught us anything, it is that some of these differences do matter and that they are not merely mistakes." Gordley, *supra* note 38, at 31.

have nonetheless attempted to meet that objection by suggesting that legal systems in fact comprise two kinds of rules, only one of which is determined through correspondence with the Law of Nature. Coordination rules (e.g. driving on the right or left side of the road) and the above described 'adjectival' law (that relating to the implementation rather than the formulation of the Law of Nature)[46] they regard as examples of 'morally indifferent' rules, which are determined as matters of prudence and convenience, and accordingly admit of a variety of equally valid answers.[47] In their view, then, one can only conclude that traditional comparative law doctrine has focused on the morally indifferent parts of legal systems. That conclusion however if anything confirms the incomparability of legal systems under natural law, as it entails that morally indifferent rules are comparable precisely because they on that account are 'political' rather than 'legal' rules proper.[48] Precisely because, that is, morally indifferent rules by definition do not partake in the synthesizing competition but rather stand altogether outside the legal system *qua* synthetic system – outside the *legal* realm proper.

The second problem with the natural lawyers' account of legal systems and comparative law should be more troubling to them as it is internal to that account. To reduce comparative law to just rule comparison projects legal rules as self-standing entities, which we well know they are not.[49] As legal rules are conceptually linked to other legal rules, they cannot be properly understood outside the context of their respective systems, and hence can hardly be regarded as self-standing conceptual units. This too is evident from the common core projects. That such a purportedly rule-focused project would insist on supplementing their surveys with (at times extensive) explanations as to where the various rules fit in their respective systems confirms that legal rules in fact are not understandable as such, and that comparative law ultimately cannot be reduced to just rule pooling and comparison.[50]

Having eliminated rule–rule comparison as a plausible option under the natural lawyers' own account, the only option remaining is that of referent–referent comparison – comparing the Law of Nature to itself – which indeed is just like comparing a particular apple to itself.

---

[46] See *supra*, text accompanying notes 38–39.

[47] JOHN FINNIS, *NATURAL LAW AND NATURAL RIGHTS* 284–89, 351 (1980); Gordley, *supra* note 38.

[48] "then comparatists have reached the limit of analysis. The explanation [for the difference between the morally indifferent parts of legal systems] can only be historical: to describe the previous choices which are like this one and which made the societies what they are." Gordley, *supra* note 38, at 45. (That limit however is reached more quickly here than on Gordley's account, as that account targets not the "later rationalist" strand of natural law (used here) but rather the Aristotelian strand, wherein the implementation of the Law of Nature is as much an essential part of law as its formulation.) See *supra*, text accompanying note 37.

[49] See our discussion *infra*, Chapter 3.

[50] See *supra* note 43.

III. LEGAL SYSTEMS UNDER POSITIVISM

Like natural law, positivism allows for conceptualizing law as a 'system' yet one resistant to system–system comparisons, but for the opposite reason. Whereas the legal system of natural law as we just saw fails on the first of the two requirements for meaningful comparison ('distinctness'), that of positivism fails on the second ('connectedness'). Indeed, though positivistic legal systems clearly are 'structurally distinct and prima facie equal,' their distinctness is so extreme that comparing them is tantamount to comparing an apple with love.

Law under positivism undoubtedly qualifies as a 'system' in the generic sense used above – a "unified, self-contained whole"[51] – insofar as its various elements are connected to one another rather than merely juxtaposed.[52] As Hans Kelsen himself described it, "[l]aw is not, as it is sometimes said, a rule. It is a set of rules having the kind of unity we understand by a system."[53] The connection between the rules here is material rather than conceptual, however: whereas under natural law the rules are tied together through their reflecting a same set of moral ideals, under positivism they are interconnected through their originating from a same set of institutions.[54]

The legal system of positivism consequently is of an altogether different kind than that of natural law. In contrast to the latter, which we just saw belongs among synthetic systems, the legal system of positivism arguably falls among organic systems.[55] As explained, the main difference between these two kinds of systems has to do with their particular relations to reality and truth: whereas synthetic systems mimic an external reality and hence entail a correspondence theory or truth, organic systems produce an altogether new reality and accordingly allow for a variety of different truths (one per individual system).[56] This central feature of organic systems, their reality-generating quality, is best understood against the backdrop of the biological context in which they were originally formalized.[57] As their label confirms, these systems indeed originated from the physical sciences, only later making their way

---

[51] ARNAUD, *supra* note 22.

[52] See generally: S. ROMANO, *L'ORDRE JURIDIQUE* 7 (2nd ed., 1976); Gerald Postema, Law's System: The Necessity of System in Common Law, *NEW ZEALAND L. REV.* 69, 77–79 (2014).

[53] HANS KELSEN, *GENERAL THEORY OF LAW AND STATE* 3 (1961) (1945). See also: JOSEPH RAZ, *THE CONCEPT OF A LEGAL SYSTEM: AN INTRODUCTION TO THE THEORY OF LEGAL SYSTEM* 1, 2 (1970); Michel Troper, Système juridique et État 31 *ARCH. DE PHIL. DU DROIT* 29, 31 (1986).

[54] On these two kinds of systematicity, see: S. Rials, Supraconstitutionnalité et systématicité du droit, 31 *ARCH. DE PHIL. DU DROIT* 57, 71–72 (1986); Combacau, *supra* note 21, at 86–87; Grzegorczyk, *supra* note 25, at 289–92.

[55] *Ibid.* at 284–85.

[56] See *supra* text accompanying notes 26–28.

[57] See: HUMBERTO MATURANA & FRANCISCO VARELA, *AUTOPOIESIS AND COGNITION: THE REALIZATION OF THE LIVING* (1980); FRANCISCO VARELA, *PRINCIPLES OF BIOLOGICAL AUTONOMY* (1979); Milan Zeleny, What is Autopoiesis?, *in AUTOPOIESIS: A THEORY OF LIVING ORGANIZATION* 4, 6 (Milan Zeleny ed., 1981); LUDWIG VON BERTALANFFY, *GENERAL SYSTEM THEORY* (1968).

(not without friction)[58] into such human sciences as anthropology and sociology,[59] and eventually surfacing in legal scholarship as well.[60]

An offshoot of nineteenth-century holism,[61] the organic system emulates an intuition that complex objects may not be fully explained through an analysis of their constitutive elements, as the whole may be greater than the sum of its parts. It epitomizes groups of interconnected elements that are teleologically self-regenerative, i.e. that self-regenerate with a view to fulfilling a particular purpose.[62] Living organisms are one example of such systems for sure, but so are artificial intelligence devices, which likewise constantly self-regenerate in the sense that they *both use and produce the means of their own production.*[63] Living and artificial things however differ in that the purposes for which they self-regenerate are respectively endogenous and exogenous. A rabbit, to return to a familiar example,[64] regenerates with a view to furthering its (inherent) rabbit-ness: it will engage in whatever activities (finding food and shelter, self-protection, mate selection) will best sustain it as a rabbit.[65] Deep Blue in contrast regenerates with a view to furthering whatever function is programmed into it, typically playing chess, but it could be any other; whichever it is, Deep Blue will adjust accordingly. Organic systems hence subdivide into two categories: 'autopoietic' such systems, which regenerate towards an endogenous purpose, and 'cybernetic' ones, whose regenerative purpose is instead exogenous.[66]

---

[58] The two co-authors Maturana and Varela themselves disagreed on this point: see MATURANA & VARELA, *supra* note 57, at 118; see VARELA, *supra* note 57, at 54ff. See also: Hubert Rottleuthner, Les métaphores biologiques dans la pensée juridique, 31 ARCH. DE PHIL. DU DROIT 215 (1986); M. Gutsatz, Les dangers de l'"auto", *in* L'AUTO-ORGANISATION: DE LA PHYSIQUE AU POLITIQUE 29ff (Paul Dumouchel & Jean Pierre Dupuy eds., 1983).

[59] One glaring example is Herbert Spencer's famous transposition of this model from the theory of natural selection to the realm of social organization: HERBERT SPENCER, *SOCIAL STATICS* (1954).

[60] NIKLAS LUHMANN, *A SOCIOLOGICAL THEORY OF LAW* (1985); Rottleuthner, *supra* note 58; GUNTHER TEUBNER, *LAW AS AN AUTOPOIETIC SYSTEM* (1993); Lynn M. LoPucki, The Systems Approach to Law, 82 CORNELL L. REV. 479 (1996–1997); Von Bertalanffy, *Foreword* to LASZLO, *supra* note 23, at xvii–xviii; WEINBERG, *supra* note 25, at 35–38.

[61] "Methodological holism" arose in the nineteenth century in reaction to the hitherto prevailing "methodological individualism," informed by Cartesian nominalism and Newtonian mechanism. See: ERNEST NAGEL, *THE STRUCTURE OF SCIENCE* 336–97, 536–46 (1961).

[62] GIBSON & HUGHES, *supra* note 25, at 5; LICKER, *supra* note 25, at 5; LoPucki, *supra* note 60, at 485.

[63] "They produce by themselves what they use as units, by means of what they use as units, their unity as system lying precisely in that." Niklas Luhmann, L'unité du système juridique, 31 ARCH. DE PHIL. DU DROIT 163, 166 (my translation). See also: MATURANA & VARELA, *supra* note 57, at 85–89.

[64] See *supra* Chapter 1, Part I, section iv.

[65] LoPucki, *supra* note 60, at 485.

[66] Patrick Nerhot, Le fait du droit, 31 ARCH. DE PHIL. DU DROIT 261 (1986) ("When we describe a system as autopoietic, we essentially mean (and that is the crucial difference with traditional systemism or with cybernetics) that it is the system itself that determines what is and what is not part of it." (my translation)). See generally: MATURANA & VARELA, *supra* note 57, at 80–81; Francisco Varela, L'auto-organisation: de l'apparence au mécanisme, *in* L'AUTO-ORGANISATION: DE LA PHYSIQUE AU POLITIQUE, *supra* note 58, at 149–53; Grzegorczyk, *supra* note 25, at 285.

In autopoietic and cybernetic organic systems alike, however, the regenerative process is centrally determined through the system's special 'matrix,' or 'code': rabbits eat only what their (rabbit-ness) matrix earmarks as appropriate rabbit food; Deep Blue modifies its chess moves only as mandated by its (chess-playing) matrix.[67] The matrix of the organic system hence ultimately is what enables it to absorb and respond to external stimuli in a way consistent with the system's particular purpose, to sustain interaction with the outside world without losing its distinct identity as system. System theorists have dubbed this feature "cognitive openness/functional closure."[68] Organic systems are 'cognitively open' in that there is no limit on the kind of external stimuli to which they may be called upon to respond. At the same time, their integrity as systems demands that the various reactions they marshal in response to such stimuli all be filtered through the system's peculiar matrix, i.e. that they be 'functionally closed.' In some cases, the stimuli will simply be too violent to be absorbed and will consequently result in the system's disintegration pure and simple. (The rabbit may get killed by a hunter; Deep Blue may perhaps get terminally confused by a completely erratic opponent.) But any shock short of fatal will be absorbed and will in fact contribute to the matrix reprogramming itself towards greater system adaptability for the future.[69] It therefore is through their combined cognitive openness/functional closure that organic systems generate and sustain altogether new realities – rabbits, chess games – each of which can be considered a free-standing organism (autopoietic, cybernetic) in its own right.

It has been rightly suggested that the legal system of positivism in many respects matches the description just given.[70] It is a system centred on a process – the lawmaking process – that indeed is largely self-regenerative. We saw that legal analysis under positivism centres on the question of institutional validity determined as a matter of pedigree: a given rule or order is considered valid only insofar as it is determined such by some prior element of the system, itself considered valid by the same test, and so on.[71] Judicial orders are executed only insofar as they can be justified

---

[67] "Magnetic field" or "prism" ("charging" or "filtering" incoming information) are other metaphors for the same idea: Julen Etxabe, The Legal Universe After Robert Cover, 4 LAW AND HUMANITIES 115, 124 (2010) (discussing Robert M. Cover, The Supreme Court, 1982 Term: Nomos and Narrative, 97 HARV. L. REV. 4, 9 (1983) and James Boyd White, Legal Knowledge, 115 HARV. L. REV. 1396 (2002)).

[68] Luhmann, *supra* note 63, at 173; Pfersmann, *supra* note 40, at 278; Nerhot, *supra* note 66, at 262 ("[functionality] lies within the … system itself, it is not determined by the environment"); W. R. ASHBY, INTRODUCTION TO CYBERNETICS 4 (1956) ("open to energy, but closed to information and control"). See more generally: HENRI ATLAN, ENTRE LE CRISTAL ET LA FUMÉE 41, 56, 87–88 (1979).

[69] VARELA, *supra* note 57, at 32–33, 50ff. This theory found its most famous application in Darwin's theory of evolution, which posited that species 'adapt' to new circumstances, not so much through natural genetic manipulation, as had previously been advanced by Lamarck, but rather through natural elimination of the genetically ill-equipped.

[70] R. Sève, Introduction, 31 ARCH. DE PHIL. DU DROIT 1, 9–10 (1986); François Ost, Entre ordre et désordre: le jeu du droit. Discussion du paradigme autopoiétique appliqué au droit, 31 ARCH. DE PHIL. DU DROIT 133, 141–44 (1986).

[71] See *supra*, Chapter 1, Part II, section ii.

under some pre-existing rule or regulation that is itself statutorily or constitutionally authorized, and the same is true of any act, rule or order issued by a legal official.[72] Once a new valid element has entered the system, moreover, it in turn serves to determine the validity of other potential new entrants, and so on ad infinitum.[73] In that sense it can be asserted, as did Kelsen himself, that "[a] peculiarity of the law [under a positivistic theory is] that it regulates its own creation."[74]

The self-regenerative process of the positivistic legal system furthermore is far from aimless. It is not self-regeneration for the sake of self-regeneration, but rather self-regeneration aimed, as with all organic systems, at a particular purpose, namely, whichever happens to be dictated by the sovereign. For, as Kelsen again explained, "the acts constituting the law-creating facts are ... only the continuations of the process of the creation of the so-called will of the state."[75]

Finally, 'cognitive openness' and 'functional (or, in the case of law, 'normative')[76] closure' arguably aptly capture the relation of positive law to its environment. These indeed are just more abstract sociological terms for what positivists have in the legal context dubbed 'content-neutrality' or 'a matter of pedigree,'[77] and which would explain that law can be 'relatively autonomous'[78] from society. Positivist scholars have long insisted that any kind of information (such as religious, economic, historical) can become 'law,' a part of the 'legal system,' provided it is processed in the requisite manner by the requisite institutions – viz. in the manner prescribed by the system's 'matrix.'[79] On that basis, some foreign legal materials endorsed by a court arguably would *ipso facto* become domestic law in common law systems, but

---

[72] "The norm which confers upon an act the meaning of legality or illegality is itself created by an act, which, in turn receives its legal character from yet another norm." KELSEN, *supra* note 51, at 4.

[73] "The legal nature of an act can only be established ... on the basis of prior legal acts, on the basis of elements already part of the system; [and as] a new element of the system, [that act] in turn will condition the legality of other acts subsequently submitted to the system." ARNAUD, *supra* note 22, at 51 (my translation).

[74] KELSEN, *supra* note 53, at 221. Likewise: "[the] process, in which law keeps renewing itself, as it were" (*ibid.* at 237).

[75] *Ibid.* at 281–82.

[76] Luhmann, *supra* note 63, at 173.

[77] See *supra* note 132, Chapter 1, Part II, section ii.

[78] "the degree to which the legal system looks to itself rather than to the standards of some external social, political or ethical system for guidance in making or applying law." Richard Lempert, The Autonomy of Law: Two Visions Compared, *in* AUTOPOIETIC LAW: A NEW APPROACH TO LAW AND SOCIETY, 152, 159 (Gunther Teubner ed., 1988); see also: LAWRENCE M. FRIEDMAN, TOTAL JUSTICE 27 (New York, 1985).

[79] "[Wherever] positive law itself delegates meta-legal norms like morals or justice ... these norms are transformed into norms of positive law." KELSEN, *supra* note 53, at 354. And at 278: "law is like King Midas: just as everything he touched turned to gold, so everything to which the law refers assumes legal character." Self-professed "non-positivists" have likewise asserted that "when the rest of the world is filtered through the normative lens of the nomos, the latter acts like a 'magnetic field' with the capacity to charge it juridically ... the normative universe is ... the prism or pervasive filter through which the rest of the world is perceived (and assessed)." Etxabe (discussing Cover and White), *supra* note 67, at 124.

perhaps not in civil law systems, where judges may not qualify as official law makers.[80] And doctrinally-endorsed foreign materials likewise might have constituted
'law' in the Roman legal system, where scholarly writings were considered a formal
source of law,[81] but less likely so in contemporary civil law systems, and clearly not
in common law systems of any era. In both these examples, moreover, the newly
endorsed materials can be expected to contribute to reprogramming the respective systems in the same way that new entries do in any organic system: as more
and more foreign materials come to be endorsed by common law judges, common
law systems likely grow more receptive to such materials, and likewise with Roman
law vis-à-vis doctrinally-endorsed foreign materials. Finally, the legal system of positivism appears to react to extreme external stimuli in exactly the same way as do
organic systems. Revolutions and enemy occupation, for example, cause the legal
system not merely to change, but in fact to disintegrate and subsume within another,[82] as would the rabbit eaten by the wolf, or Deep Blue reprogrammed to play
Scrabble rather than chess.

Thus, whereas the legal system of natural law, which aims to do no more than
reproduce the Law of Nature, matches the synthetic system, the legal system of
positivism, which constantly renews itself towards the purpose ascribed to it by the
sovereign, in contrast resembles the organic system. For present purposes, however,
a first significant difference between these two kinds of systems is that the latter,
unlike the former, meets the first requirement for meaningful comparison. That
is, unlike synthetic systems, organic systems are amenable, not just to internal and
meta-plurality, but also to precisely the kind of plurality that is required for system–
system comparisons.

Like synthetic systems, organic systems are divisible into subsystems. The lines
of division expectedly are material rather than conceptual, however. For, as already
noted, a synthesis by definition is just a conceptual reproduction of a reality, whereas
an organism is a reality unto itself. A synthesis therefore can correspondingly be
partitioned only conceptually, whereas an organism is amenable to material parti-
tioning. Our rabbit certainly can be analyzed as the sum total of its various organs
(brain, heart, lungs, etc.), and Deep Blue similarly can be regarded as the amal-
gam of its various physical parts (processor, hard drive, memory, etc.). Likewise
with the legal system of positivism, which, being the legal counterpart of the geo-
political nation state,[83] can be materially partitioned.[84] Nations indeed divide into

[80] RAOUL VAN CAENEGEM, *JUDGES, LEGISLATORS AND PROFESSORS: CHAPTERS IN EUROPEAN LEGAL HISTORY*
67–113 (1987).

[81] BARRY NICHOLAS, *AN INTRODUCTION TO ROMAN LAW* (1962).

[82] H. L. A. HART, *THE CONCEPT OF LAW* 114–15 (1961).

[83] KELSEN, *supra* note 53, at 286–319 ("§41. The Identity of State and Law").

[84] Even Kelsen, who insisted that there could only be one legal system in force on any given territory
(see KELSEN, *supra* note 53, at 181), agreed that systems can be divided so long as the place and
status of each division can be justified by appeal to the system's rules of organization: HANS KELSEN,

smaller territorial or population units (regions, provinces or states – cultural, ethnic or linguistic groups), to which typically correspond an equal number of distinct legal jurisdictions. Thus does the Canadian legal system, for example, divide into thirteen territorial and provincial jurisdictions, as well as a variety of personality-based regimes (e.g. corporate law, aboriginal law), each endowed with its own set of lawmaking institutions.[85] Also like synthetic systems, moreover, organic systems allow for meta-plurality insofar as each can in turn be seen as a component of a larger super-structure: rabbits contribute to the larger eco-system; Deep Blue is just one of many players in the IT network; and the legal system of positivism is to international law what the nation state is to the international community.

But the possibility of conceptualizing organic systems in terms of sub- or meta-units ultimately is no more helpful than it was with synthetic systems, for the types of comparisons enabled by such conceptualization are not those typically carried out in comparative law. (We return to this in Chapter 4,[86] devoted to the particular delineation process of organic systems.) Because all Canadian legal regimes end up wired into the same Canadian matrix, investigating these regimes' interrelations is just bread and butter Canadian law; it is the stuff of Canadian federal or constitutional law, not of comparative law as such. Where the regimes in question are genealogically rooted in different foreign systems (e.g. the provinces of Quebec and Ontario, respectively originating from the French civil law and the English common law system), their investigation admittedly might include a comparative dimension. But that is so precisely because these regimes differ in pedigrees. As between like-pedigreed regimes (e.g. Ontario and Manitoba, two common law systems), the investigation would more likely be treated as a strictly internal, domestic rather than comparative matter. This arguably also explains why such pluralistic systems as Canada, which combine differently pedigreed subsystems, are specifically labelled 'mixed' legal systems.[87]

INTRODUCTION TO THE PROBLEMS OF LEGAL THEORY 99 (1992). See also: Luhmann, *supra* note 63, at 172.

[85] For a similar, yet much more detailed description of Africa, see: JACQUES VANDERLINDEN, COMPARER LES DROITS 384–85 (1995).

[86] In particular Chapter 4, Parts I and III, section iii (1).

[87] As the different, in this case civil law and common law, contents are "structurally determined" within the Canadian system (VERNON V. PALMER, MIXED JURISDICTIONS WORLDWIDE—THE THIRD LEGAL FAMILY 8 (2001); H. Patrick Glenn, Quebec: Mixité and Monism, in STUDIES IN LEGAL SYSTEMS: MIXED AND MIXING 1, 3 (Esin Örücü, Elspeth Attwooll & Sean Coyle eds., 1996)), that system is pluralistic only in the "weak" sense described above (text accompanying notes 31–32): "Within such a pluralistic legal system, parallel legal regimes, dependent from the overarching and controlling state system, result from 'recognition' by the state" (Griffiths, *supra* note 32, at 5; underline omitted). See also: David Goldberg & Elspeth Attwooll, Legal Orders, Systemic Relationships and Cultural Characteristics: Towards Spectral Jurisprudence, in STUDIES IN LEGAL SYSTEMS: MIXED AND MIXING, *supra*, at 315; Michael Garfield Smith, Some Developments in the Analytic Framework of Pluralism in PLURALISM IN AFRICA 415 (Leo Kuper & Michael Garfield Smith eds., 1969).

More helpful for present purposes is the fact that organic systems, unlike synthetic ones, are amenable to the sort of plurality required for system–system comparisons. Whereas, as argued, distinct syntheses of one and the same reality are highly unstable entities as they inevitably dissolve into a sea of disparate elements, there is no reason to doubt that organisms are stable, distinct and prima facie equal generic entities. Rabbits clearly are distinct and equal entities, each one being (at least a priori) as much of a rabbit as the next – and the same can be said of computers. Likewise with legal systems under positivism. Positivism defines law as whatever emerges from the law-making institutions of a given territory, and as institutions and territories can be many and diverse, so can law. Each legal system indeed is endowed with its own matrix and set of law-making institutions, programmed to further the wishes of its particular sovereign on that sovereign's defined territory, and as such constitutes a fully fledged self-contained system, distinct from other such systems. Moreover, as each sovereign by definition has full powers over its territory and its territory *only*, neither system is subordinated to any other, at least in principle, and all are deemed prima facie equal.[88] Legal systems under positivism in other words are not *competing* with one another the way they are under natural law, and their peaceful coexistence accordingly is possible, in just the same way that the non-competing units entailed by internal and meta-plurality can coexist, under natural law and positivism alike. In sum, the legal system of positivism being as distinct and autonomous as is the state, there necessarily are, under that conception, at least as many distinct and autonomous legal systems as there are states, which indicates that these systems meet the first, 'distinctness' requirement for meaningful comparison.

They fail to meet the second, however. This is so because they are cybernetic rather than autopoietic organic systems – Deep Blues rather than rabbits. Recall that the central difference between these two subcategories has to do with the systems' ultimate purpose being endogenous or exogenous: unlike autopoietic organic systems, cybernetic ones regenerate towards an exogenous purpose. Deep Blue plays chess not because that is what computers are (inherently) meant to do but because that is what was (externally) programmed into it.

This central difference carries important structural implications. Because cybernetic systems are outwardly determined, they operate in a vertical, linear fashion – they boast inputs and outputs, beginnings and ends. Their various elements consequently are hierarchically ordered; they are triggered into action in accordance with some fixed, rigorously synchronized sequence, stretching from one to the other of the process's two endpoints – from the programmer's first input, through the various processing stages, and on to the final chess move. And their functional/normative closure as a result is merely provisional: the system is closed given a particular programmed function, but it is reopened each time a new function, say, Scrabble or

[88] "*not* habitually obeying the orders of other [States]." HART, *supra* note 82, at 25. (Italics in original.)

Monopoly, is programmed into it. Autopoietic systems in contrast are circular, thus seamless: the rabbit's various organs respond to and determine one another in an unscripted, network-like fashion. No single organ is prior or more prominent than the others; none leads or closes the pack. While the various organs clearly work together in a coordinated way, that coordination is their own doing; it is not the product of some external force. As a result, autopoietic systems never stand to be reopened. Whatever reprogramming may be needed to adjust for external shocks or internal failures will come from within or not at all, in which case the system will just crash. Unlike cybernetic systems, they are definitively, not just provisionally, closed.

That the legal system of positivism is a cybernetic rather than autopoietic organic system should be obvious from the description given so far.[89] At the outset, the system's finality is whatever its ultimate programmer – the sovereign – intends it to be, which makes it an exogenous finality given that any kind of intention by definition stands, on the positivist account, outside the system. This in turn causes that system to be linear and hierarchical, as well as only provisionally closed. It is linear and hierarchical insofar as it is structured like a pyramid, every one of its components being connected upwards to the level of authority immediately above it, and downwards to the level just below. Investigations into the validity of legal materials thus proceed vertically, by retracing lines of authority through the system's various levels, from the most particular (private contracts, wills, etc.),[90] through mid-level materials (case law, legislation, regulations, ordinances) to the most general (constitutional provisions or equivalent).[91] The fact that intentions are external to the system moreover entails that appealing to them involves cracking the system open.[92] Whenever the legislator inputs new ideas or reformulates old ones, whenever judges act like legislators – in 'hard' cases – the system is reopened and its matrix reprogrammed. In easy cases, facts are processed into judgments that merely reproduce the existing matrix, which judgments accordingly are just the last of a long chain of regular entries into the system's database.[93] In hard cases, however, the existing database

---

[89] See *supra* Chapter 1, Part II, section ii.

[90] "the individual norms are also 'law,' just as much parts of the legal order as the general norms on which their creation is based" (KELSEN, *supra* note 53, at 232).

[91] "[Law] proceeds from the general (abstract) to the individual (particular); it is a process of increasing individualization and concretization." *Ibid.* at 237.

[92] *Contra* Kelsen, who aimed "to understand all law ... as one closed whole." (*Ibid.* at 328.) Kelsen like Hart attempted to close law's circle by describing the highest norm as at least partially determined by acceptance from the system's lower organs, but their success in this respect is mitigated at best. See: Troper, *supra* note 53; Ost, *supra* note 70, at 143; Rials, *supra* note 54, at 57.

[93] "The structure of the legal system is like some gigantic computer program, coded to deal with millions of problems that are fed daily into the machine. Rules of organization, jurisdiction, and procedure are part of the coding. Equally important are the substantive rules of law. They are the output of the system, but one that serves to cut future outputs to shape." LAWRENCE M. FRIEDMAN, *THE LEGAL SYSTEM: A SOCIAL SCIENCE PERSPECTIVE* 12 (1975).

is insufficient for the matrix to generate the requisite output. Some reprogramming hence is needed, which involves judges retracing the programming sequence all the way up to the programmer's first intention. Thus, whereas the same vertical, pedigree investigation takes place in easy and hard cases, that investigation is taken one step further, altogether bursting out of the system, in hard cases. The legal systems of positivism being therefore vertically structured and ultimately open to external determination, they clearly qualify as cybernetic organic systems.

The reason that they fail to meet the connectedness requirement is that they each have their own sovereign programmer, *ex hypothesi* acting entirely independently from all others. These systems therefore fail to meet the connectedness requirement for the very same reason that they succeed at meeting the distinctness requirement: as cybernetic systems, they are distinct and connected entities to the same extent and in the same way that their respective programmers are, and their programmers in fact are categorically distinct and *dis*connected. They of course have in common that all qualify as (positivistic) 'legal' systems – as cybernetic systems, capable of processing an infinite variety of different contents into 'legal' rules proper. But, while such limited connectedness might suffice to make these systems comparable, it is insufficient to make them comparable in a meaningful way. For comparing such thinly connected systems indeed would, as with comparing an apple to love,[94] merely serve to reiterate the diagnosis of radical difference that is already obvious from their definition: "these radically differently programmed systems are radically different."[95]

Positivists of course recognize that comparative law has traditionally moved beyond such pointless reiterations into more meaningful comparisons of the various purposes actually programmed into the different systems. Comparative law has not been content, that is, to just point out that France and the US are differently programmed systems; it has delved into the substance of that difference and concluded that France has been programmed *to favour privacy over free expression* whereas the US has conversely been programmed *to favour free expression*. But as such conclusions involve probing the intentions of the French and US programmers, which intentions under positivism as we saw are necessarily external to the French and US systems, positivists cannot but regard such comparisons as exercises in 'comparative politics' or 'comparative political philosophy' rather than 'comparative law' proper: though they undoubtedly are meaningful and interesting, they focus on dimensions of legal systems that, on the positivists' account, are merely contingent. Under

94 See *supra* Part I.
95 "Il n'y a donc pas réellement de droit comparé : il n'y a tout juste ... que des droits comparés, puisque l'essence du droit le condamne, sur le plan des contenus, à demeurer éclaté, divers, pluriel à l'infini : concrètement, il n'y a que des droits et non plus un droit, si ce n'est cette structure normative précisément vide de tout contenu, et dont la substance juridique doit rester totalement creuse afin de rester ouverte à tout contenu possible arbitrairement déterminé par les souverainetés étatiques ou législatives." Picard, *supra* note 6, at 905.

positivism, then, legal systems are but differently programmed cybernetic systems whose only point of connection is that they indeed all are differently programmed cybernetic systems.

Like natural law, therefore, positivism fails to account for the possibility of meaningful legal comparison (and for traditional comparative law scholarship), but for the opposite reason. Whereas law does not boast the requisite distinctness under the natural lawyers' ideal account, legal systems do not boast the requisite connectedness under the positivists' material account. Thus, whereas comparing law under natural law is like comparing a particular apple to itself, under positivism it is akin to comparing an apple to love. What we need is something in between: a conception of law sufficiently broad to accommodate plurality – one or several 'others' – but not so broad as to lose all sense of unity and of 'self.' Only then can legal comparison be tantamount to comparing apples and oranges.

IV. LEGAL SYSTEMS UNDER LAW AS COLLECTIVE COMMITMENT

I would suggest that law as collective commitment is just such a conception. As it combines the ideal dimension of natural law and the material dimension of positivism, it also combines their respective unity and plurality. Legal systems on that conception hence are distinct and presumptively equal entities, as per the first requirement for meaningful comparison, yet also adequately interconnected, as per the second.

Concerning the first requirement, recall that law under that conception is a *practice* – a practice that reflects as well as forms and transforms a community's legal ideals.[96] Like law under positivism, then, law as collective commitment is a material conduit for ideals. It accordingly follows that its legal system is, like that of positivism, an organic system. Law as collective commitment indeed is self-regenerative in that every new argument that the community comes to accept as valid in turn impacts on the validity of future arguments. In that sense it clearly qualifies as a system that "uses and produces the means of its own production."[97] That regenerative process moreover is purposive: it is aimed at fostering the community's peculiar set of ideal(s). It also is informationally open and normatively closed, finally. We saw that, on the one hand, there is a priori no limit on the kinds of arguments that can come to be accepted as legally valid in any given community but that, on the other hand, for any argument to be deemed so valid, it must be accepted as such in the context of the community's formal legal settings. And like any organism, the organic system of law as collective commitment indeed is replicable into a plurality of stable, for non-competing, iterations: each community looks to its own legal practice to further its own ideals, and as there are many such communities, there clearly are

---

[96] See *supra* Chapter 1, Part I.
[97] *Supra* note 63.

many legal systems. The community in sum is to law as collective commitment what the sovereign state is to positivism: legal systems under law as collective commitment are as numerous, distinct and prima facie equal as are communities, in just the same way that under positivism legal systems are as numerous, distinct and equal as are sovereign states. (The further questions of what entities qualify as 'communities' and the extent to which they can be conceptualized separately from nation states are addressed in Chapter 4. Suffice to say for now that nothing said so far commits us to viewing the two as either coextensive or non-coextensive.)

The organic system of law as collective commitment however differs from that of positivism in one crucial respect. Whereas the latter as mentioned is a cybernetic organic system, thus vertical and open to outside reprogramming, the former is an autopoietic system, a rabbit rather than a computer, thus circular and fully closed. For, whereas the ultimate finality of the positivistic legal system (the sovereign's ideal(s)) lies outside the system, that of the legal system under law as collective commitment (the community's ideal(s)) – lies within.[98] In the above description of law as collective commitment, the ideals indeed are part and parcel of the practice since they at once inform and emerge from it. The legal system hence is ideal through and through as well as material through and through – rather than one part material and one part ideal – and its unity as system consequently is conceptual (as under natural law) as much as it is material (as under positivism).[99]

As the system's ultimate referent is internal to it, that system indeed is circular. The community enforces only the ideals that qualify as its formal legal ideals, at the same time as only the ideals it in fact enforces qualify as such; legal analysis involves adducing valid arguments as to how best to interpret legal materials, which best interpretation in turn determines what counts as valid legal arguments; judicial decisions are based on legislative materials, the meaning of which is itself determined through judicial decisions; and so on.[100] As the systems' various elements constantly feed on one another, none of them can be described as prior or subsequent to

---

[98] Luhmann, *supra* note 63 at 173 ("Law's normativity has no external goal. Its function consists in its possibility to recreate itself continuously, instant by instant, case by case, stroke by stroke, and it is precisely destined not to find an [external] end."); Nerhot, *supra* note 66, at 262 ("[N]ormativity lies within the legal system itself, it is not determined by the environment."). In such sociological accounts of the legal system as autopoietic system, ideals expectedly are represented through such material forms as "communications" and "messages": e.g., see Luhmann at 168–70; LoPucki, *supra* note 60, at 479; Ost, *supra* note 70, at 133; ARNAUD, *supra* note 22; AUTOPOIETIC LAW: A NEW APPROACH TO LAW AND SOCIETY, *supra* note 78, at 35 (1988).

[99] See *supra* Chapter 1, Part II.

[100] Luhmann, *supra* note 63, at 174 ("The laws are normative rules *only because* they are to be applied in judgments, in the same way that these judgments are normatively to resolve situations *only because* that is provided for by the laws." My emphasis.). Mark Walters likewise describes law as "embedded within a network of interlocking strands of normative value that bend back upon themselves never reaching an end. The relevant image on this account is not a string but a web of strings shaped into a globe or sphere." (Mark Walters, The Unwritten Constitution as a Legal Concept, *in* PHILOSOPHICAL FOUNDATIONS OF CONSTITUTIONAL LAW 33–34 (David Dyzenhaus & Malcolm Thorburn eds., 2016).)

any other – the system is seamless. All elements are interconnected at all levels, in a network rather than linear fashion, and their mutual consistency accordingly offers as good a test of their membership in the system as do their respective pedigrees.[101]

Being circular, the system of law as collective commitment is also closed. Though it does need to be continually reprogrammed, if only to adjust for new fact scenarios not solvable through pre-existing arguments, all such reprogramming is carried out on the inside. For the programmers themselves are located within the system. As explained,[102] the legislative, adjudicative and litigating functions are more difficult to delineate under law as commitment than under positivism or natural law because all actors are there involved in fundamentally the same, collective argumentative/interpretive exercise. Since what counts as law in the community comes to be determined through this collective exercise, all legal actors can to some extent be regarded as programmers of the system. Thus, while the system does need constant reprogramming, no external intervention is required to that end because to operate the system necessarily *is* to reprogram it, under law as collective commitment. In sum, unlike the cybernetic system of positivism, which constantly renews itself so as to better realize the ideal(s) externally imposed upon it, and accordingly is vertical and ultimately open, the autopoietic system of law as collective commitment regenerates with the view to realizing its own, inherent ideals, with the result that it is in contrast circular and closed.

This difference is crucial because it explains why the latter system succeeds and the former fails in meeting the second requirement for meaningful comparison, that of adequate interconnectedness. As explained in Chapter 1, the ideals inherent in law as collective commitment are of two kinds: whereas such substantive ideals as freedom of expression and crime reduction are contingent ideals, which different systems accordingly might choose or decline to endorse, such formal ideals as effectiveness, argumentativeness, publicness, internal coherence and formality are non-contingent, and hence necessarily present to some extent in all systems.[103] Importantly, non-contingent ideals are as internal to the systems as are contingent ones, seeing that the first are just possibility conditions of the second. That is, a substantive ideal that would not be pursued in a somewhat effective, argumentative, public and internally coherent fashion simply would not, as discussed,[104] qualify as a 'collective commitment' of that community.[105] Under law as collective commitment, then, whereas different legal systems pursue different substantive ideals, all

---

[101] See Peter Benson's discussion of "validation through fit": Peter Benson, The Idea of a Public Basis of Justification for Contract, 33 OSGOODE HALL L. J. 275, 325–26 (1995).

[102] See *supra* Chapter 1, Part II, section iii.

[103] See *supra* Chapter 1, Part I, section vi. In the same vein, Fuller describes his set of eight essential desiderata as "procedural natural law" (LON L. FULLER, THE MORALITY OF LAW 96 (1969)).

[104] *Ibid.*

[105] NIGEL SIMMONDS, LAW AS MORAL IDEA 60 (2007). See also: Étienne Picard, Le droit comparé est-il du droit?, 1 ANN. INST. MICHEL VILLEY 173, 210 (2009): "[T]he law obeys to objectivities that impose

systems nonetheless remain connected to one another through the common set of formal ideals that makes such pursuits possible. This in turn causes the systems to be amenable to meaningful mutual comparison, in terms of effectiveness, transparency, internal consistency – just like apples and oranges can be meaningfully compared in terms of weight, sweetness and ripeness.

CONCLUSION

This chapter aimed to show that the conception of law as collective commitment laid out in Chapter 1 offers a promising basis on which to build an account of comparative law inasmuch as it accounts for a very wide variety of 'legal systems' that can be meaningfully compared to one another.

We saw in Chapter 1 that law as collective commitments is so thin as to allow for even such borderline cases as religious, ethnic, international, 'soft' transnational or even 'sham' law to potentially qualify as *law* proper. If so, the various corresponding communities – religious, ethnic, transnational network, etc. – presumably would themselves potentially qualify as *legal systems*, and any research project seeking to compare these systems, as projects in *comparative law*. Such is the large breadth of coverage presumptively allowed for under a conception as thin as law as collective commitment.

Yet we here saw that that conception is nonetheless thick enough to weed out comparative projects that would be meaningless in the sense of inviting nothing but trivial preordained conclusions. As also seen in Chapter 1, law is respectively essentially ideal and material (and incidentally material and ideal) under natural law and positivism, whereas it is essentially ideal *as well as* material under law as collective commitments. We here saw that it follows that whatever entities qualify as legal systems under that conception indeed are systems in their own right, systems that combine rather than merely juxtapose ideality and materiality, and the attendant connectedness and distinctness required for meaningful mutual comparison. Unlike the systems of natural law, the systems of law as collective commitment are organic rather than synthetic systems, thus conceptualizable as a plurality of stable, distinct and prima facie equal entities. Unlike the systems of positivism, they are autopoietic rather than cybernetic organic systems, internally determined through ideals, at least some of which are present in all systems. As a result, whereas to compare legal systems under natural law is like comparing an identical apple to itself, and under positivism like comparing an apple to love, it is a meaningful comparison – much like comparing apples and oranges – under law as collective commitment.

In sum, law as collective commitment appears to be a highly inclusive conception that could nonetheless serve to weed out meaningless legal comparisons – precisely the kind of conception we need, I would suggest, for a sound account of comparative law.

themselves upon its positive norms." And at 242–43: "These [objectivities] do not relate to a constraint that would be external to law … they are rules endogenous to law itself." (My translation.)

3

Engaging with Legal Systems

Epistemology

INTRODUCTION

Having determined that legal systems can be the apples and oranges of comparative law, we now turn to what may be the thorniest preliminary issue facing comparatists, namely, that of the proper stance or perspective from which to engage with such systems. In particular, comparatists must decide whether to study foreign legal systems from an external perspective (observer), an internal perspective (participant) or some combination thereof.

As this epistemological dilemma is neither new nor unique to law, Part I briefly recounts the historical debate over the external and internal perspectives (cognitivism versus constructivism) in the humanities in general, with particular emphasis on the philosophy of history. Part II then carries this reflection over to law, suggesting that the natural law and positivism ideal-types elaborated in Chapters 1 and 2 both motion to an external perspective whereas law as collective commitment mandates an internal perspective. We move to the comparative context in Part III, which aims to respond to the standard 'home bias objection' against adopting an internal perspective on foreign law. I there argue that law as comparative collective commitment allows for the possibility that outsiders contribute to the same, internal understanding of legal systems as insiders strive to unpack, though they do so through a process that itself oscillates between the internal and external perspectives, the peculiarity of the outsiders' (comparative) contribution to legal understanding lying precisely in that oscillating process.

I. INTERNAL AND EXTERNAL PERSPECTIVES IN THE SOCIAL SCIENCES

Unlike apples and oranges – which, as natural things, can only be apprehended from a scientific, external observer perspective – law involves a human dimension, apprehensible from an external or internal perspective. All scientifically relevant

aspects of apples and oranges indeed carry material manifestations, externally analyzable in terms of cause and effect; apples and oranges simply do not have an
'inside' that might elude proper accounting in those terms. Not so with law which,
while admittedly boasting 'hard data' (texts, orders, actions, institutions, statistics,
incentive structures, etc.), amenable to mechanistic analysis, cannot be reduced
to these. Any set of legal materials can be considered from the perspective of such
externally observable data *or else* from a perspective internal to their human authors,
one aiming to identify the particular beliefs, ideals, intentions and purposes that
these materials were meant to embody. Unlike the botanist, then, the comparative
lawyer must ponder which of the external or internal perspective, or combination
thereof, is best suited to her purposes.

This question harps back to the much larger cognitivism/constructivism debate,
which has captivated academics of all stripes for centuries.[1] As many Renaissance
astronomers, physicists and medical practitioners were moving away from the super-
natural towards a more objective, spectator method, Descartes was laying down the
foundations for cognitivism. Most significantly, the Cartesian method presupposes
a strict divide between object and subject, proclaiming that cognition results from
the unilateral impact of the first on the second. As such, cognitivism stands for the
possibility of investigating external objects 'as they are,' unaffected, that is, by the
investigative process and, in particular, the investigating subject's personal inclinations. This in turn allows for verifiability and refutability, as a plurality of subjects can henceforth neutrally investigate and cross-check observations on the same
objects. A 'correspondence' theory of truth emerged from this whereby subjective
affirmations about the world would be considered true only insofar as they could be
shown to be congruent with an objective reality.[2] Seeing the resounding success that
cognitivism and the correspondence theory of truth had wielded across the natural
sciences, many came to think that the same approach could be profitably deployed
in the realm of human affairs.[3]

---

[1] Particularly in history (Dilthey, Collingwood), anthropology (Geertz), philosophy (Vico, Hegel)
and literature, notably from the German romantics (Herder). See generally: Patrick Gardiner *in
Introduction to* THE PHILOSOPHY OF HISTORY (Patrick Gardiner ed., 1974); James Whitman, The
Neo-Romantic Turn, *in* COMPARATIVE LEGAL STUDIES: TRADITIONS AND TRANSITIONS 312 (Pierre
Legrand & Roderick Munday eds., 2003); Geoffrey Samuel, Epistemology and Comparative Law,
in EPISTEMOLOGY AND METHODOLOGY OF COMPARATIVE LAW 35 (Mark Van Hoecke ed., 2004); Étienne
Picard, Le droit comparé est-il du droit? 1 ANN. INST. MICHEL VILLEY 173 (2009); Simone Glanert,
Method?, *in* METHODS OF COMPARATIVE LAW 61 (Pier Giuseppe Monateri ed., 2012).

[2] See generally: Andrei Marmor, Three Concepts of Objectivity, *in* LAW AND INTERPRETATION: ESSAYS IN
LEGAL PHILOSOPHY (Andrei Marmor ed., 1995); MATTHEW H. KRAMER, OBJECTIVITY AND THE RULE OF
LAW (2007); KENT GREENAWALT, LAW AND OBJECTIVITY (1992); Matti Ilmari Niemi, Objective Legal
Reasoning: Objectivity Without Objects, *in* OBJECTIVITY IN LAW AND LEGAL REASONING 69 (Jaakko Husa
& Mark Van Hoecke eds., 2013); Samuel, *supra* note 1.

[3] E.g. the classical British empiricists and later such figures as Mill, Comte and Hempel. ("[G]iven
the motives present to an individual's mind, and given likewise the character and disposition of the
individual, the manner in which he will act maybe unerringly inferred; that if we knew the person

Some resisted that move, however, notably the neo-Kantians of the nineteenth century. To these scholars, the cognitivist dichotomy between object and subject was far too stark to begin with, inasmuch as, even in the natural sciences, the investigating subject arguably plays an active role in the cognitive process.[4] After all, Kant had taught that knowledge proceeds from the human mind filtering external stimuli through innate 'categories of understanding,' which are at least partially established a priori rather than experientially. *All* knowledge therefore would to some extent be phenomenological, 'constructed' by the knowing subject.[5]

But even thus qualified, the object/subject dynamic could not, the neo-Kantians stressed, operate the same way in the human as in the natural realm for the simple reason that the former involves human agency.[6] If freedom, the capacity for free choice, sets humans aside from the rest of nature, humans ultimately are not determined by the natural laws so much as *self*-determined, with the result that causal analysis would be particularly ill-suited, or at least highly incomplete (some would say 'so incomplete as to be misleading'), for the purpose of understanding them: "[T]he categories in terms of which we deliberate and choose cannot be accommodated into the same logical space as the categories in terms of which we causally explain events: on the one hand, freedom, meaning, responsibility, value and the 'ought'; on the other, necessity and causality."[7]

Understanding humans accordingly requires seizing on the intentions, the 'oughts' that drive the individual actors to act the way they do. It involves deciphering *meaning*, the *reasons* behind the acts, those *that the actors themselves* ascribe to those acts.[8] As R. G. Collingwood aptly remarked with respect to historical research,

[t]he historian, investigating any event in the past, makes a distinction between what may be called the outside and the inside of an event. By the outside of the event I mean everything belonging to it which can be described in terms of bodies

thoroughly, and knew all the inducements which are acting upon him, we could foretell his conduct with as much certainty as we can predict any physical event." JOHN STUART MILL, *A SYSTEM OF LOGIC* 522 (1864).)

4 See Nietzsche's critical depiction of "the ascetic ideal": FRIEDRICH NIETZSCHE, *THE GAY SCIENCE* 307 (Walter Kaufmann trans., 1974) (1882). Likewise: THOMAS S. KUHN, *THE STRUCTURE OF SCIENTIFIC REVOLUTIONS* 5 (2nd ed. 1970) ("[N]ormal science ... [is] a strenuous and devoted attempt to force nature into the conceptual boxes supplied by professional education."); CARL G. HEMPEL, *FUNDAMENTALS OF CONCEPT FORMATION IN EMPIRICAL SCIENCE* (1952); JÜRGEN HABERMAS, *THE THEORY OF COMMUNICATIVE ACTION* 102–11 (Thomas McCarthy trans., 1984); GILLES-GASTON GRANGER, *LA SCIENCE ET LES SCIENCES* (1st ed. 1993) (discussed in Samuel, *supra* note 1); DOMINIQUE LECOURT, *LA PHILOSOPHIE DES SCIENCES* 117 (2001).

5 See Kant's 'transcendental idealism': IMMANUEL KANT, *CRITIQUE OF PURE REASON* A369 (Guyer & Wood trans., 1998).

6 Picard, *supra* note 1, at 200.

7 NIGEL SIMMONDS, *LAW AS A MORAL IDEA* 115 (2008).

8 HANS PETER RICKMAN, *UNDERSTANDING AND THE HUMAN STUDIES* 23 (1967); PETER WINCH, *THE IDEA OF A SOCIAL SCIENCE* 45 (1958).

and their movements ... By the inside of the event I mean that in it which can only be described in terms of thought ... The historian is never concerned with either of these to the exclusion of the other ... In the case of nature, the distinction between the outside and the inside of an event does not arise ... It is true that the scientist, like the historian, has to go beyond the mere discovery of events; but the direction in which he moves is very different ... When a scientist asks, "why did that piece of litmus paper turn pink?" he means "on what kinds of occasions do pieces of litmus paper turn pink?" When a historian asks "why did Brutus stab Caesar?" he means "what did Brutus think, which made him decide to stab Caesar?" The cause of the event, for him, means the thought in the mind of the person by whose agency the event came about: and this is not something other than the event, it is the inside of the event itself.[9]

If this is right, the constructivist element in human studies indeed is qualitatively different from that at play in natural studies. Whereas the investigating subject constructs the concepts that she needs in order to make sense of her natural surroundings, there is a sense in which she in fact constructs *the very object* of her analysis where human phenomena are concerned. For, meaning is not something 'out there,' prior to and independent from the investigation process, waiting to be cognitively apprehended. It rather is *created* through that very process:

> There existed electrical storms and thunder long before there were human beings to form concepts of them or establish that there was any connection between them. But it does not make sense to suppose that human beings might have been issuing commands and obeying them before they came to form the concept of command and obedience. For their performance of such acts is itself the chief manifestation of their possession of those concepts.[10]

Understanding human affairs thus requires from the subject that she engage in (active) construction rather than just (passive) cognition.[11] It differs from understanding

---

9   Robin George Collingwood, Human Nature and Human History, *in* GARDINER, *supra* note 1 at 24–25. See also: Arthur O. Lovejoy, Present Standpoints and Past History, *in* THE PHILOSOPHY OF HISTORY IN OUR TIME (Hans Meyerhoff ed., 1959); HANS PETER RICKMAN, MEANING IN HISTORY: DILTHEY'S THOUGHT ON HISTORY AND SOCIETY (1962); Quentin Skinner, 'Social Meaning' and the Explanation of Social Action, *in* GARDINER, *supra* note 1, at 106.

10 Peter Winch, *Concepts and Actions*, *in* GARDINER, *supra* note 1, at 41, 43. Likewise at 45: "The idea of war, for instance ... was not simply invented by people who wanted to *explain* what happens when societies come into armed conflict. It is an idea which provides the criteria of what is appropriate in the behaviour of members of the conflicting societies ... The concept of war belongs essentially to my behaviour. But the concept of gravity does not belong *essentially* to the behaviour of a falling apple in the same way: it belongs rather to the physicist's *explanation* of the apple's behaviour."

11 "'[C]ognitivism' can be contrasted with 'constructivism', which instead posits that the knowing acts themselves contribute to constituting their objects, which accordingly no longer enjoy such already there ... such autonomy of being in relation to the knowledge initiatives that construct them." Picard, *supra* note 1, at 199 (my translation). As Samuel explains (Samuel, *supra* note 1, at 188–89), the

natural events in that it amounts to "the understanding of understanding"[12] – *das Verstehen* rather than *die Erklärung*.[13]

It follows that the correspondence theory of truth is flatly inadequate in the realm of human affairs: such things as are amenable to *Verstehen* cannot be apprehended 'as they are,' only 'as they are constructed.' *Verstehen* thus commands the adoption of a different standard of validity, one centred on the quality of the subject's construction rather than on its congruence with some external object.[14] From 'correspondence' we accordingly move to the weaker standard of 'coherence'[15] or 'intelligibility'[16] – 'constructive objectivity,'[17] 'epistemic objectivity'[18] or 'objectivity without objects'[19] – according to which a 'valid' interpretation of a particular occurrence is one that "enables us to see that occurrence as flowing intelligibly from a human agent's intentions, motives, passions and purposes."[20] Like the correspondence standard, then, this one presupposes the possibility of distinguishing the 'passions and purposes' of the agent(s) being interpreted from those of the agent doing the interpreting, and to control for the latter.[21] Unlike the correspondence standard, however, it admits of degree variations, for interpretations typically are not categorically 'right' or 'wrong' so much as 'better' or 'worse' – *more or less* plausible or intelligible.[22]

It should be clear at this point how it is that *Erklärung* and *Verstehen* can respectively be described as 'external' and 'internal.' These labels do not, as it is sometimes thought, refer merely to the object of understanding lying inside or

---

postmodernists went one step further than the neo-Kantians to argue that knowledge of natural events and human affairs alike are "constructed." (See e.g. Derrida's denial of Lévi-Strauss's distinction between scientific and *bricoleur* discourses, insisting that "every discourse is *bricoleur*": JACQUES DERRIDA, WRITING AND DIFFERENCE, 285 (Alan Bass trans., 1978).) In short, whereas the positivists collapsed the distinction between natural and human sciences by lumping both within cognitivism, the postmodernists collapsed it by lumping them within constructivism.

[12] CLIFFORD GEERTZ, LOCAL KNOWLEDGE: FURTHER ESSAYS IN INTERPRETIVE ANTHROPOLOGY 5 (2000).

[13] G. H. VON WRIGHT, EXPLANATION AND UNDERSTANDING (1971).

[14] "[O]bjectivity [so conceived] does not depend on its having external reference ... [it] is concerned not with the description and explanation of what happens but with decisions and their justifications." THOMAS NAGEL, THE LAST WORD 101, 102 (1997). See likewise: ROBERT ALEXY, A THEORY OF LEGAL ARGUMENTATION 187 (1989) (setting out general rules of legal reasoning); Aleksander Peczenik, SCIENTIA JURIS: LEGAL DOCTRINE AS KNOWLEDGE OF LAW AND AS A SOURCE OF LAW 4 (2005) ("[to call legal doctrine explanatory is] to conceal justification behind a façade of explanation").

[15] "Here the emphasis is on the formal qualities of the abstract elements and relations; and if an explanation or prediction is exempt from internal contradiction in respect of all the other explanations and predictions that can be drawn from the model then this will act in itself as a means of verification." Samuel, *supra* note 1, at 44.

[16] ALASDAIR MACINTYRE, AFTER VIRTUE 209ff (3rd ed., 2011).

[17] JOHN RAWLS, POLITICAL LIBERALISM 110, 115 (1993).

[18] KRAMER, *supra* note 2, at 46. Kramer also uses "trans-individual discernibility."

[19] Niemi, *supra* note 2, at 79.

[20] MACINTYRE, *supra* note 16, at 209.

[21] "the ability to depart from the individual point of view and join the common and general discourse." Rawls, *supra* note 17, as paraphrased by Niemi, *supra* note 2, at 79.

[22] Niemi, *supra* note 2, at 79.

outside the human mind.[23] To illustrate, were it possible to extract past thoughts from a human brain, these presumably might be considered objects of cognition like any others. They would be 'intellectual facts,' externally observable, analyzable and refutable in just the same way that natural facts are. The external/internal distinction however has more to do with process. The foregoing discussion indeed presupposes that thoughts are such as *can only be retrieved through interpretation* rather than cognition. And interpretation does qualify as 'internal,' insofar as it involves "re-enacting"[24] an actor's (internal) thought process – *re-creating* (to the extent possible) the context of choice in which the actor found herself immediately prior to the action and the manner in which that choice was specifically exercised. It is a creative, imaginative exercise, one that literally entails repositioning oneself *inside* the agent's mind so as to experience their actions the way they did.[25]

The external/internal distinction in short is epistemological rather than ontological. It does not pertain to *what* is being investigated so much as to *how* the investigation is to proceed – the standpoint, and corresponding method and standard of validity, that the investigator is to adopt.[26] Whereas natural phenomena may perhaps be adequately understood from a strictly external, thus cognitivist and correspondence-referenced standpoint, a proper understanding of human affairs requires an internal, hermeneutic and coherence-governed perspective.

II. INTERNAL AND EXTERNAL PERSPECTIVES IN LAW

As just described, the external and internal perspectives respectively seem to track, or so do I propose to argue now, the natural law and positivist ideal-types developed in Chapters 1 and 2, on the one hand, and law as collective commitment, on the other.

---

[23] E.g., RANDY E. BARNETT, CONTRACTS 68–75 (2010) ("'Subjective' refers to what is in a person's head.").

[24] "There is only one way in which it can be done: by rethinking them in his own mind ... The history of thought, and therefore all history, is the re-enactment of past thought in the historian's own mind." Collingwood, *supra* note 9, at 26. See also: *ibid.* at 28–29.

[25] "an effort of imaginative understanding ... which allowed him to comprehend what processes of the human will had produced it." Whitman, *supra* note 1, at 320.

[26] This distinction is obfuscated where it is claimed, for example in legal studies, that the internal perspective focuses on formal legal rules whereas the external targets the context (social, economic, historical) surrounding the rules (e.g. David Ibbetson, Historical Research in Law, *in* OXFORD HANDBOOK OF LEGAL STUDIES 863, 864 (Peter Cane & Mark V. Tushnet eds., 2003)). In line with the above, it would be more appropriate to say that the internal and external perspectives entail dealing with the rules as do legal actors and social scientists respectively. It may well be that legal actors and social scientists typically focus on different aspects of the rules – say, their coherence rather than economic impact – but that is merely contingent: should economic impact play a role in legal argumentation, that aspect of legal rules would feature in the legal actor's and the social scientist's perspective alike (Christopher McCrudden, Legal Research and the Social Sciences, 122 LAW Q. REV. 632, 635 (2006)). Likewise, the social scientist like the legal actor may be interested in rule coherence, for example, in tracing patterns of rule coherence or identifying the circumstances in which societies have worried about coherence.

i. An External Perspective Under the Natural Law
and Positivist Ideal-Types

Under either of the natural law or positivist ideal-types, law is conceptualized as some-thing 'out there,' to be observed and analyzed from a distance, in the same way that the law of gravity is analyzed by the physicist, or the photosynthesis process, by the botanist.[27] It is reducible to a set of facts – albeit of different kinds: 'moral facts'[28] under natural law and 'material facts' under positivism – presupposed to exist prior to, and independently of, the investigating subject. And a legal proposition accordingly is true or false depending on whether it (objectively) 'corresponds' to the relevant facts.

As discussed, the natural lawyers viewed the Law of Nature, their model for human laws, as the moral counterpart of the laws of physics.[29] The moral laws in their view were, just like the laws of physics, immanent in the natural order of things. Only, the 'natural order' at stake was not nature writ large so much as nature that is pecu-liarly human, defined as human reason and hence apprehensible through logical deduction. The distant stance adopted in the physical sciences accordingly would be available in 'legal science' as well: whereas the requisite distance is secured through empirical constraints in the first, it obtains through the rigours of logic in the second. Also like the physical sciences, then, legal science could be described as subject-neutral: there can only be one Law of Nature valid for all human beings in just the same way that the law of gravity operates the same way everywhere on earth.[30] Variations in the laws governing human affairs to them were no more conceivable than are variations in the laws of physics. This is confirmed by the fact that the defenders of 'legal science' (commonly described as 'transnational')[31] have typically also been involved in the study of legal convergence, the convergence of legal systems towards the one and only objective model of the Law of Nature.[32] The cognitivist slant of such an approach is further underscored by its neo-Kantian critique, according to which that approach ultimately fails to take seriously human volition and responsibility.[33]

---

[27] See generally: Samuel, *supra* note 1, at 193ff.

[28] "The world contains many facts about what we are doing ... But it also contains, it would seem, facts about what we ought to do ... [which] envisage a state of affairs which may differ from the state that currently obtains. How can such claims be themselves amongst the existing features of the world?" SIMMONDS, *supra* note 7, at 113. The view according to which such claims "derive their meaning from an abstract essence with a metaphysical status independent of linguistic usage" (*ibid.* at 57) is known as "essentialism."

[29] See *supra* Chapter 1, Part II, section i.

[30] See *supra* Chapter 2, Part II.

[31] Arthur T. von Mehren, The Rise of Transnational Legal Practice and the Task of Comparative Law, 75 TUL. L. REV. 1215 (2001).

[32] E.g., James Gordley, Comparative Legal Research: Its Function in the Development of Harmonized Law, 43 AM. J. COMP. L. 555, 567 (1995).

[33] "In purely naturalistic terms, there is no such thing as responsibility: if we trace an action back, we find out that everything one does and everything one is is determined by causal factors, lying outside of one's control." Arthur Ripstein, Equality, Luck and Responsibility, 23 PHIL. & PUB. AFF. 3 (1994).

We then saw that the positivist ideal-type in contrast allows for legal diversity, so much diversity, in fact, that it is no longer clear what if anything the various elements have in common that warrants labelling them all 'legal' in the first place.[34] Law on that account is not a *natural* fact (physical or moral), but a *conventional* fact – a human creation pure and simple. This suggests that the positivist ideal-type, unlike the naturalist one, carries at least the conceptual possibility of an internal understanding. For, as discussed, all that is humanly created can potentially be understood from the perspective of its external, tangible manifestations or else from the perspective of the intentions of its human creators. Positivism however ended up turning its back on the latter. From the outset, it put itself forward as a sociological account of law, one very much based on law's material dimension; cleaned out, that is, of any kind of reference to such intangibles as intentions, beliefs and aspirations.[35] A human creation for sure, therefore, but one of which only the material, externally observable dimension counts. The proper analogy here is not to the physical sciences so much as to the social sciences, then, the sciences dealing in the hard data of human action. Yet we in any event remain firmly ensconced within cognitivism and the correspondence theory of truth.

ii. *An Internal Perspective Under Law As Collective Commitment*

In contrast to both the natural law and positivist models, law as collective commitment clearly motions to an internal standpoint, thus a hermeneutic approach and coherence standard of validity. Recall that law on that account is "an argumentative social practice that both reflects and constitutes a community's commitment to governing itself in accordance with certain ideals."[36] Law here is neither just materials (texts, orders, coercion, etc.), as it is under positivism, nor just ideals (justice, equality, freedom, etc.), as it is under natural law. It rather is the practice of dialogically relating these two sets through arguments: legal actors argue over what ideals are embodied in the materials which justify their coercive enforcement, thereby creating new materials, the interpretation of which in turn will have to be debated, and so on.[37] The facts that make up law as collective commitment hence are what Neil MacCormick

---

[34] See *supra* Chapter 2, Part III.

[35] See *supra* Chapter 1, Part II, section ii, esp. Raz citation, note 105. See also: Samuel, *supra* note 1, at 193–94. Hart's famous struggle with what he described as 'the internal point of view' indeed suggests that he stands at some distance from the extreme materialism of the positivistic ideal-type of Chapter 2 (but see Jeremy Waldron, The Concept and the Rule of Law, 43 GEORGIA L. REV. 1, 14 (2008)).

[36] See *supra* p. 1 of Chapter 1.

[37] See *supra* Chapter 1, Part II, section iii.

calls "institutional facts":[38] "facts which we invest with meaning within a particular set of social relations ... not a set of 'natural facts', but a set of facts that become significant within a legal context."[39] And the point of legal practice accordingly is to argue over meaning, over the meaning of the relevant set of institutional facts.

Charles Taylor gets us to the same place via the notion of 'expressivism.'[40] Drawing on Herder,[41] Taylor analyzes expressivism in terms of two dimensions, the first of which is the representation of social phenomena as *expressing* something. That is, social phenomena as speech acts, as acts of 'self-affirmation,' rather than as cause and effect (as they are under 'functionalism').[42] Law as collective commitment certainly comprises that first dimension insofar as it portrays law as primarily made up of (meaning-infused) *arguments*.[43] The second of Taylor's dimensions directly appeals to constructivism, as it involves showing that the content and form of what is being expressed are dialectically interrelated.[44] That is to say, the content of the message is shown to become more precise, more determinate as it is being expressed, the formulating act hence serving to *construct* as much as to *convey* that message.[45] That

---

[38] Neil MacCormick, Institutions of Law: An Essay in Legal Theory 295 (2007) [hereinafter MacCormick, Institutions of Law]; Neil MacCormick, Rhetoric and the Rule of Law: A Theory of Legal Reasoning 65ff (2005) [hereinafter MacCormick, A Theory of Legal Reasoning]. See likewise: Eerik Lagerspetz, The Opposite Mirrors Chap. 1 ("conventional facts") (1995); Ota Weinberger, The Norm as Thought and as Reality, in An Institutional Theory of Law 31, 32–38 (Neil MacCormick & Ota Weinberger eds., 1986) ("humanly conditioned facts").

[39] John Bell, Legal Research and the Distinctiveness of Comparative Law, in Methodologies of Legal Research: Which Kind of Method for What Kind of Discipline? 155, 161 (Mark Van Hoecke ed., 2011). Likewise: Postema, supra note 1 (Law's Rule), at 11 ("The rule of law ... comprises not only (a) a set of standards for laws and for the conduct of governmental agents, and (b) a set of core legal institutions and procedures for administration of these laws, but also and crucially a third component (c) an ethos, a set of relationships and responsibilities rooted in core convictions and commitments.").

[40] Charles Taylor, Hegel 15ff (1975).

[41] Simmonds (supra note 7, at 149) attributes the same idea to Aristotle and Gadamer.

[42] "[Self-affirmation] imposing itself on external reality." Taylor, supra note 40. See likewise: Ronald Dworkin, Law's Empire (1986); John Henry Merryman, Civil Law Tradition, 35 Am. J. Comp. L. 438, 441 (1987) ("To understand [law] you have to know ... what its image of itself is."); Cass R. Sunstein, On the Expressive Function of Law, 144 U. Penn. L. Rev. 2021 (1996); Mark Tushnet, The Possibilities of Comparative Constitutional Law, 108 Yale L. J. 1226, 1255 (1999); Geertz, supra note 12, at 233 ("conceiving of human behaviour and the products of human behaviour as saying something"); Mitchel Lasser, The Question of Understanding, in Comparative Legal Studies, supra note 1, at 197, 207 ("how the legal system understands itself to function."); Sean Coyle, From Positivism to Idealism 6–7 (2007) ("the sense in which the legal order embodies the expression of a society's self-understanding and its views of human nature and the good life."); Richard Hyland, Gifts: A Study in Comparative Law, 98ff (2009); Joseph Vining, The Resilience of Law, in Law and Democracy in the Empire of Force 151 (H. Jefferson Powell & James Boyd White eds., 2009).

[43] See supra Chapter 1, Part I, section vi.

[44] "[T]he notion that the realization of a form clarifies or makes determinate what the form is ... Thus the notion of human life as expression sees this not only as the realization of purposes but also as the clarification of these purposes." Taylor, supra note 40, at 16–17. Neil Walker refers to the same idea as "intimation" (Neil Walker, Intimations of Global Law 149 (2015)).

[45] "[It] tells stories about the culture that helped to shape it and which it in turn helps to shape." Mary Ann Glendon, Abortion and Divorce in Western Law 8 (1987). This is where law differs

too is present in law as collective commitment, wherein new arguments necessarily build on past ones, which they in turn serve to modify, refine and improve.[46]

Now, law so conceived arguably can only be fully understood from within, from the perspective of the argument makers.[47] To understand legal arguments is to grasp how it is that they can be considered compelling, how it is that they can be seen as providing "authoritative reasons for action."[48] And this requires "engaging in [the very same] justificatory project"[49] as the argument makers themselves. For if law is not just mechanical behaviour but in fact an *ethos* proper,[50] understanding it requires *experiencing* its normative pull; it involves active (re)construction rather than passive cognition insofar as the referenced ideals are internalized and processed as such, not merely observed from a distance. And as said ideals inevitably end up somewhat transformed in the process, the would-be distant observer in fact cannot but become a participant pure and simple: "[h]e ... *joins* the practice he proposes to understand; his conclusions are then not neutral reports about what the citizens ... think but claims ... *competitive* with theirs."[51] Briefly, if law is, as per law as collective commitments, essentially made up of debate and argument, a strictly external, observer perspective is bound to prove sourly defective.

iii. *A Midway Position?*

A number of legal theorists have resisted the observer/participant dichotomy and defended a kind of Humean midpoint – a position of "normative inertness"[52] – from which it would be possible to grasp and report on a legal practice without for that

---

from anthropology in Whitman's view (WHITMAN, *supra* note 1, at 341): "[Unlike lawyers, c]ultural anthropologists ... aim to document the 'cultures' they study; and they assume that, if they change those cultures, they have in some fundamental way tainted or destroyed them." See likewise: MACCORMICK, RHETORIC AND THE RULE OF LAW, *supra* note 38, at 29 ("This is an intellectual process involving a new imagining and describing of the implicit order in potential disorder ... It is not a literal rebuilding of something originally present that has somehow fallen apart.").

[46] See *supra* Chapter 1, Part I, section ii, esp. text accompanying notes 22–28.

[47] "in terms of what makes them intelligible and worthwhile, or at least on balance worthwhile, to their human participants." MACCORMICK, INSTITUTIONS OF LAW, *supra* note 38 at 295. A most forceful plea for understanding law on the inside appears in William Ewald's seminal work: William Ewald, Comparative Jurisprudence (I): What Was It Like to Try a Rat?, 143 U. PA. L. REV. 1898 (1994–95). See also: JOHN FINNIS, NATURAL LAW AND NATURAL RIGHTS 3–4 (1980) ("[T]he actions, practices, etc. [that make up law] can be fully understood only by understanding their point, that is to say their objective, their value, their significance or importance, as conceived by the people who performed them, engaged in them, etc."); JOSEPH RAZ, PRACTICAL REASON AND NORMS (2nd ed. 1999); FREDERICK SCHAUER, THE FORCE OF LAW (2015), chap. 3 (discussing H. L. A. Hart's famous "internal point of view").

[48] Bell, *supra* note 39, at 159 (discussing G. Samuel, Is Law Really a Social Science? A View from Comparative Law, 67 CAMBRIDGE L. J. 292–96 (2008)).

[49] John Gardner, What Is Tort Law For?, The Place of Corrective Justice, 30 LAW & PHIL. 1, 3 (2011).

[50] Postema, *supra* note 1 (*Law's Rule*), at 12. E.g. the Herderian conception of law as "ethical self-realization and perfection" (FREDERICK C. BEISER, THE GERMAN HISTORICIST TRADITION 156 (2011)).

[51] DWORKIN, *supra* note 42, at 64. (Italics in original.)

[52] John Gardner, Legal Positivism: 5 1/2 Myths, 46 AM. J. OF JURIS. 199, 203 (2001) (Gardner is himself critical of that position).

matter joining it. MacCormick himself, for instance, maintained that in between the "front-line actors" (legislators, judges, advocates) and the "purely external observers" (legal sociologists, economists, anthropologists) stand the "observers from within," who share the front-liners' "cognitive" approach though not their "volitional" involvement.[53] Students and scholars are such observers, he claimed, as they are "concerned with jurisprudential or doctrinal exposition of [law while retaining] a certain detachment by contrast with front-line actors [and] a relatively high degree of engagement by contrast with purely external observers."[54] In other words, they aim "to give the right answer from within the system, but need not be wishing to achieve that result."[55] Finally, Kerchove and Ost describe the same as the "moderate external" standpoint. As they define it, the "moderate external" standpoint is that which investigators adopt in order to "account in the most exhaustive way possible ... for the systematicity inherent in law ... without undertaking to pursue such systematization themselves."[56] Hans Kelsen likewise insisted, finally, that it was entirely possible "to be an excellent law professor and an anarchist."[57]

I would contend that such midway position is untenable for, as Taylor's analysis of expressivism makes clear, it simply is not possible to recount "thought objects"[58] (including legal arguments) without transforming them to some extent. Even assuming that thoughts can be conceptualized separately from their formulation,[59] no two formulations of a same thought, even identically-worded, will likely be exactly the same. This is so for at least three reasons. First, the formulation process is itself, as the neo-Kantians indicated, a critical process, engaging some measure of the formulator's subjectivity: "[t]he historian not only re-enacts past thought, he re-enacts it in the context of his own knowledge and therefore, in re-enacting it, criticizes it, forms his own judgement of its value."[60] Insofar as different formulations are produced

---

[53] NEIL MACCORMICK, *LEGAL REASONING AND LEGAL THEORY* 289 (1978); NEIL MACCORMICK, *H. L. A. HART* 37–40 (1981) [hereinafter; MACCORMICK, *H. L. A. HART*]; MACCORMICK, *RHETORIC AND THE RULE OF LAW, supra* note 38, at 67 ("So indeed the law-settling decision is different from the interpretative discourse that leads into it."). Brian Tamanaha likewise distinguishes between "participant-" and "non-participant observers," suggesting the former comprises judges only: Brian Z. Tamanaha, A Socio-Legal Methodology for the Internal/External Distinction: Jurisprudential Implications, 75 *FORDHAM L. REV.* 1255 (2006).

[54] MACCORMICK, *INSTITUTIONS OF LAW, supra* note 38, at 5–6. And at 5: "a mixture of detached description and value oriented activity."

[55] Bell, *supra* note 39, at 159.

[56] MICHEL VAN DE KERCHOVE & FRANCOIS OST, *LEGAL SYSTEM BETWEEN ORDER AND DISORDER* 29 (1994). See likewise: Bell, *supra* note 39, at 168 (suggesting the local jurist, unlike the comparative lawyer, is "the continuance of the system"); J. De Koning, The Functional Method of Comparative Law: Quo Vadis?, 74 *RABELSZ* 318, 342 (2010) ("it is perfectly possible to make non-normative statements about normative issues"); Lasser, *supra* note 42, at 206 ("an external perspective on the internal"). See our discussion of the "subjectivity objection" *infra* pp. 106–107.

[57] HANS KELSEN, *A PURE THEORY OF LAW* 218 (1967), discussed in Bell, *supra* note 39, at 159.

[58] Weinberger, *supra* note 38, at 32–38.

[59] "[Y]ou think of the meaning as a thing of the same kind as the word, though also different from the word. Here the word, there the meaning. The money, and the cow that you can buy with it." LUDWIG WITTGENSTEIN, *PHILOSOPHICAL INVESTIGATIONS* §120 (2009) (criticizing this view).

[60] Collingwood, *supra* note 9, at 26.

by differently subjective formulators,[61] then, they probably differ to some extent. In addition, it is by now widely accepted that formulations take on meaning only within particular 'contexts of meaning,' which cannot but evolve from one formulation to the next.[62] Even identically-worded formulations might mean different things in different contexts, therefore. Finally, to formulate something *ipso facto* is to offer it up for transformation, "to subject it to the process of articulate normative critique, [since w]hat has been *expressed* ... must inevitably be debated and defended."[63] To formulate something hence is to contribute to its transformation at least in the sense of inviting the process of such transformation. Quite simply,

> whereas we [may] accept that the scientific formulation of the laws of thermodynamics does not add anything at all to thermodynamics as such, one has never seen a treatise on the civil law, for example, be just the transcription of the civil code: it adds something, necessarily, lest it be absolutely useless. And what it adds is meaning, if not supplemental meaning, at least the means to determinate it better.[64]

That at any rate is arguably why legal scholars and law students (whose own formulations of the law at times enlighten their teacher, whose own writings at times enlighten the judges, whose own judgments guide the legislators, and so on) are portrayed as fully fledged legal participants in Chapter 1[65] – and in fact considered such (at least with respect to published scholars) in many legal systems. In particular, it is well known that scholarly writings are treated like quasi-official sources of law in France and Germany, for example, much like they were in Ancient Rome.[66]

iv. *The Heterogeneity Objection*

It has however been objected that there can be no *single* 'participant standpoint' on any law insofar as, in all legal systems, the participants hardly form a homogeneous

---

[61] Or even, perhaps, the same formulator but at different points in time, as one's critical process presumably evolves over time.

[62] "[A] form of life sufficiently concrete ... that the one can recognize sense and purpose in what the other says and does." Wittgenstein, quoted in DWORKIN, *supra* note 42, at 63–64; "Any understanding is therefore inscribed in finitude." Heidegger, as paraphrased by Glanert, *supra* note 1, at 72; "[A legal text] will not and should not say the same thing always; it will in fact yield different meanings to different minds in different situations, differences that themselves become the topic of thought and argument." JAMES BOYD WHITE, *LIVING SPEECH* 142 (2006).

[63] Whitman, *supra* note 1, at 340.

[64] Picard, *supra* note 1, at 213 (my translation). Dworkin agrees: "[S]truggling to show what is good about [equality], why we should honour it as a value, and the extent to which we should, is the only sensible way to proceed in order to decide what that value really is." (François Du Dubois, Ronald Dworkin, The Practice of Integrity, 2004 ACTA JURIDICA 1, 3 (2004).) Likewise: Lasser, *supra* note 42, at 217–19; Ugo Mattei, Why the Wind Changed: Intellectual Leadership in Western Law, 42 AM. J. COMP. L. 195, 211 (1994) (discussing the effect of Schlesinger's purportedly "descriptive" scholarship on US and European law alike).

[65] See *supra* text following note 152, Chapter 1, Part II, section iii.

[66] See *supra* Chapter 1, Part I, section v.

whole.[67] Unlike Collingwood's historian seizing on Brutus' mind, the person investigating an entire legal system has a great many minds to choose from. At least, this is so under law as collective commitment. Under some versions of positivism, where all law-making powers ultimately lie in a unique sovereign, the question may not arise: the only actor whose mind it might be interesting to explore for the purpose of understanding the legal system arguably is that of the sovereign. But where law is conceptualized as it is here, as the collective product of *many* minds, it may seem that a determination needs to be made as to which of these will count: exactly "whose 'mind' should we have in mind?"[68]

More difficult still, the many minds in question rarely if ever agree. Uniform agreement as to the meaning of legal rules after all is never present as a matter of fact, nor is it typically aspired to. But even mere consensus is usually elusive. Insofar as law is, as here assumed, essentially made up of debate and argument, it in fact *presupposes* a divergence of views (given that people argue only where they disagree with one another).

Perhaps, then, does an inside understanding of the system require that we statistically *aggregate* the individual actors' diverging views of it through polls and surveys?[69] But this in turn would suppose that all those views are equally worthy, whereas there is little reason for thinking that that is the case. If anything, personal experience reveals that legal actors are highly *un*equal when it comes to understanding their law, some of them being in fact squarely deficient in that respect.[70] One scholar even goes so far as to impugn *all* actors, collectively or individually, as "*unusually poor informants*"[71] about their system. So how is the comparative lawyer to go about understanding law "from the perspective of the participants" if said participants' own accounts of that law cannot even be relied upon to begin with? Should we just resign ourselves to the fact that law might just be "too complex and diverse to be said to have an inside"?[72]

In response, that line of reasoning appears misguided insofar as it equates an internal understanding of the law with an internal understanding of individual legal actors, which law as collective commitment rejects. Recall that that conception shows law to be 'public' in a deeper sense than just mere transparency, namely, in the Rawlsian sense of transcending particular actors (even the sum of them all) and hence pertaining

---

[67] Lasser, *supra* note 42; Pierre Legrand, Comparative Legal Studies and the Matter of Authenticity 1 *J. Comp. L.* 365, 381–82 (2008); Bell, *supra* note 39, at 166.

[68] See Lasser at 215.

[69] E.g. *ibid.* at 209 (surveying the private views of French judges for the purpose of understanding French official legal discourse). Yet see *ibid.* at 223 (legal education aiming to teach students, not so much to "think like a lawyer" as to "speak or argue like a lawyer").

[70] Lasser, *supra* note 42, at 231.

[71] Whitman, *supra* note 1, at 334. (Emphasis in original.) Likewise: Mauro Bussani & Ugo Mattei, The Common Core Approach to European Private Law, 3 *Colum. J. Eur. L.* 339, 352–53 (1997–98).

[72] Lasser, *supra* note 42, at 217.

to the community as "altogether separate from its individual members."[73] We just saw that law on that account is not 'out there' ("items in the physical furniture of the universe"),[74] as it might be under natural law or positivism.[75] But nor is it, for that matter, purely subjective ("part of the psychic state of any particular person at any given time").[76] As per the above discussion concerning the coherence standard,[77] it rather lies somewhere in between, in what Karl Popper calls the "third" or the "inter-subjective" world:[78] "[the world] of inter-subjective meanings available to human understanding through interpretation."[79] Given that law accordingly exists *across* rather than *inside* people, what particular individuals might privately think of it is of no relevance, at least for the purpose of the kind of understanding we are here after.[80]

The entity to be explored from within hence is not the mind(s) of particular actor(s) but rather that of the law itself, the *collective* mind at play in and through the social practice that is law.[81] The goal is to reconstruct how *the law as such* sees itself – *its* ideal self-representation. Indeed, the actors' own behaviour suggests as much.[82] The actors themselves, that is, distinguish between the (homogeneous) collective ideals embedded in their law and the (heterogeneous) private ideals that that law was meant to transcend,[83] and direct their arguments to the former: "the claims and arguments participants make, licensed and encouraged by the practice, are about what *it* means, not what *they* mean."[84] Polls and surveys are out, therefore,

---

73 See *supra* Chapter 1, Part I, section iv, esp. text accompanying notes 44–48. See also: Ewald, *supra* note 47, at 1949, 2149.

74 MacCormick, Institutions of Law, *supra* note 38, at 292.

75 See *supra* section ii.

76 MacCormick, Institutions of Law, *supra* note 38, at 292.

77 See *supra* text accompanying notes 14–22.

78 Karl Popper, Objective Knowledge: An Evolutionary Approach (1972) chap. 4, esp. p. 159: "[the world of that which is]" "man-made and, in a very clear sense, superhuman at the same time. It transcends its makers." See likewise Hannah Arendt's claim that it is possible to acknowledge the part of subjectivity in the realm of judgment and decision without for that matter accepting that that realm is necessarily governed by individual preferences: Hannah Arendt, Crisis in Culture, in Between Past and Future (1961).

79 MacCormick, Institutions of Law, *supra* note 38, at 292. See likewise, Mark Van Hoecke, Matt Ilmari Niemi, Bertjan Wolthuis & Mustapha El Karouni, in Objectivity in Law and Legal Reasoning, *supra* note 2.

80 It may of course be relevant from a sociological or anthropological perspective.

81 The "total, organic whole" that is the "quasi-mystical *Geist*," in Whitman's words (Whitman, *supra* note 1, at 320–21 (discussing Dilthey)). See also: Aulis Aarnio, On Legal Reasoning 297–98 (1977); MacCormick, H.L.A. Hart, *supra* note 53, at 29, 33–43; Geertz, *supra* note 12, at 57; Vittorio Villa, Legal Science Between Natural and Human Sciences, 4 Leg. Stud. 243 (1984); Jacco Bomhoff, Comparing Legal Argument, in Practice and Theory in Comparative Law 4, 5 (Maurice Adams & Jacco Bomhoff eds., 2012).

82 On the duty of "fidelity" to the object of analysis, see: Lasser, *supra* note 42, at 224; Winch, *supra* note 10, at 41.

83 See *supra* text accompanying notes 46–48, Chapter 1, Part I, section iv.

84 Dworkin, *supra* note 42, at 63. (Emphasis in original.) See also: Lasser, *supra* note 42, at 205 ("[the legal actors] come to terms with the discursive and conceptual universe of a legal system *in the terms and according to the logic of [their legal] system*") (emphasis in original).

for the simple reason that the participants themselves exclude them.[85] What the participants are after can only be pursued through public debate and interpretation, and we are after just what the participants are.

The internal standpoint is 'univocal' rather than heterogeneous, then, inasmuch as it targets the actors *qua* participants in the system rather than *qua* actual persons. *Qua* participants, the actors speak in one voice insofar as *they act as if their law did.* That simply is the ground rule for all interpretative acts: interpreters are to treat the object of interpretation as if it spoke 'with one voice,' which single voice it is precisely their task to collectively piece together.[86] This is well conveyed through Max Weber's concept of the ideal interpreter, according to which interpreters always seek to articulate "*the* theoretically conceived pure type of subjective meaning attributed to the hypothetical actor or actors in a given type of action."[87] Participants in a legal system indeed typically aim to produce not just any odd interpretation of their law but rather the single 'best' one, that which the (single most) *Herculean* participant in their system would produce.[88] Though such 'best' interpretation as we saw is constantly challenged and revised, it nonetheless serves as the exclusive benchmark for any and all punctual interpretive acts.

Ronald Dworkin helpfully illustrates the same idea through an analogy with artistic interpretation as theorized by Stanley Cavell.[89] Cavell rejects the standard view

---

[85] Bell, *supra* note 39, at 158, 167 (discussing the "frailty" of the comparative method whereby foreign law is researched through questionnaires).

[86] "From an internal point of view, [legal interpretation involves a] good faith and best shot at showing ... that the legal order speaks with one voice on [any given] issue." David Dyzenhaus, Deliberative Constitutionalism Through the Lens of the Administrative State *in* Cambridge Handbook of Deliberative Constitutionalism 15 (Ron Levy *et al.* eds., forthcoming 2018); "The empirical claim, made from the outside, on an 'unsystematic collage' does not in any way undermine ... committed interpretative claims, made from the inside, that 'our law' ... should be interpreted, other things equal, in a way that contributes to its coherence." Martijn W. Hesselink, How Many Systems of Private Law Are There in Europe? On Plural Legal Sources, Multiple Identities and the Unity of Law, *in* Pluralism and European Private Law 199 (Leone Niglia ed., 2013).

[87] Max Weber, *Economy and State—An Outline of Interpretive Sociology*, vol. I, 4 (Guenther Roth & Claus Wittich eds., 1978). (Emphasis added.)

[88] Ronald Dworkin, *Taking Rights Seriously* 81–130 (1977). A significant difference remains between my and Dworkin's accounts, however. In Dworkin, there can ultimately be just one single most ideal interpreter for all law, as the standard against which to assess "best" interpretations in all cases is political morality as a single, universal concept ("purposes and motives of larger social units, ultimately of life or mind itself," Dworkin, *supra* note 42, at 422–23). As a result, the internal and external standpoints arguably end up being merged in Dworkin. (Simmonds, *supra* note 7, at 33; William Twining, Institutions of Law From a Global Perspective, *in* 20 Law as Institutional Normative Order 22 (Maksymillian Del Mar & Zenon Bankowski eds., 2010).) The present account in contrast posits (see Chapter 2) a plurality of political moralities/ideal interpreters – one per legal system – with the result that the external/internal distinction remains. (Dworkin comes closest to allowing for such plurality when he discusses family circles (Ronald Dworkin, *Justice for Hedgehogs*, chapter on "Law" (2011)). My thanks go to David Dyzenhaus for pointing this out to me.)

[89] Dworkin, *supra* note 42, at 57ff (discussing Stanley Cavell, *Must We Mean What We Say?* (1969), chap. 8).

of artistic intention as "crude conscious-mental-state"[90] and instead conceptualizes that intention as what the artist would *ex post facto* accept as consistent with it, or even a *better* representation of it. Accordingly, "the interpreter's judgement of what [the] author would have accepted will be guided by his sense of what the author *should* have accepted, that is, his sense of which readings would make the work *better* and which would make it *worse*."[91] Dworkin calls this "creative interpretation," and suggests it also aptly describes what legal actors do.[92]

Another useful analogy, to which we return later, is found in game playing.[93] A game involves different players, with different personalities and life goals, yet also boasts a distinct inherent purpose, which all players take on as their own when they play the game (i.e. when they act qua players). Winning involves furthering the purpose of the game by making the best possible moves consistent with it. This involves creativity, as such 'best' moves may never have been played before. They can nonetheless be recognized as such by the players after the fact, insofar as all are generally agreed as to the game's purpose and attendant rules. That is not to say that said purpose and rules are fixed, and they do tend to evolve as the game is being played. But one thing remains clear throughout: any given move is determined 'good' or 'bad' *by reference to the object of the game, not that of individual players*.[94] The internal perspective on law likewise involves doing what legal players do, namely, conceptualizing the local law as infused with some single overall purpose and advancing the best possible arguments consistent with that purpose, regardless of any personal purposes the players might also incidentally harbour.

In sum, the heterogeneity objection simply misses the mark. It targets legal actors in their individual capacity whereas on the present account "[t]he search for univocal meaning within a [legal] practice can only be conducted from the perspective of one who seeks to follow and continue the practice [as such]."[95]

v. *The Subjectivity Objection*

The argument just offered also bears on another, related objection, according to which law being normative, any understanding of it is necessarily 'subjective.'[96] At least three versions of this objection seem to be on offer. Under the first, the claim

---

[90] *Ibid.* at 57.

[91] *Ibid.*

[92] *Ibid.* at 50 ("like artistic interpretation [legal interpretation aims] to interpret something created by people as an entity distinct from them rather than what people say, as in conversational interpretation.").

[93] RICHARD RORTY, *PHILOSOPHY AND THE MIRROR OF NATURE* 11 (1979); KERCHOVE & OST, *supra* note 56.

[94] "[D]ifferentiated thought within a legal culture or tradition must assume a measure of epistemological commonality if it is to lay any claim to cognitive ... effectivity." Legrand, *supra* note 67, at note 66.

[95] SIMMONDS, *supra* note 7, at 33.

[96] Anne Peters & Heiner Schwenke, Comparative Law Beyond Post-Modernism, 49 INT'L & COMP. L. Q. 800, 820ff (2000).

is that the ideals furthered through legal argumentation are not law's ideals so much as the legal actors' *perception* of such ideals, which perception inevitably is somewhat subjective. The second version in contrast stipulates that the understandings of the law advanced by the actors reflect their views of how the law *should be*, not just of how it *is*. The third version, finally, claims that the legal actors covertly or unconsciously act so as to channel the law in the direction of their personal interests, in other words that, while purporting to pursue the law's ideals, they will in fact be pursuing *their own*. Let me address each version in turn.

With respect to the first, it admittedly seems inevitable that the actors can only go on law's ideals as they perceive them.[97] But we saw that such residual kind of subjectivity is probably present in all knowledge, not just legal knowledge.[98] As philosopher John Passmore remarked, "if only those inquiries are objective in which the inquirer begins with a blank mind, then no inquiry whatsoever is objective."[99] While such residual discretion most likely is present in law, then, it ought to be viewed as no more problematic than in other fields of study.

Under its second version, likewise, the objection describes a state of affairs that is unavoidable yet also unobjectionable. Arguing over ideals as we saw necessarily involves passing judgment on those ideals, parcelling them out, ranking them, showing them to be incomplete or inapposite, etc. Even purported mere 'recounting' of ideals in fact cannot be purely descriptive as we saw.[100] And the present account does conceptualize legal argumentation as an exercise in critical thinking, one in which the various actors compete to defend their respective 'best' interpretations of the law, their views of how the law *should* be.[101] These are 'subjective' views in much the same way that, as just indicated, the 'law' they argue over is in fact their 'subjective' perception of it. Still, they are views of how the law should be *given its own* (not the actors') purposes[102] – what Niklas Luhmann calls 'eigenvalues.'[103] As such, they remain properly *legal* interpretations, ones of which Dworkin would say that they aim 'to make the law the best *it* can be.'[104] Ernest Weinrib puts the same point as follows:

[97] "There can only be a situated understanding of law ... No understanding — no matter the extent of mimetic fealty — will capture the law 'as it is'." Legrand, *supra* note 67, at 448 (emphasis in original).

[98] See *supra* text accompanying notes 4–5 and 60.

[99] John A. Passmore, The Objectivity of History, *in* GARDINER, *supra* note 1, at 145, 146.

[100] *Contra*: Lasser, *supra* note 42, at 224–26; von Mehren, *supra* note 31, at 1215 (discussing "purely descriptive" comparative law). See generally: H. Patrick Glenn, Aims of Comparative Law, *in* ELGAR ENCYCLOPEDIA OF COMPARATIVE LAW 57, 58–89 (Jan M. Smits ed., 2006); *supra* section iii.

[101] See *supra* Chapter 1, Part I, section ii, esp. text accompanying notes 22–28, and Chapter 1, Part II, section iii, text accompanying note 145.

[102] Bell, *supra* note 39, at 175 ("The researcher is stating what ought to be done *according to the legal point of view within a particular legal system*." Emphasis added.)

[103] NIKLAS LUHMANN, LAW AS A SOCIAL SYSTEM 47 (Fatima Kastner *et al.* eds., Klaus Ziegart trans., 2009) ("the values expressed through the repetition of the system's operations").

[104] "the best possible example of the form or genre to which it is taken to belong"; Dworkin, *supra* note 40, at 52. Likewise: Whitman, *supra* note 1, at 336 ("Dworkin is right: the 'inner' perspective always

Of course, all understandings are the activities of the individual minds that understand. But in orienting their efforts to the law, these minds are themselves possessed by the idea of that which they are trying to understand, so that this idea is not only the object of their attentions but the subject that animates them to work toward its realization and to subordinate their personalities to its intelligible requirements. The understandings of jurists count to the extent that they are not personal opinions but are expressions of what is demanded of law if it is to remain true to its own nature.[105]

The kind of 'subjectivity' at play under the second version of the objection hence is ultimately no more problematic than that under the first.

As for the different worry just alluded to – that the actors' 'best' interpretations might actually be determined by reference to their personal purposes – it in fact is the object of the third and last version of the objection. This last version is problematic or not depending on whether we consider it in principle or in reality. In principle, there is no reason to assume that legal argumentation will be highjacked by private interests, given the actors' above-discussed (ideal) ability and willingness to distinguish between their and the law's purposes. In reality, however, it must be recognized that the exact line between these two sets may not be so clear, and the actors' private purposes, never so far. The legal actors accordingly may find it difficult, as a matter of fact, to resist the temptation of opportunistic behaviour.

As with the first version, though, this problem is not unique to law: it affects any area of social life that stages groups and individuals. But in addition, it must be noted that some forces operate to constrain such behaviour.[106] For one, the actors' arguments will prove effective to modify the law only insofar as they are accepted as legal arguments proper by the larger legal community, which acceptance in turn will depend on those arguments cohering with what that community takes to be its legal ideals.[107] These ideals can be identified with some degree of specificity, moreover,

represents an effort at normative beautification, an effort at improving and reconceiving the principles of the law.").

[105] ERNEST J. WEINRIB, THE IDEA OF PRIVATE LAW 15–16 (1995). Likewise: Neil MacCormick, The Ideal and the Actual of Law and Society, in LAW, VALUES AND SOCIAL PRACTICES 15ff (John Tasioulas ed., 1997); Kenneth I. Winston, The Ideal Element in a Definition of Law, 5 LAW & PHIL 89, 106 (1986), paraphrasing Ernst Nagel, Fact, Value, and Human Purpose, 4 NAT. L. F. 30 (1959) ("approximation to an ideal is a feature of legal experience itself ... a significant definition will be value-laden without being arbitrary or personal.").

[106] See generally: Gerald J. Postema, A Similibus ad Similia: Analogical Thinking in Law, in COMMON LAW THEORY 102, 124–26 (Douglas E. Edlin ed., 2007).

[107] MACCORMICK, LEGAL REASONING AND LEGAL THEORY, supra note 53, at chap. 8. See also: Stefan Oeter, Theorizing the Global Legal Order: An Institutionalist Perspective, in THEORISING THE GLOBAL LEGAL ORDER 61, 67 (Andrew Halpin & Volker Roeben eds., 2009). ("Framing positions in opinio juris language forces actors to argue primarily in terms of normative beliefs and values, and not in terms of interests. Such 'encoding' ... develops its own dynamic [wherein i]nterests are not only translated in terms of normative beliefs, but to a certain degree also transcended in norms and values. ... Actors [thus experience a] loss of discursive control."); Julen Etxabe, The Legal Universe After Robert Cover,

as they are not 'purely mental imaginings.'[108] Their embodiment in the community's legal materials to some extent renders them 'externally recognizable,'[109] 'publicly available as symbols.'[110] Admittedly, these materials not being self-explanatory, they call for interpretation, which itself remains unconstrained (at least by the materials themselves). Legal materials simply do not stand as some kind of fixed objects 'out there,' against which to determine, on a correspondence basis, the absolute 'rightness' or 'wrongness' of legal arguments (assuming such determinations are even possible). Nonetheless, the less stringent coherence standard applies to them which as explained does wield a certain measure of constraining power: it allows for the determination of 'better' and 'worse' arguments, and hence the ultimate dismissal of at least some of them.[111] Finally, to the extent that all legal actors are vulnerable to the same opportunistic inclinations, each has an incentive to expose and confront those who might be acting on them.[112] Quite simply, citizens covertly attempting to move the law in the direction of their personal interests will be pressed to defend their positions through publicly acceptable arguments. And the larger the group of citizens, the greater the chance that the various subjectivities accordingly will end up fending off if not offsetting one another.[113]

In sum, of the three versions of the subjectivity objection just surveyed, only the third might be worth worrying about. And even as concerns this last one, we can draw comfort from the fact that citizens are not free to engage in opportunistic, self-serving legal practice entirely unconstrained, at least not under the present account of law. For, on that account, the law's own aspirations of coherence and

---

4 LAW & HUMANITIES 115, 124 (2010) ("The limit of a valid claim is hence set by the imagination of the speaker and the persuasiveness of the claim (ie the ability to frame the legal argument in ways that can be accepted by others as valid.").

[108] WEINRIB, *supra* note 105, at 104.

[109] *Ibid.* at 104 ("On stepping into a world of interaction, the freely willing actor establishes a presence there through acts that have an externally recognizable nature.); Picard, *supra* note 1, at 199–202, 217–19.

[110] GEERTZ, *supra* note 12, at 31 ("the object of cultural study is not to be found in an informant's unspoken subjectivity but is rather what is publicly available as symbols—the inscription in writing, the fixation of meaning.").

[111] See *supra* text accompanying note 22; MACCORMICK, *LEGAL REASONING AND LEGAL THEORY*, *supra* note 53, at 12: "We distinguish between good and bad, more sound and less sound, relevant and irrelevant, acceptable or unacceptable arguments in relation to ... legal disputation."

[112] Pierre Legrand, The Impossibility of 'Legal Transplants,' 4 *MAASTRICHT J.* 111, 115 (1997) ("interpretation [i]s an 'intersubjective' phenomenon interpretation in the sense that it is the product of the interpreter's subjectivity as it interacts with the network of all subjectivities within an interpretive community."); Peters & Schwenke, *supra* note 96, at 831, discussing HENRY H. BAUER, *SCIENTIFIC LITERACY AND THE MYTH OF THE SCIENTIFIC METHOD* 43–62 (1992) ("So scholarship escapes the prejudice of the point of view of those constructing it through testing and mutual criticism.").

[113] "the greater the number of us attempting to draw meaning from the same data, the more that meaning becomes objective, and in turn serves to inform the collective juridical thought." Simmonds, *supra* note 7, at 217–18. See also: Andrew Halpin, Conceptual Collisions, 2 *JURIS* 507, 1 (2015) (concepts opening themselves to challenge the moment they claim to be more than one person's concept).

publicness operate to counter such behaviour. That is to say that, as concerns the only form of subjectivity here worthy of worry, checks operate which originate from within the law itself. Though these checks are not such as to guarantee anything like a single 'objectively right' understanding of the law, they do serve to filter out such of these understandings as would fall below the threshold of 'inter-subjective acceptability.' In so doing, they also allow for some kind of progression towards increasingly 'better' collective understandings. And that is probably as much as one can hope for in the realm of human affairs.

III. INTERNAL AND EXTERNAL PERSPECTIVES IN COMPARATIVE LAW

Having hopefully established that law as collective commitments can only be properly apprehended from an internal perspective, which included dismissing both the heterogeneity and subjectivity objections, we now examine the extent to which if at all the same conclusion can be applied to comparative law. That further step requires us to account, in particular, for the fact that the party engaging in the reconstruction exercise is now an outsider, someone already acquainted with another legal system. This involves addressing what I will call the 'home bias objection'[114] – a central issue in the cognitivism/constructivism debate recounted earlier, and the object of a voluminous literature ever since.[115] Heidegger referred to it as "thrownness," Gadamer, as "prejudices," Popper, as "framework theory."[116] More recent designations include "situatedness," "entrapment," "embeddedness."[117] While the home bias objection, however labelled, clearly bears on all disciplines involving a cross-cultural dimension, it is particularly significant for comparative law, which altogether fuels on otherness.[118]

---

[114] The plethora of alternative labels in circulation includes "cultural blinkers" (BERNHARD GROβFELD, THE STRENGTH AND WEAKNESS OF COMPARATIVE LAW 38 (Tony Weir trans., 1990)), the "perspective problem" (Günter Frankenberg, Critical Comparisons: Re-thinking Comparative Law, 26 HARV. INT'L. L. J. 411 (1985)), the "unconscious spell" (SIMMONDS, *supra* note 7, at 414), and the "ethnocentric gaze" (Brenda Cossman, Turning the Gaze Back on Itself: Comparative Law, Feminist Legal Studies, and the Postcolonial Project, UTAH L. REV. 525, 526 (1997)).

[115] See generally: Frankenberg, *supra* note 114; V. Grosswald Curran, Cultural Immersion, Difference and Categories in U.S. Comparative Law, 46 AM. J. COMP. L. 43 (1998); Nora Demleitner, Challenge, Opportunity and Risk: An Era of Change in Comparative Law, 46 AM. J. COMP. L. 647 (1998) (esp. her description of the "critical Utah group"); Peters & Schwenke, *supra* note 96, at 811–12 (on US and German scholarship); Legrand, *supra* note 67, at 444ff.

[116] MARTIN HEIDEGGER, BEING AND TIME 417 (John Macquarrie & Edward Robinson trans., 1962) (*Geworfenheit*); HANS GEORGE GADAMER, TRUTH AND METHOD 295 (Joel Weinsheimer & Donald G. Marshall trans., 2004) (*Vorurteile*); KARL POPPER, THE MYTH OF THE FRAMEWORK: IN DEFENCE OF SCIENCE AND RATIONALITY (1994).

[117] Respectively: MACINTYRE, *supra* note 16, at x, 197; DWORKIN, *supra* note 42, at 422–23; STANLEY FISH, DOING WHAT COMES NATURALLY 141 (1989).

[118] Should it entail "nothing else but *total incomparability*," as some have suggested, it would indeed call "into question the very essence of comparative legal scholarship." Peters & Schwenke, *supra* note 96, at 820.

This last Part accordingly examines the extent to which an internal perspective seems to be at play in extant comparative law scholarship while being perhaps impaired by home bias. We begin by outlining some features of that scholarship that indeed motion to an internal perspective, and thereafter focus on the home bias objection as such. While that objection does deserve to be taken seriously, I conclude, it is not fatal to an internal understanding of foreign law. Although the outsider's engagement with the law differs in process and contribution from that of the local actors, it might nonetheless qualify as 'internal.' Only, the outsider necessarily participates in several legal games at once, namely, the reconstruction of the local law, that of their home law, and that of comparative law as such.

i. *The Outsider's Internal Perspective*

While comparative law scholarship has, as we saw, been derided for amounting to little more than rule hoarding,[119] there is little reason to think that such hoarding has been pursued for its own sake rather than as just a necessary first step to an internal reconstruction of legal systems. Indeed, very few if any comparative law projects in fact stop at that preliminary stage. The classic two- or three-jurisdiction study on a given issue commonly aims to assist in case litigation and hence goes the extra step of embodying the rules into arguments proper, thus providing the reader with a somewhat fuller account of the treatment of the issue in each jurisdiction.[120] The same can be said of many broader subject matter studies, which aim to encompass entire legal fields (e.g. comparative contract law, comparative constitutional law, etc.).[121] The legal family literature likewise pays attention to arguments and reasoning styles, as these recur among the criteria there used for classifying legal systems.[122] Even the common core projects to some extent remain attuned to the internal standpoint, moreover. While such projects as mentioned are ostensibly geared to surveying rules rather than systems,[123] they too evince at least an admission that either is meaningless without the other, for the inventories provided are typically supplemented with short explanations as to how the various rules from given systems fit together and in the larger context of their respective systems.[124] Although these explanations

---

[119] See *supra*, Prologue.
[120] E.g. Adrian Popovici, Le sort des honoraires extrajudiciaires 62 *Revue du Barreau* 53 (2002).
[121] E.g. Barry Nicholas, *The French Law of Contract* (2nd ed. 1992); René David & David Pugsley, *Les Contrats en droit anglais* (1985).
[122] E.g. Konrad Zweigert & Hein Kötz, *An Introduction to Comparative Law* (Tony Weir trans., 3rd ed. 1998); H. Patrick Glenn, *Legal Traditions of the World* (2004); René David & John E.C. Brierley, *Major Legal Systems in the World Today: An Introduction to the Comparative Study of Law* (3rd ed. 1985).
[123] See *supra* text following note 42, Chapter 2.
[124] E.g. *The Enforceability of Promises in European Contract Law* (James Gordley ed., 2001).

admittedly remain quite superficial, their mere presence arguably testifies to their authors being at least sensitive to the importance of the internal perspective.

Then again, if the internal perspective entails, as indicated, first-hand involvement in the shaping of the local law, the real test lies with the front line: have comparative lawyers' writings in fact permeated the local legal debate or have they remained peripheral, perhaps even altogether irrelevant to it?[125] On this score too, however, comparative lawyers fare quite well, for it seems clear that they have had at least some impact on the form and substance of domestic legal systems.[126] Certainly in constitutional matters, high-level courts in various jurisdictions routinely rely on comparative lawyers' reports as to what is being done elsewhere.[127] And domestic judges have at times remarked on outsiders' accounts of their law being particularly "illuminating."[128] It seems quite clear, then, comparative lawyers have to some extent directly contributed to the internal transformation of the law in their target jurisdictions.

At the same time, it cannot be denied that some comparative endeavours, notably among the legal transplants and legal origins projects, have been resounding failures.[129] Here again, however, the analysis given of the reasons for such failures is instructive as to the pull exerted by the internal perspective on comparative lawyers. For, the primary reason identified for the failure of legal transplants has to do with the treatment of the transplanted rules at the hands of the local actors in the recipient systems. That is to say that, however competent, careful and well-intentioned donor actors might be individually, a transplant's success or failure would ultimately lie with the (legal) cultural fit, or lack thereof, between the donor and recipient systems.[130] In a similar vein, many legal origins projects have been criticized for deploying evaluative criteria that are external to the legal systems under consideration.[131] The relative inefficiency of any given legal system can legitimately be considered

---

[125] "a final and essential test must be passed: are the comparatist's descriptions and discursive reproductions more or less recognizable to those who operate within the studied system?" Lasser, *supra* note 42, at 223–24. See likewise: L.-J. CONSTANTINESCO, TRAITÉ DE DROIT COMPARÉ, VOL. II— LA MÉTHODE COMPARATIVE 155 (1974); GEOFFREY SAMUEL, AN INTRODUCTION TO COMPARATIVE LAW THEORY AND METHOD 17 (2014).

[126] MARTIN SHAPIRO, COURTS: A COMPARATIVE AND POLITICAL ANALYSIS (1981).

[127] DIETER GRIMM, CONSTITUTIONALISM: PAST, PRESENT AND FUTURE (2016); Aharon Barak, Response to The Judge as Comparatist: Comparison in Public Law 80 TULANE LAW REVIEW 195 (2005).

[128] *Chartbrook Ltd. v. Persimmon Homes Ltd. et al.*, [2009] UKHL at para. 39 (House of Lords, *per* Lord Hoffmann, citing Catherine Valcke, On Comparing French and English Contract Law: Insights from Social Contract Theory, IV JOURNAL OF COMPARATIVE LAW 69).

[129] Yves DEZALAY & BRYANT GARTH, THE INTERNATIONALIZATION OF PALACE WARS: LAWYERS, ECONOMISTS, AND THE CONTEST TO TRANSFORM LATIN AMERICAN STATES (2002); William Twining, Social Science and Diffusion of Law 32 JOURNAL OF LAW AND SOCIETY 203 (2005); JEDIDIAH J. KRONCKE, THE FUTILITY OF LAW AND DEVELOPMENT (2016).

[130] See KRONCKE, *ibid.*

[131] See generally: THE SHIFTING MEANING OF LEGAL CERTAINTY IN COMPARATIVE AND TRANSNATIONAL LAW (Mark Fenwick *et al.* eds., 2017).

a 'defect' of that system, the critique goes, only where efficiency in fact appears among its internally determined collective commitments.[132] (Such projects having stirred far greater interest among economists than comparative lawyers[133] arguably further attests to the importance that the latter, in contrast with the former, attach to the internal standpoint.) With respect to both these kinds of projects, then, failure would be blamed on a lack of awareness of the local legal culture and/or more general downplaying of the impact of culture on legal practice. As in both cases the finger ultimately points to some kind of home bias objection, I will now analyze that objection in more detail.

ii. *The Outsider's Home Bias*

The home bias objection centres on the fact that participating in a game, any game, requires knowledge of the rules, whereas many rules of the legal game are not explicit and as such might be beyond the reach of outsiders. The formal rules of course are somewhat easily accessible, but the larger 'context of meaning' might not be. That is to say, the formal rules are embedded in an unarticulated web of cultural assumptions, "ideas, attitudes, opinions and expectations with regard to the legal system"[134] – "shared social meanings," "styles of thought," "mental softwares," "conceptual molds," "background knowledge," "habits of thought," "cryptotypes," "ideolects," "primary epistemologies"[135] – none of which are articulated for the simple

---

[132] See the debate surrounding the World Bank's *Doing Business* reports: Catherine Valcke, The French Response to the World's Bank 'Doing Business' Response, 60 UNIVERSITY OF TORONTO LAW JOURNAL 197 (2010).

[133] Ralf Michaels, Comparative Law by Numbers? Legal Origins Thesis, Doing Business Reports, and the Silence of Traditional Comparative Law, 57 AM. J. COMP. L. 765, 786 (2009).

[134] Lawrence M. Friedman, The Place of Legal Culture in the Sociology of Law, *in* LAW AND SOCIOLOGY: CURRENT LEGAL ISSUES (Michael Freedman ed., 2006). See also: MICHAEL OAKESHOTT, EXPERIENCE AND ITS MODES (1933); James Boyd White, Legal Knowledge, 115 HARV. L. REV. 1396 (2002); Christopher McCrudden, What Does It Mean to Compare, and What Should It Mean? in COMPARING COMPARATIVE LAW 61, 77ff (Samantha Besson *et al.* eds., 2017); DWORKIN, *supra* note 42, at 63 ("[Participants need] to share a vocabulary, they must understand the world in sufficiently similar ways and have interests and convictions sufficiently similar to recognize the sense in each other's claims, to treat them *as* claims rather than just noises."); WEINRIB, *supra* note 105, at 13 ("Shared understandings on such basic matters [the institutional and conceptual features that law presupposes] are indispensable to effective participation in juristic activity. Indeed, to participate in that activity is to be animated by those understandings.").

[135] Respectively: WEINRIB, *supra* note 105, at 13; Ewald, *supra* note 47, at 1948, 2140; GEERT HOFSTEDE ET AL., CULTURES AND ORGANIZATIONS: SOFTWARE AND THE MIND (2nd ed. 1997); Mireille Delmas-Marty, Le pluralisme ordonné et les interactions entre ensembles juridiques, 14 RECUEIL DALLOZ 937, 952 (2006); JOHN R. SEARLE, THE CONSTRUCTION OF SOCIAL REALITY (1995); Jennifer Nedelsky, Receptivity and Judgment, 4 ETHICS & GLOBAL POLITICS 231, 235 (2011); Rodolfo Sacco, Legal Formants: A Dynamic Approach to Comparative Law (Installment II of II), 39 AM. J. COMP. L. 343 (1991); Lasser, *supra* note 42, at 222 (referring to literary theorist Mikhail Bakhtin); Jaakko Husa, Kaleidoscopic Cultural Views and Legal Theory: Dethroning the Objectivity?, *in* OBJECTIVITY IN LAW AND LEGAL REASONING, *supra* note 2, at 197.

reason that, at least on a local level, they need not be. These unwritten rules being 'in the background,' a part of the 'cultural unconscious'[136] or *mentalité*,[137] they have come to the local actors naturally, merely "as a function of belonging to the community."[138] The local actors consequently typically go about their legal game without thinking much about them, just taking them for granted, even possibly unable to describe them if asked.

The problem is that the outsider by definition is not privy to those background rules. Nor is she able to decipher them through deduction and logic, as they are cultural in nature, and hence impermeable to such heuristics. Yet recourse to some such rules as we saw is essential to understanding the local formal rules (as it is of any text).[139] After all, therein lies the requisite *Vorverständnis*, without which no *Verständnis* proper can even begin to unfold.[140] The worry accordingly is that the outsider, being barred from the local background rules of understanding, will import her own, those at play in her home community, thus landing a distorted understanding of the local law.[141] This understanding will be 'distorted' in that it will be 'culturally subjective,' which form of subjectivity is both qualitatively different from, and far more problematic than, the three forms examined above. Or so goes the objection.

Not surprisingly, most legal comparatists seem simply unaware of the issue or else dismiss it as unproblematic. Those who dismiss it do so by denying one or several of the objection's three crucial segments, namely, (1) acquaintance with a legal system's background rules of understanding is essential for understanding its formal legal rules; (2) background rules of understanding differ across legal systems; and (3) being cultural in nature, these rules cannot be internalized through conscious reflection. As none of these three segments can be denied under law as

---

[136] Pierre Legrand, Sur l'analyse différentielle des juriscultures, 51 *R. I. D. C.* 1053, 1056 (1999).

[137] On the wide use of that term in the comparative law literature, see: Mathias Reimann, The Progress and Failure of Comparative Law in the Second Half of the Twentieth Century, 50 AM. J. COMP. L. 671, 678, note 40 (2002).

[138] Pierre Legrand, European Legal Systems Are Not Converging, 45 INT'L. & COMP. L. Q., 52, 56 (1996) (here clearly motioning to Savigny's *Volksgeist* and Herder's *Zeitgeist*). Likewise: PIERRE LEGRAND, FRAGMENTS ON LAW-AS-CULTURE 27 (1999) ("the framework of intangibles within which an interpretive community operates, which has normative force for this community ... and which, over the *longue durée*, determines the identity of a community as community"); HOFSTEDE, *supra* note 135 ("the collective programming of the mind which distinguishes the members of one group or category of people from another"). For a valuable empirical study, see: Vito Breda, The Objectivity of Judicial Decisions: A Comparative Analysis of Nine Jurisdictions, *in* STUDIES IN POLITICS, SECURITY AND SOCIETY (Stanislaw Sulowski ed., forthcoming).

[139] *Supra* note 62, and accompanying text.

[140] GADAMER, *supra* note 116, discussed inter alia in JOHN BELL, FRENCH LEGAL CULTURES 8 (2001); Whitman, *supra* note 1; Glanert, *supra* note 1.

[141] Frankenberg (*supra* note 114) refers to this phenomenon as "cognitive control." Likewise in history: "the limitations of the intellectual framework which the historian derives from his particular cultural milieu would be liable to render his interpretations of previous ages inherently problematic"; Gardiner, *supra* note 1, at 10.

collective commitment, however, the objection as a whole must indeed be contended with here.

The remainder of this subsection is devoted to examining each segment in turn, and confirming that none of them can be simply dismissed under comparative law as comparative collective commitments. In the following subsection I explain how I nonetheless consider that the home bias objection, while serious, is ultimately not fatal to the comparative enterprise as here envisioned.

(1) 'Acquaintance with Background Rules Is Required for Understanding Formal Rules'

Consistently with the cognitivist slant of both our natural law and positivist ideal-types (law being 'out there,' a set of moral or material 'facts,' objectively discoverable and analyzable),[142] some comparatists seem to endorse the "insulation thesis,"[143] according to which legal rules are largely self-explanatory, i.e. meaningful per se, independently of context. Recall that natural lawyers and positivists alike are portrayed above as endorsing the dichotomy between 'easy' and 'hard' cases, diverging only as to which of these qualitatively different judicial activities should qualify as 'legal proper.'[144] Comparatists aligning with either of these ideal-types hence consider that interpretation is called for only in 'hard cases,' as the law governing 'easy cases' somehow comes readily interpreted. That is to say that the rules in question would boast some kind of fixed meaning fully determinative of their application in new settings. If so, it should be possible to sever such rules from their respective contexts, perhaps even transfer them to another, with no or little loss/change of meaning.[145]

That view however is inconsistent with the conception adopted here, according to which law is not black letter rules so much as arguments over the meaning of such rules. As indicated, no hard line in fact can be drawn here between 'easy' and 'hard' cases, seeing that meaning always is externally constructed, through interpretation

---

[142] See *supra*, Part II, section i.
[143] William Ewald, Comparative Jurisprudence II: The Logic of Legal Transplant, 43 Am. J. Comp. L. 489, 506 (1995).
[144] See *supra*, note 130 and accompanying text.
[145] In this vein, Alan Watson famously asserted that "[a] law student of the age of Justinian, confronted with a modern civil code ... would not be greatly astonished by the substance of the law ... Differences ... there certainly are, but scarcely what might be termed major developments." Alan Watson, The Making of the Civil Law 179–80 (1981). See also: Alan Watson, Legal Transplants and European Private Law, Electronic J. Comp. L. (2000) (www.ejcl.org/44/art44-2.html). At the same time, Watson's own work on legal transplants (Alan Watson, Legal Transplants: An Approach to Comparative Law (2nd ed. 1993)) clearly shows the transformative effect of context on transplanted rules. For a suggestion that Watson's writings on this point have indeed been misinterpreted, see: Ewald, *supra* note 143. Yet Ewald later rejects Watson's "textualist" approach to comparative law as "untenable": William Ewald, The Jurisprudential Approach to Comparative Law: A Field Guide to Rats 46 Am. J. Comp. L. 701, 701–707 (1998).

and the interpreter actively engaging with the object of interpretation.[146] As the interpreter hence plays a central role in the determination of meaning, meaning is not static but rather variable across interpreters.[147] However, unlike in private conversation, where the interpreter is an individual person, the interpreter in legal interpretation is an entire community, tied together through a common set of background rules of interpretation. In effect, then, legal meaning emerges from the text coming into contact with, or being processed through, the relevant set of background rules. (This explains how it is that even identically-worded formal rules can generate different implications in practice.[148])

There seems to be little choice, therefore, about our having to accept the first segment of the home bias objection: law as collective commitment clearly presupposes that formal rules are meaningless in abstraction from the relevant set of background rules of interpretation, with the result that acquaintance with the latter is essential for understanding the former.

(2) 'Background Rules Differ Across Legal Systems'

This second segment of the home bias objection can be denied in two ways, one more radical than the other. Radical denial is exemplified by hardcore universalists who would insist that, even though meaning might require interpretation, and interpretation might vary across interpretive communities, the interpretive exercise at issue here ultimately involves just one such community, namely, the community of world citizens.[149] If world law can be conceptualized (as per our natural law ideal-type) as forming just one legal system, all humans indeed are privy to the set of background rules required for interpreting that system. The very idea of an 'outsider' in fact becomes nonsensical here: all humans are now 'insiders' proper, fully engaged in the one and only legal game there is – the universal game of world law, the essential rules of which naturally come to them with humanness. That position however is clearly ruled out by the discussion of Chapter 2, for it effectively amounts to denying that law can be plural, whereas such plurality is essential for meaningful comparison: there simply cannot be meaningful comparative law where law is conceptualized as forming just one system.

Most of the comparatists who deny the second segment accordingly do so only partially. That is, they recognize that the world comprises more than one legal system, and that some (perhaps even most) of these systems' background rules might differ. Only, they deny that *all* do. For these 'partial deniers,' there is a core set of these rules

---

[146] See *supra* paragraph following note 141 in Chapter 1, Part II, section iii.
[147] See *supra* Part II, section iii.
[148] See *supra* text accompanying notes 57–61.
[149] See *supra* Chapter 2, Part II.

(e.g. basic logic and rationality, the Kantian categories of causality, time and space, such moral precepts as life preservation and cruelty avoidance, perhaps some kind of human empathy) that is shared across interpretive communities.[150] Without such universal core, they note, the home bias objector would be unable even to express her objection in the first place, as she would lack the requisite disengaged stance from which to do so. She would find herself in the same intractable position as radical moral relativists, who object to the possibility of transcending the very relativity that they thereby purport to transcend, thus simultaneously asserting and defeating their own objection.[151] The partial deniers avoid this incoherence by distinguishing two levels of background rules: a core set, common to all humans, and from which it is possible to observe the many local sets, that differ from one another.[152] Relativity hence *can* be observed, they maintain, but only from such plane as transcends it.

Law as collective commitment follows the partial deniers on this point. Recall that that account makes it possible to distinguish the core conception of law as collective commitment as such (Chapter 1) from the wide variety of legal systems potentially materializing under that conception (Chapter 2).[153] Like the partial deniers, then, the proponents of law as collective commitments are able to deflect the incoherence charges weighing against radical relativists: from the disengaged, abstract position described in Chapter 1, they can coherently assert that the multiple systems unfastened under Chapter 2 can only be properly understood from the engaged, concrete position of the actors in each system.[154] (This in any event is how we have been proceeding so far.)

---

[150] E.g. the proponents of "transnational legal science," *supra* notes 31–32; R. B. SCHLESINGER ET AL., COMPARATIVE LAW: CASES-TEXT-MATERIALS 34–35 (5th ed. 1988) ("there exists a common core of legal concepts and precepts shared by some, or even by a multitude, of the world's legal systems."). For authors claiming to articulate such core concepts, see: J. KOHLER, EINLEITUNG IN DIE VERGLEICHENDE RECHTSWISSENSCHAFT (1885), reported in Peters & Schwenke, *supra* note 96, at 804 ("immanent aspiration to development," "higher reasonableness"); DWORKIN, *supra* note 42 (universal moral standards determining 'best' legal interpretations); Max Scheler, discussed in Whitman, *supra* note 1, at 339 ("normative empathic identification with the other"); Max Weber, paraphrased in *ibid.* at 324 ("[w]e can understand *that* another person should be rationally pursuing some end, even if we cannot always understand *why*").

[151] Peters & Schwenke, *supra* note 96, at 821. See generally: BERNARD WILLIAMS, MORALITY: AN INTRODUCTION TO ETHICS 20–25 (1972); JEAN-PIERRE DUPUY, ORDRES ET DÉSORDRES. ENQUÊTE SUR UN NOUVEAU PARADIGME 226 (1982) (explaining that, even in Hofstader's example of the 'self-modifying' chess game, the meta-rule that the players' moves determine the rules of the game must itself be posited a priori).

[152] Despite being often cited in support of radical relativism, Thomas Kuhn believed that paradigm differences could in principle be mediated: THOMAS S. KUHN, THE STRUCTURE OF SCIENTIFIC REVOLUTIONS 198–204 (3rd ed. 1996), cited in Peters & Schwenke, *supra* note 96, at 817. Such mediation of course is not available to postmodernists, who deny even the possibility of meta-narratives (e.g. JEAN-FRANÇOIS LYOTARD, LA CONDITION POSTMODERNE: RAPPORT SUR LE SAVOIR (1979)).

[153] See *supra* Chapter 1, Part I, section vi as well as Chapter 2, Part IV.

[154] Compare Baudouin Dupret (The Concept of Law: A Wittgensteinian Approach with some Ethnomethodological Specifications, *in* CONCEPTS OF LAW: COMPARATIVE, JURISPRUDENTIAL, AND SOCIAL SCIENCE PERSPECTIVES (Sean Patrick Donlan & Lukas Heckendorn eds., 2013) ("Law is whatever

But the partial denial option ultimately does little to rid us of the home bias problem, for that problem continues to afflict whichever background rules are *not* included in the core. Indeed, our disengaged conception of law as collective commitment, as such, does little to help us uncover the various sets of (cultural, historical) background rules that we need in order to actually engage in each system. At least this is so if the remaining, third segment holds up. In order to definitively dispose of the home bias objection, then, those who partially deny the second segment need also to deny the third.

(3) 'Background Rules Cannot Be Internalized Through Conscious Reflection'

Of the three segments, this one is perhaps the most widely denied by comparative lawyers. This is hardly surprising given that this segment might effectively entail that no amount of efforts or good intentions on their part can get them through the door of a foreign legal system.[155] It of course is still open to them to show awareness of the issue ("heightened reflexivity,"[156] "differencing",[157] or what Gadamer called "historically-effected consciousness"[158]) and resist *assuming* that the background rules they will encounter in foreign systems will be the same as their native ones.[159] They could even adopt the stronger assumption that these rules will in fact *be different*.[160] But that is still a far cry from getting them *into* the foreign legal game. The door to any form of internal investigation of foreign law just seems destined to stay shut. The comparative lawyers who recognize that background rules may be both essential for understanding formal rules (first segment) and at least partially different from

---

local actors say is law")) and BRIAN TAMANAHA (*A GENERAL JURISPRUDENCE OF LAW AND SOCIETY* 193 (2001) ("What law is and what law does cannot be captured in any single concept … Law is whatever we attach the label law to.")) with JULIUS STONE (*LEGAL SYSTEM AND LAWYERS' REASONINGS* 166–67 (1964)) ("Law is a limit-concept, a 'category' in the sense which Kant showed to be undefinable, an independent self-contained body of knowledge, of which any definition would have to be 'meta-juristic'") and MACINTYRE, *supra* note 16, at 79 ("[philosophers of science are now largely agreed that w]hat each observer takes himself or herself to perceive is identified and has to be identified by theory-laden concepts. Perceivers without concepts, as Kant almost said, are blind.").

[155] GADAMER, *supra* note 116, at 295: "The prejudices and fore-meanings that occupy the interpreter's consciousness are not at his free disposal." And at 398: "To try to escape from one's own concepts in interpretation is not only impossible but manifestly absurd."

[156] Peters & Schwenke, *supra* note 96, at 829.

[157] GÜNTER FRANKENBERG, *COMPARATIVE LAW AS CRITIQUE* 72–76 (2016).

[158] GADAMER, *supra* note 116, at 301.

[159] E.g. HYLAND, *supra* note 42, at 112. See generally: Mary Ann Glendon, Comparative Law as Shock Treatment: A Tribute to Jacob W. F. Sundberg, *in Särtryck* UR: *FESTSKRIFT TILL JACOB W. F. SUNDBERG* 69 (Erik Nerep & Wiweka Warnling-Nerep eds., 1993); Cossman, *supra* note 114, at 537; Frankenberg, *supra* note 114.

[160] See Pierre Legrand's suggested *"praesumptio dissimilitudinis"* (Pierre Legrand, The Return of the Repressed: Moving Comparative Legal Studies Beyond Pleasure, 75 *TUL. L. REV.* 1033, 1048–49 (2001)).

system to system (second segment) hence typically end up diffusing the home bias objection by insisting that all background rules, foreign or otherwise, can ultimately be apprehended through conscious reflection (third segment).

As with the second segment, it is here worth distinguishing between categorical and more hesitant such reactions. The categorical deniers claim that any investigator is potentially able to access any local set of background rules merely by virtue of their being human, as all humans are naturally endowed with the core set. That is to say, their being even just minimally rational, empathetic, concerned to preserve life, etc., automatically translates into the capacity to access different cultures – as per the famous Roman phrase "nothing human can be alien to me."[161] The core set would thus supply the requisite '*tertium comparationis*,' or neutral point of entry into otherwise incommensurable legal cultures.[162] And any objectivity-minded investigator accordingly would be able to *consciously decide* to check their home bias at the door of the foreign system so as to make themselves fully receptive to the local background rules.[163] Zweigert and Kötz, for example, exhort legal comparatists to just "eradicate the preconceptions of [their] native legal system[s] ... [as o]ne must never *allow* one's vision to be clouded by the concepts of one's own national system."[164] Other scholars have likewise pointed to so-called 'mixed' legal systems as instances of legal communities in which such deliberate mindset switches would be a common occurrence.[165] Perhaps surprisingly, the same manner of speech is found in some post-modernist writings, wherein comparatists are commonly called upon to launch the likes of the "breaking down of the conceptual repression."[166]

In contrast, the more hesitant deniers consider that, while cultural norms cannot be grabbed or dropped at will, they can be internalized *over time*, in more or less the

---

[161] From his play *Heauton Timorumenos*, https://en.wikipedia.org/wiki/Terence.

[162] See *infra* Chapter 5, Part I, section i. Historians and philosophers have respectively referred to roughly the same notion as "Archimedian historical consciousness" (RICKMAN, *supra* note 9) and "the unity of the human mind" (GIORGIO DEL VECCHIO, MAN AND NATURE: SELECTED ESSAYS 31–33 (Ralph A. Newman ed., A. H. Campbell trans., 1969)).

[163] The notion of 'mindfulness' put forward by certain neuro-scientists seems to convey roughly the same idea, as it involves people "intentionally suspend[ing] their usual frame of reference ... for a while, and simply watch[ing] their own minds." JON KABAT-ZINN, COMING TO OUR SENSES: HEALING OURSELVES AND THE WORLD THROUGH MINDFULNESS 147 (2005), quoted in Nedelsky, *supra* note 135, at 237.

[164] ZWEIGERT & KÖTZ, *supra* note 122, at 35 (emphasis added). See likewise: Jan M. Smits, Legal Culture as Mental Software, or: How to Overcome National Legal Culture?, *in* PRIVATE LAW AND THE CULTURES OF EUROPE 133, 134–35 (Thomas Wilhelmsson *et al.* eds., 2007) (arguing that, culture being "learned," it can be taken on or dropped at will). Smits's examples however suggest that he (confusingly) equates choosing one's legal culture with choosing to be governed by a given law or jurisdiction.

[165] Nikolas Roos, NICE Dreams and Realities of European Private Law, *in* EPISTEMOLOGY AND METHODOLOGY OF COMPARATIVE LAW, *supra* note 1, at 197, 212; J. M. Smits, *The Making of European Private Law: towards a 'Ius Comme Europeanum' as a Mixed Legal System* chaps. 6–8 (2002).

[166] Günter Frankenberg, Stranger than Paradise: Identity & Politics in Comparative Law, UTAH L. REV. 259, 270 (1997).

same way that the local actors do.[167] Culture, including legal culture, is not innate
and fixed, they say, but rather acquired and in constant flux, and its bounds are fuzzy
and porous, with the result that individuals can move in and out of cultural groups
as well as cumulate multiple group memberships.[168] One indeed is not born a lawyer
but rather educated as one, which educational opportunity presumably is open to
outsiders and insiders alike. Thus, whereas the outside investigator might not be
able to simply decide to substitute the foreign cultural norms for her own, she could
decide to acquire an education in the foreign legal culture, to undergo the same
'acculturation process'[169] as did the local actors.

Law as collective commitment rules out the first, categorical position, but allows
for the hesitant one, with some qualifications. The categorical position is ruled out
because, again, it ultimately clashes with the plurality requirement articulated in
Chapter 2. Recall that, under the autopoietic model there endorsed, legal systems
are plural insofar as they emerge from distinct local communities processing their
law through their peculiar matrix, which peculiarity does have to do with these
matrixes reflecting the local culture, including the local background rules of understanding.[170] Much like language games, then, each system there constitutes a distinct legal game only insofar as it is essentially (though not exclusively) determined
by the background rules peculiar to it. The problem is, that essential peculiarity
disappears from the moment that the various sets of background rules become
bridgeable through the common set. For then, the latter effectively subsumes the
former, which accordingly differ among themselves only superficially, at any rate
insufficiently deeply to sustain the plurality requirement of Chapter 2.

In sum, while law as collective commitment allows for the possibility that the
common background rules might in some way open the door to understanding the
local ones, it also needs the common and local rules to be *dis*connected from each
other in a non-insignificant way. It needs, in other words, local background rules,
while perhaps prolonging or building on universal intellectual frameworks, to also
include a strictly local dimension, not determined by or analyzable in terms of such
frameworks.[171] For present purposes, then, the 'culturalness' of the local background

---

[167] Peters & Schwenke, *supra* note 96, at 816; Whitman, *supra* note 1, at 325, 340; Daniel Jutras, Énoncer l'indicible: le droit entre langues et traditions, 52 R.I.D.C. 781, esp. 786, 792–793 (2000); GEERT HOFSTEDE, CULTURE'S CONSEQUENCES 5 (1980).

[168] Peters & Schwenke, *supra* note 96, at 814.

[169] Lasser, *supra* note 42, at 223. And in MITCHEL DE S.-O.-L'E LASSER, *JUDICIAL DELIBERATIONS: A COMPARATIVE ANALYSIS OF JUDICIAL TRANSPARENCY AND LEGITIMACY* 11 (2004): "There can be no question, at least in the context of non-radically different legal cultures, that the comparatist can attain sufficient fluency to get a very good sense of the conceptual parameters and formal structures within which and through which a foreign jurist tends to conceptualize, articulate, debate, and resolve legal problems."

[170] See *supra* Chapter 2, Part III, esp. text following note 84.

[171] "[W]e should not forget the sheer difficulties of translating and understanding other cultures—what Clifford Geertz famously called the difficulty of grasping 'local knowledge'." David Nelken, Signaling

rules must be such that these rules cannot, against the categorical deniers' claim, be endorsed or dropped at will.[172]

But what might stand in the way of the outsider gradually gaining fluency in the local rules through education, in the incremental way suggested by the hesitant deniers? A priori nothing, and it indeed is not uncommon for, say, a French native to come to England to study English law alongside English natives. Such French native admittedly might find it more difficult than her English classmates, given that, in addition to having to learn the rules of English law, she needs to catch up on English cultural norms (let alone the English language), which her classmates need not worry about.[173] The difficulty may perhaps be further compounded, moreover, where she already has a background in French law, as such background might have served to crystallize her French linguistic and cultural norms into an altogether different approach to law and legal reasoning. In such cases, after all, the French native would be a 'legal' as well as 'cultural' outsider. But it admittedly does not follow from the bar being high, even very high, that it cannot ultimately be crossed.

Even so, it remains to be seen whether the French and English natives would end up in exactly the same place. For, while legal culture undeniably is porous and open to new entrants, it may not be so easily shed.[174] The human brain is thus wired that it lets new knowledge in without for that matter evacuating the old one: whereas we at times 'forget' things, we do not 'stop knowing' them, even such things as we no longer need or are interested in. So the French jurist learning about the English legal system does not *substitute* the English background rules of understanding for the French ones, already installed in her brain. Rather, the English cultural norms slowly come to be, if not woven into, at least *superimposed upon* the French, in just the same way that the English language would be added to, but would not supplant, her mother tongue: "[o]ne comes to the new (*i.e.* the other) without having freed oneself from the old (*i.e.* the self)."[175] Her understanding of the English legal system – formal and informal rules alike – hence cannot but be somewhat coloured by her French cultural/legal background: it will always be a French jurist's rather than an

---

Conformity: Changing Norms in Japan and China, 27 MICH. J. OF INT'L L. 1, 14 (2006). See also: WEINRIB, *supra* note 105, at 104 ("[M]eaningful acts are, therefore, historically variable and relative to societal contexts and understanding. For example, in order to appropriate, a person will perform the act that signifies appropriation in that person's society: in one society the act may be the shoe's stepping, in another the hand's seizure or the laying on of a spear."); Rodolfo Sacco, Legal Formants: A Dynamic Approach to Comparative Law (Installment I of II), 39 AM. J. COMP. L. 1, 16 (1991) ("An abstract idea finds concrete expression in a given legal language much as, in biology, a genotype or distinctive set of genes is expressed in the phenotype or outward form of a plant or animal. The jurist of an individual country studies the phenotype.").

[172] Simmonds writes likewise: "Any understanding of human society that we have available to us may be dependent on our education into practices and structures of meaning that are inhabited before they are reflected on, and the requirements of which are independent of the choices of any individual." SIMMONDS, *supra* note 7, at 32–33.

[173] Bell, *supra* note 39, at 168–69.

[174] Sacco, *supra* note 135, at 387.

[175] Pierre Legrand, Au lieu de soi, in COMPARER LES DROITS 20 (Pierre Legrand ed., 2009) (my translation).

English lawyer's understanding of English law. "Understanding there will be," in short, "but a *different* understanding it will *have* to be."[176]

To that extent, the third segment of the home bias objection, like the first two, and hence the objection as a whole, must here be contended with.

iii. *The Outsider's Internal/External Process*

Assuming, then, that an outsider's understanding of the law will necessarily differ from that of the local actors, we now explore whether and to what extent such different understanding might nonetheless qualify as 'internal' in the sense used so far. This we do through a closer look at the situation of our French jurist studying English law.

Her coming to English law from the outside indeed will cause her educational experience to differ significantly from that of her English classmates. For one, it will be preceded by a 'set up' stage that will involve settling a number of important questions.[177] The most important of these is likely to be: why English law? Why pick English law over any other possible foreign legal system? Would another civil law system not be easier for her? Or, to the extent that she is in fact looking to widen her juridical horizons, would something further afield (say, aboriginal or Shariah law) not be a better choice? Another set of questions relate to method: assuming she does choose to study English law, what is the best way to go about it? Is law school so clearly preferable to, say, some form of collaboration with an English lawyer? Is learning English and moving to England even necessary, or can she not draw all the English law she needs from French secondary sources? Whereas none of these questions ever really arise for the English students, they are immediate and prominent for the French jurist. For, those are questions of a kind that can only be pondered (as they are in this book) from an external standpoint, from the position of someone *not yet* involved in the foreign legal system.[178]

---

[176] Legrand, *supra* note 138, at 78. (Emphasis in original.) Legrand here echoes Wittgenstein, who reportedly considered (THOMAS NAGEL, THE VIEW FROM NOWHERE 20 (1986)) that "extending the idea of what we immediately feel into other people's bodies will only give us an idea of having feelings in their bodies—it will not give us an idea of how *they* feel." See likewise: Bell, *supra* note 39, at 171 ("this will not be necessarily unfaithful to the original, it will simply be different."); Glanert, *supra* note 1, at 69 ("Since the intelligibility of the law can only happen through schemes that interpreters impose upon it *a priori*, a French comparatist's method, then, will differ from a German comparatist's, such that each comparison will, in the end, generate a local version of English law which simply cannot reasonably pretend to being 'English law understanding'"; Winch, *supra* note 10, at 48 ("The medieval knight did not have to use [historiographical] methods in order to view his lady in terms of the notions of courtly love: he just thought of her in those terms. Historical research may enable me to achieve some understanding of what was involved in this way of thinking, but that will not make it open to me to think of *my* lady in those terms ... And naturally, it is even more impossible for me to think of *his* lady as he did.").

[177] Ewald, *supra* note 47, at 1945ff.

[178] Lasser, *supra* note 42, at 205–206 (the method for investigating law on the inside necessarily is itself devised from the outside); Ewald, *supra* note 145, at 705 ("What is law? How can we study the legal thinking of a foreign culture? Should we study rules, or norms, or economic relations, or ideas,

But there is more. Insofar as the French jurist's overall objective is expressly comparative, her involvement with the English law will likewise be *followed* by another such external moment. Having completed her stint as local legal participant, she may want to regain her initial observer position so as to consider yet another set of questions, this time answerable only from the position of someone *no longer* engaged in the foreign law (call it the 'final comparison' phase). Among those are: is English law more efficient, fairer or in some way 'better' than French law? Are the 'law in books' and the 'law in action' of English law closer together or further apart than those of French law? Is English law more or less idealistic/pragmatic, elitist/democratic, opaque/transparent, etc.? As these are comparative questions proper, they can only be answered from the perspective of someone seeing the two legal systems at once, thus standing outside them both. Unlike her English classmates, then, the French jurist – like any comparative lawyer – will adopt an external perspective on English law both before and after actually engaging with it on the inside.

Finally, the middle phase too, that of her actual engagement, will be different. Inasmuch as her knowledge of French law as mentioned remains prominent at all times, she will inevitably tend to compare *as she goes*. Like her English peers, she will aim to do precisely what English lawyers do, viz. reconstruct the various English rules and concepts brought to her knowledge into the most coherent story possible. Only, that reconstruction exercise will inevitably be influenced by the law that she already knows. She will tend, that is, to assimilate any new rule of English law to its closest French equivalent so that it can be made to fit within her old (French) mental framework: "[the reflex automatically is] to bring the other back to the self, at the risk of reducing the other to the self, denying or occulting differences."[179] As discussed, she may be keenly aware of that risk, and genuinely determined to curb it. But she simply will be unable to proceed any differently at that point, for alternative reference points will not yet be available to her. Such 'homecoming,' as it has been called, is part and parcel of the learning process:[180] all new knowledge inevitably

---

and how are these things related?—[these] *are* questions of legal philosophy: certainly they are not questions of law."); Villa, *supra* note 81.

[179] SIMMONDS, *supra* note 7, at 217. See also: Christian von Bar, Comparative Law of Obligations: Methodology and Epistemology, in EPISTEMOLOGY AND METHODOLOGY OF COMPARATIVE LAW 123 (Mark Van Hoecke ed., 2004), at 130 (comparative reflex is pedagogically sound); Sacco, *supra* note 171, at 5 (new knowledge develops *through* comparison); Jaako Husa, Farewell to Functionalism or Methodological Tolerance?, 67 RABELS Z 419, 429–30 (2003) ("the starting point can be found in the comparativists themselves; paradigmatically this starting point is one's own legal system"); Bomhoff, *supra* note 81, at 77 ("a dialectical process that switches between internal and external perspectives of comparison"); Annelise Riles, Comparative Law and Socio-Legal Studies, in OXFORD HANDBOOK OF COMPARATIVE LAW 775, 801–802 (Mathias Remann & Reinhard Zimmerman eds., 2006) (comparative lawyer's outlook cannot be strictly internal); Frankenberg, *supra* note 114, at 413 ("The new information has to be processed ... to be integrated and contextualized with the known to make sense to us") and 423 ("The comparatist always returns to the original and prior conception.").

[180] SAMUEL, *supra* note 125, at 11; Pierre Legrand, *Comparing in Circles*, Preface to COMPARATIVE LEGAL STUDIES IN ASIA (Helen J Nicholson & Sarah Biddulph eds., 2008) (evoking Heidegger's three-fold

is assessed as against the background of what we already know, what we each have come to take as 'the normal,' our respective cognitive baselines.

This shoehorning exercise can only be pressed so far, however, as legal rules and concepts are not infinitely malleable. There will come a point where inserting yet another rule of English law into her French framework will either require serious distortion of that rule or else cause the whole framework to unravel. To the extent that the English rules are (as posited here) at least somewhat different from the French, each of them being inserted will indeed result in increased structural pressure on the framework, to the point where any new insertion will simply be too much. At that point, the French jurist will have no choice, in order to accommodate the next rule, let alone the others yet to come, to begin elaborating an altogether new framework, one better adapted to these rules and hence entirely distinct from the French. She will continue to bounce off any new rule against her French framework, but instead of trying to force them into that framework, she will now quickly reposition them into the independent English framework simultaneously gradually emerging. As more and more rules are brought in, the French jurist will, through this continuous shuttlecock movement, come to reconstruct a separate understanding for English law, one that will grow richer and more peculiar as it moves further away from the French.

As illustration, consider her first encounter with contract formation at English law.[181] Upon discovering that the three requirements of a valid contract at English law are offer, acceptance and consideration, the French jurist will instinctively assume that the first two are identical to the French eponyms (*offre* and *acceptation*), and that the third is just a different word for the traditional French *causa*. She will soon find out, however, that consideration is framed objectively, as bargain, and hence excludes donative intent. This will cause her to revisit her initial equation of consideration with *causa*, as well as, in fact, the larger equation of English contract with the French *convention*. She will dig further within the various rules on offer and acceptance, and discover that they too are understood far less subjectively, and hence differ significantly, actually, from the French *offre* and *acceptation*. She will then encounter the rules of Equity, which will comfort her with a certain sense of familiarity, only to realize that at English law these rules are considered 'exceptional,' a body of law altogether separate, not just from the common law of contracts, but from contract law as a whole. This will further confirm how different, and far apart, English contract law really is from the French law of contractual obligations. And so on as

---

structure (*Vorhabe, Vorsicht, Vorgriff*) according to which understanding anything involves positioning it in whatever particular context and set of preconceptions are then available to us, i.e., our own (Heidegger, *supra* note 116, at 191–92) and Gadamer's "hermeneutic circle," whereby understanding comes from "the interplay of the movement of tradition and the movement of the interpreter" (Gadamer, *supra* note 116, at 293)).

[181] See likewise Whitman's comparative depiction of the US and German concepts of 'dignity' (Whitman, *supra* note 1, at 338).

she proceeds through the rest of private law, public law and all the other parts of the English legal system.

Gerald Postema offers a similar, dialectic account of the comparative operation at play in analogical reasoning. Building on models developed by cognitive scientists, Postema analyzes analogical reasoning in terms of the four components of "encoding," "retrieval," "mapping" and "evaluation."[182] He then writes:

> Initially the target analogue [here, the new English rule] is encoded: Salient features are identified ... then a search for source analogues [French rules] is undertaken. A profile of the target analogue, albeit tentative and revisable, is needed to guide the retrieval search ... Once source analogue candidates are retrieved, features of the source are mapped to target features, and the results are evaluated for closeness of fit (relative to the constraints of the context). Evaluations confirm the analogy, reject it, or force further retrieval and mapping. The initial encoding and retrieval processes yield a context of comparables, finding judgments of threshold relevance of similarities and differences. These are then tested in the mapping and evaluating stages, which can call for revisions and refinement in a dynamic process. Eventually, in equilibrium judgments of robust relevance and analogical inference are formed.[183]

Postema's account is instructive in several respects, some of which will be outlined later. Not only does it aptly formalize our French jurist's learning process, it does so by striking a middle course between the Charybdis and Scylla of 'rule-rationalism' and 'particularism' – much as law as collective commitment is shown to do in Chapters 1 and 2, between the positivist and naturalist ideal-types.[184] On a rule-rationalist account, the comparison of the target and source analogues necessarily involves referring to some higher rule that subsumes them both[185] whereas the same comparison is direct and immediate, for intuitive and altogether a-theoretical, on a particularist account.[186] Postema shows that the former is ultimately flawed, for

---

[182] Postema, *supra* note 106, at 119.

[183] *Ibid.* Postema however then goes on to suggest that this model leaves out two further crucial elements of analogical reasoning in law, namely, it being 'normative' and 'discursive,' both of which flow from the fact that legal reasoning involves "making and assessing *judgments* of relevance and conclusions drawn from them." I would suggest these two elements are in fact accounted for, insofar as they partake of the definition of the relevant reasoning 'context,' which the model does refer to.

[184] *Ibid.* at 110 ("how to escape the incoherence of particularism without succumbing to rule-rationalist dogma."). Frankenberg (*supra* note 114, at 415) likewise affirms that the universal ("going rational") and relativist ("going local") approaches "are [both] non-dialectical in the sense that they either come up with 'bad' abstractions or with no abstractions at all."

[185] E.g. "One can never declare A to be legally similar to B without first formulating a legal rule of treatment by which they are rendered relevantly identical." Peter Westen, On "Confusing Ideas", 91 YALE L. J. 1153, 1163 (1982), quoted in *ibid.* at 110.

[186] "looking at [the cases] side by side and rubbing them together we may perhaps make justice flash forth as from fire-sticks." *Ibid.* at 109, quoting Plato (REPUBLIC 434C–435A).

internally incoherent, on a general level.[187] In addition, rule-rationalism turns out to be particularly problematic for us, as it presupposes some higher rule or set of rules – the aforementioned legal *tertium comparationis*[188] – that, as discussed, simply does not exist under law as collective commitment. As for particularism, Postema suggests that it in fact is no account at all, insofar as to say of a phenomenon that it is 'just what it is,' – a matter of ineffable and unconstrained 'intuition' or 'perception,' 'feeling,' or 'imagination'[189] – is simply to fail to explain it in any serious way.[190]

Postema's proposed account in contrast is an account proper, one that depicts a particular mode of reasoning, with specific components interacting in a specific way, yet requires no overarching mediating referent between the new and the existing knowledge.[191] Instead, the comparative reasoning there merely involves "fitting something into its place in an intelligible, sense-making context, like fitting a piece into a jigsaw puzzle."[192] It follows that that reasoning is *structurally* rather than *externally* constrained, the relevant constraints inhering in, rather than transcending, the context of the comparative operation. As such, Postema's account arguably serves to confirm the possibility evoked here, namely, that of coming to understand a body of foreign law through a process of *direct* back and forth with the native law, unmediated, that is, by some higher common ground.[193]

In sum, the outsider partakes of the very same legal game as the local actors but through a process that is quite different. Unlike the local actors, who remain present at all times, the outsider cannot but step out of the room before every move, as her moves, unlike theirs, are at least partially determined by something operating on

---

[187] "The rule-rationalist argues that it is not possible to judge one case relevantly similar to another without the guidance of a rule that brings them under some category or description ... However ... [i]t is possible to identify something as an instance of the rule or concept only if one judges that it is relevantly similar to cases already falling under the rule, and that is possible only if at some point it is possible to judge cases as relevantly similar without appeal to a mediating rule. If every such judgment presupposed a rule to guide it, we would be caught in an infinite regress." *Ibid.* at 114.

[188] See *supra*, note 162 and accompanying text. See however the possibility of non-legal *tertia comparationis* discussed in Chapter 5, Part I.

[189] Postema, *supra* note 106, at 109, respectively quoting Aristotle (*Nichomachean Ethics*), Mill (*System of Logic*, Bk. I, chap. 3, §11) and Hume (*Enquiries Concerning Human Understanding and Concerning the Principles of Morals*).

[190] "the reason-giving or reason-constituting facts cannot be logically particular, because in order to count as *reasons*, they must be logically repeatable, and so their descriptions must be universalizable." *Ibid.* at 109. (Emphasis in original.)

[191] See likewise Arendt's distinction between "determinative" and "reflective" judgment, the former unlike the latter involving "judg[ing] particulars without subsuming them within a general concept" (Nedelsky, *supra* note 135, at 235).

[192] Postema, *supra* note 106, at 117. Likewise: MacCormick, *Rhetoric and the Rule of Law, supra* note 38, at 208.

[193] The sequencing here is conceptual, not temporal. Temporally, it could be that the comparative lawyer has to oscillate between the internal and external standpoints, in a constant movement of back-and-forth, throughout the study. The determination of the right temporal sequence would require a much deeper analysis than is both necessary and possible within the present chapter, however. The only point that needs to be made for present purposes is that legal comparison cannot but trigger a combination of (conceptually distinct) epistemological moments.

the outside. The game itself however is one and the same: for outsiders and insiders alike, it involves regenerating the local law through the production of 'best possible' interpretations of it, interpretations that resonate as such locally.[194] In that sense it can arguably be said that the outsider pursues an understanding of the local law that is 'internal' in much the same way that is the understanding pursued by the insider.

iv. *The Outsider's Comparative Contribution*

But if the game indeed is the same, what is it, exactly, that the outsider brings to the table that insiders are not in a position to contribute? What does the outsider's in-and-out engagement with the local law produce that cannot be produced through the local actors' strictly internal engagement?

Her contribution is peculiar precisely in that it, as discussed, evolves from a cognitive process that is significantly different from the local, namely, one that is inherently *comparative*. The outsider comes to the local law equipped with knowledge of what that law is *not*, a possible alternative, which gives her a serious head start for understanding what it *is*.[195] This again is well explained by Postema on analogical reasoning:

> Contrast is essential to cognition. To grasp something meaningful is to recognize its boundaries or determinacy. This presupposes a context in which it can be distinguished. The context cannot just be some background of indeterminate light; it must be populated by other relatively determinate and contrasting elements — the sharper their outlines, the more determinate will be its features.[196]

The French jurist being already acquainted with one determinate element (French law) is in a position to consider any new element (here, English law) in relation to it, in a larger picture that includes both. Seeing both elements at once, she can identify their respective outlines and distinguish them as against one another, thereby

---

[194] Picard, *supra* note 1, at 227 ("Comparative law ... contributes to elaborating [the local concepts], thereby contributing ... to the law's very production."); Bell, *supra* note 39, at 167 ("The internal lawyer has to select amongst [fragmentary statements of the law] to make the law the best it could be. The same is true of the comparative lawyer ... As a result, I am not sure there is as much difference epistemologically between the law as it is perceived within the system and how an outside lawyer views it. Both are trying to interpret it from the inside, but the purposes may be different.").

[195] Hence the existentialist's famous designation of the other as *"das andere Ich."* (JEAN PAUL SARTRE, BEING AND NOTHINGNESS 361–430 (H. Barnes trans., 1965), echoing Aristotle's contention that "the want of harmony between two things is emphasized by their being placed side by side" (cited in Sir John Fortescue, *On the Laws and Governance of England* 14 (Shelley Lockwood ed., 1997)).

[196] Postema, *supra* note 106, at 118. Legal sociologists (e.g. Niklas Luhmann, L'unité du système juridique, 31 ARCH. PHIL. DRT 163, 171 (1989); François Ost, Entre ordre et désordre: le jeu du droit. Discussion du paradigme autopoiétique appliqué au droit 31 ARCH. PHIL. DRT 133, 139 (1986); ANDRÉ-JEAN ARNAUD ET AL., DICTIONNAIRE ENCYCLOPÉDIQUE DE THÉORIE ET DE SOCIOLOGIE DU DROIT 51 (2nd ed., 1993)) convey the same idea through the notion of background 'noise': from a perspective internal to any one system, other systems are apprehensible only as noise. They are apprehensible as such only from a perspective that is external to them all.

recognizing their relative, contingent nature.[197] From this she gains a sharpened understanding of each element on its own, unavailable to anyone privy to just one of them. As Postema describes it, that sharpened understanding naturally flows from her privileged access to the larger contrasting context. This accounts for such common remarks as: "outsiders and spectators gain a sharper and deeper insight into the actual meaning of what happens to go on before or around them than would be possible for the actual actors or participants, entirely absorbed as they must be in the events."[198] The outsider's particularly refined internal perspective in short stems, somewhat paradoxically, from her unique ability to exit that very perspective.

In particular, outsiders are uniquely positioned to develop a particularly keen understanding of the local background rules of understanding.[199] Recall that the local actors themselves are at best dimly aware of those rules. As these actors are all operating under roughly the same cultural framework, there is no need to specify, justify or even discuss that framework so long as they are arguing only among themselves. That framework comes into the limelight, however, as soon as someone carrying a different one enters the scene. For, the new entrant as discussed will bring to the table an interpretation of the local law most likely informed by that different framework, which will become clear from the moment she proceeds to defend her interpretation as against the local ones already on the table.[200] She will then naturally be called upon to articulate and defend her own framework, which will serve to

---

[197] "[W]hat sets comparatists apart is their knowledge of other possible normative conceptions, and a scepticism about the existence of definitive answers." (Whitman, *supra* note 1, at 344).

[198] Hannah Arendt, cited in ELISABETH YOUNG-BRUEHL, *HANNAH ARENDT: FOR LOVE OF THE WORLD* xi (1982). See likewise: Gardiner, *supra* note 1, at 11 ("There is ... a clear sense in which the historian's retrospective vantage-point enables him to discriminate pervasive patterns or themes in the past and thereby to accord to events a significance not the less real for having been unenvisaged, and possibly unenvisageable, by contemporary participants or observers.").

[199] A most significant contribution of the comparative law literature to date indeed has been to shed light on the different cultural unconscious, reasoning structures, internal logics, conceptions of law, etc. at play in different legal systems. E.g.: F. H. Lawson, "The Contribution of Roman Law to Western Civilization" in *Selected Essays*, vol. 1 (*Many Laws*) (Elsevier North-Holland, 1977); JOHN BELL, *FRENCH LEGAL CULTURES* (2001); DAVID & BRIERLEY, *supra* note 122; MIRJAN R. DAMASKA, *THE FACES OF JUSTICE AND STATE AUTHORITY: A COMPARATIVE APPROACH TO THE LEGAL PROCESS* (1986); R. C. VAN CAENEGEM, *AN HISTORICAL INTRODUCTION TO PRIVATE LAW* (1988); GLENN, *supra* note 122; PIERRE LEGRAND & GEOFFREY SAMUEL, *INTRODUCTION AU COMMON LAW* (2008); LASSER, *supra* note 169; Ewald, *supra* note 47; WATSON, *supra* note 145; MAX WEBER, *THE PROTESTANT ETHIC AND THE SPIRIT OF CAPITALISM* (1992); GRIMM, *supra* note 127; NICHOLAS KASIRER, *LE DROIT CIVIL: AVANT TOUT UN STYLE?* (2003); JAMES Q. WHITMAN, *HARSH JUSTICE: CRIMINAL PUNISHMENT AND THE WIDENING DIVIDE BETWEEN AMERICA AND EUROPE* (2003); LIONEL SMITH, *THE WORLDS OF TRUSTS* (2013); JACCO BOMHOFF, *BALANCING CONSTITUTIONAL RIGHTS: THE ORIGINS OF POSTWAR LEGAL DISCOURSE* (2015); HYLAND, *supra* note 42; R. DANIEL KELEMEN, *EUROLEGALISM: THE TRANSFORMATION OF LAW AND REGULATION IN THE EUROPEAN UNION* (2011); SUJIT CHOUDHRY, *THE MIGRATION OF CONSTITUTIONAL IDEAS* (2002); STEFAN VOGENAUER, *DIE AUSLEGUNG VON GESETZEN IN ENGLAND UND AUF DEM KONTINENT* (2001); MARKUS DUBBER & TATJANA HÖRNLE, *CRIMINAL LAW: A COMPARATIVE APPROACH* (2014).

[200] Lasser, *supra* note 42, at 219, 232.

corner the local actors into doing the same with theirs, and a full, open framework debate will ensue.

To illustrate, consider the reaction of the French jurist moving through the validity requirements of English contracts and coming across Pollock's circularity objection concerning the doctrine of consideration applied to mutual promises.[201] As Pollock sees it, neither promise can act as valid consideration for the other unless it is itself binding, which it cannot be unless the other one already is, and so on ad infinitum. The French jurist will be puzzled by that objection, as she can diffuse the contentious conundrum quite easily, by distinguishing the factual from the normative dimension of consideration (the *performance* actually contemplated from the *obligation* to so perform) and retaining only the former for definitional purposes – as arguably is commonly done with *causa* and in other areas of French law.[202]

She will be even more puzzled, though, by the resistance that the local English actors will manifest towards her proposed solution. She will try to understand that resistance, pressing the point and generating further discussion, until the heart of their disagreement finally comes to light: such Cartesian factual/normative dissociations as come naturally to the French may be much less natural, if not plainly counterintuitive, to the more pragmatic English psyche. Only then will the French jurist truly understand Pollock's conundrum (and the consideration requirement, and English contract): *in a context where the normative cannot easily be dissociated from the factual*, consideration indeed might be problematized in the way suggested. More significantly, though, her coming to that realization will have prompted the English actors to bring to the fore and articulate some rules of interpretation ("the factual and normative dimensions of legal concepts are never to come apart") that had hitherto remained hidden in their background.

Perhaps more striking still, this applies with equal force with respect to the outsider's *own* native rules of interpretation. Prior to her encounter with English law, the French jurist was no more aware of the French background rules than the English actors were of the English. She likely had never really thought about, let alone openly discussed, the opportunity of dissociating the factual and normative dimensions of legal concepts with her previous, exclusively French interlocutors, as they too always took such moves for granted, as 'givens' not calling for discussion. Only when the French jurist is confronted with the English actors' different 'givens' is she "shocked"[203] into full awareness of hers. As Nigel Simmonds describes it:

> what is most remarkable is that this elucidation [of foreign law] often presents a double dimension, direct and reflexive: the comparatist thought he was shedding

[201] FREDERICK POLLOCK, CONTRACTS 144 (13th ed. 1950) (1876).
[202] Catherine Valcke, English Consideration and French Causa: The Best of Faux Amis, *in* COMPARATIVISTICA YEARBOOK 2012: COMPARATIVE JURISPRUDENCE, COMPARATIVE STATE STUDIES, COMPARATIVE POLITICAL STUDIES 120 (Oleksij Kresin ed., 2013).
[203] Glendon, *supra* note 159.

light on a foreign concept whereas, by that same process, he also sheds light on his own law pertaining to a counterpart concept, which he may not have fully understood ... The knowledge process becomes circular and cumulative. More precisely, it shapes itself into a growing spiral: the more I understand the other system and the more I understand mine, and reciprocally.[204]

In sum, the native and foreign law here interact perfectly symmetrically, as "equal partners in dialogue."[205] The outsider's contribution boils down to forcing a direct confrontation wherein the formal and informal rules on each side are laid out on the table for all to see and assess.

It follows that we can now harp back to the home bias objection and conclude, again with Simmonds, that

> [t]he philosopher who seeks some Archimedean point outside of history will find that he has nowhere left to stand ... [Whereas] some sort of escape from the cave of conventional understanding might be an intelligible goal, the basis for the escape must begin in reflection upon the beliefs that shape our lives within the cave ... [for t]he overall enlightenment gained [ultimately comes from] a grasp of the conditional nature of the conventional understandings, rather than a denunciation of the totality of such understandings as sheer error.[206]

v. *The Outsider's Many Legal Games*

The foregoing discussion stages the outsider as a player in at least three games at once. The first two should by now be obvious: as the outsider oscillates between the foreign and her native law, she contributes to both legal debates at once and in

---

[204] SIMMONDS, *supra* note 7, at 217–18.

[205] Glanert, *supra* note 1, at 73. And: "[a]s the dialogue progresses, the interpreter revises his prejudices, rethinks his questions and expects new answers." (*Ibid.*) Likewise: Lasser, *supra* note 42, at 19 ("[I]t is precisely a sensitivity to other ways of organizing and conceptualizing the legal universe that affords the comparatist the opportunity to approach and present foreign legal systems in such a way as to do them justice. Such epistemological awareness ... affords ... the possibility of shifting in and out of analytic perspectives in such a way as to grant the observer very different vistas of the foreign and domestic objects ... as well as of the intellectual constructs used to visualize and organize them."); Sacco, *supra* note 135, at 387 ("Cryptotypes may be identified and explored only through the use of comparison at a systematic and institutional level."); GEERTZ, *supra* note 12, at 233 ("We need, in the end, something rather more than local knowledge ... a way of turning its varieties into commentaries one upon another, the one lighting what the other darkens."); BELL, *supra* note 140, at 21 ((citing Garapon) "The best way of abstracting oneself from one's own culture is to look at it from the outside in confronting it with other cultures."); Whitman, *supra* note 1, at 340 ("foreign law, as an articulated normative position, always presents a challenge to domestic law, which claims to be normatively justified, and so, forces the domestic system to reflect on the question.").

[206] SIMMONDS, *supra* note 7, at 35. Likewise: See GEERTZ, *supra* note 12, at 10 and 233; Tushnet, *supra* note 42, esp. at 1236; Pierre Legrand, Comparative Legal Studies and Commitment to Theory, 58 MOD. L. REV. 262, 266.

the same way, viz. by deepening the understanding of each through contrast with the other, which the local, strictly internal players could not achieve on their own. In particular, her contribution causes those rules of each game as would otherwise remain obscure to shine light on one another so that each set can respectively be seen, questioned, reiterated or revisited, and ultimately reinforced.

The outsider's necessarily different understanding of the local law accordingly appears to be so in degree only: it is just a more acute version of the heterogeneous understandings that the local actors advance and debate among themselves, which heterogeneity, it is worth recalling, is not a legal pathology so much as a distinctive feature of a healthy legal system.[207] As such, the outsider's different understanding does not prevent her from participating in the local debate, quite the contrary. Her intervention if anything serves to broaden the realm of possible interpretations, as well as tighten the collective check on personal bias and interpretative mistakes that is already operating on the local level:[208] as the circle of interveners grows larger and more diversified (perhaps including outsiders from more than just one foreign system), so does the likelihood that mistakes and opportunistic behaviour be caught and neutralized. The outsider hence participates in at least two local legal games at once, more where a greater number of legal systems are being compared, seeing that she necessarily contributes to however many legal systems are included in her study.

But there will always be yet another. From the moment that one participates in a number of local legal games, one automatically belongs, in addition, to the distinct 'outsider interpretive community' – the game of *comparative* law.[209] Comparative lawyers have their own set of questions to debate, questions that are altogether distinct from those debated at the local level: in addition to arguing over the best interpretation of particular bodies of local law, they ask themselves what is to be done with these bodies, however interpreted. In what sense can these be mutually compared? What might be the point of such comparisons? How should one go about them? Does it make sense to compare local systems by reference to standards locally treated as legally irrelevant? What significance if any should be attached to the respective local internal perspectives? And what if these perspectives differ to the point of revealing altogether different underlying conceptions of 'law'? These are, in short, the very questions being pursued in this book.[210]

To say that comparative law constitutes a legal game separate from the local ones however is not to say that it does not impact on them. To the contrary, it seems clear that one's moves in the local legal game will probably reflect one's positions

---

[207] See *supra* Part II, section iv.

[208] See *supra* Part II, section v.

[209] Mark Tushnet, The Boundaries of Comparative Law, 13 EUROPEAN CONSTITUTIONAL LAW REVIEW 13 (2017).

[210] That these indeed are qualitatively different questions is confirmed by the fact that, in Luhmann's jargon (see *infra* Chapter 4, Part II, section i), they call for true/false, not legal/illegal, coding.

on the various comparative questions just listed.[211] A 'convergence' comparative law scholar,[212] for example, might tend to debate the meaning of some local law by emphasizing features of it that seem to be also traceable within other systems. In contrast, a 'difference' scholar (viewing comparative law as primarily concerned with the local)[213] will tend to privilege features of the local law that seem unique to it. Likewise, the local arguments advanced by 'legal family' scholars[214] might underscore whatever features of the local law happen to answer to their particular family classification criteria, whereas efficiency considerations will be prominent in the arguments of 'legal origin' scholars,[215] and historical considerations, in those of 'legal transplant' scholars.[216] These connections also run in the reverse, moreover: one's moves in the comparative game will likely bear the mark of one's experiences at the local level. For it is most likely that the local experiences of the scholars making up the various groups just mentioned played a role in their joining those groups in the first place. The convergence scholar probably came to be so upon discovering certain features or patterns recurring in his various local arguments; the difference scholar, upon being in contrast struck by the diversity in these arguments; and so on.

Given this interaction between the comparative and local legal games, finally, one would naturally expect the same heterogeneity and subjectivity issues as beset the local level to arise here as well. Indeed, any comparative lawyer's conception of comparative (and hence, indirectly, any local) law reflects her personal views as to what comparative (and local) law *should* be about, much like the local actors' 'best' interpretations of their law ultimately are what they subjectively take to be so. Yet such subjectivity and consequent heterogeneity are no more avoidable, or problematic, than they were concluded to be on the local level: the comparative debate presupposes that the debaters hold different views on comparative law in much the same way that the local debate presupposes the local actors holding heterogeneous views about their law. At the same time, their debating these different views broadly and publicly allows them to transcend these differences to some extent. For the same collective process of mutual correction as operates on the local level presumably operates here as well: as any comparative lawyer is too immersed in her belief system to be fully aware of it, she naturally relies on the others to signal and control

---

[211] "focus, the knack of ignoring some details and attending to others. Focus is the product of ... one's cognitive frame. Frame is constituted by the cognizer's sense of the point of [the analogy/comparison] ... Together, they trigger certain experience-based dispositions to look for certain things and to ignore others. Frame and focus suggest a context of comparables." Postema, *supra* note 106, at 118.
[212] See *supra* note 32.
[213] See *supra* note 30 of Chapter 1.
[214] See *supra* note 11 of Chapter 1.
[215] See the survey of that literature in 57 AM. J. COMP. L. (2009).
[216] See *supra* note 145.

for its existence – and is in turn expected to signal and control for the belief systems of the others.[217] As with the local legal games, then, the more expansive and diversified the comparative game is, the better: "the results will very likely become sound in the long run, if criticism comes from all investigated legal cultures."[218] Here likewise, 'enlarging' the hermeneutic circle is the ultimate aim.[219]

CONCLUSION

This chapter aimed to show that it is possible, as the best hermeneutic scholars thought it might be, "not to surrender to 'otherness,' but explain how understanding is possible *despite* otherness."[220] Like local legal actors, the outsider seeks to show the local law in its 'best' possible light, 'best' in terms of fit with extant legal materials and the system's underlying commitments. Unlike the local actors, however, the outsider comes to this interpretive exercise from the outside, and must hence face up to the home bias objection, according to which her interpretation ultimately will necessarily differ from that of the local actors. But therein lies the outsider's peculiar contribution: as the outsider brings her home system in direct, unmediated confrontation with the local law, she causes the cultural unconscious on both sides to come to light, which in time serves to reaffirm and strengthen the peculiar character of each. An internal perspective, then, but one whose peculiarity, and peculiar contribution, lies precisely in its proceeding from a constant back and forth between the inside and the outside, between the one and the other.

---

[217] "The possible effect of this [home bias] can only be measured by reading concrete comparative studies ... in order to evaluate to what extent the comparativist in question has been a prisoner." Husa, *supra* note 179, at 437. For the suggestion that that is just a feature of scientific research in general, see: GARY KING ET AL., DESIGNING SOCIAL INQUIRY: SCIENTIFIC INFERENCE IN QUALITATIVE RESEARCH 8 (1994) ("The process for gathering the data and inferring the conclusions must be such that the reliability of those data and conclusions can be assessed widely, by individuals other than the original researchers.").

[218] Peters & Schwenke, *supra* note 96, at 837. See also: Jean Michel Berthelot, Les sciences du social, in ÉPISTÉMOLOGIE DES SCIENCES SOCIALES 203–65 (Jean Michel Berthelot ed., 2001); Michaels, *supra* note 133; Lasser, *supra* note 42, at 235.

[219] Legrand, *supra* note 180.

[220] Whitman, *supra* note 1, at 323. (Emphasis in original.)

4

Delineating Legal Systems

Geography

INTRODUCTION

In Chapter 2, we identified the legal system as the most appropriate analytical unit for comparative law on the basis that, from among all possible 'legal things' (laws, rules, institutions), only legal systems, it was argued, can be seen as self-standing units amenable to meaningful mutual comparison. The conclusions reached in Chapter 3 however made it clear that it is one thing to settle on the legal system as the right analytical unit, and quite another to delineate its contours in any particular case: if all who partake in shaping the local legal discourse, including foreigners, are to count as actors of the system, where does that system begin and end, demographically speaking? And if the foreign actors' contributions are based on foreign sources, values, materials and intellectual frameworks, where do the system's normative, material and intellectual boundaries lie? No actual comparison of legal systems can begin before we get a clearer sense of how to go about disentangling the 'foreign' from the 'local' in any given case.

While this 'problem of individuation'[1] is not new, it is particularly acute in the present, globalized environment. Comparative lawyers are routinely criticized for having long 'individuated' their target legal systems through an external approach, insofar as they would have traditionally just coopted to that end the territorial criterion used in politics for delineating nation states, hence effectively reducing legal systems to their corresponding states.[2] It has been objected that such methodological

---

[1] "[W]hat can be treated as a legal order? What counts as one rule? What counts as one law?" WILLIAM TWINING & DAVID MIERS, *HOW TO DO THINGS WITH RULES?* 143–46 (4th ed. 1999). More generally: WILLIAM TWINING, *GENERAL JURISPRUDENCE* chap. 15 (2009); Laura Nader, The Anthropological Study of Law, 67 *AMERICAN ANTHROPOLOGIST* 3 (1965).

[2] Mathias Reimann, Beyond National Systems: A Comparative Law for the International Age, 75 *TUL. L. REV.* 1103 (2001); T. W. Bennett, Comparative Law and African Customary Law, *in* THE *OXFORD HANDBOOK OF COMPARATIVE LAW* 641; Ralf Michaels, *Transnationalizing Comparative Law,*

shortcut, while perhaps warranted when law was produced through physically proximate actors and resources, is ill-advised at best in a global world, where governance takes the form of such ill-defined and occasionally clashing transnational instruments as are international treaties, extra-territorial adjudication, transnational regulatory networks and so on.[3] The current global legal environment would thus serve to confirm that legal systems in fact are best conceptualized as epistemic rather than territorial communities, the contours of which can only be properly delineated from an internal perspective, that of the various minds making up each one of them. Hence does there seem to be wide consensus that the traditional, state-based analytical framework of comparative law is due for a serious overhaul.[4]

This fourth chapter aims to show that that critique is unfounded. First, comparative lawyers in fact have not been individuating their target systems in the reductive way just described. Second, the more subtle way in which they have actually proceeded is defensible, at least inasmuch as it can be shown to cohere with the present account of comparative law as comparative collective commitments. While comparative lawyers have focused on state courts, which clearly are to some extent territorially connected, they have not for that matter projected legal systems as coextensive with the corresponding, territorially bound nation states. Their approach to individuating legal systems therefore can at most be described as 'somewhat territorial': though it does entail minimal territorial connection, it also accounts for the fundamental epistemic quality (and consequent importance of deferring to the respective internal delineation processes) of legal systems.

The argument proceeds in three Parts. In line with the internal/external distinction structuring the last chapter, Part I argues that, just like the contents of legal systems, their contours are best apprehended from a mixed internal/external perspective. We take up the internal standpoint in Part II, which investigates the process by which legal systems, as epistemic communities, *self*-delineate. It is there

---

MAASTRICHT J. EUR. & COMP. L. 303ff (2016); David Goldberg & Elspeth Attwooll, Legal Orders, Systemic Relationships and Cultural Characteristics, *in* STUDIES IN LEGAL SYSTEMS 313 (Esin Örücü *et al.* eds., 1996); Stepan Wood, Transnational Governance Interactions: A Critical Review of the Legal Literature, *in* 11 OSGOODE LEGAL STUDIES RESEARCH PAPER SERIES 14, 13 (Osgoode Hall Law School, Research Paper No. 35, 2015).

3   For a helpful survey of the voluminous literature on topic, see Wood, *supra* note 2.

4   UGO MATTEI, COMPARATIVE LAW AND ECONOMICS xii, 74 (1997); WERNER F. MENSKI, COMPARATIVE LAW IN A GLOBAL CONTEXT: THE LEGAL SYSTEMS OF ASIA AND AFRICA (2nd ed., 2006); Mads Andenas & Duncan Fairgrieve, Intent On Making Mischief: Seven Ways of Using Comparative Law, *in* METHODS OF COMPARATIVE LAW 25, 26 (Pier Giuseppe Monateri ed., 2012); Horatia Muir Watt, Globalization and Comparative Law, *in* THE OXFORD HANDBOOK OF COMPARATIVE LAW, *supra* note 2, at 579, 580–83; Ralf Michaels, Globalization and Law: Law Beyond the State, *in* LAW AND SOCIAL THEORY 287, 303 (Reza Banaker & Max Travers eds., 2nd ed. 2013); Wolf Heydebrand, From Globalization of Law to Law under Globalization, *in* ADAPTING LEGAL CULTURES 117ff (David Nelken & Johannes Feest eds., 2001); Lawrence Rosen, Beyond Compare, *in* COMPARATIVE LEGAL STUDIES: TRADITIONS AND TRANSITIONS 493, 510 (Pierre Legrand & Roderick Munday eds., 2003); TWINING, *supra* note 1, at chap. 12 (2009); William Twining, Globalisation and Comparative Law, *in* COMPARATIVE LAW: A HANDBOOK 69, 70–71 (Esin Örücü & David Nelken eds., 2007).

suggested that that self-delineation process causes legal systems to look very much like … bee swarms. In the same way that bee swarms boast elusive and fickle edges surrounding a clearly identifiable queen bee, legal systems can be conceptualized as cloud-like structures anchored in a comparatively well-defined and stable centre of gravity, in particular, the rulings of their central adjudicative bodies.[5] In Part III, we exit the internal perspective so as to observe from a distance how the various swarm-like systems interact among themselves in the global universe. That external standpoint takes us into the legal pluralism debate as it allows us to assess which of the various accounts of global law currently on offer fit with our swarm model and the more general account of comparative law built so far. The upshot of Parts II and III is that the traditional, state-based analytic framework of comparative law, properly understood, is in fact fine as it is, at least for the time being.

I. INTERNAL AND EXTERNAL LEGAL SYSTEM DELINEATION

To the extent that legal systems can be described as 'epistemic communities,' their contours would be, just like their contents, a priori best identified from within each system. Yet as those systems interact with one another, which interaction is bound to impact on their compositions and overall structures, an external perspective seems also warranted. For, whatever happens *between* the various systems can only be observed and analyzed from *outside* those systems. Particularly where the exercise is ultimately geared at comparing them: as discussed, any act of comparison involves considering each object *as it relates to the other*, which requires standing back from them both.[6] We accordingly first investigate the extent to which legal systems qualify as epistemic communities, and the corollary requirement of delineating their contours from an internal standpoint, and thereafter recount the need to complement that internal investigation with an external one.

i. *Internal Delineation*

Initially defined by sociologists of knowledge as "socially segregated sub-universes of meaning,"[7] the notion of 'epistemic community' has been applied in a wide variety of intellectual contexts. Natural scientists are said to form such a community based

---

[5] I first raised, but did not develop, the analogy between legal systems and bee swarms in: Catherine Valcke, 'Precedent' and 'Legal Systems' in Comparative Law: A Canadian Perspective, *in* PRECEDENT IN COMPARATIVE LAW (Ewoud Hondius ed., 2007). Legal systems have similarly been likened to clouds (MIREILLE DELMAS-MARTY, ORDERING PLURALISM 162 (2009)) and "clusters of gnats or small flies" (Karl Popper, Of Clouds and Clocks, *in* OBJECTIVE KNOWLEDGE: AN EVOLUTIONARY APPROACH (1972) referred to by Delmas-Marty, *ibid.*) (My thanks to Max Del Mar for pointing this out to me.). Bee swarms better suit my purposes as, unlike clouds and gnat/fly clusters, their respective queen bees provide clearly identifiable centres of gravity.

[6] See *supra* Chapter 3, Part III.

[7] PETER L. BERGER & THOMAS LUCKMANN, THE SOCIAL CONSTRUCTION OF REALITY 65 (1967).

on their "shared faith in the scientific method as a way of generating truth."[8] Literary
and art theory commonly evoke in a similar way 'hermeneutic' or 'interpretive communities.'[9] The social science scholarship on group definition[10] likewise is replete
with such labels as '*Gemeinschaft*,'[11] '*aires culturelles*'[12] or 'imagined communities,'[13]
all of which connote groups bound together by "share[d] collective understandings
[of] what they are doing and why."[14] Perhaps most notorious in this regard is international relations scholar Peter Haas's analysis of 'epistemic communities' in terms of
the following four components:

> (1) a shared set of normative and principled beliefs, which provide a value-based
> rationale for the social action of community members; (2) shared causal beliefs,
> which are derived from their analysis of practices leading or contributing to a cen-
> tral set of problems in their domain ... (3) shared notions of validity— that is, inter-
> subjective, internally defined criteria for weighing and validating knowledge in the
> domain of their expertise; and (4) ... a set of common practices associated with a set
> of problems to which their professional competence is directed.[15]

The same notion made its way into law, finally, under such various denom-
inations as 'legal consciousness,'[16] 'nomos' or 'normative universe,'[17] 'expert

[8] BURKART HOLZNER & JOHN H. MARX, KNOWLEDGE APPLICATION: THE KNOWLEDGE SYSTEM IN
SOCIETY 107–11 (1979), paraphrased in Peter M. Haas, Knowledge, Power, and International Policy
Coordination, 46 INT'L ORG. 1, 3, n. 4 (1992). See likewise: LUDWIK FLECK, GENESIS AND DEVELOPMENT
OF A SCIENTIFIC FACT (German ed., 1935) (describing as 'thought collective' any "sociological group
with a common style of thinking," as paraphrased by Haas, *supra*); THOMAS S. KUHN, THE STRUCTURE
OF SCIENTIFIC REVOLUTIONS 175, 180 (2nd ed. 1970) ('paradigm' as "an entire constellation of beliefs,
values, techniques ... shared by members of a given community [and governing] not a subject matter
but a group of practitioners.").
[9] STANLEY FISH, IS THERE A TEXT IN THIS CLASS? THE AUTHORITY OF INTERPRETIVE COMMUNITIES (1982).
[10] See generally: Samuel L. Gaertner et al., Reducing Intergroup Bias: The Benefits of Recategorization,
in INTERGROUP RELATIONS: ESSENTIAL READINGS 356 (Michael A. Hogg & Dominic Abrams eds., 2001);
PENELOPE J. OAKES & S. ALEXANDER HASLAM, STEREOTYPING AND SOCIAL REALITY 147–51 (1994).
[11] TÖNNIES: COMMUNITY AND CIVIL SOCIETY xli (Jose Harris ed., Margaret Hollis trans., 2001) (1887),
discussing FERDINAND TÖNNIES, GEMEINSCHAFT AND GESELLSCHAFT (1887) ("a community unified by
shared experience, values and norms").
[12] 2 LÉONTIN-JEAN CONSTANTINESCO, LA MÉTHODE COMPARATIVE 95ff (1974).
[13] BENEDICT ANDERSON, IMAGINED COMMUNITIES: REFLECTIONS ON THE ORIGINS AND SPREAD OF
NATIONALISM (1983).
[14] EMANUEL ADLER, COMMUNITARIAN INTERNATIONAL RELATIONS: THE EPISTEMIC FOUNDATIONS OF
INTERNATIONAL RELATIONS 22 (2005).
[15] Haas, *supra* note 8, at 3.
[16] Duncan Kennedy, Towards an Historical Understanding of Legal Consciousness: The Case of
Classical Legal Thought in America, 1850–1940, in 3 RESEARCH IN LAW AND SOCIOLOGY 3, 6 (Rita J.
Simon & Steven Spitzer eds., 1980) ("something more influential than a checklist of facts, techniques,
and opinions").
[17] Julen Extabe, The Legal Universe after Robert Cover, 4 LAW & HUMAN. 115, 118–19 (2010) ("the entire
battery of resources for normative thought and action that are immanent in any living community ...
[in particular:] (a) a well-constituted and fully blossomed human collective; (b) a self-consciousness

community,'[18] 'epistemic cluster,'[19] *'espace normatif,'*[20] *'fonctionnel, voire structurel'*[21] and 'organizational network.'[22] Most importantly for our purposes, the common thread in all variations of 'epistemic communities,' in and outside law, is the insistence on a group bond that is intellectual rather than physical,[23] on a common space that is 'discursive' rather than territorial.[24]

The working conception of law used here is clearly laced with the same thread. Chapter 1 described law as the collective commitment of an entire community by and to itself to foster a set of shared ideals, which commitment is primarily expressed through a particular form of argumentation.[25] Law accordingly is here seen as a collective normative discourse, a fundamentally intellectual, though publicly constructed, phenomenon. And what ties the community together on that account, what defines it as a 'community' in the first place, hence likewise is an intellectual, epistemic bond. The references to publicly shared ideals and epistemic bonds are unmistakable indicators that legal communities, on the present account, are 'epistemic communities' as described in the literature.

Importantly, one key feature of 'epistemic communities' under that description is that although they are not boundless,[26] their boundaries are set internally: epistemic

---

of their collective identity (to think of themselves *as* a group); (c) a perception of sharing and being bound by common authoritative texts; and (d) certain normative life-projects.").

[18] Stefan Oeter, Theorising the Global Legal Order – An Institutionalist Perspective, *in* THEORISING THE GLOBAL LEGAL ORDER 61, 72 (Andrew Halpin & Volker Roeben eds., 2009).

[19] John Gillespie, Developing a Framework for Understanding the Localisation of Global Script in East Asia, *in* THEORISING THE GLOBAL LEGAL ORDER, ibid. at 209, 227.

[20] Béatrice Jaluzot, Cartographier les droits, *in* MÉLANGES EN L'HONNEUR DE CAMILLE JAUFFRET-SPINOSI 679, 680 (2013).

[21] MIREILLE DELMAS-MARTY, LE PLURALISME ORDONNÉ 134 (2006) ("functional, possibly even structural space"); Watt, *supra* note 4, at 589–90 ("epistemic communities").

[22] Respectively, Olga Frishman, Should Courts Fear Transnational Engagement?, 49 VAND. J. TRANSNAT'L L. 59 (2016), Part II at 10 ("a community of organizations that partakes of a common meaning system and whose participants interact more frequently and fatefully with one another than with actors outside the field").

[23] Gillespie, *supra* note 19, at 227 ("These epistemic clusters should not be thought of as communities in a physical sense, but rather as abstract bonds with the potential to generate cooperation and shared understandings."); Watt, *supra* note 4, at 588 referring to David Nelken, Comparatists and Transferability, *in* COMPARATIVE LEGAL STUDIES: TRADITIONS AND TRANSITIONS, *supra* note 4, at 445ff; H. PATRICK GLENN, LEGAL TRADITIONS OF THE WORLD: SUSTAINABLE DIVERSITY IN LAW 22ff, 49ff (2004) ("The identity of cultural or epistemic communities needs to dissociate from geo-political divisions of the globe."); Filomena Chirico & Pierre Larouche, Convergence and Divergence, *in* NATIONAL LEGAL SYSTEMS AND GLOBALIZATION 9, 16 (Pierre Larouche & Péter Cserne eds., 2013) ("[Our] point of reference is not a geographical territory ... but rather a legal epistemic community.").

[24] Gunther Teubner, Global Bukowina: Legal Pluralism in the World Society, *in* GLOBAL LAW WITHOUT A STATE 3 (Gunther Teubner ed., 1996).

[25] See *supra* Chapter 1, Part I.

[26] Ralf Michaels, Global Legal Pluralism, 5 ANN. REV. L. SOC. SCI. 243, 253 (2009) ("Even a deterritorialized locality would require some kind of boundaries, a distinction of inside and outside").

communities *self*-delineate.[27] That is to say that it falls to the members of those communities acting collectively to determine what is in and out for the purpose of constructing their particular discourse: whose voices will be listened to, and considered the loudest, what arguments of theirs will be accepted as persuasive and why, what values will be regarded as relevant and in what order of priority, and so on. And as the community itself ultimately is no other than that very discourse, it is their community that the participants are effectively constructing in this way. Shortly, the very contours of the community being, like its discursive content, intellectual in nature, they too are ultimately determined by the various minds making up that community.

The self-definition feature of epistemic communities is as widely recognized in law as it is elsewhere. If Hart's rule of recognition, or Kelsen's Grundnorm – the ultimate determinant of what is to count as 'legal' in any legal system – is itself contained in those systems (which question has so troubled positivists of all stripes), legal systems indeed are self-delineating.[28] If Dworkin's "pre-interpretive stage," the identification of the object for interpretation, is itself a matter of interpretation, and if such (pre-interpretive) interpretation is carried out by the very same actors as carry out the (subsequent) act of interpretation proper (implicit in Dworkin's argument), the contours of the legal interpretation exercise similarly are internally defined.[29]

Self-definition likewise is central to Niklas Luhmann's account of legal systems, which we used in Chapter 2 to explain those systems' inherent comparability.[30] On Luhmann's account, it will be recalled, legal systems are a particular kind of organic systems, namely, "autopoietic" such systems. They qualify as organic systems

---

[27] Haas, *supra* note 8, at 35; John Gerard Ruggie, International Responses to Technology, 29 INT'L ORG. 557, 569–70 (1975) (describing the community's spontaneous emergence around a particular *episteme*); Gordon Pask, Developments in Conversation Theory: Actual and Potential Applications, *in* 3 APPLIED SYSTEMS AND CYBERNETICS 1326, 1327 (George E. Lasker ed., 1978) (analogizing discursive communities to computing systems, which "comput[e] their own boundaries"); Francisco J. Varela, On Being Autonomous: The Lessons of Natural History for Systems Theory, *in* APPLIED GENERAL SYSTEMS RESEARCH 77, 77 (George J. Klir ed., 1978); Mark van Hoecke, Do "Legal Systems" Exist? The Concept of Law and Comparative Law, *in* CONCEPTS OF LAW: COMPARATIVE, JURISPRUDENTIAL, AND SOCIAL SCIENCE PERSPECTIVES 43, 54 (Seán Donlan & Lukas Heckendorm Urscheler eds., 2014).

[28] Nils Jansen, Comparative Law and Comparative Knowledge, *in* THE OXFORD HANDBOOK OF COMPARATIVE LAW, *supra* note 2, at 320 (citing Hart for the proposition that "[l]egal systems ... are normally understood as individual entities defining their boundaries from within."). If so, neither Hart nor Kelsen is a perfect match for the 'positivist ideal-type' laid out in Chapter 1.

[29] RONALD DWORKIN, LAW'S EMPIRE 65ff, 91ff (1988); see also note 22 at p. 425: "So we disagree about whether one can be unjust to animals, or only cruel, and about whether relations between groups, as distinct from individuals, are matters of justice."

[30] For an argument on system theory's compatibility with hermeneutic accounts of law, see: Neil MacCormick, Beyond the Sovereign State, 56 MOD. L. REV 1, 10 (1990). It should however be noted that such system theorists as Luhmann and Teubner consider that all of world law constitutes a single 'system' (the *legal* system, by contrast with the *economic, religious*, etc. systems), thus resisting the suggestion that what are commonly viewed as the world's legal systems indeed are distinct 'systems' proper. For an argument that there should be no reason to resist crossing that extra step and regard world legal systems as at least distinct 'subsystems' of the world's larger legal 'system,' see: Ralf Michaels, *The Global Legal System* (on file with author).

insofar as they self-regenerate – "they both use and produce the means of their own production."[31] But what makes them 'autopoietic,' in addition to just organic, is that the purpose towards which that self-regeneration process is oriented is itself endogenously rather than exogenously determined, the latter being true of other ('cybernetic') organic systems. That is to say that what ultimately dictates the structure and contours of autopoietic systems, their respective purposes, are themselves determined from within the respective systems.

But Luhmann's explanation for the internal purpose-definition of legal systems is particular. Whereas most legal theorists recognize that purpose-definition, like content-building more generally, is achieved within the systems, they nonetheless insist on separating these functions. Hart distinguishes 'primary' from 'secondary' rules; Dworkin describes the 'pre-interpretive' and 'interpretive' stages of legal interpretation sequentially. In contrast, Luhmann insists that the purpose-defining operations are, in autopoietic unlike in other organic systems, *qualitatively indistinguishable* from the systems' other operations:

> [There is no] difference in essence or any material difference between operation and structure ... Law-related communications have, as operations of the legal system, always a double function as factors for production and as preservers of structure ... The operation provides its unity as an autopoietic element precisely by serving both ... It is in this sense that we shall define the legal system also as a system with a (self-) determined structure.[32]

I would suggest that legal practice everywhere largely bears out Luhmann's insight on this point. In any adjudicative context, the adjudicator is faced with a host of so-called 'preliminary' dispositions, procedural issues of standing and jurisdictions that must be disposed of before deciding on the substance of the claim. Does she have jurisdiction over the matter? Have all other requisite recourses been properly exhausted? Do the litigants have standing? Was the ruling they are appealing from ultra vires of the ruling body's administrative powers? Is the statute they are invoking even constitutional? Yet such so-called 'preliminary' issues are dealt with in essentially the same way as are 'substantive' issues proper. They are decided by the very same decision maker, relying on the very same pool of legal materials, deploying the very same interpretive process. When, say, a Canadian judge has to rule on a transnational contract dispute, she uses Canadian (private international) law to determine whether she has jurisdiction over the matter. In the affirmative, she then consults Canadian (procedural) law to determine whether the litigants have standing. Should

---

[31] See *supra* Chapter 2, text accompanying note 63.

[32] NIKLAS LUHMANN, *LAW AS A SOCIAL SYSTEM* 84–85 (Fatima Kastner *et al.* eds., Klaus A. Ziegert trans., 2009) (1993). The same idea is conveyed by Postema, when discussing laws setting out "performance conditions for other laws." Gerald Postema, Law's System: The Necessity of System in Common Law, *New Zealand L. Rev.* 69, 79–80 (2014).

any issue arise as to the authority of some case or statute, she likewise would turn to Canadian (administrative or constitutional) law to determine the matter. At each point, moreover, she proceeds to interpret the relevant (private international, procedural, administrative or constitutional) law by appeal to the requisite Canadian standards. And the same can arguably be said of judges all over the world.[33]

But there is more. Not only are the actors, resources and process exactly the same for 'preliminary' and 'substantive' issues, the latter arguably are as 'structure-defining' as the former.[34] That is, when finally disposing of the issue of contract law – the 'substantive' issue – our Canadian (or other) judge will be contributing to defining the contours of the Canadian legal system in much the same way as she does when disposing of the various 'preliminary' issues. Such dispositions indeed will involve referring to the 'colour' of Canadian law as against any other law, which peculiar colour will necessarily be reaffirmed and refined in the process. And that is the very same (peculiarly Canadian) 'colour' as will taint the determination of all issues to come, 'preliminary' ones included. In Luhmann's own words, she then "codes"[35] said contract (or contractual stipulation or action) as "legal/illegal," which operation simultaneously serves to specify what "legal/illegal" means at Canadian law.

If Luhmann's analysis is right and all legal operations ('preliminary' or otherwise) are structure-defining, an external definition of legal systems is ill-advised indeed. For one, to the extent that one might want (as per the argument of the last chapter) to abide by an internal perspective when it comes to exploring the contents of their target systems, the delineation of the respective domains for internal and external investigation would end up being somewhat arbitrary. Additionally, the undifferentiated use of a single external definitional criterion for all legal systems is bound to clash with the internal criteria of at least some of them, yielding distorted understandings of these systems' contents and boundaries alike.

The experience of 'mixed' legal systems offers a case in point. Those systems emerged post colonization, from an attempt to institutionalize the peaceful cohabitation of (divergent) colonizer and colonized legal cultures within a same national territory.[36] The Canadian constitution, for example, allocates exclusive jurisdiction

---

[33] "Insofar as jurisdiction establishes the boundary between law and non-law, every claim of jurisdiction — as well as its denial—is constitutive of a norm." Extabe, *supra* note 17, at 135. For examples of legal systems internally defining in particular domains, see: Efrat Arbel, Bordering the Constitution, Constituting the Border, 53 OSGOODE HALL L. J. 824 (on the reflexive identification of asylum seekers entitled to basic constitutional protection in the US and Canada); Judith Resnik, Bordering by Law: The Migration of Law, Crimes, Sovereignty, and the Mail, *in Namos: Immigration and Emigration* 79 (Jack Knight ed., 2015).

[34] "[S]o what is a law and what are the contents of a compleat body of the laws are questions of which neither can well be answer'd without the other." Jeremy Bentham, *Of the Limits of the Penal Branch of Jurisprudence (Collected Works)*, 2 (P. Schofield, ed., 2010). But see: Friedman, *supra* note 93, Chapter 2, at 84.

[35] See *infra* note 69.

[36] See generally: VERNON V. PALMER, *MIXED JURISDICTIONS WORLDWIDE: THE THIRD LEGAL FAMILY* (2001); H. Patrick Glenn, Quebec: Mixité and Monism, *in COMPARATIVE LAW: A HANDBOOK*, *supra* note 4, at 1.

over 'property and private law' to the Canadian provinces,[37] thus purportedly allow-ing the province of Quebec to rule itself in accordance with its French-inherited civil law tradition with respect to these matters, while remaining governed by the Canadian common law tradition in other matters. To the extent that Quebec accord-ingly is in a position to reflexively regenerate its law regarding property and private rights, it would be an example of a 'legal system' (or at least 'subsystem')[38] whose contours are externally defined: the contents of Quebec property and private law are internally determined, but within the contours externally set by the Canadian constitution.[39]

Canadian legal practice however has revealed such compartmentalization attempts to be only mildly successful at best. As the Canadian system, like all legal systems, strives towards internal consistency, its legal actors across Canada have felt considerable pressure to harmonize provincial law in all matters, *contra* Canada's self-professed, formal ideal of provincial autonomy in certain domains. And the constitutional barriers instituted to that end have proven insufficient to prevent the infiltration of Canadian juridical standards and authorities in all areas of provincial law, Quebec's included.[40] As a result, it is often said of Quebec (and Louisiana, Puerto Rico, Scotland) private law today that it can only ambivalently be described as 'civilian.'[41]

Arbitrariness and distortion aside, however, the most immediate problem of an exclusively external definition of legal systems appears to be that it would cause comparatists to simply miss out on substantial amounts of information that, on the present account, should be highly valuable to them. If comparative law involves, as suggested in Chapter 3, extracting collective commitments from legal materials, it presumably is best to have available for that purpose the largest possible pool of such materials, all else equal. And if the argument just given is right, there is no reason to exclude from that pool the materials pertaining to 'preliminary' issues.[42] For the

---

[37] Art. 92 of the BNA Act.

[38] The question of whether such 'mixed' legal systems are best described as 'subsystems' or 'systems' proper, already flagged in Chapter 2, Part III (see text accompanying notes 86–87), is discussed in more detail in Part III, section iii (1), below.

[39] PALMER, *supra* note 36, at 8 (mixed systems as "structurally" so mixed); Glenn, *supra* note 36, at 3 ("structural *mixité*"); Goldberg & Attwooll, *supra* note 2, at 333–34 (giving a similar description of the relation of the English Court of Session (Lord Osborne) to the Church of Scotland).

[40] JOHN E. C. BRIERLEY & RODERICK A. MCDONALD, QUEBEC CIVIL LAW: AN INTRODUCTION TO QUEBEC PRIVATE LAW (1993); PALMER, *supra* note 36; Glenn, *supra* note 36.

[41] See generally: STUDIES IN LEGAL SYSTEMS: MIXED AND MIXING (Esin Örücü *et al.* eds., 1996).

[42] On the great variation of jurisdiction and authority criteria across legal systems, see respectively: Ralf Michaels, Two Paradigms of Jurisdiction, 27 MICH. J INT'L L. 1003 (2007) (comparing European and US 'paradigms' and arguing, at 1012, that overall functional equivalence has in fact fomented, not diminished, such variations); Martijn W. Hesselink, How Many Systems of Private Law Are There in Europe? On Plural Legal Sources, Multiple Identities and the Unity of Law, *in* PLURALISM AND EUROPEAN PRIVATE LAW 199, 203, note 12 (Leone Niglia ed., 2013) (referring to RAOUL VAN CAENEGEM, JUDGES, LEGISLATORS AND PROFESSORS: CHAPTERS IN EUROPEAN LEGAL HISTORY (1987)).

'expressive value' of such materials – their value for the purpose of expressing the system's underlying collective commitments – would clearly be as high as that of any other materials in that system. Yet such of those materials as would clash with the external definition would, under an exclusively external definition, be excluded from the outset. What is more, such clashing materials arguably are those that might in fact prove *most* informative here: comparatists presumably are primarily interested in identifying the set of collective commitments *peculiar* to each system, and self-defining materials that clash with the system's external definition are those that most likely reveal a *peculiar* set of commitments, one different, at the very least, from the standard set presupposed by that definition. In any event, those are the very materials that should attract the attention of all comparatists intent on countering their inevitable 'home bias,'[43], given that the set of commitments embodied in any external definition most likely is that at play in the definition setter's home system.[44]

Returning to the above example, we did see that, under the external definition embodied in the Canadian constitution, Quebec should be considered an autonomous system/subsystem with respect to property and private law matters yet one parasitic upon the Canadian system with respect to all other matters. That suggests not only that Quebec should be considered peculiarly 'civilian' with respect to the first matters (which we saw is dubious at best), but also that it should be slotted among common law systems with respect to the second. Any comparatist interested in the peculiarity of Quebec law should therefore presumably focus on Quebec private law, disregarding Quebec courts' treatment of public law. Yet some authors have reported that cultural and linguistic differences in reality have caused Quebec courts to operate very differently from other provincial courts *even in certain areas of public law*, notably administrative law, to the point where it might now be appropriate to describe Quebec as an autonomous subsystem with respect to both private and at least some branches of public law.[45] If so, to stick to the external definition embodied in the Canadian constitution, and exclude all public law from a study designed to assess Quebec's juridical exceptionalism, would be wrongheaded indeed, as it would risk bypassing what might prove the most informative materials for that purpose.

An internal exploration of legal systems' 'preliminary' and 'substantive' materials alike accordingly seems best all around for the purpose, here pursued, of identifying the collective commitments peculiar to each such system.[46]

---

[43] As per our earlier discussion (see *supra* Chapter 3, Part III) of the home-bias objection.

[44] The ideological neutrality of the Westphalian conception of law has often been called into question, e.g.: GLENN, *supra* note 23, at 35, 50 (criticizing that conception as reflecting a Western bias); Van Hoecke, *supra* note 27.

[45] Robert Leckey, Prescribed by Law/Une Règle de Droit, 45 OSGOODE HALL L. J. 571 (2007).

[46] For comparatists adopting and/or advocating an internal delineation of legal systems, as against the traditional, external approach, see: TWINING, *supra* note 1, at 83 (referring to system definition through "active involvement of the participants"); BRIAN Z. TAMANAHA, *A GENERAL JURISPRUDENCE OF LAW* AND

ii. *External Delineation*

Of course, the argument of section i (and of this entire book) can itself only be marshalled from an external standpoint. It is an argument concerning the proper analytic parameters for our investigation, which as discussed necessarily takes place prior to, and as premise for, that investigation (internal or otherwise). As per the discussion of the last chapter, it is because comparatists partake of their own, academic community at the same time as they partake of the various communities of legal actors that they propose to investigate and compare – because they are external observers *as well as* internal participants – that they can engage in such arguments in the first place.[47] Crucially, the external and internal perspectives are here, as in any scientific inquiry,[48] dialectically rather than sequentially related.

With respect to mixed legal systems, in particular, our critique of a strictly external standpoint necessarily presupposed, and in fact proceeded from, such a standpoint. Before we could launch into that critique, we had to identify, even if only provisionally, Quebec as a 'mixed' legal system. That is, we had to go back in history (adopt a historical standpoint) and identify the political implications of English and French colonization on Canadian territories, as crystallized in current Canadian constitutional documents. We started off, in other words, from the external definition of the Canadian legal system embodied in the Canadian constitution, and tested it as against the inner workings of Quebec legal practice.[49]

Importantly, that external definition was not set aside from the moment that it was determined to sit uneasily with legal practice. As any legal practice constantly strives

---

SOCIETY 194 (2001) ("Law is whatever people identify and treat through their social practices as 'law'"); H. Patrick Glenn, Legal Traditions and Legal Traditions, 2 J. COMP. L. 69, 71 (2007) ("Legal theorists (or legal comparatists), therefore, need not formulate a definition of a legal tradition because the (various) definitions are out there. One must simply work with them."); LUHMANN, *supra* note 32, at 84–85 ("Only the law itself can say what law is."); NICO KRISCH, BEYOND CONSTITUTIONALISM: THE PLURALIST STRUCTURE OF POSTNATIONAL LAW 92 (2010); Hesselink, *supra* note 42, at 228; Julie Dickson, How Many Legal Systems? Some Puzzles Regarding the Identity Conditions of, and Relations Between, Legal Systems in the European Union, 9 PROBLEMA 9 (2008) Jacco Bomhoff, The Constitution of the Conflict of Laws 7 (London Sch. of Ec., Law Soc. and Ec. Working Paper Series, Paper No. 4, 2014) (assimilating 'constitutions' to "[sites for] deliberation and contestation over the character and boundaries of the[ir] identities and responsibilities," there borrowing from Gunther Teubner, CONSTITUTIONAL FRAGMENTS (2012) and JOSEPH STORY, COMMENTARIES ON THE CONFLICT OF LAWS para. 34 (1834) ("[E]very nation must judge for itself what is its true duty in the administration of justice.")).

[47] See *supra* Chapter 3, Part III, section iv. That seems to be Simmonds' point (NIGEL E. SIMMONDS, LAW AS MORAL IDEA 156–58 (2007), when he argues that the question of what qualifies as a 'legal system' calls for a different kind of answer (in terms of each contender's relative proximity to Fuller's 'archetype') than that of what is contained in each system (in categorical binary terms of valid/invalid).

[48] See Karl Popper's description of the analytic framework and substantive yield of the scientific process as necessarily constantly feeding on one another: POPPER, OBJECTIVE KNOWLEDGE, *supra* note 5, at 142–46.

[49] Legal practice in the other Canadian provinces of course is likewise relevant for that purpose. I offer an analysis of the Canadian legal system that spans provincial legal practice in and outside Quebec in Valcke, *supra* note 5.

to align itself back with its framing documents, those documents are never very far. Indeed, the discrepancy between Quebec and general Canadian administrative law is one that Quebec legal actors must account for on a regular basis, in the context of any administrative law litigation on appeal before the Canadian Supreme Court for sure, but also within Quebec, whenever litigants choose to present arguments based on pan-Canadian authorities (as such authorities remain, under the Canadian constitution, formally binding in Quebec). To be sure, it is doubtful that one could even make sense of Quebec legal practice abstracted from its larger, Canadian constitutional context. The internal and external definitions of a legal system hence always operate in tandem, as they demand to be constantly bounced against one another, in a dialectic rather than sequential motion – which the discussion of section i hopefully illustrates.

Also noteworthy, finally, is that the discussion left hanging one central question, namely, that of the extent to which Quebec should ultimately be viewed as a 'system' autonomous from, or at least a 'subsystem' included in, the Canadian legal system. That fact alone arguably confirms the point just made about the internal and external perspectives being dialectically related. For a proper answer indeed is unattainable from a strictly internal perspective but rather requires that the question be considered from alternating internal and external standpoints. This we do in the next two Parts below, as Part II investigates the internal structure of legal systems whereas Part III stands back to consider how those systems interact with one another in the global universe. The two Parts being dialectically related is underscored by the fact that the conclusions of Part II cannot but be provisional, as confirmed by the fact that they end up being revisited and adjusted in light of the conclusions of Part III.

II. LEGAL SYSTEMS AS BEE SWARMS

The hallmarks of bee swarms for present purposes is that they project fluid edges around a, if not fixed, at least relatively well-defined centre of gravity, namely, their respective queen bees. I here contend that legal systems, as internally delineating epistemic communities, likewise boast a well-defined institutional grounding (i) encircled by fluid edges (ii).

i. *A Well-Defined (Material) Centre of Gravity*

Under the above description emerging from the literature, epistemic communities in and outside law are shown as revolving around "actual practices in the field."[50] Haas's analysis refers to the community members' "social *actions*" and "common *practices*."[51] Others evoke "concrete patterns of social ordering"[52] or "what people

---

[50] Baudouin Dupret, Legal Pluralism, Plurality of Laws, and Legal Practices, 1 Eur. J. Leg. Stud. 1 (2007).

[51] Haas, *supra* note 8.

[52] Marc Galanter, Justice in Many Rooms, 19 J. Legal Pluralism 1, 17 (1981).

actually do."[53] Yet others point to sets of "common documents,"[54] "texts,"[55] "check-list[s] of facts [and] techniques,"[56] all of which connote concrete things and actions, situated in time and space. Martijn Hesselink makes the same point when he bemuses that a community being "imaginary" does not mean it is "imagined."[57] In the realm of international relations, Emmanuel Adler recently went as far as to suggest that what he had described as "epistemic communities"[58] would be best re-conceptualized as "communities of practice."[59] And the present account of law as collective commitment likewise focuses on such commitments as emerge from a community's legal *practice*.[60] Of course, the communities in question draw their soul from the *meaning* attached to those things and actions: it is the similar way in which the community members go about interpreting them that ultimately causes them to come together as a community, however labelled. But as Max Weber outlined, before there can be 'meaning,' there must be 'meaningful *acts*'[61] – any interpretation is interpretation *of* 'something out there.'[62]

So what are, exactly, the 'meaningful acts' of law? Legal practice is commonly described as the combination of argumentation and implementation.[63] I would suggest that a better, for more specific, description would be to say that it is argumentation *geared at* implementation: argumentation as to *what ought to be ultimately*

---

[53] Brian Z. Tamanaha, The Folly of the Social Scientific Concept of Legal Pluralism, 20 J. L. Soc'y 217 note 71 (1993). See likewise: TWINING, *supra* note 1, at 119 (comparing accounts of 'culture' as mere transmission of ideas (Glenn) and as including ideas and actual behaviour (Bell, Kluckhohn)).

[54] Annelise Riles, The Anti-Network: Global Private Law, Legal Knowledge, and the Legitimacy of the State, 56 AM. J. COMP. L. 605 (2008).

[55] Extabe, *supra* note 17.

[56] Kennedy, *supra* note 16.

[57] Hesselink, *supra* note 42, at 214 (referring to ANDERSON, *supra* note 13); Jeremy Waldron, The Concept and the Rule of Law, 43 GEOR. L. REV 1, 13–14 ("Not every system of command and control that calls itself a legal system *is* a legal system.").

[58] ADLER, *supra* note 14.

[59] Emanuel Adler & Vincent Pouliot, International Practices: Introduction and Framework, *in* INTERNATIONAL PRACTICES 3 (Emanuel Adler & Vincent Pouliot eds., 2011). I am grateful to Jutta Brunnée for pointing that out to me. Consistently with the account of law and legal practice given in Chapter 1, Adler and Pouliot define (*ibid.* at 6) "practices" as "socially meaningful patterns of action which, in being performed more or less competently, simultaneously embody, act out, and possibly reify background knowledge and discourse in and on the material world."

[60] See *supra* Chapter 1, Part I.

[61] MAX WEBER, 1 ECONOMY AND STATE 4 (1968). Weber here follows Hegel's contention that ethical life requires concrete expression in a community, expression situated in public space: CHARLES TAYLOR, HEGEL AND MODERN SOCIETY 84–95 (1979); HANNAH ARENDT, THE HUMAN CONDITION, chap. 2 (1958). Likewise: CLIFFORD GEERTZ, LOCAL KNOWLEDGE 31 (3rd ed. 2000) ("the object of cultural study is not to be found in an informant's unspoken subjectivity but is rather what is publicly available as symbols — the inscription in writing, the fixation of meaning.").

[62] "[P]ractices are not self-identifying." Luc Wintgens, Legisprudence and Comparative Law, *in* EPISTEMOLOGY AND METHODOLOGY OF COMPARATIVE LAW 299, 309 (Mark van Hoecke ed., 2004).

[63] E.g., Jutta Brunnée & Stephen J. Toope, Interactional Legal Theory, the International Rule of Law, and Global Constitutionalism *in* HANDBOOK OF GLOBAL CONSTITUTIONALISM 170, 175 (Anthony F. Lang & Antje Wiener eds., 2017).

coded by the courts as legal or illegal, and enforced as such.[64] That clearly describes the behaviour of litigating parties before a court, of lawyers advising clients as to their legal predicaments, and of private parties drafting such legal instruments as contracts, for example. But it arguably also characterizes the behaviour of all other legal actors, though perhaps with lesser degrees of immediacy.

It seems clear that arbitrators and lower court judges worry about their rulings standing up to a higher court's review, and hence aim at least to some extent to replicate what they speculate would be those courts' pronouncements on the issue before them. Legal scholars can likewise be described, I would suggest, as discussing and debating what they consider *should* be – or else *should* count as valid arguments towards – the courts' ultimate rulings on various questions. For one, their own pupils are constantly being reminded to 'think like lawyers,' to adduce only 'valid legal arguments,' i.e. arguments that could be found persuasive by a local court. That description moreover seems apt whether the scholars in question are local or foreign: as we saw,[65] comparative lawyers might similarly be constrained to reconstructing the local legal discourse in ways that would be found acceptable to the local actors, hence to their judges.

The same might even be true of legislators, regulators and administrative tribunals, moreover. On one conception of legislation at least, "its content will get progressively filled as one goes down the ladder [of official authority, that content being] not determined until the law has been applied ... the sovereign's act of making a law [hence] is only completed when that (provisional) resting point has been reached."[66] To be sure, that conception sits well with the fact that statutes and regulations are typically drafted with a view to maximizing judicial enforcement: unconstitutional wording is generally avoided, as are texts so inconsistent with the system's other legal materials that they might end up being altogether ignored by the judges. As for administrative tribunals, finally, while they clearly are endowed with extensive discretionary powers and the concomitant high degree of institutional independence, they too ultimately operate 'in the shadow of the law,' so to speak, with an eye to 'the judge over their shoulder' – as some government documentation explicitly recognizes and openly addresses.[67]

---

[64] "For law to perform its expressive function well, it is important that law communicate well ... [L]aw ... receives articulation through the anticipation and enforcement of sanctions." Cass R. Sunstein, On the Expressive Function of Law, 144 *U. PENN. L. REV.* 2021, 2050–51 (1996).

[65] See *supra* Chapter 3, Part III, section ii.

[66] David Dyzenhaus, Deliberative Constitutionalism Through the Lens of the Administrative State *in* CAMBRIDGE HANDBOOK OF DELIBERATIVE CONSTITUTIONALISM 13 (Ron Levy *et al.* eds., forthcoming 2018).

[67] Gus O'Donnell, Foreword to THE JUDGE OVER YOUR SHOULDER (Treasury Solicitor's Department ed., 4th ed. 2006). The opening line of the first edition sets the tone of the whole document as follows: "You are sitting at your desk granting licences on behalf of your Minister. Your enabling statutory powers are in the widest possible terms: 'The Secretary of State may grant licences on such conditions as he thinks fit'. With power like that you might think that there could be no possible ground for legal

In that sense it can plausibly be asserted, I would suggest, that all the various rules, arguments, source materials and so on that make up legal systems are more or less directly aimed at the single binary question of what will or will not end up being implemented by the courts. If so, while what is in fact coded legal or illegal by the judges in the different systems varies,[68] that binary coding structure is constant.[69] We will see below that the arguments themselves of course can only be *relatively* 'good' or 'bad' (depending on how likely they are to lead to the particular legal/illegal coding sought). But the point for now is that all legal arguments are ultimately directed at such binary coding.

And if that is an accurate description of legal practice everywhere, it arguably makes sense to count as 'meaningful acts' in any given legal community all and only those operations ultimately directed at the community's particular legal/illegal coding. Indeed, the only arguments, etc., that really *matter* are those aired in front of the community's judges. For judges are uniquely empowered to trigger implementation, to turn 'mere' arguments into concrete measures directly affecting people's lives. Unlike other legal actors, judges in all legal systems are bound (explicitly or implicitly) by "the prohibition of denial of justice,"[70] the requirement to "decide all cases brought to them by themselves,"[71] even those where there seems to be no good reason to favour one or the other of the 'legal' or 'illegal' coding options.[72] Moreover, only their decisions are final, thus amenable to imminent and irreversible implementation: the finality that individuals pine for in all legal communities[73] – having matters 'settled' once and for all – comes from the judges, and them

challenge in the courts whatever you do. But you would be wrong." I am grateful to David Dyzenhaus for pointing out that document to me.

[68] Extabe, *supra* note 17, at 124 ("practical decisions of validity are reached on a case by case basis and according to rhetorically tailored criteria of relevance that are contingent (because they depend on temporal and spatial considerations), heterogenous (because they are not enclosed on any list of permissible sources), and evaluative (because they depend on judgements)."), but for Extabe such contingence confirms, *contra* the present argument, that legal systems cannot be described as 'systems' proper (at 120 and 124).

[69] "The important point is that [all legal] communication defers to its regulation through coding"; LUHMANN, *supra* note 32, at 100. "All systems code their environment ... But while the code is essential ... the content of these programmes is contingent." Richard Nobles & David Schiff, *Introduction* to LUHMANN, *supra* note 32, at 10.

[70] See LUHMANN, *supra* note 32, at 279.

[71] *Ibid.*

[72] As there is no third, "neither legal nor illegal" option open to them, they "inevitably, and regularly, have to decide the undecidable": "Contracts and statutes can be drafted (or avoided) on the assumption that the legality of a particular matter cannot be known prior to the matter being decided ... But this avoidance is not open to the courts." Nobles & Schiff, *supra* note 69, at 32. And at 34: "arguments are operations of the legal system, but unlike decisions, they do not assign symbols of validity... [T]his special role of the courts explains how it is that 'errors' — decisions without reasons or applying inconsistent reasons, are nonetheless part of the system."

[73] For an account of finality as inherent to justice and the rule of law, see: A. Ripstein, The Rule of Law and Times' Arrow, *in Private Law and the Rule of Law*, chap. 14 (Lisa M. Austin & Dennis Klimchuk eds, 2014). See *contra*: Leone Niglia, Pluralism in a New Key – Between Plurality and Normativity,

alone. The arguments directed at them accordingly should be considered particularly weighty expressions of the community's underlying collective commitments: precisely because such arguments carry the potential of real, imminent, irreversible consequences for the parties involved, they likely reflect a degree of thoughtfulness unrivalled by inconsequential arguments, which in contrast are 'free' and 'easy to make,' thus probably less carefully thought through.[74] That is arguably confirmed by the notorious distinction drawn in common law systems between the *ratio decidendi* and *obiter dicta* of judicial decisions: *ratios* would be particularly significant precisely because they bear directly on the outcome of the case, thus on what will materially affect the parties, whereas *obiters* would be less significant because they are by definition devoid of such imminent material consequences.

But it has been claimed that such strong emphasis on judges and adjudication, while perhaps warranted with respect to common law systems (as the example just given would confirm), is unrepresentative of most legal communities, in particular, civil law systems.[75] I would resist such a claim on the basis that French and German legal scholars alike commonly echo their Anglo-Saxon counterparts[76] in describing their law as adjudication-centred.[77] And while the *ratio/dicta* language indeed is peculiar to common law argumentation, the same notion is arguably also present, though expressed differently, in civil law systems. While judicial decisions admittedly are considered less authoritative than written law, or perhaps even doctrinal writings, in civil law systems (at least in French and French-inspired ones, less so in German-inspired systems), that arguably is so only because their judicial decisions

---

in PLURALISM AND EUROPEAN PRIVATE LAW, *supra* note 42, at 254 (suggesting that finality matters *merely* for 'law as integrity' as purportedly distinct from law's normativity); H. Patrick Glenn, *supra* note 46, at 70 (linking finality with legal hierarchy, which he views as normatively unattractive, though elsewhere recognizing (H. Patrick Glenn, Cosmopolitan Legal Orders, in THEORISING THE GLOBAL LEGAL ORDER, *supra* note 18, at 25) the importance of finality at the level of individual rulings).

[74] I accordingly would object to describing 'legal systems' as mere 'sites of contestation' (e.g. Hans Lindahl, A-Legality: Postnationalism and the Question of Legal Boundaries, 73 MOD. L. R. 30, 44 (2010); KRISCH, *supra* note 46) on the same basis, namely, that only contestation conducted *in the shadow of implementation* 'matters' and hence ought to be seen as 'meaningful.'

[75] Hesselink, *supra* note 42, at 209.

[76] Most famously Justice Holmes, who described law as the 'bad man's prediction' of what the courts will do in any particular case (Oliver Wendell Holmes, The Path of the Law, 10 HARV. L. R. 457 (1897)), and Dworkin (RONALD DWORKIN, TAKING RIGHTS SERIOUSLY (1978)).

[77] Jean Carbonnier, Les hypothèses fondamentales de la sociologie juridique, in FLEXIBLE DROIT: POUR UNE SOCIOLOGIE DU DROIT SANS RIGUEUR 21 (8th ed., 1995) ("est juridique ce qui est propre à provoquer un jugement, ce qui est susceptible de procès, justiciable de cette activité très particulière d'un tiers personnage qu'on appelle arbitre ou juge."); Jaluzot, *supra* note 20, in 689 ("il s'agit de s'intéresser ... au droit tel qu'il est dans la réalité et vérifié par l'expérience. Cette vérification est obtenue par la justiciabilité des règles observées, par leur aptitude à conduire à une décision judiciaire dotée d'une force contraignante étatique."). The same moreover has been said of Confucian jurisprudence (Norman P. Ho, Confucian Jurisprudence, Dworkin, and Hard Cases, 10 WASH. U. JURIS. REV. (forthcoming)) and contemporary Chinese law more generally (Mark Jia, Chinese Common Law? Guiding Cases and Judicial Reform, 129 HARV. L. REV. 2213 (2016)). See generally: MIRJAN R. DAMAŠKA, THE FACES OF JUSTICE AND STATE AUTHORITY 3–6 (1986).

are much less explicit than the typical English case. The classic French judgment offers no more than the bare disposition of the case – what at common law is considered the judgment's 'conclusion' – leaving it to the scholars to articulate the full reasoning. Considered on their own, French judgments accordingly offer very little juridical information. But the arguments afterwards expounded by the scholars very much are those that *they attribute to their judges*. Another possible explanation for the apparent lesser importance of judicial decisions at French law might be that it is meant to signal a general preference for reason-based arguments of principles, directly derived from the Code, over casuistic argumentation, which instead proceeds from analogies across specific rulings. But here again, I would argue, the collective reflection is ultimately more about the kind of arguments likely to find judicial favour than about any kind of downplaying of the judges' role.

Insofar as it can be accepted that all legal systems are (for good reasons) ultimately centred on adjudication, then, it would seem that although these are discursive communities, self-defined in and through particular discourses, those discourses remain materially anchored in the specific institutions capable of implementing them on the community members.[78] And insofar as implementation might require coercion,[79] which in turn requires at least minimal territorial connection with the bodies and/or assets of the individuals involved,[80] the systems themselves can arguably be described as necessarily ultimately so connected.[81]

ii. *Fluid (Intellectual) Edges*

While legal systems, then, boast a relatively well-defined institutional, material centre of gravity, their edges as indicated are determined intellectually, which causes them to be fluid. Notably, that fluidity is spatial and temporal. That is to say, the

---

[78] Hence did Dworkin describe precedential decisions as exerting "gravitational force": Ronald Dworkin, *Taking Rights Seriously* 111 (1978).

[79] See *supra* Chapter 1, Part I, section i.

[80] "the foundation of jurisdiction is physical power"; *McDonald v. Mabee* 243 U.S. 90, 91 (1917) (*per* J. Holmes); "a state ought to assume jurisdiction only if it has a real and substantial link to the event." *R. v. Hape*, [2007] 2 S.C.R. 292 (Can.) at para. 62. See also para. 65 (enforcement jurisdiction ultimately is strictly territorial); Bomhoff, *supra* note 46, at 6 (scholarly consensus on the geographical limitations of enforcement powers); Sarah Song, The Significance of Territorial Presence and the Rights of Immigrants, *in* MIGRATION IN POLITICAL THEORY: THE ETHICS OF MOVEMENT AND MEMBERSHIP 225 (Sarah Fine & Lea Ypi eds., 2014); Kurt Siehr, Global Jurisdiction of Local Courts and Recognition of Their Judgments Abroad, *in* FESTSCHRIFT FÜR ULRICH MAGNUS ZUM 70, 515 (Peter Mankowski & Wolfgang Wurmnest eds., 2014) (state courts refusing enforcement of judgment entered on basis of 'transient jurisdiction' – individuals only temporarily present on state territory). The requisite degree of material connection may however vary across legal systems. For example, Continental inquisitorial procedure arguably presupposes a lesser such degree than Anglo-Saxon adversarial procedure.

[81] Whether such minimal territorial connection necessarily entails that only (territory controlling) nation states can qualify as legal systems proper remains an open question, as indicated in Part III, section iii, *infra*. See in particular note 134, *infra*.

exact geography of legal systems, unlike that of their judicial institutions, is difficult to ascertain demographically (who counts as an actor of the system) and in
terms of materials (what norms, rules, sources, etc. can be considered a part of the
system). That geographic indeterminacy moreover is compounded by historic indeterminacy: whatever individuals and materials can be earmarked as partaking of the
system at any given point in time changes constantly, and the precise moment at
which those changes occur cannot be pinpointed with any certainty. We will first
look to the temporal indeterminacy of legal systems and thereafter consider their
spatial indeterminacy.

(1) Time

There is little debate that legal systems are dynamic systems, whose reflexive quality
results in their shape and content changing constantly.[82] As every legal operation,
we saw, involves looking backwards to prior legal operations while also projecting
forward via speculations as to future such operations – what some call 'intimation'[83]
and others view as just inherent to the notion of 'tradition'[84] – and as every new
operation in turn is included into the stockpile of operations that will inform future
ones, the overall size of that stockpile is bound to increase. But its content is likewise
modified at each turn, since every new operation involves reinterpreting the existing stockpile, and interpretation as we know contributes to modifying, even ever so
slightly, what is being interpreted.[85] It is therefore the system's size and content alike
that is bound to evolve through its self-regeneration process: the legal actors "not
only have to rebuild the ship as it sails, but they have to do so in a shifting sea whose
nautical charts are subject to continuous adjustment."[86]

---

[82] "Contrary to entities or substances, which can be grasped in a reified way, practices have no existence
other than in their unfolding or process." Adler & Pouliot, *supra* note 59, at 7. See generally: MICHEL
VAN DE KERCHOVE & FRANÇOIS OST, *LEGAL SYSTEM BETWEEN ORDER AND DISORDER* (Ian Stewart
trans., 1994); Hesselink, *supra* note 42, at 209; Heydebrand, *supra* note 4, at 117ff; Rosen, *supra* note
4, at 503ff; Ugo Mattei, Three Patterns of Law: Taxonomy and Change in the World's Legal Systems,
45 AM J. COMP. L. 1997.

[83] NEIL WALKER, *INTIMATIONS OF GLOBAL LAW* 157–58 (2014) ("Intimation ... is as much about what
is implicit in the world as it stands and as it unfolds, as it is about our explicit pronouncements on
the world to come ... as much about anticipation as veneration."). And though Walker first suggests
intimation "is distinctive about global law," he later acknowledges (at 157) that it is present in "any
type of [legal or non-legal] normativity intimation."

[84] Martin Krygier, Law as Tradition, 5 LAW & PHIL. 237 (1986) ('tradition' as central feature of any
jurisdictionally bounded legal system's generic claim to authority); GLENN, *supra* note 23, at chap. 1;
see WALKER at 152 (tradition as "selective specification in accordance with a recognised transmission
procedure or formula which consciously ensures continuity between past and present").

[85] See *supra* discussion of Chapter 3, Part II, section iii.

[86] WALKER, *supra* note 83, at 162. See also, *ibid.* at 149–50: "it is on account of that doubly 'intimated'
object—actively projected and obliquely sourced ... that ... law retains a fluid and contentious quality";
and at 151, referring to "[law's] complex relationship to the legal past and to the legal future and so to
legal 'time' in general." Likewise: SIMMONDS, *supra* note 47, at 162 ("never fully reducible to a great

The precise whereabouts of that process remain somewhat obscure, however. In particular, the thorny question of how the system first emerges calls for further reflection: if every new operation appeals to the existing stock of past operations, which themselves presumably appealed to similarly pre-existing such operations, what did the very first operations appeal to? We are faced with a chicken and egg dilemma. For it now seems that, just like bee swarms which start in some elusive fashion but clearly self-magnify from the moment that they have in fact started, legal systems can really come into existence only from the moment that ... they already exist.[87]

It is worth emphasizing at the outset that that dilemma arises only under an internal definition of legal systems. That is clear, again, from colonial history: although the colonizing powers typically took it upon themselves to (externally) set a precise date at which their respective colonies would be considered created, those colonies did not *really* (internally) establish themselves as autonomous legal systems until they had already accumulated a minimum of local materials on which to draw for the purpose of adjudicating local disputes – as per the above paradox.[88] Further compounding the problem, moreover, as colonial legal materials naturally accumulated at different paces for different areas of law, it presumably could be said that the colonial legal system came into existence at different times depending on the area of law. So if colonial legal systems were not born on the precise date externally set in colonial law, when did they, in fact, come into existence?

As it turns out, that dilemma is not quite as intractable as first appears, at least not when it comes to law. (We can, fortunately, safely leave it to entomologists to deal with actual bee swarms.) Here again, Luhmann's sociological insights prove enlightening. On his account, the formation of legal systems proceeds in three stages.[89] First comes an accumulation of individual rulings: social life inevitably entails interpersonal conflicts, which need to be resolved one way or the other.[90] The individuals charged with those resolutions at that point proceed on no other basis than their personal sense of right and wrong. They can gather inspiration from the

assemblage of enacted rules, but ... always a system awaiting construction from those materials."); SEAN COYLE, *FROM POSITIVISM TO IDEALISM* 16 (2007) ("constant revision and fragmentation [as] endemic to political ideals"); LUHMANN, *supra* note 32, at 91 ("Law is a historical machine in the sense that each autopoietic operation changes the system, changes the state of the machine, and creates changed conditions for further operations ... It is a machine that involves its own condition in each operation and so constructs a new machine with each operation.").

[87] CONSTANTINESCO, *supra* note 12, at 216ff; VAN DE KERCHOVE & OST, *supra* note 82, at 147ff.

[88] David B. Schorr, Questioning Harmonization: Legal Transplantation in the Colonial Context, 10 *THEORETICAL INQUIRIES IN L.* 49–53 (2009). On Canadian colonial history, see: Howard P. Glenn, Persuasive Authority, 32 *MCGILL L. J.* 261 (1987). On the US experience, see: RENÉ DAVID, MARIE GORÉ & CAMILLE JAUFFRET-SPINOSI, *LES GRANDS SYSTÈMES DE DROIT CONTEMPORAINS* 301ff (2002); ALAN WATSON, *LEGAL TRANSPLANTS* 65ff (2006).

[89] LUHMANN, *supra* note 32, at 230ff. See likewise Adler & Pouliot's very similar account of the emergence of practices writ large: Adler & Pouliot, *supra* note 59, at 18–21.

[90] Nobles & Schiff, *supra* note 69, at 25 ("long experience in arbitrating normative conflicts with the code legal/illegal").

Bible, Greek mythology, or whatever, or just go on their individual preferences. The sources determining conflict resolution at that early stage are infinite and infinitely varied: we are in a state of complete 'porosity,' 'permeability' or, as Luhmann calls it, "informational openness."[91]

Once a number of those rulings have taken place, however, the intellectual urge arises to "attempt to order what is happening."[92] The rulings are first recorded, in writing or, in the case of oral legal traditions, through memory and narrative.[93] Patterns can then be detected in the justifications given for the various resolutions, some of which seem particularly consistent, robust or somehow more legitimate, and hence worth retaining over the others. Only at this second stage, when a sufficient number of (actual) rulings have been gathered that it becomes possible to (intellectually) reflect back on them, can a form of 'legal consciousness' begin to emerge.[94] As the justification patterns initially retained recur in new conflict resolutions, their salience increases,[95] to the point of gradually acquiring the status of 'norms,'[96] which in turn allows community members to form 'normative expectations' as to future conflict resolutions.[97] The sum of those henceforth 'normative' rules, maxims, arguments, concepts and so on congeals over time into a body of 'legal materials' proper, soon to be attended with a particular technique ('legal

---

[91] Twining, *supra* note 4, at 85 ("the imprecision and porosity of the social contexts of most normative orders"); Extabe, *supra* note 17, at 124 ("law [as] an essentially porous entity, distinguishable from, and yet permeable by, its exterior"); Jaluzot, *supra* note 20, at 691 ("relativité, mobilité et permeabilité de l'ordre juridique"); LUHMANN, *supra* note 32.

[92] Nobles & Schiff, *supra* note 69, at 27.

[93] LUHMANN, *supra* note 32, at 234; Nobles & Schiff, *supra* note 69, at 25 ("[We witness the] establishment of a level of secondary self-observation ... writing recorded transactions that were worth recording.").

[94] Nobles & Schiff, *supra* note 69, at 51 ("a continued connection between consciousness and legal systems"); Extabe, *supra* note 17, at 118; Gillespie, *supra* note 19, at 227 ("social institutions and regulatory practices are first created in the mind"); Kennedy, *supra* note 16, at 15 (explaining how legal consciousness is experienced by legal actors: "if your position about X puts a good deal of moral and intellectual pressure on you to take a particular position with respect to Y, then the two are part of [the same legal system]. If you experience no such pressure, they are not.").

[95] "The differentiation process ... can thus begin somewhere or other and somehow or other and reinforce the deviation that has arisen. One settlement among many comes to be preferred where the advantages of centralization are mutually reinforcing." NIKLAS LUHMANN, 4 THEORY OF SOCIETY 3 (2012).

[96] That distinction variously appears in the legal literature as that between 'what people actually do' and their 'felt sense of obligation' (Tamanaha, *supra* note 53), 'actual behaviour' and 'beliefs or attitudes concerning its legitimacy, obligatoriness, and prescriptive power' (TWINING, *supra* note 1, at 118), 'existence empirique' and 'validité' (Jaluzot, *supra* note 20, at 690).

[97] "The function of law is to maintain normative expectations in the face of disappointment. Law's communications about what ought to occur must, if they are to continue as expectations, remain meaningful despite the inevitability that what ought to occur will not always occur." Nobles & Schiff, *supra* note 69, at 9 (paraphrasing Luhmann at 94). And at 15: "The presence of expectations that captured and convicted thieves will be punished stabilizes expectations represented by the law of theft even if only a few criminals are punished relative to the amount of crime." See likewise, Postema's description of law's 'normative guidance': Postema, *Law's System*, *supra* note 32 at 88–91.

dogmatics')[98] and concomitant body of expertise ('legal professionals').[99] Only then does the initial 'informational openness' come to be accompanied by minimal 'normative closure,'[100] the closure required for organic 'systems' to be recognizable as such.[101] As legal materials, legal dogmatics and legal professionals slowly come together, so does a somewhat enclosed 'legal practice,' distinguishable from other social practices.

Then comes the third and final stage of the formation process, on Luhmann's account, that of reflecting back on the practice itself. That is, it is now possible for, say, scholars to reflect on (and debate) not just the punctual outcomes of the conflict resolution process, but also the growing body of professional arguments that simultaneously supports and emerges from that resolution process, i.e. the practice as such. We now have 'law' proper – law reflecting upon itself *as law* – as well as a 'legal system' proper: a system wherein individual conflicts are resolved by appeal to an objective law rather than via the subjective opinions of unconnected arbitrators operating on an individual basis.[102]

Three consecutive steps, then, respectively staging judges, lawyers and scholars. While Luhmann himself does not say so explicitly, moreover, the *disappearance* of legal systems presumably proceeds in the same way, through the same three steps in reverse. As particular materials, techniques and voices somehow come to be ignored by the judges, they in turn move out of sight of the lawyers, and of the scholars.[103] They gradually exit adjudication, legal practice, and in time legal consciousness as a whole, thus the system itself – which shrinks, possibly to the point of extinction.

To say of legal systems that they 'really come into existence only from the moment that they already exist' – or, in the reverse, that they 'really come out of existence only from the moment that they no longer exist' – hence is not quite as tautological as might have first appeared. For the apparent circularity of such statements quickly subsides under the present (and Luhmann's) conception of law as inherently factual *and* intellectual. (*Quid* of bee swarms, which do not boast the same duality?)

---

[98] LUHMANN, *supra* note 32, at 256.

[99] LUHMANN, *supra* note 32, at 298.

[100] LUHMANN, *supra* note 32, at chap. 2; NIKLAS LUHMANN, A SOCIOLOGICAL THEORY OF LAW 174–83 (1985); Niklas Luhmann, The Unity of the Legal System, in AUTOPOIETIC LAW – A NEW APPROACH TO LAW AND SOCIETY 16 (Gunther Teubner ed., 1988). See also: Hubert Rottleuthner, Les métaphores biologiques dans la pensée juridique, 31 ARCH. DE PHIL. DU DROIT 215 (1986); VAN DE KERCHOVE & OST, *supra* note 82.

[101] See *supra* Chapter 2, Part IV.

[102] "The long-term effect of all of this is a base of concepts, maxims, principles, and rules for decisions that forms the materials which are applied partly formally, partly critically, and which enable the judge to reject ad hoc and ad hominem arguments." LUHMANN, *supra* note 95, at 249. See also above the discussions of 'Publicness' in *supra* Chapter 1, Part I, section iv, and of 'The Subjectivity Objection' in Chapter 3, Part II, section v.

[103] See our earlier discussion in Chapter 1, Part II, section iii.

Precisely because law as collective commitment allows to distinguish between what *is* in fact implemented as legal/illegal (the *facts* of law) and what *ought* to be so implemented (the *norms* of law),[104] it can coherently be said of law on that account that it exists or does not exist (normatively) only from the moment that it already exists or no longer exists (factually). Or, in Luhmann's words, that "autopoietic systems are always historical systems, which start from the state in which they have put themselves,"[105] and that "[l]egal practice [as one such system] always operates with a law that has historically always been there because it could not otherwise entertain the notion of distinguishing itself as legal practice."[106] (Note that the circularity of such statements in contrast really is intractable under either of the above described positivist and natural law ideal-types, where law is respectively strictly factual and strictly intellectual, and hence lacks the complementing dimension needed to unravel the circle.)

The temporal indeterminacy of legal systems should be clear at this point. Under the picture just laid out, there is no exact moment at which one can categorically affirm that a legal system, or any of its components, 'exists' or 'does not exist' ... *normatively* speaking. Whereas the legal/illegal rulings that ground the system are categorical and punctual, the normative significance of those rulings, like that of the system's various other components – or of the entire system for that matter – is a matter of interpretation, thus relative and never fixed once and for all, but rather gradually increased or decreased over time.[107]

Consider again how the judicial reasoning process operates. In common law systems, the stockpile of accumulated legal operations consulted by the judges in any given case as we know is largely made up of judicial decisions, in particular, the parts of those decisions considered 'binding' (*ratio*), in contrast with their parts considered merely 'persuasive' (*obiter*). A similar distinction is arguably drawn in civil law systems between ('binding') legislative diktats and ('persuasive') diktats emerging from a *jurisprudence constante* (in France) or *ständige Rechtsprechung* (in Germany).[108] Yet analysts of the judicial process report that, despite such dichotomous labelling, no

---

[104] See *supra* Chapter 1, Part II, section iii.

[105] LUHMANN, *supra* note 95, at 85.

[106] *Ibid.* at 91.

[107] As obtains more generally under a 'coherence' rather than 'correspondence' standard of truth, as discussed above: see *supra* text accompanying note 106 in "Subjectivity Objection," Chapter 3, Part II, section v. See likewise Adler & Pouliot's account (Adler & Pouliot, *supra* note 59, at 6) of 'practice' as "socially meaningful patterns of action [that are] performed *more or less* competently." (Emphasis added.)

[108] A. Harvison Young, Stare Decisis—Quebec Court of Appeal, 72 CAN. BAR REV. 91, 98, 101 (1993). The same can be said of the Italian *dottrina giuridica* and the Spanish *doctrina juridica*. See generally: Robert Alexy & Ralph Dreier, Precedent in the Federal Republic of Germany, *in* INTERPRETING PRECEDENTS: A COMPARATIVE STUDY 17, 50 (Neil MacCormick & Robert S. Summers eds., 1997); Jean Carbonnier, Authorities in Civil Law: France, *in* THE ROLE OF JUDICIAL DECISIONS AND DOCTRINE IN CIVIL LAW AND IN MIXED JURISDICTIONS 91, 102 (Joseph Dainow ed., 1974); Michele Taruffo & Massimo La Torre, Precedent in Italy, *in* INTERPRETING PRECEDENTS: A COMPARATIVE STUDY, *supra*,

authority is, in fact, ever considered absolutely determinative (or not) by the judges in any legal system.[109] Common law judges rather treat (purportedly 'binding') precedents as additional, more or less constraining reasons to favour one conclusion over the other, one important factor in that determination being the authoritative salience of the courts that issued them.[110] In other words, the weight of past decisions would be proportional to how 'loud' the particular decision maker's voice is taken to be in the system at that particular time. In civil law systems likewise, the legislative voice will be considered 'louder' than the judicial voices at the source of any *jurisprudence constante* or *ständige Rechtsprechung* (though the difference is less marked with respect to the latter). In certain (easy) cases, of course, relevant authorities exist whose loudness seems well established and enduring. But where the stockpile of previous operations does not cover the case at hand, or is internally contradictory, the judge has no choice but to rely on less authoritative, perhaps even hitherto legally irrelevant, materials. So soon as that happens, however, those materials *ipso facto* become more authoritative – their normative salience increases – which in turn causes them to be reused in other cases (as per Luhmann's second stage of the formation process above), to a point where they might eventually come to be treated as clearly entrenched and enduringly 'loud' materials. That arguably explains the rise to prominence of policy arguments in common law jurisdictions and enviable status of doctrinal writings in civil law jurisdiction.[111]

The normative significance of each of the system's components, and the system's corresponding overall normative tightness, would accordingly be a matter of degree and one that varies over time. That presumably is why legal systems are typically described as 'forming,' 'emerging,' 'developing' or else as 'declining,' 'fading,' 'deteriorating,' rather than as categorically 'existing' or 'not existing'[112] – as is typically done with bee swarms. Unlike the centre of gravity of legal systems, then, their temporal boundaries are fluid: the size and content of these systems change constantly, and the exact moments at which those changes take place cannot be precisely identified.

(2) Space

Luhmann's account of the formation of legal systems arguably likewise underscores these systems' spatial indeterminacy. The three stages of their formation confirm,

---

at 141, 180–81; Alfonso Ruiz Miguel & Francisco J. Laporta, Precedent in Spain, *in* INTERPRETING PRECEDENTS: A COMPARATIVE STUDY, *supra*, at 259, 272–73, 282–83.

[109] See that point's discussion in *supra* Chapter 1, Part II, section iii.

[110] DWORKIN, *supra* note 29, at 24ff (1986); Stephen R. Perry, Judicial Obligation, Precedent and the Common Law, 7 OXF. J. LEG. STUD. 215, 239–45 (1987).

[111] See *supra*, Chapter 1, Part I, section v.

[112] "If efficacy of law is a matter of degree, then we might have to concede that law's existence is likewise and thereby a matter of degree." Gerald J. Postema, Fidelity in Law's Commonwealth, *in* PRIVATE LAW AND THE RULE OF LAW n. 19 (Lisa M. Austin & Dennis Klimchuk eds., 2014).

he suggests, that these systems are not structured hierarchically but rather circularly, in terms of 'centre' and 'periphery.'[113] So far, so good, but he and I part company in the next step, when it comes to specifying the internal spatial organization of that circular structure (the system's "internal differentiation").[114]

Luhmann's account motions to an internal organization in terms of three concentric layers, corresponding to the three stages of the system's formation. The first layer as expected is made up of the judges – the system's very heart, its 'centre of gravity,' as I described it. The second layer gathers the lawyers, who reflect on the judges' rulings with a view to extracting the rules and arguments that will inform future rulings – what Luhmann describes as 'second order' legal reasoning. Besides lawyers, that second layer includes all those who 'think like lawyers' – those who engage in 'second order' legal reasoning: the legislators, the contract drafters, even the judges themselves (in common law systems), when they overtly interpret previous cases rather than just finally dispose of that before them. The third layer, finally, comprises the scholars, as we saw, but also all those who 'think like scholars' – those who reflect on the materials produced through the second layer with a view to questioning and ultimately honing these materials' overall consistency and desirability. As the reflection of that last group of actors accordingly amounts to 'reflection on reflections,' Luhmann dubs it "third order" legal reasoning. Three concentric layers, then – much like the heart of an onion – corresponding to the three forms of reasoning deployed at the three stages of formation.

I would resist that account of the internal organization of legal systems on the ground that while I do see the 'first order' reasoning deployed in the first layer (ruling on cases) as qualitatively different from the 'second' and 'third order' reasoning deployed in the next two (arguing over rulings), what Luhmann distinguishes as 'second' and 'third order' reasoning are in my view one and the same.[115] That is to say, that while the scholars' 'third order' reflection admittedly is in a sense further removed from the judges' rulings than, say, the lawyers' 'second order' arguments before those very judges, it proceeds in exactly the same way. We indeed saw that any kind of legal interpretation necessarily involves passing judgment on the internal consistency and normative desirability of the materials interpreted.[116] If so, the task of extracting rules from past rulings is 'normative' in exactly the same way as is that of overtly assessing those rulings' quality however defined: in both cases, the debate ultimately centres on how judges *ought* to rule in any given case.[117]

---

[113] Nobles & Schiff, *supra* note 69, at 30 (referring to Luhmann, chap. 7). Likewise: Gérard Timsit, L'ordre juridique comme métaphore, 33 *Droits* 8 (2001) ("un système d'appartenances ou d'inclusion des normes dans un ensemble non-hiérarchisé").

[114] LUHMANN, *supra* note 95.

[115] My earlier denial of the possibility of a sustainable midway position between the internal and external perspectives (see *supra* Chapter 3, Part II, section iii) proceeds from the same argument.

[116] See *supra* Chapter 1 and Chapter 3.

[117] Of course, the judges' own reasoning could likewise be described as 'normative' in so far as they in principle should decide their cases by asking the very same question of how judges (here, themselves)

Of course, there are scholars and scholars. Some scholars are more interested in reinventing the legal system along normative lines borrowed from neighbouring social systems (economics, literature, politics) than in honing the system's own normative apparatus. Theirs are the so-called 'external' critiques, by contrast to 'internal' ones, which instead seek to evaluate the system 'on its own terms.' Such external-critique scholars admittedly might be engaging in an intellectual exercise qualitatively different from that deployed by any of the actors just discussed. But as Luhmann himself seems to recognize, that may well militate in favour of positioning them, not so much on a separate layer, as altogether outside the system[118] – they would be economists, literary critics, political scientists more than 'legal scholars' proper. My point accordingly only applies to the internal-critique scholars, insofar as their reasoning would in fact be qualitatively indistinguishable from that of any actor populating the purported second and third layers.[119] In sum, while I would retain (in fact insist on) the distinction drawn by Luhmann between the (first order) centre and the periphery of legal systems, I would resist his further (second/third order) distinction within the periphery.

That is not to say, however, that all legal actors and materials should be seen as equidistant from the centre, thus as forming a single homogenous peripheral layer. Rather, their differences in normative salience warrants, I would argue, positioning them at correspondingly different distances from one another and the centre. At any given time, that is, the most salient actors and materials, those most likely to convince the judges – 'slam dunk' arguments, for example – can be pictured as sitting tightly together, very close to these judges. Conversely, the least salient actors and materials, those only remotely likely to convince the judges – highly 'creative' arguments – would sit further apart from one another and the judges. And in between would lay a flurry of unevenly distributed 'somewhat salient' actors and materials – arguments 'worth a shot.' Now, we saw that the actors' and materials' relative degrees of salience change over time, which would suggest that their relative distances from one another and the centre do as well. Indeed, when judges undertake to rely on hitherto ignored sources or materials, the resulting salience increase is reflected in those sources/materials moving correspondingly closer to the ones crowding the system centre. Conversely, as particular sources and materials become less frequently used in adjudication, their resulting diminishing salience is matched by a corresponding movement away from the centre.

---

objectively *ought to* decide the case at hand. But, crucially, we saw that they can in fact base their decisions on their own personal values (as they do in the first stage of the formation process). Those decisions would nonetheless count as 'legal,' whereas only the arguments based on the objective values of the system as a whole count as properly 'legal normative judgment.'

[118] Nobles & Schiff, *supra* note 69, at 35. That would confirm the claim made in Chapter 3 to the effect that a 'midpoint' position between the internal and external perspectives is ultimately unsustainable.

[119] Oddly, Luhmann seems to agree: "the observation is itself an operation, and therefore everything applies to it that has been shown to apply to operations ... In this sense, self-reference always implies external reference, and vice versa." (LUHMANN, *supra* note 32).

If we now stand back to consider what that does to the spatial configuration of the system as a whole, we observe that any punctual movement of a system component towards or away from the centre, as it gains or loses salience, translates into a corresponding marginal variation in the system's overall coverage and density. The first judicial reference to hitherto ignored materials causes the system to stretch its boundary to reach to and include the new materials, thus marginally increasing its overall coverage. But as those materials are being reused in subsequent cases, they make their way towards the centre, resulting in the system shrinking back, and its density proportionally increasing. And conversely, materials moving away from the centre first cause an extension of the system's coverage, with the corresponding decrease in density. But if those materials move even further out, and exit the system altogether, the system's boundary then pops back to a smaller overall coverage, yet without the proportional recovery in density, as the system is now short of some of its initial components. That entails that older, more mature legal systems, whose composition has had time to stabilize over time, are knit more tightly, their breadth and density being respectively smaller and higher than those of younger, emerging such systems – as are long-standing compared to emerging bee swarms. In Luhmann's words, the 'normative closure' of mature systems is stronger, as those have had time to include and weave together high quantities of materials, and their informational openness correspondingly becomes less significant, as said strong normative closure eliminates the need, all else equal, to fish for new materials outside the system.

In sum, the fundamental normative character of legal systems, which makes it impossible to categorically affirm that those systems, or any of their elements, 'exist' or 'do not exist' at any particular *time*, also makes it impossible to ascribe exact *locations* to them or their elements at any given point in time. Certainly, there is no reason to assume that their locations can be determined territorially, by reference to the fixed territorial locations of the central adjudicative bodies that first produced them. All adjudicative bodies remain free to, and in fact commonly do, coopt materials originating from other state territories. A Canadian judge referring to an English judicial decision for the first time, for example, has the effect of extending the reach of the Canadian swarm into English territories (without for that matter undermining the structural integrity of the Canadian and English swarms, as we see below).[120] Confirmed patterns of such citations indeed are what prompted comparative lawyers to classify the Canadian and English legal systems within the same, common law 'family' or 'tradition.'[121]

---

[120] See *infra*, text accompanying notes 134–35.

[121] E.g. the Canadian and English systems being grouped within the same, common law 'family' or 'tradition': INTRODUCTION TO COMPARATIVE LAW (Konrad Zweigert & Hein Koetz eds., Tony Weir trans., 1987); GLENN, *supra* note 23; DAVID, GORÉ & JAUFFRET-SPINOSI, *supra* note 88, at 301ff; CONSTANTINESCO, *supra* note 12.

Legal systems hence emerge from their self-delineating process resembling, I would contend, bee swarms more than onions. Whereas onions boast stable and well-defined concentric layers, legal systems are ill-shaped, elusively contoured and unevenly dense at any particular time. Moreover, such shape, contours and density change constantly. From static and dynamic perspectives alike, then, they look very much like bee swarms, whose ever-fluctuating edges and opacity levels are determined by their elements' relative proximity to, and constant movement towards or away from, the queen bee.

III. BEE SWARMS IN GLOBAL LAW

We now exit the internal perspective and move from the local to the global with a view to exploring the implications of the conception of legal systems just laid out for the legal pluralism debate: to what extent, if at all, does our swarm model allow for dissociating law from the state? How does that model account for law that apparently spans more than one state (EC, the Commonwealth) or less than one (provincial law, municipal law)? What does it say of international law or any other form of 'soft' transnational law (cross-border regulatory networks, extra-territorial adjudication)? How does it deal with law that targets only certain people (aboriginal law, religious law) or certain sectors of activity (human rights law, environmental law)? What of informal or even underground social and economic organizations (sports clubs, cultural associations, chambers of commerce, mafia groups)? How many swarms are at play in each of these cases, and where does each one begin and end? Are they mutually exclusive or do they clash and intersect? Such questions need to be answered before comparatists can proceed to identify and delineate the particular swarm-like systems that they will be comparing.

Several competing accounts of global law emerge from the legal pluralism literature, which dictate respectively different answers to the above questions. I here propose to review these accounts with a view to identifying those consistent with the swarm model of Part II, section ii. Note that the goal here is not to select or reconstruct an account of global law that might prove 'best all around' but merely to unpack the global implications of our swarm model and the more general account of comparative law built so far. Of course, as with all working conceptions, one would here hope for global (or any other) implications that prove somewhat intuitively appealing independently of their fit with the particular model at play.[122] In any event, much more would be needed beyond the fit assessment just proposed if our ultimate target were global rather than comparative law.

The various accounts of global law currently on offer are here organized in terms of three categories and subcategories, and discussed in that order. At a most general

---

[122] See *supra* Prologue.

level, accounts of global law can be described as either 'monistic' or 'pluralistic' (section i). Pluralistic such accounts in turn are so either 'strongly' or merely 'weakly' (section ii). Among weakly pluralist accounts, finally, we distinguish between those targeting 'subnational' and 'supranational' law (section iii).

i. Monism Versus Pluralism

As 'monism' and 'pluralism' mean different things to different people, it bears specifying at the outset how I use these terms here. I call 'monistic' (or 'non-pluralist') any account of global law wherein *all legal systems share one and the same kind of juridicity.*[123] That is to say that, under monism as I see it, however many different kinds of juridicity may coexist in the global universe, just one of them is at play in all that qualifies as a 'legal system' proper. A pluralist account in contrast allows for 'legal systems' possibly being grounded in different kinds of juridicity.

Perhaps the most obvious example of monism so defined is the traditional Westphalian model – also dubbed 'sovereignism'[124] or 'nationalism'[125] – wherein state law represents the only possible kind of juridicity, state legal orders represent the only possible 'legal systems,' and world law accordingly divides into exactly as many legal systems as there are nation states. Another example of monism is the 'universalism' – or 'anti-sovereignism'[126] – which in contrast merges all world law into just one, universal legal system. Universalists do typically contend that the rise in cross-border traffic of legal products and ideas that has attended globalization justify conceptualizing state and non-state actors as joined (or at least steadfastly joining) into a single 'world legal community,'[127] and all of world law as correspondingly form-

---

[123] Compare the above definition with that proposed by Woodman (Gordon Woodman, Ideological Combat and Social Observation: Recent Debate about Legal Pluralism, 42 J. LEG. PLUR. 21 (1988)), according to which an account of global law projects all legal systems as ultimately 'defined by, and subordinated to' state law – which others have described as 'methodological nationalism' (GUNTHER TEUBNER, CONSTITUTIONAL FRAGMENTS 10 (2012)) or 'state centrism' (Michaels, *supra* note 26, at 251).

[124] Niglia, *supra* note 73, at 250; Paul Schiff Berman, How Legal Pluralism Is and Is Not Distinct from Liberalism: A Response to Dennis Patterson and Alexis Galán, 11 INT'L J. CONST. L. 801, 802 (2013).

[125] Hesselink, *supra* note 42.

[126] 'Universalism' and 'sovereignism' are often described as opposite extremes on a same spectrum, e.g. Niglia, *supra* note 73, at 250.

[127] See elsewhere: Anne-Marie Slaughter, Judicial Globalization, 40 VA J. INT'L L. 1103 (2000) (though admitting that transnational judicial dialogue need not result in "blurring of the lines": ANNE-MARIE SLAUGHTER, A NEW WORLD ORDER 10 (2004)); Ronald J. Krotoszynski, I'd Like to Teach the World to Sing (in Perfect Harmony): International Judicial Dialogue and the Muses, 104 MICH. L. REV. 1321, 1322–23, 1327–36 (2006); LAWRENCE BAUM, JUDGES AND THEIR AUDIENCES (2008); MARY ANN GLENDON, RIGHTS TALK: THE IMPOVERISHMENT OF POLITICAL DISCOURSE 158 (1991) ("international traffic in ideas"); Itamar Mann, Dialectic of Transnationalism: Unauthorized Migration and Human Rights, 1993–2013, 54 HARV. INT'L L. J. 315, 391 (2013) (redefining "human rights law as a global *Grundnorm*"); JULIAN D. M. LEW, ACHIEVING THE DREAM: AUTONOMOUS ARBITRATION 179 (2006) (Arbitration "exists in its own space—a non-national or transnational or, if you prefer, an international domain. It has its own space independent of all national jurisdiction."); Glenn, *supra* note 73, at 29 (describing international arbitration as self-standing); JOHN KEANE, GLOBAL CIVIL SOCIETY 94 (2003);

ing a single, stateless legal system. Like sovereignism, universalism here qualifies as monistic insofar as it too ultimately reduces legal systems proper to just one kind of judicity, only, world rather than state juridicity, which in turn translates into a single (world versus state) legal system model.[128]

But some 'cosmopolitanist' accounts of global law, commonly portrayed as sitting in between sovereignism and universalism, likewise so qualify. Whereas under sovereignism and universalism alike, the selected model represents the one and only possible form of legal system *as well as the only possible form of juridicity*, cosmopolitanism posits the possibility of numerous juridical forms, not all of which necessarily qualify as 'legal systems.' Cosmopolitanists indeed agree with universalists, against sovereignists, that the heightened transnational interaction of state and non-state actors under globalization is juridically (not just politically) significant insofar as it has caused extant legal systems to harmonize their contents and altogether new forms of (transnational) juridicity to emerge. At the same time, cosmopolitanists agree with sovereignists, against universalists, that it does not follow from that observation that national legal systems have disintegrated and unified into one world system: so long as the national systems' interaction can properly be described as one of mutual 'engagement' – rather than, say, 'merger' or 'subordination' – their integrity as distinct systems is preserved, and might in fact be reinforced.[129] International law, for example, they view as a transnational juridical form distinct from yet on a par with (i.e. no more no less 'juridical' than) that underlying state legal systems, whereas sovereignists and universalists view it as, respectively, altogether non-juridical and the only juridical form that can be.

Ernst Heinrichsohn, World State, World Citizenship: How a New Consciousness Can Save the World from Self-Destruction (2000); Klaus-Peter Berger, The Creeping Codification of the New Lex Mercatoria (2nd ed. 2010); Gralf-Peter Calliess, Lex Mercatoria: A Reflexive Law Guide to An Autonomous Legal System, 2 German L. J. 17 (2001); Ralf Michaels, The True Lex Mercatoria: Law Beyond the State, 14 Indiana J. of Global Leg Stud. 447; Emmanuel Gaillard, Legal Theory of International Arbitration (2010); Vlad Perju, Cosmopolitanism in Constitutional Law, 35 Cardozo L. Rev. 711, 727 (2013) (all legal actors "inhabiting shared constitutional spaces"); Olga Frishman, Should Courts Fear Transnational Engagement?, Vand. J. Transnat'l L. (2016), Part II ("transnational organizational field of courts").

[128] Both "revolve around imagined 'centres'—whether universal or particular"; Niglia, *supra* note 73, at 253; "[b]oth sovereigntist territorialism and universalist harmonization try to wipe out pluralism"; Berman, *supra* note 124, at 2.

[129] See: Vicki Jackson, Constitutional Engagement in a Transnational Era 71 (2010) (distinguishing between 'engagement' and 'dialogue,' and privileging the former on the basis that "the posture of engagement may or may not imply felt obligations of reciprocity"); Mann, *supra* note 127, at 384 (defending "a heroic obliteration of the dialectic of transnationalism through a return to state sovereignty"); Catherine Dupré, Globalisation and Judicial Reasoning: Building Blocks for a Method of Interpretation, *in* Theorising the Global Legal Order 107, *supra* note 18, at 107 (examples of cross-system 'engagement'); Gillespie, *supra* note 19, at 209 (distinguishing 'hybridity,' 'resistance' and 'difference'). Jackson however links 'dialogue' to 'convergence' (Jackson, *supra*, at 1–8, 284), which alignment is specifically resisted here, as we place 'convergence' on an altogether different (substantive) plane. See *infra* note 165.

A cosmopolitan account of global law would then be monistic or pluralistic, under the present definition, depending on whether it projects all 'legal systems' as necessarily grounded in one and the same kind of juridicity (monistic cosmopolitanism) or else allows for different kinds of 'legal systems,' grounded in different kinds of juridicity (pluralistic cosmopolitanism). Kantian cosmopolitanism[130] would be an example of monistic cosmopolitanism, since it projects international law ('cosmopolitan right') as properly juridical yet of a kind of juridicity altogether different from that underlying state legal systems, those remaining the only 'legal systems' proper.[131] In contrast, the kind of cosmopolitanism currently advanced by many globalization scholars would here qualify as 'pluralistic' insofar as it accounts for international law (and other areas of infra- or transnational 'soft' law) as just one of many different kinds of 'legal systems' making up the global universe, those systems differing precisely in their boasting respectively different kinds of juridicity.[132]

[130] IMMANUEL KANT, PERPETUAL PEACE, A PHILOSOPHICAL SKETCH (1795), reprinted in KANT: POLITICAL WRITINGS (H. S. Reiss ed., H. B. Nisbet trans., 1991); JOHN RAWLS, THE LAW OF PEOPLES (2001); JEREMY WALDRON, PARTLY LAWS COMMON TO ALL MANKIND (2012). On Kantian cosmopolitanism more generally, see: GARRETT W. BROWN & DAVID HELD, THE COSMOPOLITAN READER (2010); SEYLA BENHABIB, ANOTHER COSMOPOLITANISM 24 (Robert Post ed., 2008); Claudio Corradetti, Kant's Legacy and the Idea of Transitional Jus Cosmopoliticum, 29 RATIO JURIS 105 (2014); Christophe Petermann, Kant, Précurseur de la mondialisation du droit, in LE DROIT SAISI PAR LA MONDIALISATION 171 (Charles-Albert Morand ed., 2001); Pavlos Eleftheriadis, Cosmopolitan Law, 9 EUR. L. J. 241 (2003).
[131] GARRETT WALLACE BROWN, GROUNDING COSMOPOLITANISM: FROM KANT TO THE IDEA OF A COSMOPOLITAN CONSTITUTION 45 (2009) ("domestic justice is the cornerstone of Kant's overall cosmopolitan vision"); OTFRIED HÖFFE, KANT'S COSMOPOLITAN THEORY OF LAW AND PEACE 196 (Alexandra Newton trans., 2006) (Kant's cosmopolitanism being "both a complementary and subsidiary"); Perju, supra note 127, at 727, "accounts for the supranational constitutional phenomena without subsuming municipal constitutional orders or otherwise compromising their integrity"). For critiques, see: Stan Van Hooft, Cosmopolitanism as Virtue, 3 J. GLOBAL ETHICS 303 (2007) ("national borders and national sovereignty are irrelevant [to the cosmopolitan debate]"); THOMAS W. POGGE, WORLD POVERTY AND HUMAN RIGHTS (2002) (criticizing Rawls's use of the state as consenting unit); David Held, Democratic Accountability and Political Effectiveness from a Cosmopolitan Perspective, in GLOBAL GOVERNANCE AND THE ROLE OF NON-STATE ACTORS (G. Folk Schuppert ed., 2005) (death of the Westphalian state); AMARTYA SEN, REASON BEFORE IDENTITY 31 (1999); Allen Buchanan, Rawls's Law of Peoples: Rules for a Vanished Westphalian World, 110 ETHICS 697, 701 (2000).
[132] Paul Schiff Berman, The Globalization of Jurisdiction, 151 U. PENN. L. REV. 311, 480 (2002) (the acknowledgment of multiple communities, rather than the erasure of all communities except the most encompassing); SLAUGHTER, supra note 127, at 29; KWAME ANTHONY APPIAH, COSMOPOLITANISM: ETHICS IN A WORLD OF STRANGERS (2006); Heydebrand, supra note 4, at 123–29 (2001); Andrew Halpin, Introduction to THEORISING THE GLOBAL LEGAL ORDER, supra note 18, at 9 ("a resistance to closure... [in particular] that sponsored by a restrictive notion of the western legal system"); Cassandra Steer, Legal Transplants or Legal Patchworking? The Creation of International Criminal Law as a Pluralistic Body of Law, in PLURALISM IN INTERNATIONAL CRIMINAL LAW 2, 3, 28 (Elies van Sliedregt & Sergey Vasiliev eds., 2014) (cosmopolitanism steering clear of both deep pluralism and statism); David A. Hollinger, Not Universalists, Not Pluralists: The New Cosmopolitans Find Their Own Way, in CONCEIVING COSMOPOLITANISM: THEORY, CONTEXT AND PRACTICE 227, 228 (Steven Vertovec & Robin Cohen eds., 2003); Glenn, supra note 73, at 28; DELMAS-MARTY, supra note 21. The case of international law, in particular, is taken up below, pp. 181–82.

While this may seem like petty label quibbling, I would submit that it is not, at least not in the context of the present argument. For it allows us to immediately proceed with a first round of triage of the available accounts of global law. Indeed, we can say at once that universalism is 'out' and that sovereignism and monistic cosmopolitanism as just defined are 'in.' Universalism is 'out' because, quite apart from its possible inherent plausibility and/or desirability as an account of global law (and also, in fact, from its qualifying as 'monistic' under the present definition), it *ex hypothesi* allows for no more than one legal system whereas comparative law evidently requires a minimum of two.[133] Sovereignism and monistic cosmopolitanism in contrast are clearly 'in,' as they both provide for a plurality of legal systems that are distinct yet of a same kind (state law) – precisely what we determined in Chapter 2 to be necessary for any two entities to be amenable to meaningful mutual comparison.

Moreover, the fact that sovereignism and monistic cosmopolitanism both reduce legal systems to *state* legal systems, in particular, causes them to be pointedly consistent with our swarm model. For, in the current Westphalian context at least, state courts are uniquely endowed with the kind of real and immediate enforcement powers required to qualify as swarm centre under that model. Note that that is not to say that no other adjudicative body can ever so qualify, only that state courts clearly do.[134] In principle, any central conflict resolution process that is collective, systematic and sanction-backed could serve as proper swarm centre, and the corresponding state or non-state community, stand as an autonomous swarm, under our model. The point being made here is merely that any account of global law that equates legal systems with state legal systems can immediately be retained, whatever other account(s) we may later want to add to that list.

It is also worth emphasizing, finally, that the fact that cosmopolitanism (monistic or pluralistic) has state legal systems interacting with one another to the point of harmonizing their contents and generating altogether new juridical forms is no reason to cross monistic cosmopolitanism off our list. To the contrary, Chapter 2 established that the structural integrity of legal systems under the present account ends up being preserved if not strengthened through their mutual interaction, at least where that interaction is 'informational' rather than 'normative.'[135] Chapter 2

---

[133] The natural law ideal-type was rejected above (see *supra* Chapter 2, Part II, section i) on the same basis.

[134] "Within this global community, states constitute the fundamental political element, for in the present historical stage, all individuals and groups are linked to one state or another." Antonio Cassese, Remarks on Scelle's Theory of "Role Splitting" (dédoublement fonctionnel) in International Law, 1 EUR. J. INT'L L. 210, 211 (1990). For a taste of the vigorous contemporary debate on whether law is tied to the state essentially or merely contingently, see the literature listed in note 212, *infra*.

[135] See *supra* Chapter 2, Part IV. Luhmann conceptualizes cross-system 'engagement' ('structural coupling': LUHMANN, *supra* note 32, at chap. 9) as involving the systems working together to decrease the level of mutual 'irritation,' suggesting that it serves if anything to confirm, in fact strengthen, the systems' respective identities as autonomous systems. See: Gunther Teubner, Legal Irritants: Good Faith in British Law or How Unifying Law Ends up in New Divergences, 61 MOD. L. REV. 11 (1998). See likewise: Oliver Wendell Holmes, The Path of the Law, 10 HARV. L. REV. 457 (1897)) ("The Law

also underscored, moreover, that comparative law needs its objects of comparison to be (structurally) distinct, not (substantively) different, that is, conceptualizable as distinct entities, regardless of their contents being otherwise possibly similar or different.[136] As cosmopolitanism likewise insists on structural integrity over contents difference, it clearly sits well with the present account, certainly as well as does sovereignism.

The rest of this chapter is devoted to investigating whether any 'pluralistic' accounts of global law might likewise belong on our list, alongside sovereignism and monistic cosmopolitanism.

ii. 'Strong' Versus 'Weak' Legal Pluralism

The most general distinction lacing the globalization literature is that between 'strong' and 'weak' legal pluralism, seminally so-coined by John Griffiths back in 1986.[137] Strong and weak legal pluralism alike dissociate the legal system from the nation state given that both allow for a greater number of legal systems than states. But they differ in that strong legal pluralism allows for *overlapping* legal systems whereas weak legal pluralism does not.

---

can accept directly normative premises from morals or from other social sources, but only through an explicit transformation."); Nobles & Schiff, *supra* note 69, at 20 ("law can borrow the values of other systems but not their codes") and at 22 ("Moral imperatives can become incorporated into law, juridified, but this is no different from having conditional programmes that refer to accountancy standards.").

   It follows that the concerns voiced by some national courts, notably the US Supreme Court, that reliance on foreign materials in domestic adjudication might erode the authority of the domestic materials, thus also the domestic system's integrity as a sovereign national system, would be unwarranted under the present account: so long as the national judges *reserve to themselves* the task of accepting or rejecting the foreign materials under consideration – so long as "the operation of [external] referring remains an operation of the system" (LUHMANN, *supra* note 32, at 106) – the integration of those materials should pose no threat to the system's integrity. On the general debate over foreign citations, see: CASS R. SUNSTEIN, *A CONSTITUTION OF MANY MINDS* (2009); Raymond Legeais, L'utilisation du droit comparé par les tribunaux, 2 *R. I. D. C.* 339 (1994); Mark Tushnet, The Possibilities of Comparative Constitutional Law, 108 *YALE L. J.* 1225, 1307 (1999); Martin Gelter & Mathias M. Siems, Citations to Foreign Courts—Illegitimate and Superfluous, or Unavoidable? Evidence from Europe, 62 *AM. J. COMP. L.* 35 (2014); Ulrich Drobnig & Sjef van Erp, The Use of Comparative Law by Courts, *in* THE USE OF COMPARATIVE LAW BY COURTS (Ulrich Drobnig & Sjef van Erp eds., 1999); Shirley S. Abrahamson & Michael J. Fischer, All the World's a Courtroom: Judging in the New Millennium, 26 *HOFSTRA L. REV.* 273 (1997–98); Bruce Ackerman, The Rise of World Constitutionalism, 83 *VA. L. REV.* 771 (1997); Taavi Annus, Comparative Constitutional Reasoning: The Law and Strategy of Selecting Human Rights Arguments, 14 *DUKE J. COMP. & INT'L L.* 301, 309ff (2004); Eric A. Posner & Cass R. Sunstein, The Law of Other States, 59 *STAN. L. REV.* 131 (2006); Response: Eric A. Posner & Cass R. Sunstein, On Learning from Others, 59 *STAN. L REV.* 1309, 1313 (2007); Frederick Schauer, Authority and Authorities, 94 *VA. L. REV.* 1931 (2008)

[136] See *supra* Chapter 2, Part I, section i and Part IV.

[137] John Griffiths, What is Legal Pluralism?, 24 *J. LEG. PLURALISM* 1, 2–3 (1986). See *supra* note 32, Chapter 2.

Though strong (or "deep,"[138] "true,"[139] "horizontal,"[140] "external,"[141] "new"[142]) pluralism originally emerged as a reaction against "the ideological heritage of the bourgeois revolution and liberal hegemony,"[143] such ideological bent arguably is not essential to it.[144] At its core, strong legal pluralism merely stands for the proposition that "two or more legal systems [can] coexist in the same social field."[145] That is to say that the global universe would stage a plurality of distinct legal regimes whose competing authority claims over the same matters would a priori all be equally valid as there would be "no clear hierarchical relation that could establish priorities" among them.[146] As strong legal pluralism hence rejects "a logic of exclusion/ inclusion [and] criticizes any kind of centralisation and monopolisation of law,"[147] it naturally defects from the idea that legal systems ought to be mutually exclusive. Because it sees each system autonomously determining its own reach on the inside, in complete disregard of any other system's similar determination, it precludes the possibility of the various systems coordinating so as to avoid authority overlaps.[148]

---

[138] BOAVENTURA DE SOUSA SANTOS, TOWARD A NEW LEGAL COMMON SENSE: LAW, GLOBALIZATION AND EMANCIPATION (2nd ed. 2002).

[139] Hesselink, *supra* note 42; Niglia, *supra* note 73.

[140] GEORGES GURVITCH, THE SOCIOLOGY OF LAW 181 (1942).

[141] GAVIN W. ANDERSON, CONSTITUTIONAL RIGHTS AFTER GLOBALIZATION 53–54 (Hart 2005).

[142] Gunther Teubner, The Two Faces of Janus: Rethinking Legal Pluralism, 13 CARDOZO L. REV. 1443, 1451 (1992).

[143] Griffiths, *supra* note 137, at 2–3. See likewise: ANDERSON, *supra* note 141, at 39ff.

[144] Ralf Michaels, On Liberalism and Legal Pluralism, *in* TRANSNATIONAL LAW: RETHINKING EUROPEAN LAW AND LEGAL THINKING 122 (Miguel Maduro, Kaarlo Tuori & Suvi Sankari eds., 2014).

[145] Sally Engle Merry, Legal Pluralism, 22 LAW & SOC'Y REV 869, 870 (1988). And at 873: "Instead of mutual influences between two separate entities, this perspective sees plural forms of ordering as participating in the same social field." See also: Marc Hertogh, What Is Non-State Law? Mapping the Other Hemisphere of the Legal World, *in* INTERNATIONAL GOVERNANCE AND LAW: STATE REGULATION AND NON-STATE LAW 11, 12 (Hanneke van Schooten & Jonathan Verschuuren eds., 2008) ("two or more legal orders can exist ... within the same territory"); DENIS GALLIGAN, LAW IN MODERN SOCIETY 162 (2007) ("legal systems derive from sources other than the state and exist as independent fields of law"). For a suggestion that true legal pluralism needs to go beyond overlapping systems of authority to a multiplicity of inconsistent rules of recognition within the same system, see: N. W. Barber, Legal Pluralism and the European Union, 12 EUR. L. J. 306, 325–26 (2006).

[146] Ralf Michaels, Why We Have No Theory of European Private Law, *in* PLURALISM AND EUROPEAN PRIVATE LAW 139, *supra* note 42, at 149 (footnotes omitted). See likewise: Neil Walker & Stephen Tierney, Introduction: A Constitutional Mosaic? Exploring the New Frontiers of Europe's Constitutionalism *in* EUROPE'S CONSTITUTIONAL MOSAIC 1 (Neil Walker, Jo Shaw & Stephen Tierney eds., 2011) ("It is a pattern based on *plurality* rather than the *singularity* of the constitutional field; the *diversity* rather that the *uniformity* of its parts; the *heterarchical* rather the *hierarchical* quality of the relations between these parts; and the *fluidity* rather than the *fixity* of the internal and external boundaries.").

[147] Niglia, *supra* note 73, at 252. See likewise: Twining, *supra* note 1, at 364; H. Patrick Glenn, The Nationalist Heritage, *in* COMPARATIVE LEGAL STUDIES: TRADITIONS AND TRANSITIONS 76, *supra* note 4.

[148] WILLIAM TWINING, GLOBALISATION AND LEGAL THEORY 151 (2000) ("a multiplicity of overlapping orders co-existing within the same territorial or social space"); Boaventura de Sousa Santos, Law: a Map of Misreading, 14 J. L. & SOC'Y 279, 298 (1987) ("Our legal life is constituted by an intersection of different legal orders, that is by interlegality ... a highly dynamic process because the different legal spaces are non-synchronic and thus result in uneven and unstable mixings of legal codes.");

It is important not to confuse strong legal pluralism with other forms of law-related pluralism commonly associated with it, in particular, 'norm pluralism,' 'voice pluralism' and 'market pluralism.'[149] 'Norm pluralism' generally evokes situations of overlapping spheres of normativity as inevitably obtain from individuals combining multiple group memberships – families, college alumni, professional, social or religious organizations – all of which come with particular sets of rules, expectations, commitments, and so on.[150] But that same label is at times also used to evoke the very different situations of several legal systems sharing same sets of legal rules or legal values (rule/value 'sharing')[151] or one legal system gathering rules/values from

---

PAUL SCHIFF BERMAN, GLOBAL LEGAL PLURALISM: JURISPRUDENCE BEYOND BORDERS 1 (2012) ("multiple overlapping normative communities"); NICOLE ROUGHAN, AUTHORITIES: CONFLICTS, COOPERATION, AND TRANSNATIONAL LEGAL THEORY 1 (2013) (describing the claims for a global jurisprudence analyzing "purported instances of law beyond, between, within, and/or outside state borders; and any resulting interactions or overlaps between different legal systems" by such authors as Keith Culver & Michael Giudice, LEGALITY'S BORDERS: AN ESSAY IN GENERAL JURISPRUDENCE (2010); Detlef Von Daniels, THE CONCEPT OF LAW FROM A TRANSNATIONAL PERSPECTIVE (2010); NICO KRISCH, BEYOND CONSTITUTIONALISM: THE PLURALIST STRUCTURE OF POSTNATIONAL LAW (2010); GRALF-PETER CALLIESS & PEER ZUMBANSEN, ROUGH CONSENSUS AND RUNNING CODE: A THEORY OF TRANSNATIONAL PRIVATE LAW (2010); TAMANAHA, supra note 46).

[149] For overviews of the various 'pluralisms' on offer, see: Hesselink, supra note 42, at 200–201, 244 ("plurality of legal sources and materials, or of relevant epistemological claims, normative theories, values, relevant communities and senses of belonging").

[150] See generally: MICHAEL WALZER, SPHERES OF JUSTICE: A DEFENSE OF PLURALITY AND EQUALITY (1983); CHARLES TAYLOR, SOURCES OF THE SELF: THE MAKING OF MODERN IDENTITY (1993); MICHAEL J. SANDEL, DEMOCRACY'S DISCONTENT, AMERICA IN SEARCH OF A PUBLIC PHILOSOPHY 345 (1996); AMARTYA SEN, IDENTITY AND VIOLENCE: THE ILLUSION OF DESTINY (2006); Martha Craven Nussbaum, Patriotism and Cosmopolitanism, in FOR LOVE OF COUNTRY: DEBATING THE LIMITS OF PATRIOTISM 1, 9 (Joshua Cohen ed., 1996); JOSEPH H. H. WEILER, THE CONSTITUTION OF EUROPE: "DO THE NEW CLOTHES HAVE AN EMPEROR?" AND OTHER ESSAYS ON EUROPEAN INTEGRATION 328 (1999); Michaels, supra note 4, at 11 ("different aspects of our identities may be relevant—and in potential conflict—in different contexts, or even in the very same context"); Michaels, supra note 146, at 144–46 (discussing Pierre Legrand, Antivonbar, 1 J. COMP. L. 13, 36 (2005), arguably wrongly associating Legrand's argument with a defence of nationalism); Hesselink, supra note 42, at 234 (multiplicity of allegiances in the European context); SLAUGHTER, supra note 127, at 36–64, 131–65 ("the state is just one of many social contracts entered by individuals," but concluding therefrom, contra the above argument, that such multiple senses of belonging result in "disaggregated [state] sovereignty").

[151] What Hesselink dubs 'plural legalism'; Hesselink, supra note 42, at 199. The extent to which legal rules are such as to be 'shareable' by several systems of course is an open question. (See supra Part II, section ii (1) in this chapter, and Chapter 2, Part IV, section iii, and more generally: Teubner, supra note 135; THE PRACTICE OF HUMAN RIGHTS (Mark Goodale & Sally Engle Merry eds., 2007); Michaels, supra note 4, at 4 (diversification of US/English commercial law ensuing from universal borrowal of it); Stephen Allen, The UN Declaration of the Rights of Indigenous Peoples: Towards a Global Legal Order on Indigenous Rights?, in THEORISING THE GLOBAL LEGAL ORDER, supra note 18, at 187; Gillespie, supra note 19, at 228; Antje Wiener & Philip Liste, Lost Without Translation? Cross-Referencing and a New Global Community of Courts, 21 IND. J. GLOB. LEG. STUD. 263, 264 (2014).) If it is the case that, while such legal canons and values as constitutional provisions, 'freedom of contract,' 'due process,' etc. clearly travel across systems, their meanings do not, only 'rules' abstracted from their (locally determined) meanings can properly be described as 'shareable' – which may or may not fit what we commonly take 'rules' to be about.

different legal origins (rule/value 'hybridization').[152] 'Voice pluralism' in contrast emphasizes the diverse authorships of (legal or non-legal) canons of normativity, as it seeks to "bring multiple norm-generating communities into greater dialogue with each other,"[153] thus to maximize the overall number of voices being heard more than the overall diversity of what is in fact being said.[154] 'Market pluralism,' finally, refers to the pluralism naturally yielded through forum and/or applicable law shopping by private parties, and more general legal rule/value shopping by law makers (as per the second kind of 'norm pluralism').[155]

While these three kinds of pluralism are at times advocated by the same people as advocate strong legal pluralism, and simultaneously with it, I would argue that they remain conceptually distinct from it, and in fact carry no special connection to it. For, all three can be accounted for under just a weakly or even altogether *non*-pluralist vision of global law, only differently than under strong legal pluralism. Whereas strong legal pluralism equates normativity with legality, and hence dictates that overlapping spheres of *normative* authority necessarily represent as many overlapping spheres of *legal* authority,[156] the traditional, Westphalian model, for one, distinguishes normativity from legality, and insists that such 'norm pluralism' (individuals cumulating membership in many normative communities) is best governed via a structure of legal authority that is itself overlap free. Rule/value 'sharing' and 'hybridization' likewise can easily be accounted for under the Westphalian model, given that such situations, as explained, need not be viewed as undermining the structural integrity of the (national) systems involved.[157] Similarly with respect to 'voice pluralism': a Westphalian account might recognize the value of promoting voice diversity yet resist the (strong legal pluralist) suggestion that such diversity would be best achieved through ascribing formal legal status to every voice involved. As for 'market pluralism,' finally, while it has been dubbed 'radical pluralism,' it actually is hardly radical at all[158] seeing that it not only *avails under*, but might in fact *presuppose*, the most conventional account of global law: forum/law

---

[152] Hans-W. Micklitz, Monistic Ideology versus Pluralistic Reality: Toward a Normative Design for European Private Law, *in* PLURALISM AND EUROPEAN PRIVATE LAW 29, *supra* note 42, at 47 ("hybridization"); Glenn, *supra* note 36, at 9 ("conceptual mixité"); Goldberg & Attwooll, *supra* note 2, at 332 ("legal seepage").

[153] Berman, *supra* note 124, at 805. See generally: Niglia, *supra* note 73, at 253.

[154] See Berman, *supra* note 124, at 801 ("maximize the opportunity for plural voices to be heard") and 809 ("accommodating multiple voices, recognizing multiple"); Glenn, *supra* note 73, at 32 (insisting on including legislative voices).

[155] Jan Smits, A Radical View of Legal Pluralism, *in* PLURALISM AND EUROPEAN PRIVATE LAW, *supra* note 42, at 161.

[156] Berman, *supra* text note 132, at 480ff.

[157] See *supra* text accompanying notes 135–36.

[158] Hesselink, *supra* note 42, at 236–38 ("Not only are the ideas of a law market and law as product limited to state law: the market is structured by choice of law rules"); Christian Joerges, On the Legitimacy of Europeanising Private Law: Considerations on a Justice-Making Law for the EU Multi-Level System, 7 ELECTRONIC J. COMP. L. 3 (2003), paraphrased by Michaels, *supra* note 146, at 150 ("individuals are able to choose among different laws not because they feel bound by *all* of them ... but because they

shopping indeed might prove easiest where the available options are clearly delineated and distinct from one another, as are legal systems under the (yet again)
Westphalian model. In sum, while 'norm pluralism' and 'voice pluralism' do involve
authority overlaps, those are of a different kind than avail under strong legal pluralism (overlaps of *legal* authority); and 'market pluralism' simply does not entail
overlaps of any kind.

Having distinguished strong legal pluralism from other kinds of pluralism, we
are now in a position to assess its peculiar compatibility or incompatibility with our
swarm model. At the outset, it is worth noting that not all of the various 'defects' that
have been ascribed to strong legal pluralism are problematic for present purposes.
One such defect here proving innocuous is the so-called 'logical embarrassment'
arising from strong legal pluralism affirming that different legal systems dictate different answers to the same legal questions, at the same time as it recognizes that
these systems' radical incommensurability prevents any assessment of whether
the questions indeed are the same to begin with.[159] That logical embarrassment
admittedly is intractable under an assumption of radical system incommensurability, which most strong legal pluralists appear to endorse.[160] But it could be fixed
(should we want to) by relaxing said assumption ever so slightly, so as to allow in
just a minimal measure of external perspective, and hence also a minimal measure
of inter-system commensurability.[161] Thus modified, strong legal pluralism would
have us *first* identify, from an external perspective, a common set of *strictly factual*
questions, and only *thereafter* revert to an internal exploration of these questions'
various legal treatments (allowing us to eventually conclude that the various systems
indeed dictate different answers to the same questions), which sequential reasoning
is contradiction-free. Strong legal pluralism hence is 'logically embarrassing' only
insofar as it presupposes an *exclusively* internal perspective,[162] which premise may
or may not be essential to it, and clearly does *not* hold under the present account of
comparative law. (Note that that is precisely how we proceed in Chapter 5, Part I.)

Yet there is another, deeper problem with strong legal pluralism, which ultimately causes us to reject even its modified version. In addition to being 'logically

---

feel bound by *none* of them."); Brigitta Lurger, A Radical View of Pluralism? Comments on Jan Smits,
in PLURALISM AND EUROPEAN PRIVATE LAW, *supra* note 42, at 173.

[159] Hesselink, *supra* note 42, at 230, citing Kelsen (HANS KELSEN, GENERAL THEORY OF LAW AND STATE 379
(2007) (1945)) for the proposition that, from the perspective of each system, the others simply do not
exist as such. Hesselink here borrows from, and disagrees with, Neil MacCormick, who claimed that
"[t]he problem is not logically embarrassing, because strictly the answers are from the point of view
of different systems"; NEIL MACCORMICK, QUESTIONING SOVEREIGNTY: LAW, STATE AND NATION IN THE
EUROPEAN COMMONWEALTH 119 (1999).

[160] Otto Pfersmann, Contre le pluralisme mondialisationniste, pour un monisme juridique ouvert et
différencié, 121 ARCHIVES DE PHILOSOPHIE, DE SOCIOLOGIE, ET DE DROIT 131, 139 (2010). See e.g.
GLOBAL LAW WITHOUT A STATE (Gunther Teubner ed., 1997).

[161] MacCormick, *supra* note 30, at 6.

[162] See Hesselink's suggestion (Hesselink, *supra* note 42, at 232) that allowing in any amount of externality
causes 'pluralism' to collapse into 'monism.'

embarrassing,' which as suggested is both debatable and possibly fixable, strong legal pluralism suffers from a 'practical embarrassment' that in contrast is uncontroversial and unfixable. Strong legal pluralism is 'practically embarrassed' insofar as it quite simply allows for "the same human beings or corporations ... to have and not have a certain right. How shall they act?"[163] As it posits concurrent legal orders heter-archically governing the same legal questions, strong legal pluralism does allow, as explained, for the possibility of equally valid yet clashing answers to any given question. And being given contradictory signals as to one's legal position indeed is 'practically embarrassing' for any citizen acting individually. As Luhmann would describe it, out goes the 'stabilizing of normative expectations' that any legal system essentially aims to achieve.[164]

The problem arguably looms larger still, however, as it would avail to some extent even in situations where the various orders happen to deliver converging answers.[165] For, in such situations, neither of the (admittedly converging) answers could be considered final, thus imminently implementable, as each would ultimately remain just one of several possible alternative, equally valid answers.[166] The settling of matters 'once and for all' would simply remain unattainable.[167]

That is exemplified in what might be the most tangible historical instance of strong legal pluralism on record, namely, the cohabitation of Law and Equity within English law. For centuries, the two jurisdictions competed with one another in the governance of same substantive matters by constantly readjusting their procedural requirements so as to divert litigants away from the other. As neither court stood above the other, each remained powerless to preclude the other from rehearing matters considered settled in the first. The lack of finality (and overall conceptual uncertainty) led to such intolerable social instability that an objective

---

[163] MacCormick, *supra* note 30. See also: Postema, *Law's System, supra* note 32, at 83 ("A conflict between two different legal norms or norm-regimes may arise if a legal actor or subject cannot comply with both simultaneously."); Michaels, *supra* note 146, at 152 ("In the end, an umpire seems to be needed"); Hesselink, *supra* note 42, at 229 ("the conflict remains unresolved, not merely temporarily, while the jury is out, but fundamentally").

[164] Kelsen offers the same argument in support of the impossibility of concurrent moral and legal obligations on a same issue: "an individual who regards the law as a system of valid norms has to disregard morals as such a system ... [because] no viewpoint exists from which both morals and law may simultaneously be regarded as valid normative orders. No one can serve two masters." MAX KELSEN, *A PURE THEORY OF LAW* 329 (Max Knight trans., 2nd ed., 2005) (1967).

[165] Herein lies the key difference between 'convergence' or 'harmonization,' and 'unification': whereas 'convergence' and 'harmonization' refer to a merger in the substance of legal materials from distinct jurisdictions, 'unification' refers to such substantive mergers as result from a merger of the jurisdictions themselves. See generally: Micklitz, *supra* note 152, at 49–50; DELMAS-MARTY, *supra* note 21.

[166] This assumes that the overlap cannot be resolved by appeal to some kind of primacy rule transcending the various orders, as commonly happens where jurisdiction overlaps between states are resolved through rules of private international law. See also *infra*, section iii (i). Such system overlaps as are resolvable in that way are not 'true' overlaps for present purposes as finality remains possible. My thanks go to Karen Knop for raising that point.

[167] Niglia, *supra* note 73, at 262 (referring to closure as 'settlement').

third-party, the legislator, was eventually called upon to intervene and coordinate the two jurisdictions through the enactment of the 1875 Judicature Act. Prior to that enactment, however, English law arguably was indeed in a state of strong legal pluralism, with the attendant lack of finality, precarious individual expectations and general social instability.

Individual and social instability aside, however, finality has been argued to be essential to all legal systems on the level of principle,[168] and certainly stands as a key feature of our swarm model. Recall the reasons that the swarm model has legal systems centred on their respective highest courts. As only those courts' rulings are treated as final, only they carry the potential of imminent implementation, which in turn means, we argued, that the arguments aimed at those rulings can be viewed as particularly thoughtful and deliberate. That argument confirms, it was claimed, the explanatory power of the swarm model insofar as it accounts for the special status accorded to legal arguments over other kinds of arguments, and their salience variations over time and space, in all legal systems. But it was also meant to exhibit the model's unique suitability from the standpoint of comparative law, as the particular thoughtfulness of adjudication-geared arguments in turn justifies comparative lawyers treating those, and those alone, as the 'meaningful (legal) acts' they need for the purpose of reconstructing the collective commitments underlying the various swarm-like systems they intend to compare. Removing finality thus strikes at the very core of our swarm model. It guts the various swarms from their very hearts, effectively eliminating the swarms themselves, and in the process evacuates the model's explanatory power, as well as its usefulness to legal comparatists.

In sum, the preclusion of any kind of adjudicative finality under strong legal pluralism is problematic in more ways than one. The resulting 'practical embarrassment' experienced by individuals in going about their daily affairs reveals a deeper structural defect that, from our standpoint, proves nothing short of fatal. For that reason, though strongly pluralist accounts may or may not provide a coherent account of global law as such, any such account is bound to be fundamentally at odds with our swarm model – which suffices to reject them all here. It is worth reiterating, however, that it does not follow that other forms of pluralism, in particular norm-, voice- and market pluralism, should likewise be dismissed. As the foregoing discussion hopefully makes clear, all three of the latter forms of pluralism are fully consistent with, and in fact accounted for under, the present swarm model (which if anything should serve to confirm their distinguishability from strong legal pluralism).

---

[168] See, in particular, Joseph Raz's argument that all legal systems claim supremacy over the matters internally determined as falling within their jurisdiction: JOSEPH RAZ, PRACTICAL REASON AND NORMS 151–52 (1990); JOSEPH RAZ, THE AUTHORITY OF LAW 118–19 (1979). See likewise: JOHN FINNIS, NATURAL LAW AND NATURAL RIGHTS 148–49, 267 (1980). But see contra: ANDREI MARMOR, POSITIVE LAW AND OBJECTIVE VALUES 39–42 (2001).

Having dismissed strong legal pluralism, we now turn to weak legal pluralism, i.e. accounts of global law that, while 'pluralistic' in the above sense of allowing for 'legal systems' being grounded in different kinds of juridicity, do secure adjudicative finality as they (at least in principle) preclude unresolvable system overlaps.

iii. *'Subnational'* Versus *'Supranational'* Weak Legal Pluralism

At a subnational level, weak legal pluralism entails conceptualizing the various formal (provincial, municipal, etc.) and informal (religious, athletic, professional, etc.) units making up states as distinct and mutually exclusive 'legal systems' in much the same way as are state legal systems. At a supranational level, it involves conceptualizing various forms of transnational juridicity (EC law, *lex mercatoria*, international law, etc.) as autonomous and mutually exclusive 'legal systems' on a par with and in addition to state legal systems. From the standpoint of comparative law, the subnational option means that a single swarm-like (state) system could be conceptualized as comprising several distinct and mutually exclusive sub-swarms, all of which could properly be compared to one another and their host swarm. The supranational option in contrast means that a single (transnational) swarm could span several states and still be, again, amenable to meaningful comparison with other such swarms and state swarms. As both of these options entail that there can be 'legal systems' beyond just state legal systems, either of them panning out would vindicate the compatibility of weakly pluralistic cosmopolitanism with our swarm model (in addition to sovereignism and monistic cosmopolitanism). We now discuss each of these options in turn.

(1) Subnationalism

Mutual exclusivity is not a problem under subnationalism, as it is possible to conceptualize subnational units as mutually exclusive. Although they admittedly might overlap from a membership standpoint (as any one individual, as discussed,[169] cumulates memberships in several formal and informal subunits at once), they need not overlap in terms of legal authority. Formal subunits are generally granted areas of exclusive jurisdiction under the national constitution, and situations of concurrent jurisdictions are typically resolved in favour of one or the other through the operation of primacy rules. As for informal subunits, they can likewise be conceptualized as governing mutually exclusive list of matters, determined by reference to their respective purposes – athletic competition qualifications falling to sports associations, cattle grazing rules to local cattle ranchers, and so on. As formal and informal subunits alike accordingly are "making rules, interpreting them, applying

---

[169] See above discussion of 'norm pluralism,' pp. 166–68.

them to specific cases, and sanctioning violations" on respectively different matters,[170] what might stand in the way of treating them as autonomous swarms under
our model?

The problem is, the internal rulings of formal and informal subunits in fact lack
finality despite those subunits' legal authority being possibly mutually exclusive.
Looking first to the rulings of informal subunits, we observe that while their authority
may be considered exclusive *as against one another*, none of them can be considered
exclusively authoritative *as against the state*.[171] In the current political context, at least,
an individual dissatisfied with an informal group's ruling, even on a matter recognized
as falling within that group's competence, retains the possibility of appealing it to a
national court. In order to become final, then, any such ruling must ultimately be
coopted by the state in some way, if not overtly, at least implicitly.[172] Where the ruling
is in fact appealed, the national court will confirm it, and make it final, or else over-
rule it, and effectively cancel it altogether. And where it is not appealed, the binary
logic of inclusion/exclusion at play in our swarm model suggests that the ruling is
implicitly endorsed under national law: all individual actions and decisions not formally denounced as illegal by a national court are implicitly deemed legal, under that
logic.[173] That is to say that, at least in the current political context, informal subunits are
ultimately powerless to oust, and extirpate themselves from, the authority of state law.[174]

But by the same token, it would seem that formal subunits should have that power,
precisely because they in contrast have in fact been formally endorsed as such by
the state. Where, say, a province is officially granted the power to govern certain
matters under the national constitution, that province's presumptively final rulings
on those matters can arguably be viewed as having themselves been *ex ante* officially endorsed by the state. Yet the finality problem endures, as the validity of any
such ruling remains conditional on the ruling being formally confirmed *as falling*

---

[170] "If governing involves making rules, interpreting them, applying them to specific cases, and
sanctioning violations, some or all of this is done by such different clusters of people as the Mafia,
the National Collegiate Athletic Association, the American Arbitration Association, those who run
large shopping centers, neighborhood associations, and even the regulars at Smokey's tavern." Stewart
Macaulay, Private Government, *in* LAW AND THE SOCIAL SCIENCES (Leon Lipson & Stanton Wheeler
eds., 1986), cited in Hertogh, *supra* note 145, at 11.

[171] See generally: GALLIGAN, *supra* note 145, at chap. 10; Robert Wai, Transnational Liftoff and Juridical
Touchdown: The Regulatory Function of Private International Law in an Era of Globalization, 40
COL. J. TRANSNAT'L L. 209 (2002); John Biggins, 'Targeted Touchdown' and 'Partial Liftoff': Post-Crisis
Dispute Resolution in the OTC Derivatives Markets and the Challenge for ISDA, 13 GER. L. J. 1297,
1327 (2012); Glenn, *supra* note 73, at 30 (on the relation of religious orders to state law).

[172] "All the communities existing within a state are subject to the state legal order, which conditions their
scope, validity and field of competence." Cassese, *supra* note 134, at 212.

[173] See Kelsen's notion of "voidable legal norms," discussed in LARS VINX, HANS KELSEN'S PURE THEORY
OF LAW: LEGALITY AND LEGITIMACY 89–94 (2007).

[174] See the famous Rose & Frank decision of the English Court of Appeal (UKHL 2, AC 445), where
the parties aimed to exclude their 'gentlemen's agreement' from state law yet the court accepted
jurisdiction over the matter only to thereafter declare the agreement non-binding ... under English law.

within the province's powers, which confirmation can only come from ... the state.[175] Here again such confirmation can be implicit, as where the ruling's constitutionality or administrative validity goes unchallenged. But the point stands that, even with respect to rulings eventually confirmed by the state as falling within the subunit's official powers, such state confirmation is needed for the rulings to be considered final, and immediately executable.

If informal and formal subunits alike ultimately depend on the state for supplying their rulings with finality, both lack the degree of autonomy needed to qualify as self-standing swarms under our model. For, as per our earlier remarks concerning mixed legal systems,[176] such dependence confirms that the contours of the subunits' respective realms of legal authority are ultimately set externally by their host state, rather than internally by the subunits themselves. And our model only allows for fully closed, autopoietic swarm-like systems that self-*delineate* at the same time as they self-regenerate.

It follows for comparative law in general, first, that great caution is in order when the objects for comparison include subnational units, formal or informal. As those units do not self-delineate, and hence are not fully closed, whatever collective commitments can be extracted from their law are likely infused to some extent with the collective commitments of their host state, and hence can only equivocally be ascribed to the subunits as such. Moreover, as no clear line can be drawn between structure-defining and general content-building legal operations, sorting the subunits' from their host states' commitments is hardly if at all feasible. In addition, the difficulty in delineating peculiar from non-peculiar collective commitments entails that it would likewise be difficult to determine even just *the extent to which* any given unit is in fact suffused with commitments not its own. Comparing ('untainted') national systems[177] with ('possibly tainted') subnational units, or else two ('possibly *differently* tainted') subunits to one another would accordingly run the risk of being like comparing apples and love: the two objects for comparison simply could not be assumed to qualify as the 'distinct and prima facie equal entities' required for meaningful legal comparison under the present account.[178]

---

[175] "Within such a pluralistic legal system, parallel legal regimes, dependent from the overarching and controlling state system, result from 'recognition' by the state"; Griffiths, *supra* note 137, at 5.

[176] See *supra*, Part I. See generally: Christina M. Rodriguez, *Federalism and National Consensus* 1 (Oct. 2013) (unpublished manuscript) (on file with Rodriguez) (describing the harmonising impact of supreme courts in federative arrangements). *Contra*: Goldberg & Attwooll, *supra* note 2, at 313–14 (Scotland purportedly qualifying as a 'non-statal legal order' in Kelsen's analysis, though they distinguish legal 'orders' from legal 'systems').

[177] It should be clear by now that to describe national systems as 'untainted' here is not to deny that national systems interact constantly, in ways that at times result in their contents being seriously modified. However, as such 'tainting' is ultimately processed through the systems' peculiar formal law-making institutions, the new materials, values, etc. can be taken to have become the systems' own in a way that cannot be said to happen with subnational units. See *supra* notes 135–36.

[178] See *supra* Chapter 2, Part I, section iii.

Current comparative scholarship on informal and formal subnational units arguably confirms that first observation. While studies of informal subunits within a same nation – say, the Canadian Wheat Growers Collective, Canada's Mohawk community, and Canada's National Ballet[179] – might target those communities' legal dimension, they would typically focus on the different corporate, non-profit or plain contractual structures governing those communities. Such studies accordingly might be better described as studies in *Canadian* corporate/non-profit/contract law than as studies in comparative law traditionally understood – they would be legal-domain-to-legal-domain studies, more than legal-system-to-legal-system studies.[180] As for legal comparisons of informal subunits partaking of several nations – say, the International Wheat Growers Collective, North American Mohawks, the International Association of Ballet Dancers – they would admittedly reach beyond just one nation's (here Canada's) legal authority. But such comparisons typically harp back to the various national systems connected to the informal subunit. A comparative study targeting North American Mohawks, for example, would typically compare the different treatments of traditional Mohawk rights in the US and Canadian legal systems. Such a study would clearly qualify as a legal-system-to-legal-system comparison, thus as a study in comparative law proper, yet its analytic unit ultimately is the national legal system (the US and Canadian legal systems) more than the subunit (North American Mohawks) as such.

With respect to formal subnational units, our first observation arguably is borne out by studies of mixed legal systems, which commonly involve comparing, again, not so much the subunit to its host system, as the subunit's genealogical and host national legal systems. Any comparatist intent on explaining the difference between Quebec and Canadian private law, for example, typically does so by relating whatever collective commitments emerge from Quebec's private law as clash with those emerging from the rest of Canadian private law to Quebec's peculiarly French legal heritage.[181] The systems ultimately being compared here accordingly are, really, the French and English national legal systems more than the Quebec and Canadian systems per se.

A second and more general observation suggested by the above discussion motions back to our earlier discussion of internal and external system delineation. From the strictly internal perspective adopted in Part II, formal and informal subnational units could potentially be seen as autonomous swarms, thus amenable to meaningful comparisons under the present account, insofar as they are endowed with purportedly final adjudicative bodies. It is only when we here, in Part III, reverted to an external perspective, and observed those units *as they stand to one another and the state*, that we realized that they ultimately do not so qualify, as their rulings in fact are not final.

---

[179] Any of those labels and the subsequent may be fictitious.
[180] See *supra* Chapter 2, Part II.
[181] See *supra* Chapter 2, Part III.

(Recall that the reason given above, in section i(1), for strong legal pluralists not being bothered by system overlaps was precisely that they in fact cannot *see* such overlaps from the exclusively internal perspective they cling to.) Hence the need, again, for comparative lawyers to in fact *oscillate* between the internal and external perspectives.

(2) Supranationalism

The viability of weak legal pluralism at a supranational level likely is best assessed through the analysis of a concrete example. I propose that of the European Union, as it has spurred particularly enlightening scholarship on the issue.[182]

Various universalist, sovereignist and cosmopolitanist accounts of Europe have been advanced, which expectedly differ from one another in the overall number of legal systems projected. Universalists (or in this case, where the universe is shrunk to just Europe, 'Europeanists')[183] view European unification as having resulted in the creation of a single pan-European legal system subsuming all member states' hitherto national legal systems – what Julie Dickson dubbed the "One Big Legal System" model (Figure 1).[184] At the opposite end of the spectrum, sovereignists insist that the overall number of legal systems is unchanged, as the only effect of European unification in their view has been to supplement the member states' national systems with a new layer of law, namely, EC law – the 'Part of Member States' model (Figure 2).[185] In between lie various cosmopolitanist accounts, the most prominent of which arguably is the "27 + 1" model,[186] which projects EC law as a pan-European legal system *distinct from and in addition to* the member states' systems (Figure 3).

---

[182] See generally: Raz, *supra* note 168; MacCormick, *supra* note 30; MacCormick, *supra* note 159; Van Hoecke, *supra* note 27 at 55; Mattias Kumm, The Jurisprudence of Constitutional Conflict: Constitutional Supremacy in Europe Before and After the Constitutional Treaty, 11 Eur. L. J. 262 (2005); Delmas-Marty, *supra* note 21; Niglia, *supra* note 73, at 153; Constitutionalism in Transformation: European and Theoretical Perspectives (Richard Bellamy & Dario Castiglione eds., 1996); Sovereignty in Transition (Neil Walker ed., 2003); Weiler, *supra* note 150; Alec Stone Sweet, The Judicial Construction of Europe 97 (2004); Stephen Weatherhill, Law and Integration in the European Union (1995); Karen J. Alter, Establishing the Supremacy of European Law, The Making of an International Rule of Law in Europe (2001).

[183] Hesselink, *supra* note 42.

[184] Dickson, *supra* note 46, at 2. Proponents of that view include the Spinelli group (Spinelli Group (www.spinelligroup.eu/); Guy Verhofstadt, The United States of Europe, Manifesto for a New Europe (2006).

[185] *Ibid.* In support of the 'Part of the Member States' model, one could cite such pronouncements of the European Court of Justice as "community law therefore not only imposes obligations on individuals but is also intended to confer upon them rights which become part of *their* legal heritage." Case C-26/62. *Van Gend en Loos v. Nederlandse Administratie der Belastingen,* 1963 E.C.R. 1, at 12 (emphasis added). And: "Such a clearly expressed prohibition which came into force with the treaty throughout the community, and so became an integral part of the legal system of the member states, forms part of the law of those states." Case C-6/64, *Flamino Costa v. ENEL,* 1964 E.C.R. 585, at 593.

[186] *Ibid.* Hesselink (Hesselink *supra* note 42, at 225ff) calls that model 'European dualism,' but ultimately distinguishes it from 'cosmopolitanism,' which he defines more narrowly than above.

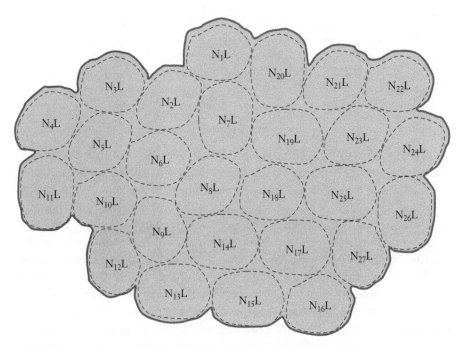

Figure 1. Universalism 'One Big Legal System': 1 European system (comprising 27 National Law parts)

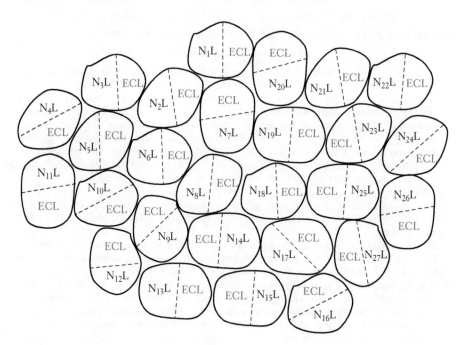

Figure 2. Sovereignism 'Part of Member States': 27 national systems (comprising 1 NL part and 1 ECL part)

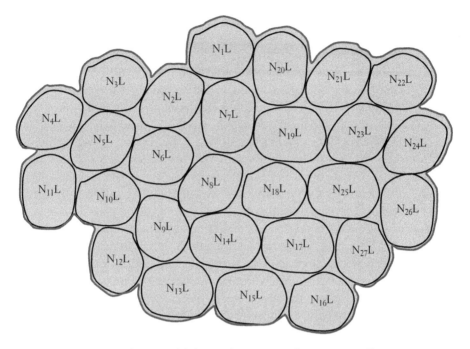

Figure 3. Cosmopolitanism (1) '27 + 1': 27 national systems + 1 European system = 28 systems

That last model is most interesting to us as it indeed is an example of 'weakly pluralistic' cosmopolitanism, by contrast with the 'strongly pluralistic' kind quickly eliminated in section iii. Insofar as the '27 + 1' model posits 'legal systems' alternatively grounded in national or supranational (European) juridicities, it qualifies as 'pluralistic'; insofar as all said 'legal systems' are mutually exclusive (the European and various national jurisdictions not overlapping), its pluralism is of the 'weak' kind. The '27 + 1' model holding up under the parameters of our swarm model would thus establish that the present account of comparative law is consistent with at least one form of global pluralism.

Justifications for the '27 + 1' model can arguably be found in the Maastricht Treaty provisions introducing European citizenship as a supplement to, rather than substitute for, national citizenship, thus resulting in member state nationals henceforth cumulating national *and* European citizenships.[187] They can also be found in numerous pronouncements of the European Court of Justice (ECJ) reiterating the independence of the European legal order as against the member states' national

---

[187] But see Treaty on the Functioning of the European Union, European Union, 1957, art. 20, making European citizenship dependent on national citizenship, which has caused some national courts to deny the existence of a European *Volk* distinct from the national *Volks*: BVerfGE 123, 267 (*Lissabon*), at 372 (cited in Hesselink, *supra* note 42, at 213).

systems. The ECJ explicitly stated, for example, that "[b]y contrast with ordinary international treaties, the EC treaty has created its own legal system"[188] and that "the law stemming from the treaty [is] an independent source of law"[189] resulting from "[t]he transfer by the states from their domestic legal system to the community legal system of the rights and obligations arising under the Treaty,"[190] which new EC law moreover would take precedence over conflicting national law.[191] Quite aside from the ECJ's own view on the matter, moreover, several key structural features of the EU point in the same direction, in particular the fact that it is endowed with peculiar "sources of law, law-making institutions and procedures, methods of policing Member States' compliance with EU obligations, [and] procedures for the judicial review of EU norms."[192] One observer even contends that European legal institutions have come to develop a peculiar legal discourse.[193]

Yet one institutional feature concerning the enforcement of EC law militates against the '27 + 1' model. Whereas the various rules and orders making up that law all directly or indirectly originate from within the European constitutional structure, their enforcement is ultimately secured through the member states' national courts.[194] Insofar as those courts are viewed as external to the European constitutional structure, then, it may be difficult to conceptualize EC law as a self-standing legal system, particularly given the importance attached to enforcement in our swarm model. (It will be recalled that in order to qualify as an autonomous swarm under that model, any legal order does need to be, not merely self-defining and self-generating, but also self-*enforced* as such.)

Perhaps, however, the national courts could be viewed as somehow *partaking* of the European constitutional structure. As the EC treaty itself designates those courts as the enforcers of EC law,[195] they arguably could be considered official delegates of the European government for enforcement purposes, in line with Georges Scelle's famous theory of "*dédoublement fonctionnel*" ('role splitting') in

---

[188] See *Van Gend en Loos*, 1963 E.C.R. 1, at 12 (cited in Dickson, *supra* note 46, at 5).

[189] See *Flamino Costa*, 1964 E.C.R. 585, at 594 (cited by Dickson, *supra*).

[190] *Ibid.* (cited by Dickson, *supra*).

[191] Case 6/64, *supra* note 189; Case 11/70 *Internationale Handelsgesellschaft* [1970] E.C.R. 1125; Case 106/77 *Amministrazione delle Finanze dello Stato v. Simmenthal SpA* [1978] E.C.R. 629 (all cited by Dickson, *supra*, note 21). On the resolution of such conflicts through the interplay of 'mandatory' and 'optional' rules, see generally: Bénédicte Fauvarque-Cosson, European Contract Law Through and Beyond Pluralism, *in* PLURALISM AND EUROPEAN PRIVATE LAW 95, *supra* note 42, at 95.

[192] See Dickson, *supra* note 46.

[193] Martijn W. Hesselink, A European Legal Method? On European Private Law and Scientific Method, 15 EUR. L. J. 20 (2009).

[194] Déirdre Dwyer, The Domestic Enforcement of Supranational Rules: The Role of Evidence in EC Competition Law, *in* THEORISING THE GLOBAL LEGAL ORDER, *supra* note 18, at 167; Gillespie *supra* note 19, at 221.

[195] See the preliminary reference procedure of art. 234 EC Treaty, discussed in Dickson, *supra* note 46, at 23.

international law.[196] Each national court would then have two hats to wear, so to speak: they would act as enforcers of their national law in the realm governed by that law, and would switch hats to become enforcers of European law when dealing with matters governed by EC law.[197] Through such conceptual hat switching or "split personality,"[198] the integrity of the distinct European and national systems would presumably be preserved: each national court would effectively double up as swarm centre for two distinct swarms, their national system and the European system – those systems intersecting only with respect to the physical persons of the judges in charge of ultimately enforcing their respective rulings (as the respective realms of legal authority would themselves purportedly remain mutually exclusive).

If so, however, the validity of the '27 + 1' model would have to be assessed by reference to the national courts' view of it, not the view embodied in the European treaties or the pronouncements of the ECJ. For it will be recalled that under our swarm model, swarm delineation is achieved internally, by the very same officials as are in charge of standard adjudication, those tasks being in fact one and the same.[199] Accordingly, as the national courts would here be the ultimate enforcers of EC law, only *their* views as to how many swarms are at play, and where each one begins and end, should count. From our perspective, then, Dickson's contention[200] that the choice among the various models must ultimately be determined by reference to the national courts' behaviour seems entirely apposite. And what interests us here is not so much how those courts in fact rule on EC law issues but rather how they *justify their authority to do so*. If the national courts ground that authority in their respective national constitutions (reading said constitutions as calling for the implementation of international treaties, including the European treaties, and all rules and court orders derived therefrom), they are clearly of the view that they are ultimately accountable to their respective national constitutions. They in other words deny being bound by some kind of European 'rule of recognition' or *Grundnorm* distinct from their national ones.[201] If the national courts instead ground their authority to

---

[196] Georges Scelle, 1 *Précis de droit des gens. Principes et systématique*, 43, 54–56, 217 (1932), discussed in Cassese, *supra* note 134. (I am grateful to Ralf Michaels for bringing Scelle's work on point to my attention.) Scelle here builds on Kelsen's idea of international law involving a 'decentralization of social functions': Hans Kelsen, Théorie générale du droit international public. Problèmes choisis, *in* RECUEIL DES COURS DE L'ACADÉMIE DE LA HAYE 124–37 (1932).

[197] "Ils sont agents et gouvernants nationaux lorsqu'ils fonctionnent dans l'ordre juridique étatique; ils sont agents et gouvernants [européens] lorsqu'ils agissent dans l'ordre juridique [européen]"; Georges Scelle, Règles générales du droit de la paix, 46 RECUEIL DES COURS DE L'ACADÉMIE DE LA HAYE 356, 358 (1933).

[198] Cassese, *supra* note 134, at 212.

[199] See *supra* Part I text accompanying notes 32–35.

[200] Dickson, *supra* note 46, at 9.

[201] For suggestions that Europe might boast distinct European and national rules of recognitions: Michaels, *supra* note 4, at 14; Michaels, *supra* note 30 at 249; Claus-Wilhelm Canaris, Die richtlinienkonforme Auslegung und Rechtsfortbildung im System der juristischen Methodenlehre,

rule on EC law matters in the European treaties and the rulings of the ECJ as such,
they clearly see themselves as agents for the European government, thus bound by a
European rule of recognition, in addition to and alongside with, their national rule
of recognition.

Dickson reports that national courts have in fact widely resorted to the first kind
of justification:

> [I]n each case, the national legal system reserves to itself the right ultimately to
> determine the relationship between the [purported] EU legal system and the
> national legal system and to impose conditions on the operation of that relation-
> ship. Even as they grant EC law supremacy over national law, then, they do so on
> a different basis from that expounded by the ECJ: for the ECJ, the supremacy of
> EC law over national law is a consequence of the very nature and purpose of EC
> law and is hence required as a doctrine of EC law itself; for many national legal
> systems, EC law has in the end usually been granted supremacy over national law
> ... on the say so, and under the terms set by, the national courts and the national
> constitutional order more broadly.[202]

Based on that behaviour from the member states' national courts, we would have
to (provisionally) conclude against the (cosmopolitanist) '27 + 1' model – and for
that matter the (universalist) 'One Big Legal System' model – and in favour of the
(sovereignist) 'Part of Member States' model.

Nonetheless, the present argument warrants pressing further the (by now apparently counterfactual) '27 + 1' model, so as to explore possible variations on it. Note
at the outset that national courts hypothetically uniformly resorting to the second of
the above two kinds of justification might not suffice, in and of itself, to definitively
conclude in favour of the '27 + 1' model. That is, even if all national courts somehow saw themselves as accountable to the European constitution when ruling on
EC law, that might not be enough to conclusively establish the existence of a distinct
European rule of recognition. I would suggest that we would also need some kind
of evidence that each of those courts worries, at least to some extent, about aligning
its EC law rulings with those of its peer EC delegates, i.e. those of the other national
courts. That is because an aspiration, or at least a claim, to internal consistency is a

---

in IM DIENSTE DER GERCHTIGKEIT (H. Koziol & P. Rummel eds., 2002); Hesselink, *supra* note 42, at
218, 226; MacCormick, *supra* note 30; MACCORMICK, *supra* note 159; Pavlos Eleftheriadis, Pluralism
and Integrity, 23 RATIO JURIS 365, 378–79 (2010); Matthias Kumm, Constitutionalism and the Moral
Point of Constitutional Pluralism: Institutional Civil Disobedience and Conscientious Objection,
in PHILOSOPHICAL FOUNDATIONS OF EU LAW (Julie Dickson & Pavlos Eleftheriadis eds., 2012);
DELMAS-MARTY, *supra* note 21; Alec Stone Sweet & Thomas Brunell, Constructing a Supranational
Constitution, *in* THE JUDICIAL CONSTRUCTION OF EUROPE, *supra* note 182; Barber, *supra* note 145, at n.
94; PAUL CRAIG & GRÁINNE DE BÚRCA, EU LAW 433 (3rd ed. 2003).
[202] Dickson, *supra* note 46, at 10.

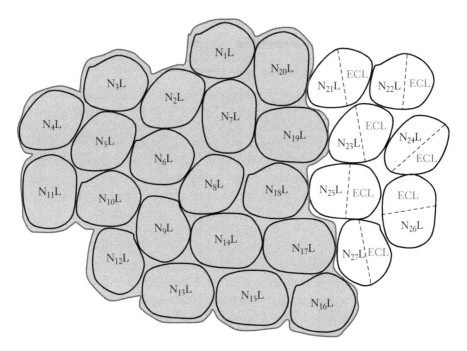

Figure 4. Cosmopolitanism (2) '(20 + 1) + 7': (20 national systems + 1 European system) + 7 independent national systems = 28 systems

defining characteristic of legal systems under our account,[203] as it arguably is to some degree under any account. Only where *both* of those two conditions are met could it plausibly be affirmed, in my view, that a distinct EC legal order exists alongside the twenty-seven member states' national legal systems.

Of course, there is no reason to assume uniformity across national courts here. A more realistic scenario in fact would have only some, say twenty, of the twenty-seven national courts meeting the two conditions, with the result that the '27 + 1' model would hold for those twenty but not for the remaining seven, which would instead be better represented by the 'Part of Member States' model (Figure 4). (It is assumed that no national court in the group of twenty sees itself as acting as EC delegate with respect to European *and* national matters, thus as having to worry about pan-European consistency on both counts. Should some of them do, they presumably would have to be carved out of the group of twenty and repositioned under the 'One Big Legal System' model.)

But there is also the possibility that some national courts meet the first but not the second condition. (The reverse is implausible, as it would be difficult to justify, on strict legal grounds, being bound by no other 'rule of recognition' than emerges

---

[203] See *supra* Chapter 1, Part I, section iii.

from one's national constitution yet having to harmonize your rulings with those of the other national courts.) For example, let us assume that, out of the group of twenty, five see themselves as bound by the European constitution with respect to EC law yet do not worry at all about aligning their EC law rulings with those of the other fifteen national courts. That would mean that although they see themselves as EC delegates, each of those five national courts would be developing its own peculiar take on the European constitution and EC law more generally, independently of any other national court doing the same – much like Quebec courts have done, as we saw, certainly in the area of private law.[204] Of course, the Quebec (or any other 'mixed jurisdiction') situation differs, in that the finality of Quebec's rulings (on any matter) is conditional upon their being recognized as such by the Canadian Supreme Court, whose own rulings are immediately enforceable, whereas in the European context, any judgment of the ECJ overruling a national court is ultimately enforceable only via that same national court. That difference is crucial insofar as it entails that the very reason that Quebec could not, I argued, be viewed as a self-standing swarm should cause us to come to the opposite conclusion in the European context, regarding the five national courts generating EC law on their own. That is, as those five courts *are* the ultimate enforcers of their EC law rulings, whatever legal practice emerges around those rulings should in contrast constitute a self-standing swarm.[205]

The overall picture emerging here would accordingly be a cosmopolitanist one (more legal systems than just belonging to the national member states) yet one that departs from the '27 + 1' model proposed by Dickson.[206] For we would now

---

[204] See *supra* Part I text accompanying notes 39 and 45.

[205] For such an account of the European codification movement, see: Ralf Michaels, Code vs Code: Nationalist and Internationalist Images of the Code civil in the French Resistance to a European Codification, 8 EUR. REV. OF CONTRACT L. 277 (2012).

[206] A further variation, wherein the various EC swarms emerging under any cosmopolitanist account would somehow qualify as 'sub-swarms' in relation to the various national swarms proper, can fortunately be safely ignored here, as it entails that national courts could somehow feel 'bound' by their national law but only 'somewhat bound' by EC law (non-national law possibly being 'binding' on national courts while not, for that matter, 'binding as *their* law'), which distinction is unavailable under the present model. See Dickson's approving discussion and citations (Dickson, *supra* note 46, at 17–23) of Raz's writings on point (RAZ, *supra* note 168, at 119 ("Quite often the courts have an obligation to apply laws of other legal systems ... although these were not and do not become part of the legal system")); Joseph Raz, Incorporation by Law, 10 LEGAL THEORY 1, 10 (2004) ("US and UK statutes give legal effect to company regulations, to university statutes, and to many other standards without thereby making them part of the law of the United Kingdom or United States ... Such references [nonetheless] make the application of the standards referred to legally required."). Likewise: Glenn, *supra* note 73, at 35 (describing the 'margin of appreciation' in ECHR since 1976 as an example of "multivalent logic"/"between legality and illegality"); ALAN WATSON, SOURCES OF LAW, LEGAL CHANGE AND AMBIGUITY 112 (1984) ("analytical two-tier system of law"); TWINING, *supra* note 1, at n. 132 ("[soft law instruments having] some legal effects even though they lack formal authority"), citing Francis Snyder, The Effectiveness of European Community Law: Institutions, Processes, Tools and Techniques, 56 MOD. L. REV. 19, 32 (1993); F. Beveridge & S. Nott, A Hard Look at Soft Law,

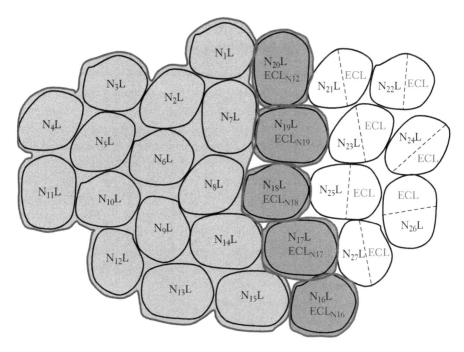

Figure 5. Cosmopolitanism (3) '(15 + 1) + 7 + (5 x 2)': (15 national systems + 1 European system) + 7 independent national systems + 5 national systems doubling up as 'localized' European systems = 33 systems

have seven national courts (meeting neither of the two conditions) acting as centres of just their respective national swarms; fifteen national courts (meeting both conditions) acting as centres of their respective national swarms *and one collective, European swarm*; and five national courts (meeting only the first condition) acting as centres of their respective national swarms *as well as of their respective, localized European swarms* – for a grand total of thirty-three swarms (7 + 16 + 10) (Figure 5). (Again assuming away the 'One Big Legal System' model, on the basis that no national courts would meet the two conditions with respect to both EC and their national law.) Of course, those numbers remain hypothetical. The real numbers would have to be settled by examining the rulings of each of the twenty-seven national courts so as to determine how many of them in fact meet both, neither, or only the first of the two conditions. The total number would accordingly vary between one (if the 'One Big Legal System' model is allowed back in) and fifty-four (where *all* twenty-seven national courts meet the first but not the second condition with respect to EC law).

in LAWMAKING IN THE EUROPEAN UNION chap. 14 (Paul Craig & Carol Harlow eds., 1998); G. Howells, "Soft Law" in EC Consumer Law, *in* LAWMAKING IN THE EUROPEAN UNION, *supra*, at chap. 15.

Now, should that analysis hold, it could presumably be carried outside the European context and applied to any realm of transnational normativity that ends up being enforced by national courts. For example, to the extent that all 194 of the sovereign national courts currently on record[207] justify their authority to rule on issues of private international law by reference to their respective national law on the matter, and do so without regard for what is done elsewhere, they would meet neither of the two conditions, which would suggest that the (sovereignist) 'Part of Member States' model best represents private international law.[208] In matters of public international law, in contrast, a cosmopolitanist model projecting anywhere from 195 (194 national + 1 collective international) to 390 (194 national + 194 localized international) legal systems might have traction. (Remember that a cosmopolitanist model by definition posits at least one system in addition to the national systems, thus rules out alternative possible counts of 1 and 194, respectively reflecting the universalist and sovereignist models.) The exact number would have to be determined based on how many of the 194 national courts (1) justify their authority to enforce rules and rulings of international law by appeal to international rather than national legal instruments and materials, and (2) take account of the international law rulings of the other national courts that do (1). Say that ninety national courts do (1) and (2), and four national courts do only (1). The overall count would then be 199 (194 national systems + 1 collective international system for the group of 90 + 4 localized international systems). And the same exercise could presumably be carried out with any area of public or private 'soft' law – transnational regulation networks, arbitration, etc. – qualifying as a 'community of practice' on account of regular enforcement by national courts.[209]

So far so good, but there is yet another glitch, having to do with the hat switching operation. Recall that that operation allowed us to conceptualize one and the same

---

[207] Total number of current sovereign states mustering the widest expert consensus according to the online World Atlas (World Atlas, *How Many Countries Are in the World?* (2016) www.worldatlas.com/nations.htm).

[208] STORY, *supra* note 46, at para. 21, cited in Bomhoff, *supra* note 46, at 14, 15 ("[W]hatever force and obligation the laws of one country have in another, depends solely upon the laws ... of the latter."); ERNST ZITELMANN, 1 *INTERNATIONALES PRIVATRECHT* 41 (1897) ("A state's authority is always exclusive."). *Contra*: various recent attempts to reconceptualize private international law as ultimately grounded in some kind of transnational conflicts of law 'constitution,' e.g., Bomhoff, *supra* note 46; Robert Wai, Private v. Private: Transnational Private Law and Contestation in Global Economic Governance, *in* PRIVATE INTERNATIONAL LAW AND GLOBAL GOVERNANCE 34, 53 (Horatia Muir Watt & Diego P. Fernández Arroyo eds., 2014) ("the complex shadow of multiple state laws ... as structuring the terrain on which transnational private ordering occurs").

[209] Adler & Pouliot, *supra* note 59. It has however been suggested that any area of international law has yet to congeal into such a 'community of practice': JUTTA BRUNNÉE & STEPHEN J. TOOPE, *LEGITIMACY AND LEGALITY IN INTERNATIONAL LAW* 8 (2010); Jutta Brunnée & Stephen J. Toope, Interactional International Law and the Practice of Legality, *in* INTERNATIONAL PRACTICES, *supra* note 59, at 108; Se-Shauna Wheatle, Comparative Law and the 'Ius Gentium', 3 CAMB. J. INT. & COMP. L. 1060, 1062 (2014); Oeter, *supra* note 18, at 78–79; Halpin, *supra* note 132, at 4.

national court serving as swarm centre for two swarms at once. Also recall, however, that (1) swarms do not come readily delineated but are rather being constantly
(re-)delineated through their respective central adjudicative operations, and that (2)
the various swarms cannot overlap. Presumably, then, the national court operating
any two swarms would have to do so in a way that avoids those swarms overlapping.
Of course, that is exactly what the European member state courts do on a daily
basis: the lion's share of their (and all EC law experts') work in fact consists of disentangling the aspects of European citizens' lives respectively falling under EC and
national law.[210]

But that suggests that each of the national and European swarms is being delineated by reference to something external to it (the other swarm), whereas they really
should be *self*-delineating, by reference to nothing other than themselves. In effect,
then, the current European situation actually *is* analogous to the Canadian one,
wherein one central court, the Canadian Supreme Court, is ultimately in charge
of coordinating, from the outside, the respective jurisdictions of the various provincial units. Also like in the Canadian situation, then, the various jurisdictions being
coordinated should, under our model, be viewed as forming just one collective
swarm. That suggests that even as official EC delegates, the national courts are not,
in fact, hat switching. As it ultimately falls to each one of them to coordinate their
national and European jurisdictions, they effectively always wear *one and the same
hat*, namely, that of a (collective) central court operating a single (two-part) swarm.

That leaves us with just two possibilities: either each of the national courts coordinating two jurisdictions heads just one national swarm – the (sovereignist) 'Part of
Member States' model (see Figure 2) – or else each is just one of several players collectively coordinating the national and European jurisdictions of a single European swarm
comprising as many national units as there are players: the (universalist) 'One Big Legal
System' model (see Figure 1). There simply is no third (cosmopolitanist) possibility,
that is, whereby any given national system could count as one swarm *separate from,
and in addition to*, some supranational swarm that would include it. Whereas the
behaviour of the group of five national courts (meeting only the first condition) presumably motions to the first conclusion, that of the group of fifteen (meeting both
conditions) would militate in favour of the second. (Note that the fact that all twenty
courts meet at least the first condition, as they coordinate the two jurisdictions by
reference to EC rulings on the matter, is ultimately irrelevant here: whatever norms
they choose to consult in that coordination process, they still *reserve to themselves*
the task of handling that process.)

[210] Roger Cotterrell, Transnational Communities and the Concept of Law, 21 RATIO JURIS 1, 15 (2008)
("a slowly emerging template in terms of which [jurisdictional disputes or conflicts over authority and
legitimacy claims] can be judged"). But see: Niglia, *supra* note 73, at 251 (deriding universalists as
purportedly "capable of determining solutions effortlessly").

It thus seems that, for our purposes at least, weakly pluralistic cosmopolitanism ultimately does not offer a viable alternative to sovereignism and universalism since, under the parameters of our swarm model, it necessarily unravels
into one or the other.[211] No more than strongly pluralistic cosmopolitanism or
weak legal pluralism at the subnational level, then, does weakly pluralistic cosmopolitanism belong on our list of accounts of global law compatible with the
present account of comparative law. That list accordingly stops at just two monistic accounts of global law, namely, sovereignism and monistic (or Kantian-like)
cosmopolitanism.

This suggests two points with regard to comparative law studies involving supranational units. The first is that, in delineating the contours of the various supranational
units at play, comparative lawyers should focus on the behaviour of the courts in
charge of actually enforcing the relevant rules and rulings, and disregard conflicting delineation tips that might be garnered from other legal instruments. The second brings us back, yet again, to our earlier point concerning the importance for
comparative lawyers to adopt a mixed, internal/external perspective: whereas our
discussion of weak legal pluralism at the subnational level emphasized that point
by expounding the perils of an exclusively internal perspective, the foregoing discussion of weak legal pluralism at the supranational level does the same but from
the opposite direction, that is, by outlining the perils of a perspective that would in
contrast be exclusively external.

CONCLUSION

The aim of Part I was to clarify that the general conclusion of the previous chapter
as to the importance of apprehending foreign law from a mixed internal/external
perspective holds whether one aims to reconstruct the contents of any given legal
system or delineate that system's contours. As legal systems are epistemic communities whose content-building and structure-defining operations are in fact identical,
whatever perspective is determined appropriate for the purpose of investigating their
contents ought to be also appropriate for the purpose of delineating their contours.

---

[211] Hesselink (Hesselink, *supra* note 42, at 213, 225) offers a similar argument against 'pluralist' models
of European private law, though the unraveling there stops at 'dualism.' See also: Michaels at 158;
Niglia, *supra* note 73, at 253 ("hierarchical thinking lies behind the most ostensibly pluralist private
law theories"). That might just confirm Michael Sandel's claim (MICHAEL J. SANDEL, DEMOCRACY'S
DISCONTENT, AMERICA IN SEARCH OF A PUBLIC PHILOSOPHY 345 (1996)) that "the cosmopolitan vision is
wrong to suggest that we can restore self-government simply by pushing sovereignty and citizenship
upward"; and Seyla Benhabib's claim (SEYLA BENHABIB, THE RIGHTS OF OTHERS: ALIENS, RESIDENTS,
AND CITIZENS 219 (2004)) that "the scope of democratic legitimacy cannot extend beyond the demos
which has circumscribed itself as a people upon a given territory."

We ourselves accordingly undertook to consider the delineation of legal systems from alternating internal (Part II) and external (Part III) perspectives.

In Part II, we compared the internal structuring process of legal systems to that of bee swarms. In the same way that bee swarms boast elusive edges surrounding a clearly identifiable queen bee, legal systems, it was argued, project an ill-defined mass of materials and arguments gravitating around a comparatively well-defined centre of gravity, in particular, their respective central adjudicative bodies. Building on Niklas Luhmann's account of the formation of legal systems, we there saw that the fluidity of the peripheral layer of legal systems is both temporal and spatial. As it is the normative salience of legal materials and arguments that determines the extent to which, and moment at which, they can be considered part of the system, both their geographical and historical parameters indeed are bound to vary with that normative salience.

In Part III, we exited the internal perspective so as to observe legal systems as they relate *inter se* in the current global context. We there determined, first, that the present account of comparative law is inconsistent with universalism and consistent with sovereignism and monistic cosmopolitanism (section i). The latter two being 'non-pluralistic,' under our definition, we thereafter turned to consider 'pluralistic' accounts of global law. We immediately dismissed 'strong legal pluralism' because it portrays legal systems as possibly overlapping in unresolvable ways, whereas our swarm model requires that matters be possibly settled once and for all, which possibility obtains only where legal systems are free of such overlaps (section ii). As weak legal pluralism in contrast presupposes legal systems' mutual exclusivity, we then proceeded to examine its sub- and supranational instantiations (section iii), only to conclude that neither is, in the end, compatible with our swarm model. Whereas formal and informal subnational units can be seen as mutually exclusive as against one another, they are not mutually exclusive as against their host state, as it ultimately falls to the courts of that host state to carve out the respective (mutually exclusive) realms of subnational and national jurisdiction (section iii (1)). As for the possibility of supranational legal systems existing alongside and in addition to national systems ('weakly pluralistic cosmopolitanism'), our analysis of the European situation revealed it to be unsustainable, at least when applying the analytical framework of our swarm model. We concluded that only sovereignism and monistic cosmopolitanism are compatible with our swarm model and the present account of comparative law more generally.

The upshot of this chapter for comparative law is two-fold. First, the conclusion reached in the previous chapter as to the importance of comparative lawyers oscillating between the internal and external perspectives is confirmed. Second, traditional comparative law scholarship, which has focused on national law, though has not for that matter projected legal systems as coextensive with territorially bound nation states, hopefully is validated. Should the day come (back) where adjudicative bodies other than national courts are endowed with real enforcement powers,[212] the traditional analytic framework of comparative law might indeed need to be revisited. But in the present context of Westphalian world politics, there does not appear to be cause for worry.

[212] As was arguably the case in medieval times, prior to the emergence of nation states. Kelsen famously denied that possibility, as he considered the political and legal realms to be inextricably interwoven, even at just a conceptual level. KELSEN, *supra* note 159; HANS KELSEN, *INTRODUCTION TO THE PROBLEMS OF LEGAL THEORY* 99 (Bonnie Litschewski Paulson & Stanley L. Paulson trans., 1992) ("When the legal system has achieved a certain degree of centralization, it is characterised as a state."). The primary aim of much of the global pluralist literature of course is to attempt to dissociate law from the political nation state. However, those who reviewed that literature seem to converge on the view that, first, it remains largely under-theorized and, second, none of it ultimately manages to steer clear of state law. See: Wood, *supra* note 2, at 35–37; Dickson, *supra* note 46, at 2; MACCORMICK, *supra* note 159, at 97–121, 102–105; Kumm, *supra* note 182, at 267, 306; Michaels, *supra* note 4, at 10, 14; Ralf Michaels, Territorial Jurisdiction after Territoriality, *in* GLOBALISATION AND JURISDICTION 105 (Piet Jan Slot & Mielle Bulterman eds., 2004); Oxana Golynker, European Union as a Single Working-Living Space: EU Law and New Forms of Intra-Community Migration, *in* THEORISING THE GLOBAL LEGAL ORDER 145, *supra* note 18, at 145; ROUGHAN, *supra* note 148, at 8; ALAIN DEGENNE & MICHEL FORSÉ, *INTRODUCING SOCIAL NETWORKS* 12 (2nd ed. 1999); Mark Granovetter, Economic Action and Social Structure: The Problem of Embeddedness, 91 AM. J. SOC. 481, 491 (1985); NATIONAL LEGAL SYSTEMS AND GLOBALIZATION: NEW ROLES, CONTINUED RELEVANCE (Pierre Larouche & Péter Cserne eds., 2013); J. E. Alvarez, State Sovereignty is Not Withering Away: A Few Lessons for the Future, *in* REALIZING UTOPIA: THE FUTURE OF INTERNATIONAL LAW 26, 27–37 (Antonio Cassese ed., 2012); Noah Feldman, Cosmopolitan Law?, 116 YALE L. J. 1022, 1032 (2007); Jack Goldsmith, Liberal Democracy and Cosmopolitan Duty, 55 STAN. L. REV. 1667, 1673–75 (2003); Alan Scott Rau & George Bermann, Gateway-Schmateway: An Exchange Between George Bermann and Alan Rau, 43 PEPPERDINE L. REV. 469, 472 (2016); David Nelken, Signaling Conformity: Changing Norms in Japan and China, 27 MICH. J. OF INT'L L. 933, 945 (2006).

5

Comparing Legal Systems

Methodology

INTRODUCTION

The last four chapters laid out the analytic framework of comparative law as comparison of the collective commitments underlying legal systems. Chapter 1 described the working conception of law, "law as collective commitment," on which that account of comparative law is based, which working conception was in turn shown in Chapter 2 to entail a conception of legal systems as uniquely suited to meaningful mutual comparison. Chapter 3 then took up the epistemological question of the proper (external and/or internal) perspective from which to engage with foreign such systems, whereas the question of their proper geographical and historical delineation was explored in Chapter 4.

The present chapter aims to operationalize that analytic framework into a three-step methodology for comparing these systems. The aim is not to develop a "comprehensive methodology" that would be a priori valid for all comparative law projects, in opposition to the seemingly wide consensus among comparatists in favour "methodological pluralism."[1] More modestly, it merely seeks to unpack the methodological implications of the particular account of comparative law evolved in the previous chapters – a methodology specifically tailored to the account of comparative law as comparative collective commitments. Of course, insofar as that account does provide that the various components of legal systems can only be properly understood in the light of their system's peculiar commitments, and insofar as all comparative law projects arguably require that whatever such components, or groups thereof, are being

---

[1] See generally: Marieke Oderkerk, The Need for a Methodological Framework for Comparative Legal Research—Sense and Nonsense of "Methodological Pluralism" in Comparative Law, 79 RABELSZ 589 (2015); Mark van Hoecke, Do "Legal Systems" Exist? The Concept of Law and Comparative Law, in CONCEPTS OF LAW: COMPARATIVE, JURISPRUDENTIAL, AND SOCIAL SCIENCE PERSPECTIVES 43 (Seán Donlan & Lukas Heckendorm Urscheler eds., 2014); Robert Leckey, Review of Comparative Law, 26 SOCIAL & LEGAL STUDIES 3 (2017).

compared first need to be properly understood, one might expect all projects to draw on the present methodology to some extent. Then again, it may also be possible to simply rely on pre-existing collective commitment understandings, produced by others, of the legal systems under study. Even where the present methodology is in fact drawn upon, however, one would expect it to be supplemented with whatever additional, more specific methodological guidelines may be appropriate for the particular project in question.[2]

Part I describes the first stage of that comparative process, namely, identifying a topic, target legal systems and the relevant legal data for each of the chosen systems, which first stage has us draw on functionalism and expressivism alike. Part II then discusses what is to be done with that data, in particular, how to reconstruct it into coherent narratives reflecting the systems' respective underlying collective commitments. We there see that such reconstruction proceeds dialectically, as the singularity of each narrative best comes to light through their being set against the others. Finally, Part III offers a way to bring these narratives together within a same comparison act without for that matter eroding their peculiar identities as distinct narratives. That comparison act can be described as 'proportional comparison' insofar as it involves the various systems under comparison being measured against their own standards, the standards each system sets for itself on the inside.

I. GATHERING THE RELEVANT LEGAL DATA

For any comparison to be meaningful, it must be impartial as between the various objects being compared. That is, it must proceed so as to avoid skewing the analysis in favour of one (or some) of them. This requires exploring the various objects through a comparative criterion that is equally applicable to all yet privileges none – an 'invariant point of reference,'[3] or *tertium comparationis*.[4]

In the context of any given comparative legal study, the *tertium comparationis* is no other than the issue, particular topic or more general area of law that the

---

[2] *Ibid.*, at 604.

[3] Gideon Sjoberg, The Comparative Method in the Social Sciences, 22 PHIL. SCI. 106, 107 (1955) ("Only through the use of invariant points of reference is it possible to test adequately various hypotheses in a cross-cultural setting.").

[4] The issue, first raised in the context of comparative law by Radbruch (Gustav Radbruch, Über die Methode der Rechtsvergleichung, R.I.D.C. 753, 758ff (1905–6)) has been the object of a voluminous literature in the field (e.g. John Henry Merryman, Comparative Law and Scientific Explanation, *in* LAW IN THE UNITED STATES OF AMERICA IN SOCIAL AND TECHNICAL REVOLUTION 81, 92 (John N. Hazard & Wenceslas J. Wagner eds., 1974); Hein Kötz, Comparative Law in Germany Today, R.I.D.C. 106–17 (1999)). LÉONTIN-JEAN CONSTANTINESCO, TRAITÉ DE DROIT COMPARÉ 143–44 (1972) [hereinafter CONSTANTINESCO, TRAITÉ DE DROIT COMPARÉ]; LÉONTIN-JEAN CONSTANTINESCO, LA MÉTHODE COMPARATIVE 34ff (1974) [hereinafter CONSTANTINESCO, LA MÉTHODE COMPARATIVE]; Ralf Michaels, The Functional Method of Comparative Law, *in* THE OXFORD HANDBOOK OF COMPARATIVE LAW 339 (Mathias Reimann & Reinhard Zimmermann eds., 2006); Esin Örücü, Methodology of Comparative Law, *in* ELGAR ENCYCLOPEDIA OF COMPARATIVE LAW 442 (Jan M. Smits ed., 2006).

comparatist proposes to explore in her target legal systems. So where one proposes to compare the treatment of, say, freedom of expression at German and US law, the *tertium comparationis* is 'freedom of expression,' whereas 'contract law' would be the (broader) *tertium comparationis* in a study aimed at covering, more broadly, all of Japanese and Argentinian contract law. And the 'objects' of the comparison here would be the German and US legal systems, and Japanese and Argentinian systems, respectively. Admittedly, the only parts of those systems that would then be of immediate interest to the comparatist would be their legal materials bearing on freedom of expression in the first case, and those partaking of contract law in the second. However, insofar as legal materials as we saw are meaningless outside the context of their respective systems, the comparatist's inquiry will necessarily have to reach to the rest of German/US or Japanese/Argentinian law – and their underlying collective commitments – and it is therefore these entire systems that will ultimately constitute the analytic unit, the 'objects,' of the comparison.

Note that the determination of the *tertium comparationis* and target legal systems is an operation necessarily accomplished from an external standpoint, that of an observer standing outside any and all legal systems.[5] That is, while the comparatist as argued ultimately aims to investigate and understand each of her target systems on the inside, from the standpoint of its participants,[6] such investigations are necessarily preceded by an externally conducted stage-setting phase, of which the determination of the *tertium comparationis* and target legal systems is a part. That is the case for any scientific investigation: investigative parameters need to be set before the investigation proper can begin.

But the stage-setting phase being prior does not mean that it is entirely insulated from the subsequent phases. For one, the parameters set in the stage-setting phase ("design") clearly channel the investigation itself ("execution") and hence are bound to bear on its results ("yield") to some extent.[7] But in addition, as is also the case for any scientific investigation, those parameters will likely be subsequently revisited, adjusted or refined in light of the results of the investigation, they being always merely provisional.[8] For example, a comparatist intent on comparing 'shareholder rights' in legal systems X and Y, only to discover during the investigation proper that system X in fact lacks anything resembling a capital market,[9] would have no choice but to modify her initial *tertium comparationis* ('shareholder rights') or else replace system X with another, capital market-endowed legal system. Thus,

---

[5] "an outsider's epistemic point of view": Jaakko Husa, Farewell to Functionalism or Methodological Tolerance?, 67 R*ABEL*Z 419, 426 (2003). See generally Chapter 4, Part II, section ii.

[6] See *supra* Chapter 3, Part III.

[7] The "design/execution/yield" designation is Ewald's: William Ewald, Comparative Jurisprudence (I): What Was It Like to Try a Rat?, 143 *U. P*A*. L. R*EV. 1189, 1889–90 (1995).

[8] Sjoberg, *supra* note 3, at 114; J*OHN* O*ULTON* W*ISDOM*, F*OUNDATIONS OF* I*NFERENCE IN* N*ATURAL* S*CIENCES* (1952), both authors drawing on K*ARL* R. P*OPPER*, O*BJECTIVE* K*NOWLEDGE* 142–46 (1972).

[9] The example is drawn from: Michaels, *supra* note 4, at 368.

while the external and internal phases of the comparative process remain conceptually distinct, at least in a scientifically sound such process, they feed on one another.

i. Choosing a Topic and Target Legal Systems

But how does the comparative lawyer proceed to choose a *tertium comparationis* and particular target legal systems in the first place? On one level, there is very little to say about such process as it is, at least initially, largely intuitive. Like all scientists, seasoned comparative lawyers naturally come to develop a 'sense' of what particular questions have yet, and deserve, to be studied in their areas of expertise, and are able to steer their and others' (students', colleagues') work accordingly.[10] While such 'hunches'[11] by definition defy strict rationalization, they are not for that matter entirely subjective, culturally tainted or arbitrary.[12] They are 'informed' insofar as they emerge from the scientist's accumulated expertise and, inasmuch as they indeed are amenable to future revisions in light of the investigation results, they remain to some extent constrained by the scientific process.[13] So an experienced comparative lawyer 'feeling' that one might gain valuable new knowledge about the German and/or US legal systems, or 'freedom of expression' writ large, from comparing its treatments in those two systems would be more than enough reason to launch into such a study.[14]

---

[10] KONRAD ZWEIGERT & HEIN KÖTZ, AN INTRODUCTION TO COMPARATIVE LAW 33 (Tony Weir trans., 3rd ed. 1998) ("[T]here will always remain ... an area where only sound judgment, common sense, or even intuition can be of any help."). They also describe the same as "feeling" (at 34) and as "imagination" (at 35). Jennifer Nedelsky (Receptivity and Judgment 4 ETHICS & GLOBAL POLITICS 231, 235 (2011)) likewise describes the initial 'oumf' triggering scientific enquiry as an act of judgment à la Kant and Arendt, thus subjective yet not for that matter arbitrary. See *supra* note 78, Chapter 3.

[11] See ZWEIGERT & KÖTZ, *supra* note 10, at 33.

[12] Such 'hunches' indeed have been denounced as 'unscientific': Ralf Michaels, The Second Wave of Comparative Law and Economics, 59 U. TORONTO L. J. 197, 212 (2009) and Michaels, *supra* note 4, at 360, discussing ZWEIGERT & KÖTZ, *supra* note 10 (E.g. Günter Frankenberg, Stranger than Paradise: Identity & Politics in Comparative Law, UTAH L. REV. 259, 270 (1997) ("comparatists [must] realize that their everyday is shaped and dominated by a grid of concepts, research techniques, professional ethics, and politics, by which the prevailing culture imposes on the individual scholar its canons of how legal scholarship is to be conducted.").) Yet they arguably are an inescapable part of the 'scientific process' proper: KARL R. POPPER, THE LOGIC OF SCIENTIFIC DISCOVERY 31–32 (1972). For, "[it can't be that w]e must understand [have a theory for] what it is we are studying before we can study it." (Andrew Halpin, Conceptual Collisions, 2 JURIS. 507 (2011)).

[13] Patrick Gardiner, *Introduction to* THE PHILOSOPHY OF HISTORY 13 (Patrick Gardiner ed., 1974) ("But to say that [the historian's] choice of problems bears the mark of current concerns is not to say that the solutions he produces must be similarly influenced or infected."); Jaakko Husa, The False Dichotomy Between Theory and Practice: Lessons from Comparative Law, *in* RECHTSWISSENSCHAFT ALS JURISTISCHE DOKTRIN 105, 116–17 (2009) ("A macro-construct gives the comparatist ... a firmer basis than reliance on one's own prejudices."); Sjoberg, *supra* note 3, at 111 ("The process of constructing an adequate set of invariant reference points must, then, be one of continual trial and error and, fundamentally, one of self-criticism.").

[14] "a choice about 'what matters', that is, which aspects of the law are relevant for the comparative lawyer, and which aspects of the law might benefit from the additional knowledge which comparison

But if the choice of topic thus remains largely a matter of intuition, its exact formulation calls for much deliberation. For, formulating the *tertium comparationis* as just 'freedom of expression' will not do here. This is because legal labels – 'freedom of expression,' 'contract law,' 'shareholder rights' – are notoriously unreliable identifiers of counterpart rules or domains across jurisdictions. In fact, if there is one observation on which all comparatists seem to converge, it is that the labels used to designate rules, concepts, institutions or even entire areas of law are not standardized across legal systems but rather determined locally, with the result that the same label may well capture different matters (and a different label, similar matters) in different legal systems.[15] It could hence be that some legal materials falling under the label 'freedom of expression' in the US legal system fall under a different label ('defamation?') in the German system. Substituting subject area for issue labels would fare no better, moreover, as the freedom of expression cases treated as 'constitutional' matters in one system might span a number of legal domains ('delictual law,' 'criminal law,' 'administrative law?') in the other, some of which might not even exist in the first. If so, the comparative lawyer confining her investigation to the 'constitutional' matters of each system would end up missing out on a whole pool of second-jurisdiction materials speaking directly to her issue.

A more pointed example would be a comparative study aimed at comparing the notion of 'contract' at French and English law. One reviewing the areas of the French and English systems locally designated as 'contract law' would naturally conclude that the notion of 'contract' differs drastically in the two systems, if only because

---

provides." Nils Jansen, Comparative Law and Comparative Knowledge *in* THE OXFORD HANDBOOK OF COMPARATIVE LAW 305, *supra* note 4, at 314.

[15] Mark Van Hoecke, Deep Level Comparative Law, *in* EPISTEMOLOGY AND METHODOLOGY OF COMPARATIVE LAW 165, 174–75 (Mark Van Hoecke ed., 2004); Arthur T. Von Mehren, Civil-Law Analogues to Consideration: An Exercise in Comparative Analysis, 72 HARV. L. REV. 1009, 1010 (1959); ZWEIGERT & KÖTZ, *supra* note 10, at 28–45; Michele Graziadei, The Functionalist Heritage, *in* COMPARATIVE LEGAL STUDIES: TRADITIONS AND TRANSITIONS (Pierre Legrand & Roderick Munday eds., 2003); Bruce Ackerman, The Rise of World Constitutionalism, 83 VA L. REV. 771, 794 (1997); Mark Tushnet, The Possibilities of Comparative Constitutional Law, 108 YALE L. J. 1225 (1999); Antje Wiener & Philip Liste, Lost Without Translation? Cross-Referencing and a New Global Community of Courts, 21 IND. J. GLOBAL LEGAL STUD. 263 (2014); Sjoberg, *supra* note 3, at 106–107, 112 ('divorce,' 'household'); Rodolfo Sacco, Legal Formants: A Dynamic Approach to Comparative Law (Installment I of II), 39 AM. J. COMP. L. 1, 10 (1991) ('revolving funds'); Étienne Picard, Le droit comparé est-il du droit?, 1 ANN. INST. MICHEL VILLEY 173, 218ff (2009) ('discretion'); CONSTANTINESCO, LA MÉTHODE COMPARATIVE *supra* note 4, at 41; Otto Pfersmann, Le droit comparé comme interpretation et comme théorie du droit, R.I.D.C. 275, 283–84 (2001) ('president,' 'immunity'); Randall Peerenboom, What Have We Learned About Law and Development? Describing, Predicting, and Asssessing Legal Reforms in China, 27 MICH. J. OF INT'L L. 823 (2006) ('due process'); Geoffrey Samuel, Does One Need an Understanding of Methodology in Law Before One Can Understand Methodology in Comparative Law?, *in* METHODOLOGIES OF LEGAL RESEARCH: WHICH KIND OF METHODOLOGY FOR WHAT KIND OF DISCIPLINE? 177, 185–86 (Mark Van Hoecke ed., 2011) ('misrepresentation,' 'good faith,' 'mistake'); John Bell, Legal Research and the Distinctiveness of Comparative Law, *in* METHODOLOGIES OF LEGAL RESEARCH: WHICH KIND OF METHODOLOGY FOR WHAT KIND OF DISCIPLINE? 155, *supra*, at 162 ('stolen').

gratuitous transfers in principle qualify as 'contracts' in the first but not the second.[16] A glimpse at French evidentiary law however quickly reveals that gratuitous transfers exceeding a certain (low) sum in fact are not enforceable unless notarized – much like unilateral transfers unsealed or unsupported by 'nominal' consideration are unenforceable at English law. In the final analysis, therefore, the difference between the French and the English 'contract' is far less stark than might initially appear. But grasping this requires reviewing all the law bearing on contracts in the two systems, whether or not it falls under what is locally labelled 'contract law,' i.e. including that falling under 'evidentiary law.' Here again, then, the comparative lawyer confining her investigation to French and English 'contract law' materials would end up missing highly relevant French legal data. Her analysis would end up skewed as she would, in effect, be comparing apples with love.[17]

ii. *Identifying Potentially Relevant Legal Data: Functionalism*

But what else is there, besides labels? Social function arguably offers a promising alternative. As noted by Ernst Rabel and others, the functions discharged by legal rules, unlike their labels, do tend to cut across jurisdictions.[18] Indeed, it seems reasonable to think that law is called upon to attend to a core of similar social

---

[16] BARRY NICHOLAS, THE FRENCH LAW OF CONTRACTS (1982).

[17] See *supra* Chapter 2, Part I. That problem admittedly could be avoided by having her settle on one or the other of the two systems' different labels as a starting point, and proceed to compare the situations covered by that label in the first system with the counterpart situations in the second. But that would in turn entail analyzing the situations in the second system through the lens of the first, given that the first group of situations would necessarily correspond to a full category in the first system, whereas the second (counterpart) group would correspond to just a sample, perhaps not even representative, of what is considered a full category in the second system (since it is here assumed that the first and second categories are not coextensive).

[18] ERNST RABEL, 1 THE CONFLICT OF LAWS: A COMPARATIVE STUDY (2nd ed. 1945); Clive M. Schmitthoff, The Science of Comparative Law, 7 CAMBRIDGE L. J. 94, 96 (1939); ZWEIGERT & KÖTZ, *supra* note 10, at 31 ("in law the only things which are comparable are those which fulfil the same function."); BASIL S. MARKESINIS, FOREIGN LAW AND COMPARATIVE METHODOLOGY 4–6 (1997); Arthur T. von Mehren, The Comparative Study of Law, 6/7 TUL. CIVIL L. FOR. 43 (1991–92); Vladimir Aleksandrovich Tumanov, On Comparing Various Types of Legal Systems, in COMPARATIVE LAW AND LEGAL SYSTEM: HISTORICAL AND SOCIO-LEGAL PERSPECTIVES 69, 76 (William Elliott Butler & W. N Kudriavstev eds., 1985); Pierre Larouche, Legal Emulation Between Regulatory Competition and Comparative Law, in NATIONAL LEGAL SYSTEMS AND GLOBALIZATION: NEW ROLES, CONTINUED RELEVANCE (Pierre Larouche & Péter Cserne eds., 2013); Filomena Chirico & Pierre Larouche, Convergence and Divergence in Law and Economics and Comparative Law, in NATIONAL LEGAL SYSTEMS AND GLOBALISATION, *supra*, at 19–20; MATTHIAS SIEMS, COMPARATIVE LAW 13–15, 35–36 (2014); Oliver Brand, Conceptual Comparisons: Towards a Coherent Methodology of Comparative Legal Studies, 32 BROOKLYN J. INT'L L. 405–66 (2007); John C. Reitz, How to Do Comparative Law, 46 AM. J. COMP. L. 617, 620–23 (1998); Geoffrey Samuel, Epistemology and Comparative Law: Contributions from the Sciences and Social Sciences, in EPISTEMOLOGY AND METHODOLOGY OF COMPARATIVE LAW, *supra* note 15, 35, at 38, 40–41, 61–64, 75ff; Nikolas Roos, NICE Dreams and Realities of European Private Law, in EPISTEMOLOGY AND METHODOLOGY OF COMPARATIVE LAW 197, *supra*, at 213ff; Luc J. Wintgens, Legisprudence and Comparative Law, in EPISTEMOLOGY AND METHODOLOGY OF COMPARATIVE LAW, *supra*, 299, at 301ff;

problems – two cars colliding at an intersection, neighbours crossing one another's lawns without permission, employees failing to show up for work, etc. – across jurisdictions. That is not to suggest that *all* social problems are the same across *all* jurisdictions, only that *some* such problems are common across *some* jurisdictions.[19] If so, the particular problems that happen to be shared by the particular systems under study might well provide the jurisdiction-neutral point of entry we are looking for.[20]

Consider again our comparative lawyer interested in freedom of expression. Rather than searching for relevant materials through such legal key words as 'freedom of expression' or 'constitutional law,' she could ask herself how the German and US legal systems typically handle the real-life situation of 'citizens bad-mouthing one another in public.' That problem-based formulation would naturally take her across legal labels and categories, to *all* the materials bearing on that aspect of freedom of expression in each jurisdiction. That these materials might attract different labels or classifications in the two jurisdictions would no longer matter, in other words.[21]

But it could be retorted that such problem-based formulations do not resolve the label issue, but only push it one level further, as they too most likely include some (system-variant) labels. For, in the formulation just suggested, the references to 'citizens' and 'in public' likewise possibly designate different matters in the two systems. Should our comparatist discover that that is in fact the case, she admittedly could try yet another formulation, more concrete still, one in which 'citizens' and 'in public' are respectively replaced with 'passport-carrying individuals' and 'in newspapers.'[22] Then again, the same label issue arguably recurs here as well with respect to 'passport' and 'newspapers.' And so on. In short, while our comparatist might be able to move to increasingly more factual, less heavily law-laden formulations, she may be unable ever to reach to a level that is entirely free of system-variant labelling. *Some* measure

Jaakko Husa & Jan M. Smits, A Dialogue on Comparative Functionalism, MAASTRICHT J. EUR & COMP. L. 18 (2011).

[19] Much comparative law scholarship critical of functionalism seems to fall prey to that confusion. E.g. James Whitman, The Neo-Romantic Turn, *in* COMPARATIVE LEGAL STUDIES: TRADITIONS AND TRANSITIONS, *supra* note 15, 312, at 313; see SIEMS at 38; Ackerman, *supra* note 15, at 771, 775 (1997).

[20] It has been suggested that 'ideals' might likewise be sufficiently removed from particular legal labelling to serve as (system-invariant) *tertia comparationis*: Reitz, *supra* note 18, at 629; Sjoberg, *supra* note 3, at 110. Yet it is hard to see how such 'ideals' could be operationalized into actual *tertia comparationis* without first being reduced to fact situations. ("a compromise between the two [empirical categories and rationalistic conceptual schemes]": *ibid.*) In testing the extent to which the French and English legal systems abide by a 'subjective' or 'objective' conception of contract, for example, it seems necessary to translate these ideas into such real world situations as obtain where parties to a contract (objectively) say one thing but (subjectively) think another, i.e. typical mistake situations. See e.g., Catherine Valcke, Convergence and Divergence among the English, French and German Conceptions of Contract, 16 EUR. REV. PRIV. L. 29 (2008).

[21] And the 'common core' literature (e.g. *infra* note 34) does typically proceed from such problem-based starting points.

[22] This would be one example of the analytic framework revisiting discussed *supra*, pp. 191–92.

of distortion and bias as between the two systems would hence remain inevitable. This is so for the simple reason that, as many comparatists have pointed out, the fact/ law distinction ultimately remains to some extent elusive in all legal systems, and the legal construction of what might externally appear to be same sets of facts – their legal relevance and particular implications – in fact varies from system to system as said construction is ultimately determined through local practice.[23] Hence has it been questioned whether (problem-based) 'function' really does offer a more promising (system-invariant) *tertium comparationis* than do (system-variant) legal labels.

I would suggest that it does, insofar as all that we really need for present purposes is not so much the possibility of reaching to some ultimate, purely factual level, lying altogether outside law, as that of moving *across* varying levels of fact/law ladenness. Recall that the scientific imperative at issue here merely is to keep the object of investigation separate from the set of a priori assumptions used to channel that investigation: "the common point of reference cannot itself be established through comparison."[24] If facts were neatly delineable from law, that imperative would obviously be well satisfied through confining the first (facts) to our investigative premises and using the second (law) as object of investigation. But such neat delineation is not absolutely necessary insofar as our primary concern remains that of identifying a point of reference *that is not also part of what is being investigated* – quite apart, that is, from the nature of that particular point of reference, specifically, whether it is heavily fact- or law-laden.

Say, for example, that our comparatist has determined through prior work that the legal definitions of 'citizen' and 'bad-mouthing' are relatively similar in the German and US systems, sufficiently similar in fact that the last proposed formulation would prove an acceptably 'neutral' common point of reference for new work involving

---

[23] NEIL MACCORMICK, *INSTITUTIONS OF LAW: AN ESSAY IN LEGAL THEORY* 290 (2007); Samuel, *supra* note 18, at 38–43; Mark Van Hoecke & Mark Warrington, Legal Cultures, Legal Paradigms and Legal Doctrine: Towards a New Model for Comparative Law, 47 INT'L & COMP. L. Q. 495, 535 (1998); Lawrence Rosen, Beyond Compare, *in* COMPARATIVE LEGAL STUDIES: TRADITIONS AND TRANSITIONS, *supra* note 15, 493, at 443; Husa, *supra* note 5, at 430; Bell, *supra* note 15, at 163; NATIONAL LEGAL SYSTEMS AND GLOBALIZATION: NEW ROLES, CONTINUED RELEVANCE, *supra* note 18, at n. 27; Whitman, *supra* note 19; Michaels, *supra* note 4, at 366; LÉON HUSSON, *NOUVELLES ÉTUDES SUR LA PENSÉE JURIDIQUE* 220 (1974); Patrick Nerhot, Le fait du droit, 31 ARCH. DE PHIL. DU DROIT 261 (1986). See generally: JEANNE PARAIN-VIAL, *LA NATURE DU FAIT DANS LES SCIENCES HUMAINES* (1966). (While Samuel, *supra* at 39, also emphasizes that a same legal concept, say 'trespass,' can play a variety of different functions in the same legal system, it is unclear why that should be considered problematic here, as it only entails that the legal concept of 'trespass' in one legal system could be arrived at through a variety of different fact scenarios. See likewise: Örücü, *supra* note 4, at 445.)

[24] Radbruch, *supra* note 4, in MKSRr 2, 423 (1906) ("Das Sein-Sollende läßt sich nimmermehr aus dem Seienden ableiten"); Chirico & Larouche, *supra* note 16, at 19–20 ("a constant exogenous point"); RICHARD HYLAND, *GIFTS: A STUDY IN COMPARATIVE LAW* 112 (2009) ("concepts that do not coincide with those of any one legal system"); JEAN-PIERRE DUPUY, *ORDRES ET DÉSORDRES. ENQUÊTE SUR UN NOUVEAU PARADIGME*, 226 (1982) (suggesting that, even in Hofstader's example of the "self-modifying" chess game, the meta-rule that the players' moves determine the rules of the game itself must be fixed a priori.).

those two systems. If so, comparing the treatment of that formulation (however legally charged it may be) would, I would suggest, qualify as a scientifically sound enterprise so long as it is confined to *those two systems*.

The point to keep, importantly, in mind hence is that the aim here pursued is methodological only: we are not after some point of reference that might somehow ontologically qualify as neutral and equally apt *for all legal systems*, only one that would so qualify for the particular comparative project at issue, thus *for the systems targeted in that particular project*.[25] From this strictly methodological standpoint, the elusive fact/law distinction, and consequent possibility that any point of reference be law-laden to some extent, is no more fatal than the fact that legal systems might not all answer to a fixed set of social problems: all that matters is that comparatists be able to find points of entry whose particular social anchors and degrees of law-ladenness happen to be suitable for the systems targeted in their respective projects.

Another common critique of functionalism is worth mentioning here, only to show that it does not apply. It has been lamented that the functionalist method assumes, it stands to reason, a correspondingly functionalistic conception of law, whereas such conception cannot be presumed to underlie all legal systems. Specifically, some legal systems (Continental systems in particular) would tend to rest on an 'expressivist' rather than 'functionalist' conception, wherein law stands as a collective expression of ideals ('law as ideals') more than as an instrument with which to resolve social problems ('law as social engineering').[26] As a functionalist method would accordingly clash with the expressivist aspirations of at least some legal systems, its use in comparisons involving such systems would be distortive and, as such, scientifically unwarranted.[27]

Responding to that second critique requires clarifying at the outset how 'functionalistic' the method just proposed really is. Indeed, the sort of 'functionalism' at play here – 'equivalence,'[28] 'thin,'[29] 'moderate'[30] or 'methodological'[31]

---

[25] "Different theories may well require different invariant reference points": Sjoberg, *supra* note 3, at 109.

[26] See *supra* Chapter 3, Part II, section ii. For legal theorists advocating an expressivist view of law, see: RONALD DWORKIN, *LAW'S EMPIRE* (1986); John Henry Merryman, Civil Law Tradition, 35 AM. J. COMP. L. 438, 441 (1987) ("To understand [law] you have to know ... what its image of itself is."); Cass R. Sunstein, On the Expressive Function of Law, 144 U. PENN. L. REV. 2021 (1996); Tushnet, *supra* note 15; Mitchel de S.O.l'E. Lasser, The Question of Understanding, COMPARATIVE LEGAL STUDIES: TRADITIONS AND TRANSITIONS 197, *supra* note 15, at 207 ("how the legal system understands itself to function."); SEAN COYLE, *FROM POSITIVISM TO IDEALISM* 6–7 (2007) ("the sense in which the legal order embodies the expression of a society's self-understanding and its views of human nature and the good life."); HYLAND, *supra* note 24; Joseph Vining, The Resilience of Law, *in LAW AND DEMOCRACY IN THE EMPIRE OF FORCE* 151 (H. Jefferson Powell & James Boyd White eds., 2009).

[27] E.g. HYLAND, *supra* note 24, at 112ff; SIEMS, *supra* note 18, at 38–39.

[28] Michaels, *supra* note 4, at 357 ("similar functions ... be[ing] fulfilled by different institutions").

[29] WILLIAM TWINING, *GENERAL JURISPRUDENCE: UNDERSTANDING LAW FROM A GLOBAL PERSPECTIVE*, 88–122 (2009).

[30] Husa, *supra* note 5, at 421.

[31] *Ibid.*

functionalism – entails just a minimal connection of law to social problems insofar as it posits no more than that the call to resolve social problems is one of possibly many characteristics of law. In comparison, what might be termed 'substantive functionalism' effectively *reduces* law to that single characteristic insofar as it analyzes it exclusively in terms of the moral, social and political factors causally impacting the production of judicial decisions, i.e. in terms of 'legal formants.'[32] One could go further still, finally, and supplement the last analysis with an empirical observation, namely, the infamous *presumptio similitudinis* according to which the social problems that law is called upon to resolve are more or less the same in all jurisdictions.[33] It could then be concluded, along with self-professed 'convergence theorists,' that law everywhere in the world is bound, and ought, to eventually converge.[34]

What should be clear from the typology just given is that all legal theorists agree that law is connected to social problems at least *to some extent*, their disagreeing only as to the intensity of that connection. Whereas some view that connection as just one of many aspects of law, others insist that it is the primary, perhaps even exclusive, such aspect. Even hardcore 'expressivists,' indeed, acknowledge that law expresses itself through the different ways in which the judges in different communities resolve the social problems brought before them. As we already saw, sociologist Max Weber famously argued that only the justifications directed at actual judicial

[32] Sacco, *supra* note 15; Rodolfo Sacco, Legal Formants: A Dynamic Approach to Comparative Law (Installment II of II), 39 AM. J. COMP. L. 343 (1991). See likewise: UGO MATTEI, COMPARATIVE LAW AND ECONOMICS, 98, 104 (1997); Gillian K. Hadfield, *Levers of Legal Design*, (U. Southern Cal. L. Sch., Law and Ec. Working Paper Series, Paper no. 78, 2008).
[33] ZWEIGERT & KÖTZ, *supra* note 10, at 36. The *praesumptio similitudinis* has been impugned as both wrong (world law being in fact far more heterogeneous than thereby suggested) and scientifically unwarranted (it assuming *ex ante* statements whose validity it should be the object of the investigation to verify *ex post*), some scholars going as far as to suggest it be replaced with a *praesumptio dissimilitudinis*: Günter Frankenberg, Critical Comparisons: Re-thinking Comparative Law, 26 HARV. INT. L. J. 411, 453 (1985); Pierre Legrand, The Return of the Repressed: Moving Comparative Legal Studies Beyond Pleasure, 75 TUL. L. REV. 1033, 1048–49 (2001); Richard Hyland, Comparative Law, *in* A COMPANION TO PHILOSOPHY OF LAW AND LEGAL THEORY 194 (Dennis Patterson ed., 1996). Others have countered that it is unobjectionable when interpreted heuristically – as just a means for framing the analysis – rather than as an ontological statement about world law: Bell, *supra* note 15, at 174 ("In any case, it is not clear what difference arises from the use of the Legrand, rather than the Zweigert and Kötz approach as heuristics."); Catherine Valcke & Matthew Grellette, Three Functions of Function in Comparative Legal Studies, *in* THE METHOD AND CULTURE OF COMPARATIVE LAW 99, 109–10 (Maurice Adams & Dirk Heirbaut eds., 2014); Husa, *supra* note 5, at 424. The former arguably is supported by at least some of the language used by its original proponents: ZWEIGERT & KÖTZ, *supra* note 10, at 36 ("As a working rule this [the *presumptio similitudinis*] is very useful, ... At the outset of a comparative study it serves as a heuristic principle ... a useful working hypothesis."). See generally: Michaels, *supra* note 4, at 369ff ("Perhaps no statement in the history of comparative law has been criticized more.").
[34] RUDOLF B. SCHLESINGER, COMPARATIVE LAW 39 (5th ed. 1988); COMPENSATION FOR EXPROPRIATION: A COMPARATIVE STUDY (Gavin M. Erasmus ed. 1990); MATTEI, *supra* note 32, at 97 (drive to efficiency common to all legal systems). See however Ralf Michaels's convincing argument as to functional equivalence in fact militating *against* convergence (Ralf Michaels, Two Paradigms of Jurisdiction, 27 MICH. J. INT'L L. 1003, 1011–12 (2006)).

decisions, hence potentially attended with real-life consequences, should count as 'interpretive acts' for the purpose of reconstructing a community's expression of collective ideals.[35] If that is right, it arguably can be concluded that social problems can be used as a reliable conduit to relevant legal materials across legal systems and comparative projects – and that the second of the above two critiques of functionalism, while perhaps effective as against 'substantive functionalism,' lacks traction as against the 'methodological functionalism' in play here.[36]

Admittedly, problem-based formulations proving an adequate starting point for all comparative law projects would be no guarantee that relevant legal materials would never be missed. But as such hazards beset any kind of (even exclusively domestic) legal research, all that can be reasonably required of the present method is that it not be *particularly* prone to them. And there is no reason to think that it would.[37]

If anything, that method risks yielding *too much* material. It likely proves overinclusive, since law being systematically connected downwards to social problems does not entail that social facts are, in turn, upwardly connected to *nothing but* law. As social problems naturally call into play a number of different responses besides just 'legal' ones, our comparative lawyer indeed might discover that, in at least some of her targeted jurisdictions, the means deployed to address 'citizens bad-mouthing one another in public' are primarily social (or economic, or religious) in nature. Some of these jurisdictions, that is, might have no formal law bearing on the matter simply because, say, the local law makers consider that public bad-mouthing is properly controlled through social stigma alone.[38] Such non-legal responses would clearly be captured here, as problem-based research does not discriminate between legal and non-legal solutions. That is not to suggest that functionalistic identification is ineffective as such, however, only that the materials thus identified may need to be sorted at a later stage, to which we now turn.

---

[35] See *supra* Chapter 4, Part II, section i.

[36] For similar arguments, see: Husa, *supra* note 5, at 426–33; Michaels, *supra* note 4, at 365; Chirico & Larouche, *supra* note 16, at 19–20. Maurice Adams & Jacco Bomhoff, Comparing Law: Practice and Theory, *in* PRACTICE AND THEORY IN COMPARATIVE LAW 1, 12–14 (Maurice Adams & Jacco Bomhoff eds., 2012); Jonathan H. Turner & Alexandra R. Maryanski, Is "Neofunctionalism" Really Functional?, 6 SOCIOLOGICAL THEORY 110–21; Kingsley Davis, The Myth of Functional Analysis as a Special Method in Sociology and Anthropology, 24 AM. SOC. REV. 757–72; HYLAND, *supra* note 24, at 104 (distinguishing 'functionalism' and 'purposivism').

[37] *Contra*: SIEMS, *supra* note 18, at 35; Brand, *supra* note 18, at 419. Brand argues that functionalistic material identification might be under-inclusive insofar as it would miss, for example, statutes never implemented by the courts despite their never having been formally abrogated, which 'inert' materials would need to be caught for certain comparative projects, namely, expressivist ones. Under the above argument, however, 'inert' materials are ultimately irrelevant for all comparative projects, including the most 'expressivist' among them. See *supra*, Chapter 1, Part I, section v and Chapter 4, Part II, section ii.

[38] ZWEIGERT & KÖTZ, *supra* note 10, at 35 (land title reliability secured through official registration in Germany but through private insurance companies in the US); Tushnet, *supra* note 15, at 1245 (free speech implemented through market competition of television stations in the US, unlike in Russia, where the state holds monopoly over television by law).

iii. *Sorting Relevant Legal Data: Expressivism*

Whereas some comparative projects might profit from considering all legal formants at play in the various target systems, that is not the case under comparative law as presently conceptualized. Under the present account, only the materials speaking to the systems' underlying collective commitments – their particular ideals, aspirations, conceptions of justice, and so on – are to be retained. That is to say that, whereas legal formants by definition represent all that can be (externally) observed as *actually* affecting the judicial resolution of social problems in those systems, comparative law on the present account centres on what those on the inside, the legal actors in each system, consider *should ideally* affect that resolution. Say that it were found that judges' racial prejudices, for example, impact to some extent on their judgments.[39] Yet such prejudices should here be taken into account only if the local legal actors collectively consider that that impact is normatively desirable, as drawn from the fact that they openly refer to racial prejudices in the course of legal argumentation. Such prejudices in fact never surfacing in public legal arguments would indicate the opposite, namely, that their causal connection to the outcome of judicial decisions is a fact of which the actors are not proud, as it clashes with their view of how law *should* operate. In sum, we need to identify, from among the various materials preliminarily identified in each system as *functionally* relevant, those that can also be considered *hermeneutically* relevant as indicators of the system's underlying ideals.[40]

The example just given confirms what should be amply clear by now, namely, that formal legal arguments – the arguments publicly deployed in the context of official or quasi-official legal proceedings[41] – will stand out from other legal formants in that respect. From the outset, arguments of whatever kind (legal or not, formal or informal) clearly are normative utterances, which embody particular values, ideals, normative aspirations.[42] They are essentially geared at persuasion, which involves appealing to values that are shared as between persuador(s) and persuadee(s): when

---

[39] Vito Breda, The Objectivity of Judicial Decisions: A Comparative Analysis of Nine Jurisdictions, *in* STUDIES IN POLITICS, SECURITY AND SOCIETY (Stanislaw Sulowski ed., 2018).

[40] "The need remains for a sound criterion to sort out the relevant from the visible: Vlad Perju, Cosmopolitanism in Constitutional Law, 35 CARDOZO L. REV. 711, 731 (2013). See also: ALAN WATSON, LEGAL TRANSPLANTS: AN APPROACH TO COMPARATIVE LAW 5 (2nd ed. 1993) ("[W]hen the starting point is the problem, the weight of the investigation will always be primarily on the comparability of the problem, only secondarily on the comparability of the law; and any discipline founded on such a starting point will be sociology rather than law."); Husa, *supra* note 5, at 442 ("The moderate version of functional comparative law does not really say what can (or should) be done with the knowledge or information gained from research, i.e. similarities and differences as well as explanations of them."); Michaels, *supra* note 4, at 373 ("[functionalism] provides surprisingly limited tools for evaluation"); Whitman, *supra* note 19, at n. 8 ("[Functionalism implicitly] understates the social consequences of the choice of one particular means over another.").

[41] See *supra* Chapter 1, Part I, section v.

[42] See generally: STEPHEN E. TOULMIN, *THE USES OF ARGUMENT* 94–145 (1958).

I try to convince you of the soundness of my position, I naturally appeal to principles, norms, values that I know you find compelling and in turn see as compelling
to me. More than any other legal formants, therefore, the arguments deployed in
support of legal conclusions in a given community can be seen as immediate reflections of the core values that the actors see as animating that community. In fact,
the sheer fact that the actors formulating the arguments view them as persuasive is
significant in itself, as we saw: as members of the community, their perception as to
what constitutes the community's values to a certain extent contributes to making it
so.[43] In a somewhat circular fashion, then, the arguments offered in support of legal
conclusions can be seen as significant both because they reflect the community's
core legal values and because the very fact that they are being heralded as such
makes them so.

But the expressive value is even greater where these arguments are formal rather
than informal. As developed in Chapter 4, formal legal arguments matter in a way
that informal ones do not insofar as they feed into decisions that are immediately
backed by state sanctions and hence materially affect people's lives. Those formulating arguments in such portentous settings thus can be viewed as signalling a considered willingness to be held accountable for those arguments, to stand in public
judgment of their force and validity as tested against community standards. Formal
legal arguments accordingly can be taken to reflect careful judgments as to the community's core legal values in a way that informal legal arguments cannot.[44]

Importantly, the present proposed focus on formal legal arguments is system-
neutral insofar as it avoids privileging any particular kind of such arguments, in fact
allowing for great cross-system variations. Whereas written law (constitution, codes,
statutes, regulations, etc.) appears most prominent in the formal legal arguments of
some legal systems, it is upstaged by judicial decisions in other systems. Likewise,
parliamentary debates and scholarly writings are officially excluded or merely less
weighty in some systems (e.g. England) but not others (e.g. France). The present
focus on 'formal legal arguments' entails that whichever materials happen to qualify
as such in any given system should be retained as the most potent indicators of the
collective commitments underlying that system.[45]

But it is also the substance, not just the form, of formal legal arguments that varies
across legal systems. It is well known that what might be viewed as 'purely economic'

---

[43] See *supra* Chapter 1, Part I, section ii.

[44] Extending the range of materials beyond just formal legal materials admittedly might be useful insofar
as it would help capture the larger legal context, which would arguably help understand the law itself.
Such an understanding however might focus upon what moves the legal actors in their personal
capacity more than in their capacity as legal actors proper, which would here be irrelevant. See *supra*
Chapter 3, Part II, section iv.

[45] "[Comparative lawyers should consider as a source of law in any given system] whatever the lawyers
there treat as a source of law, and accord to those sources the same relative weight and value as they
do." Zweigert & Kötz, *supra* note 10, at 35.

arguments, for example, have, through accepted practice, come to enter the US formal legal discourse even in cases where the directly applicable formal law says nothing about economic considerations being even relevant.[46] And the same might be said of 'purely philosophical' arguments in French advocacy. It follows that such arguments should be included in the pools of legal data respectively earmarked as relevant for the purpose of understanding US and French law. In fact, a comparative study of US and French law that would ignore them might be considered deficient, for the sheer fact that these arguments have come to integrate the US and French legal discourses likely says something important about the values animating those systems (e.g. conceptions of justice respectively consequentialist and deontological?). For one can only assume that the case for their integration was properly "made in terms of normative claims acceptable in the domestic legal system."[47]

This explains how it is that some apparently imbalanced comparative accounts of legal systems might in fact turn out to be methodologically sound. One striking discrepancy between the accounts of French and English law commonly encountered in the comparative law literature indeed is that the first are typically heavily infused with French *intellectual* history whereas the second tend instead to build on English *political* history.[48] This naturally begs the question of whether it would not be more appropriate to seize on the same – intellectual *or* political – sets of data for both systems. It would not, however, insofar as the actors in those systems have themselves seized on these respectively different sets of historical data for the purpose of explaining their law. That is, insofar as the French have long explained their own law by reference to French intellectual history, whereas the English have done the same by reference to English political history, the apparent discrepancy in the comparative accounts of those systems arguably is entirely warranted, if not required, seeing that the ultimate objective here is to understand French and English law *on their own terms.*

In the same vein, the question arises as to what comparatists should do when observing that, say, the philosophical references given by the French legal actors to justify their law are mistaken.[49] It has been argued, for example, that whereas French scholars commonly cite Grotius and Kant in support of a subjective conception of contract, these philosophers' writings, properly interpreted, in fact motion to an objective such conception.[50] If so, what data should here be retained as most

---

[46] See *supra* Chapter 1, Part I, section v.

[47] *Ibid.* at 625.

[48] E.g. Catherine Valcke, Comparative History and the Internal View of French, German, and English Private Law, 19 CANADIAN J. L. & JURIS. 133 (2006).

[49] Michel Villey, ARCHIVES DE PHILOSOPHIE DE DROIT XII 214 (1967) (derisively referring to "la philosophie des manuels" ("treatise philosophy")). More generally: Whitman, *supra* note 19, at 331 ("Anybody who has spent time with lawyers knows that their accounts of the history of their own systems are rarely correct.").

[50] Valcke, *supra* note 20.

relevant for the purpose of reconstructing French contract law: the (philosophically) proper interpretation of those writings or the French's (legal) misinterpretation of them? The latter has to be right for the same reason that, as Wittgenstein wisely remarked, a veridical picture of an indistinct object must by necessity itself be an indistinct picture. Because the ultimate purpose here is to understand French contract law on its own terms, the interpretation to be retained is that which in fact came to enter and inform French contractual discourse, quite apart from how that interpretation might otherwise measure up as against some (philosophical or other) standard altogether external to the French legal system.[51]

Of course, what does *not* count as a formal legal argument in any legal system might be as revealing as to that system's underlying ideals as what *does* so count: public policy arguments *not appearing* in the French formal legal debate arguably is as telling about French legal ideals as their *appearing* in the US formal debate is about US such ideals. This is particularly the case should it have first been revealed, at the functionalist identification stage above, that policy considerations in fact are 'legal formants' proper in France in much the same way that they are in the US, i.e. that such considerations *actually bear* on the outcome of French judicial decisions despite their not being *openly acknowledged* as such.[52] For then, their not appearing among formal legal arguments is indicative of a deliberate concerted concealment effort on the part of French legal actors, which is itself quite telling as to how much these actors *wish* their law were free of such considerations, i.e. as to French legal *ideals*.

Note how functionalism (law-as-doing) and expressivism (law-as-saying) here point in opposite directions yet ultimately reinforce one another. Whereas a functionalist analyst would conclude from the above that French and US law are *converging* (as both are in fact impacted by policy considerations), an expressivist would instead view them as *diverging* (as that impact is considered undesirable in the first yet desirable in the second).[53] Yet these opposite conclusions here build on one another

---

[51] NIKLAS LUHMANN, *LAW AS A SOCIAL SYSTEM* 34 (Fatimah Kastner *et al.* eds., Klaus A. Ziegert trans. 2009) ('errors,' decisions without reasons or applying inconsistent reasons, are nonetheless part of the system). See likewise: CLIFFORD GEERTZ, *LOCAL KNOWLEDGE: FURTHER ESSAYS IN INTERPRETIVE ANTHROPOLOGY* 185 (2000); John Henry Merryman, The Italian Style III: Interpretation, 18 STAN. L. REV. 583, 585f (1966) ("although demonstrably unsound ... [t]his kind of folklore ... tends, somewhat refined, to dominate the thinking of the profession itself."); ALAN WATSON, *THE MAKING OF THE CIVIL LAW* 6 (1981) ("Although [Sir Thomas] Hope is mistaken [about Scots statutes allowing for direct application of Roman law in Scots courts], it is in the highest degree significant for the influence of Roman law in Scotland that he could be in error on the point.").

[52] MITCHEL DE S.O.L'E. LASSER, *JUDICIAL DELIBERATIONS: A COMPARATIVE ANALYSIS OF JUDICIAL TRANSPARENCY AND LEGITIMACY* (2004), chap. 2 (demonstrating that French *magistrats* do worry about and discuss policy considerations perhaps as much as their US counterparts, though they do so only in non-courtroom settings); Raymond Legeais, L'utilisation du droit comparé par les tribunaux, 2 *R.I.D.C.* 339, 348–52 (1994) (making a similar point about the use of foreign law in French judicial practice).

[53] Valcke, *supra* note 20; David Nelken, Comparatists and Transferability, *in* COMPARATIVE LEGAL *STUDIES: TRADITIONS AND TRANSITIONS, supra* note 15, 437, at 46off ("it does not appear, at any rate, that the world is becoming more homogeneous").

insofar as the expressivist difference is bolstered by the finding of functionalist simi-larity, and conversely. It is the interplay of functionalist and expressivist perspectives that brings to light that the (non)formal/informal distinction, commonly derided as mere window-dressing,[54] in fact carries great expressive significance.[55]

Finally, it bears emphasizing that our proposed focus on (non)formal legal mate-rials does not limit the *means* that can be used to search for these in any given legal system.[56] While such materials clearly can be gathered from the system's primary sources of law – the actual codes, statutes, etc. – they can also be usefully derived from anecdotal, journalistic or even pictographic accounts of the primary sources. Some authors go as far as to include courtroom architecture, legal officials' dress eti-quette and the like in the list of relevant pictographic materials.[57] Insofar as the latter sources can be taken (as is most likely the case) to shed some kind of light on what counts or does not count as formal legal arguments in the system and why, there is

---

[54] E.g. MATTEI, *supra* note 32, at 83.

[55] "In the end, it is precisely this interplay between the official and quasi-official discourses that is so revealing about a legal system and about the ways in which it operates, both intellectually and practically." Lasser, *supra* note 26, at 231.

[56] Stefan Vogenauer, Sources of Law and Legal Method in Comparative Law, *in* THE OXFORD HANDBOOK OF COMPARATIVE LAW, *supra* note 4, 869, at 879–80 (distinguishing between "what counts as law" and "from what documents that which counts as law can be ascertained").

[57] JOHN BELL, *FRENCH LEGAL CULTURES* 20, n. 7 (2001), referring to ROBERT JACOB, *IMAGES DE LA JUSTICE* n. 7 (1994). Legrand includes in that list Jacques-Louis David's painting of Napoleon writing his code (PIERRE LEGRAND, *FRAGMENTS ON LAW-AS-CULTURE* 5 (1999)). For suggestions that total immersion in the local culture might be required, see: VOLKMAR GESSNER, ARMIN HOELAND & CSABA VARGA, *EUROPEAN LEGAL CULTURES* 245ff (1996); Vivian Grosswald Curran, Cultural Immersion, Difference and Categories in U.S. Comparative Law, 46 AM. J. COMP. L. 43 (1998); Roger Cotterrell, Comparative Law and Legal Culture, *in* THE OXFORD HANDBOOK OF COMPARATIVE LAW, *supra* note 4, 709, at 710ff; Michele Graziadei, Comparative Law, Legal History, and the Holistic Approach to Legal Cultures, 7 ZEITSCHRIFT FÜR EUROPÄISCHES PRIVATRECHT 531, 538 (1999) ("a radical version of holism holds that it is impossible to know what it is like to think like an American or an Italian lawyer unless that condition is experienced in the first person, that is to say, unless one actually becomes an American or an Italian lawyer."); Pierre Legrand, Comparative Legal Studies and the Matter of Authenticity, 1 J. COMP. L. 365, 389 (2008) ("The comparatist's range of options in the pursuit of his task is vast since there is nothing for the observer of a legal culture that is quintessentially 'legal' (or that is quintessentially outside the 'legal')"); Pierre Legrand, Issues in the Translatability of Law, *in* NATION, LANGUAGE, AND THE ETHICS OF TRANSLATION 30, 34 (Sandra Bermann & Michael Wood eds., 2005); Gary Watt, Comparison as Deep Appreciation, *in* METHODS OF COMPARATIVE LAW 82, 87 (Pier Giuseppe Monateri ed., 2012) ("why should the legislative mind ... not venture to imagine the wisdom of arts and cultures that do not carry the legal label?"); Lasser, *supra* note 26, at 205 (no end to materials to consult for cultural fluency), and at 228 ("I prefer to limit my analysis to materials [representative of] professional culture [though] *I do not believe that the legal system is in any way separate from the general culture*"; ZWEIGERT & KÖTZ, *supra* note 10, at 38 ("he should go as deep as possible into his chosen systems [including culture writ large]" (emphasis in original)). But see: Alan Watson, Legal Change: Sources of Law and Legal Culture, 131 U. PENN. L. REV. 1121, 1138–39 (1983) (minimizing cultural factor in legal change); William Ewald, The Jurisprudential Approach to Comparative Law: A Field Guide to 'Rats' 46 AM. J. COMP. L. 705 (1998) (only formally documented and recorded views of the participants are relevant); Whitman, *supra* note 19, at 344 (no need to understand the total culture of a system in order to understand legal practices). See also *supra*, Chapter 3, Part III, section iii.

every reason to include them. Experiential learning – sitting in courtrooms or in law school classrooms – might likewise be helpful despite the fact that courtroom anecdotes or law school class notes are not commonly cited as authorities in formal legal proceedings. Insofar as the legal actors themselves might resort to such indirect means to determine what qualifies as formal legal arguments in their jurisdiction, it should be open to comparative lawyers to do the same. As even a US Federal Court of Appeals recently recognized, it ultimately falls to each investigator to weigh the reliability of the indirect sources under consideration.[58]

In sum, while our (externally set) objective of uncovering the collective ideals underlying legal systems commands that comparative lawyers focus their investigations on (non)formal legal formants, that objective allows for great variations in the form and substance of what is (internally) treated as such in the various systems. In addition, that objective places no limits on the means – direct or indirect – that can be used to get at these formants.

II. RECONSTRUCTING THE DATA INTO SYSTEMS

Once the hermeneutically relevant materials in each system have been identified, the comparatist moves to the task of *explaining* them, of answering the question: *why* does our initial problem respectively set in motion materials a, b and c in System 1, and materials d, e and f in System 2? This second stage I call 'reconstruction' because the kind of explanations here at play is such that they indeed entail reconstructing the pools of materials into respectively distinct narratives reflective of the systems' peculiar collective commitments.

Comparative lawyers are commonly criticized for lacking the inter-disciplinary expertise purportedly needed to 'explain' the cross-system variations and similarities that they have been observing.[59] That critique however rests on the arguably shaky assumption that a proper such 'explanation' *necessarily* involves reaching outside the legal realm so as to link the noted legal variations/similarities to corresponding variations/similarities in the systems' economic, religious, cultural, etc., landscapes. That assumption is shaky because our discussion to date hopefully establishes that

---

[58] In Bodum USA c. La Cafetière, Inc. 621 F.3d 624 (2010), the Federal Court of Appeals for the 7th Circuit had to interpret some French legal materials dealing with the relevance of pre-contractual documents in the interpretation of commercial contracts. The court split on the issue of whether expert testimony should be used for that purpose. Whereas Justice Wood considered such testimony useful (at pp. 31ff), Justices Easterbrook and Posner (at p. 15) preferred relying on their own interpretations of the French materials.

[59] E.g. Maurice Adams & John Griffiths, Against 'Comparative Method': Explaining Similarities and Differences, *in* PRACTICE AND THEORY IN COMPARATIVE LAW, *supra* note 36, 279, at 279; Örücü, *supra* note 4, at 449; MARY ANN GLENDON ET AL., COMPARATIVE LEGAL TRADITIONS IN A NUTSHELL 21 (3rd ed. 2008); Ugo Mattei, An Opportunity Not to Be Missed: The Future of Comparative Law in the United States, 46 AM. J. COMP. L. 709, 717 (1998); Reitz, *supra* note 18, at 627; SIEMS, *supra* note 18, at 8; GÜNTER FRANKENBERG, COMPARATIVE LAW AS CRITIQUE 12–3 (2016); Oderkerk, *supra* note 1, at 619.

legal phenomena can also be properly 'explained' exclusively in terms of features that are internal to the systems under consideration, i.e. through the very same kind of 'explanations' as are typically adduced by the local actors in a litigation context.[60] That is to say, whereas it is certainly possible (and valuable) to explain the US conception of freedom of expression being broader than the French by appealing to these nations' respectively individualistic and collectivist political economies, an explanation in terms of their respectively generous and limited private law protection against defamation might prove equally apt.[61] Likewise, the existence of estoppel in the first but not the second of these systems can potentially be explained externally, by reference to the French's historical wariness of expansive judicial powers, or else strictly internally, by reference to the fact that French law is less needy of estoppel given that it already comprises a general obligation of good faith.[62] That comparative lawyers may have traditionally neglected external explanations could accordingly betray, not so much a reluctance or inability to 'explain' per se, as a predilection for explanations of a different kind, viz. explanations that are indeed internal, for properly 'legal,' as they draw on the internal consistency of the system as do those typically adduced by the actors before their judges.[63]

Such legal explanations are precisely those being sought here. The different treatments of contractual mistake at French and English law, for example, can arguably be explained by the different ways in which French and English legal actors conceptualize contractual consent, viz. the subjective such conceptualization on the French side and its objective counterpart on the English side.[64] Such connections might possibly be extended further, moreover, so as to explain many other staple features of French and English law. On the English side, it may be possible to show that the same, objectivist normative core as underlies the conception of contract and attendant treatment of contractual mistake also underlies such peculiarly English institutional features as the active role of juries, the parol evidence rule, the reticence towards parliamentary debates and the doctrine of precedent. Likewise on the French side, the subjectivist core informing contracts and contractual mistake might be shown to also inform French judicial style, the receptivity to oral evidence and parliamentary debates, and the high deference accorded to scholarly writings.[65] Indeed,

---

[60]   See: Ewald, *supra* note 7, at 1946 (describing comparative law as a "single-track" enterprise).

[61]   E.g. Tushnet, *supra* note 15.

[62]   E.g. Simon Whittaker & Reinhard Zimmerman, Good Faith in European Contract Law: Surveying the Legal Landscape *in* GOOD FAITH IN EUROPEAN CONTRACT LAW 16–39 (Simon Whittaker & Reinhard Zimmerman eds., 2000).

[63]   Peter Benson, Abstract Right and the Possibility of a Nondistributive Conception of Contract Theory, 10 CARDOZO L. REV. 1077 (1989) ("Eventually we may situate contract within private law, law generally, and politics or ethics, but we must first understand contract as distinct: the inquiry must be 'sequenced'."); Van Hoecke, *supra* note 15, at 173 ("if you do not understand fully something, you do not understand anything"); Mathias M. Siems, The End of Comparative Law, 2 J. COMP. L. 133, 140 (2007).

[64]   Valcke, *supra* note 20.

[65]   Valcke, *supra* note 48.

insofar as these respective cores might tap into the systems' very foundations – peculiar conceptions of law[66] – they might at some point be shown to radiate through, and explain, most of the various substantive and institutional features making up the French and English legal systems.

Such explanations hence involve reconstruction in the sense that the various relevant materials are being reconnected to one another and the whole via the system's underlying ideals with a view to producing an overarching narrative: "[t]he whole of the law comprises many parts, and without comprehension of the parts the whole makes little sense. Equally, however, one cannot make sense of any part without regard to its place in the whole. This so-called 'hermeneutic circle'."[67] And as it is here assumed that *all* legal systems aspire to internal coherence to some extent, there is no reason to think that that sort of explanation-via-reconstruction ought to be confined to just the French and the English systems.

Admittedly, the sheer quantity of the materials involved is such that no single comparatist can hope to recount more than small pieces of a full narrative within a single project, or even an entire career.[68] Completeness however is not the aim here, if only because such narratives can never be considered complete.[69] Law being inherently dynamic, any snapshot of a whole legal system (were it feasible) would be doomed to quick obsolescence.[70] In addition, insofar as the very act of taking the snapshot would cause the system to be modified (even if ever so slightly),[71] an undertaking to thereby capture that entire system once and for all cannot but be self-defeating. Finally, such reconstruction exercises, as we saw, proceed from setting better and worse versions of the narrative in competition with one another, with the result that no single version can ever be heralded as the single 'right' one.[72] As the point of the exercise hence cannot be substantive completeness, it must lie instead (as is so often the case with things legal) with procedural integrity: at every point the

[66] For example, it would be reasonable to infer from a legal system treating torts and contracts as distinct categories that it subscribes to a deontological conception of law (Ernest Weinrib, The Juridical Classification of Obligations, *in* THE CLASSIFICATION OF OBLIGATIONS 37 (Peter Birks ed., 1997)), seeing that these categories would dissolve into a common analysis of remedies under a functionalist such conception (Guido Calabresi & Douglas A. Melamed, Property Rules, Liability Rules, and Inalienability: One View of the Cathedral, 85 *HARV. L. REV.* 1089 (1971–72)).

[67] NEIL MACCORMICK, *RHETORIC AND THE RULE OF LAW: A THEORY OF LEGAL REASONING* 48 (2005). See generally: DWORKIN, *supra* note 26.

[68] "[C]omparatists ... do not create disjointed bits and pieces but carefully crafted building blocks for a larger edifice. As these blocks pile up, the building itself starts to take shape." Mathias Reimann, The Progress and Failure of Comparative Law in the Second Half of the Twentieth Century, 50 *AM. J. COMP. L.* 671, 695 (2002).

[69] In this respect, law in fact differs greatly from jigsaw puzzles, to which it is often analogized. E.g. Jaakko Husa, Gift: The Piece that Does Not Fit the Legal Puzzle, *MAASTRICHT J. EUR. & COMP. L.* 16 (2009); Catherine Valcke, Reflections on Comparative Law Methodology—Getting Inside Contract Law, *in* PRACTICE AND THEORY IN COMPARATIVE LAW, *supra* note 36, at 53.

[70] See *supra* Chapter 4, Part II, section i (1).

[71] See *supra* Chapter 3, Part II, section ii.

[72] See *supra* Chapter 3, Part II, section iv.

comparatist must take care to connect the various legal materials to one another and the whole with a view to reconstructing each system into the best possible overarching narrative, quite apart from the penultimate narrative possibly remaining forever out of reach. For, merely to proceed *as if* such penultimate narrative were in fact attainable insures that every new connection contribute one small step towards a richer understanding of the system on its own terms.[73] And that is all that can be aimed for here.

This suggests that the traditionally contentious distinction between comparative studies respectively centred on cross-system 'differences' and 'similarities' is evacuated on the present account.[74] As discussed, 'convergence theorists' have long aimed to uncover the (largely functionalistic) common grounds among legal systems, with a view to promoting global legal harmonization, whereas the 'legal cultures' movement has emphasized the (largely expressivist) peculiarities of legal systems, in celebration of the cultural richness emerging from legal divergence. Yet where the aim is neither convergence nor divergence but merely to understand each legal system on its own terms, it matters little whether the features seized upon are similar or different: not only is there no reason to favour one or the other a priori, as they are just opposite faces of a same coin, but these two faces in fact reinforce one another.[75] The above discussion of French and English contract law indeed served to emphasize *both* that the two systems adopt respectively different, subjective and objective conceptions of contractual consent *and* that some notion of consent lies at the root of contract in both systems. The subjective versus objective 'difference' thus is made clear, and reinforced, as against the 'similarity' (or 'non-difference') of consent-rooted contract.

But in what sense does the incremental reconstructive method just laid out qualify as 'comparative?' The question deserves to be posed in light of the common claim that merely setting narratives side by side does not as such qualify as a 'comparative' exercise, seeing that a 'comparison' proper presumably requires the further step of outlining the particular points of divergence and convergence between them.[76]

---

[73] "Little by little, step by step, the comparatist thus develops a growing sense of the myriad elements and interrelationships that constitute the complex linguistic and conceptual universe of the foreign legal system. Once such a detailed study has been performed, a final and essential test must be passed: are the comparatist's descriptions and discursive reproductions more or less recognizable to those who operate within the studied system?" Lasser, *supra* note 26, at 223–24.

[74] E.g. Rudolf B. Schlesinger, The Past and the Future of Comparative Law, 43 Am. J. Comp. L. 477 (1995); Mattei, *supra* note 32, at 80.

[75] Gerhard Dannemann, Comparative Law: Study of Similarities or Differences?, *in* The Oxford Handbook of Comparative Law, *supra* note 4, at 383–420; Jansen, *supra* note 14, at 312 ("similarity must be accompanied by corresponding dissimilarity, that is, the conceptual distance to identical properties"); James Gordley, Is Comparative Law a Distinct Discipline?, 46 Am. J. Comp. L. 607, 615 (1998) ("if we can describe our differences, it must be because of what we share. If this is so, then studying the differences will shed light on what we have in common."); Siems, *supra* note 18, at 39.

[76] E.g. Reitz, *supra* note 18; Watson, *supra* note 40, at 4; William Twining, Comparative Law and Legal Theory: The Country and Western Tradition, *in* Comparative Law in Global Perspective 21, 46 (Ian

It should however be clear from the discussion of Chapter 3[77] that, from an episte-mological standpoint, the reconstruction of any two legal narratives cannot but pro-ceed from a dialectic movement between them. As seen, the comparatist necessarily begins from her home narrative, initially attempting to shoehorn the foreign legal materials into the (familiar) conceptual framework of that first narrative, and resorts to elaborating an altogether distinct, second narrative only thereafter, when the pres-sure on the home framework becomes unmanageable. Once the foundations of the two narratives are in place, the dialectic movement involved in their parallel reconstruction can gain momentum and intensify to the point of perfect symmetry. Though that dialectic movement may not be explicit, it is, I argued, part and parcel of what is entailed in 'understanding' something foreign.[78]

That movement is even present, I would argue, in self-described 'comparative' studies that cover only one foreign legal system.[79] Insofar as the one system is not the author's native system, or is the author's native system but is described in a foreign lan-guage, or is otherwise destined to a foreign audience, the study to some extent requires bridging the local and the foreign. It entails a form of translation that necessarily is juridical in addition to linguistic,[80] which translation triggers the dialectic movement in question: "'[t]ranslation' … is not a simple recasting of others' ways of putting things in terms of our own ways of putting them … but displaying the logic of their ways

Edge ed., 2000); CONSTANTINESCO, *LA MÉTHODE COMPARATIVE, supra* note 4, at 23; Jansen, *supra* note 14, at 307.

[77] See *supra* Chapter 3, Part III, section iii.

[78] Horatia Muir Watt, Globalization and Comparative Law, *in* THE OXFORD HANDBOOK OF COMPARATIVE LAW, *supra* note 4, 579, at 587 ("Increased awareness of alterity may generate a need for identity and tradition, while accelerated contact and juxtaposition with other traditions may mean that all sides develop a sharper sense of identity (citing H. PATRICK GLENN, LEGAL TRADITIONS OF THE WORLD 30ff (5th ed. 2000))"; CONSTANTINESCO, *LA MÉTHODE COMPARATIVE, supra* note 4, at 122–23 (describing the three stages of knowing, understanding and comparing as in fact superimposed); Pfersmann, *supra* note 15, at 283 (saying of "differentiated conceptual interpretation" that it conditions the objective description of national legal systems); Marc Bloch, Pour une histoire comparée des sociétés européennes, 48 REVUE DE SYNTHÈSE HISTORIQUE 15ff (1928) ("only by comparison was it possible to observe the peculiarities of one's own history"); Roderick Munday, Accounting for an Encounter, *in* COMPARATIVE LEGAL STUDIES: TRADITIONS AND TRANSITIONS, *supra* note 15, 3, at 21ff; Pierre Legrand, L'hypothèse de la conquête des continents par le droit américain, 45 ARCH. PHIL. DRT 37ff (2003); Samuel, *supra* note 15, at 200. *Contra* Jansen, *supra* note 14, at 306 ("Only at this second stage [of comparative legal research, the first being 'understanding and describing'] does comparison come into play.").

[79] *Contra*: Reitz, *supra* note 18; Pfersmann, *supra* note 15, at 282. Merryman reports (JOHN HENRY MERRYMAN, THE LONELINESS OF THE COMPARATIVE LAWYER 4 (1999)) that articles covering just one foreign legal system "outnumber (often by a huge margin)" articles explicitly comparing several such systems in the volumes of the *American Journal of Comparative Law.*

[80] For a compelling argument that mere linguistic difference in fact hides juridical difference, and different legal communities proper, see: Robert Leckey, Prescribed by Law/Une Règle de Droit, 45 OSGOODE HALL L. J. 571 (2007) (one purported national legal debate in fact dividing into two separate conversations in officially bilingual jurisdictions).

of putting them in the locutions of ours."[81] The reconstruction of anything foreign hence is inherently 'comparative' in the sense that it necessarily proceeds, if only epistemologically, from a dialectic movement with the local referent whereby the distinct peculiarity of each is revealed and emphasized through contrast with the other.

The methodological question then arises as to how such epistemological, and possibly implicit, dialectics will be conveyed in the comparatist's writing. The answer is straightforward in the context of single system studies. The comparatist there has no choice but to structure her entire piece around the description of the foreign system as an internally unified whole, and pepper that description with pointed comparative references to the local system ('like in our law,' 'unlike in our own legal system,' etc.). The foreign system's internal unity accordingly is there conveyed through the text's overall structure, whereas its peculiarity as against the local system emerges from the punctual in-text comparative references to that system.

In the context of multi-system studies, however, different dialectic sequences are possible, which dictate different overall structures and text contents. These can be classified as falling under one of two basic patterns. Under the first, the comparatist moves in and out of her target systems only when transitioning between them (leaving aside the initial, necessarily external stage-setting phase), as each system is being reconstructed in isolation from the next. Under the second pattern, the reconstruction process is itself chopped up into alternating counterpart slices from the various systems, the thickness of which is necessarily inversely proportional to the transitioning frequency. The first pattern thus uses the legal system as structuring unit, with the result that a comparative study of Systems A, B and C would be structured as:

System A (components 1, 2, 3, ...) – System B (components 1, 2, 3, ...) – System C (components 1, 2, 3, ...)

The second pattern in contrast uses as structural unit a group of system components, thus resulting in the same three-system study now looking something like one of the following:

Components 1_A, 1_B, 1_C – Components 2_A, 2_B, 2_C – Components 3_A, 3_B, 3_C – ...

Components $(1+2)_A$, $(1+2)_B$, $(1+2)_C$ – Components $(3+4)_A$, $(3+4)_B$, $(3+4)_C$ – Components $(5+6)_A$, $(5+6)_B$, $(5+6)_C$ – ...

Components $(1+2)_A$, $(1+2)_B$, $(1+2)_C$ – Components 3_A, 3_B, 3_C – Components $(4+5+6)_A$, $(4+5+6)_B$, $(4+5+6)_C$ – ...

Applied to our French and English contract law example, the first pattern hence would entail first presenting all the relevant substantive and institutional features of the French law, in complete isolation from the English law, and only thereafter turning to the similarly self-contained presentation of the English law (or vice versa).

[81] GEERTZ, *supra* note 51, at 10.

In contrast, the second pattern would dictate describing the French and English theories of contract, then the respective admissibility and inadmissibility of parol evidence concerning pre-contractual negotiations at French and English law, thereafter the respective judicial restraint and activism of French and English judges, and so on.

As the first pattern involves diving in and out of the two systems only once (before and after describing the particular system), its structure serves to emphasize the internal unity of each system, possibly at the risk of downplaying its various points of connection with the other system. In contrast, the constant back and forth between the systems under the second pattern suggests that its structure conversely serves to underscore the connections between the systems, perhaps to the detriment of their internal unity as separate systems. As the two dimensions – the systems' interconnectedness and their distinctness as separately unified systems – are equally important, there is no principled reason to favour one over the other, with the result that either pattern is methodologically acceptable. Only, the comparatist must take care to adjust the text accordingly, using it to bolster the systems' interconnectedness under the first structure, and the systems' respective internal unity under the second (the need for the latter emphasis increasing with the thickness of the alternating slices).

Thus, since comparing two objects involves accounting for both their interconnectedness and distinctness, which two features indeed are here being accounted for, in the context of single and multi-system studies alike, the present reconstruction method clearly would seem to qualify as a 'comparative' exercise.

III. COMPARING THE SYSTEMS

Yet comparative lawyers have traditionally aimed at more direct comparisons of legal systems than just their comparative reconstruction. In addition to comparing the components of various systems – 'micro' comparisons – (whether or not with a view to ultimately reaching to the underlying collective commitments), they have sought to also (or alternatively) engage in 'macro' comparisons, wherein entire systems are compared to one another.[82] Indeed, all fields of human knowledge proceed from comparisons of the different components/aspects/features of the objects studied yet they are not, for that matter, typically known as 'comparative' disciplines.[83] Botany, to return to our favourite example, involves identifying the peculiar features of apples as against those of oranges, and walnuts, and petunias, and palm trees. Yet nobody would insist on calling it 'comparative botany' for that reason. And the

---

[82] Ralf Michaels, Comparative Law, *in* MAX PLANCK ENCYCLOPEDIA OF EUROPEAN PRIVATE LAW 1 (Jurgen Basedow *et al.* eds., 2012); Örücü, *supra* note 4, at 443, 447; SIEMS, *supra* note 18, at 40.

[83] GEOFFREY SAMUEL, AN INTRODUCTION TO COMPARATIVE LAW THEORY AND METHOD 11 (2014); Jansen, *supra* note 14, at 307 ("Is it not the case that all knowledge is based on comparison...?"); and at 330 (comparison being inherent to any scientific undertaking); Örücü, *supra* note 4, at 446.

fact that botany happens to cover plants from different countries (oranges and palm trees clearly being 'foreign' from apples on that account) makes no difference in this respect. So perhaps what has long been known as '*comparative* law' would in fact be better labelled '*global* law' (to emphasize that the law under study reaches beyond the more familiar 'national law') in the same way that 'botany' likewise implicitly denotes 'global botany.' In what sense, then, might comparative law be *differently* 'comparative' than botany?

One important difference between law and botany of course is that, as seen in Chapter 3, whereas the physical world presumably can be properly studied from an exclusively external perspective, the intellectual quality of law raises the alternative possibility of an internal perspective. 'Global law' arguably might then prove an appropriate label for strictly external studies of world law, whereas 'comparative law' would more pointedly refer to studies of that law that in contrast account for, and compare, the different systems' respective internal standpoints. The 'legal origins' literature would be a prime example of the first, as that literature aims to compare legal systems from the externally determined standard of efficiency, in the same way that botanists compare apples and oranges from whichever physical standard(s) they deem scientifically relevant – nutritional contents, ripening times, texture, or any other.

But we also saw in Chapter 3 that the legal origins literature has been heavily criticized precisely on the basis that its seizing on an exclusively external standard would cause it to misrepresent law altogether, and hence yield ultimately distorted understandings of the various legal systems at play.[84] A finding that French law might be 'less efficient' than US law would contribute very little if anything to a proper understanding of French law, it is said, insofar as French law makers, unlike their US counterparts, never so much as tried to make their law efficient, their being long geared to perfecting instead its internal coherence.[85] To compare the efficiency of French and US law would therefore be tantamount to comparing the nutritional contents of apples and airplanes, an obviously nonsensical comparative exercise. The same critique applies to some extent to the 'legal family' literature, which has aimed to classify world legal systems into 'families' based on various sets of such mixed internal and external criteria as ethnicity, religion, sources of law and reasoning styles.[86] Given that some of these criteria are bound to clash with the internal aspirations of at least some of the legal systems surveyed, the value of such mapping

---

[84] See *supra*, Chapter 3, Part III, section ii.

[85] Jacco Bomhoff, Perfectionism in European Law, *in* 14 CAMBRIDGE YEARBOOK OF EUROPEAN LEGAL STUDIES 75 (Catherine Barnard *et al.* eds., 2012).

[86] E.g. For three good critical surveys, see: ZWEIGERT & KÖTZ, *supra* note 10, at 63–7; CONSTANTINESCO, TRAITÉ DE DROIT COMPARÉ, *supra* note 4, at 154, n. 161; Jaakko Husa, *Legal Families, in* ELGAR ENCYCLOPAEDIA OF COMPARATIVE LAW, *supra* note 4, at 382.

exercises, while unquestionable in botany and other physical sciences, is less clear with respect to law.[87]

The question thus arises as to whether comparative lawyers should avoid macro (direct system to system) comparisons altogether. It has been argued that they should, notably by the 'legal cultures' movement, on the basis that, legal systems being all about legal meaning, which is locally determined, such systems would be incommensurable, and hence also incomparable.[88] That assertion combines two claims, namely (1) as collective legal ideals are locally determined, no single metric can be identified that runs across any two legal systems, with the result that legal systems are ultimately incommensurable,[89] and (2) their being incommensurable means that no valid *tertium comparationis* is available that would allow for their proper mutual comparison. In sum, their being incommensurable *necessarily entails* their being also incomparable. If so, it is argued, internally-minded comparatists indeed should just give in with respect to macro comparisons.

The first claim seems unquestionable, as even eponymous concepts, we saw, in fact materialize differently in different legal systems: while 'consent' grounds contracts in French and English law alike, that notion is interpreted very differently in the two systems. But the second claim arguably is a *non sequitur*, at least in the context of the present analytic framework. That is, whereas commensurability and comparability are often used interchangeably,[90] the present account allows for their

---

[87] Boaventura de Sousa Santos, Law: A Map of Misreading – Toward a Postmodern Conception of Law, 14 J. L. & Soc'y 279 (1987) (describing the inevitable distortions resulting from the three mechanisms of 'scale,' 'projection' and 'symbolisation'); Reza Banakar, Power, Culture and Method in Comparative Law, 5 Int. J. of Law in Context 69, 73–74 (2009); Jaakko Husa, Legal Families in Comparative Law – Are They of Any Real Use?, 24 Retfærd 15 (2001); Å. Malmström, The System of Legal Systems: Notes on a Problem of Classification in Comparative Law, 13 Scandinavian Studies in Law 129 (1969); Ugo Mattei, Three Patterns of Law: Taxonomy and Change in World's Legal Systems, 45 Am. J. Comp. L. 5 (1997). At the same time, it can hardly be denied that the legal family literature greatly contributed to improving our understanding of world legal systems. Hein Kötz, Abschied von der Rechtskreislehre?, 6 Zeitschrift für Europäisches Privatrecht 493 (1998); B. Jaluzot, Cartographier les droits, in Mélanges en l'honneur de Camille Jauffret-Spinosi (Goré et al. eds., 2013). The question hence seems to be whether that contribution lies primarily with the overall map being proposed or with the descriptions there given of the various systems being mapped.

[88] Bomhoff & Adams, *supra* note 36, at 4 ("the avowed expressivist objective of rendering legal systems as much as possible in their own terms severely constrains opportunity for systematic comparison"); Ralf Michaels, Transnationalizing Comparative Law, 23 Maastricht J. Eur. & Comp. L. 352 (2016) ("legal science itself provides no criteria for the evaluation of law other than those derived from the law itself").

[89] Alasdair MacIntyre describes as "incommensurable" two entities for which "there are no scales of quality and quantity on which to weigh them."; A. MacIntyre, After Virtue 62 (1981). See also *supra*, Chapter 2, Part I, section ii, note 9. For an enlightening general discussion of comparability and commensurability, and an argument that they are conceptually distinct, see: James Griffin, *Well-Being: Its Meaning, Measurement and Moral Importance* 75–92 (1986).

[90] E.g. John Bell, Legal Research and the Distinctiveness of Comparative Law in Methodologies of Legal Research: Which Kind of Method for What Kind of Discipline? 155, 167 (Mark van Hoecke ed., 2011); H. Patrick Glenn, Are Legal Traditions Incommensurable? 49 Am. J. Comp. L. 133 (2001).

differentiation, and hence also for the possibility that *incommensurable* legal systems might still be somehow *comparable*.

Take the case of a dog contest, wherein one dog is declared 'best dog' overall despite the contestants being of different breeds.[91] By what standard(s) can a fox terrier be considered 'better' than a poodle? The two are being compared to one another despite the fact that what makes for a 'good' fox terrier clearly is very different from what makes for a 'good' poodle. Indeed, whereas that difference would be problematic for a *cardinal* comparison,[92] it is not for a comparison that is instead *proportional*, i.e. where the various dogs are being compared in terms of their relative score as against the scale of 'goodness' that is peculiar to their breed, so that a fox terrier scoring eight out of ten on the fox terrier scale will win out against a poodle scoring seven out of ten on the poodle scale. 'Dog-ness' here provides a perfectly valid *tertium comparationis* for comparing fox terriers and poodles despite there being no single dog-ness metric running across them both. Proportional comparison is likewise at play where physicians assess their patients' relative pain levels: a patient reporting a pain level of eight on a scale of one to ten is considered at greater pain than one reporting a pain level of seven, despite their individual pain scales being different. A common notion of 'pain' exists, though it is assessed through different 'pain metrics.' In sum, "it does not follow from there being no super-value that there is no super-scale ... All that we need for the all-encompassing scale is the possibility of ranking items on the basis of their nature ... Commensurability does not require monism."[93]

The present account allows for a similar operation with legal systems. Recall that legal systems are here conceptualized as boasting respectively distinct sets of collective commitments while also all tapping into the same core conception of law ... as collective commitment.[94] Recall also that one key feature of that core conception is

---

Elsewhere, commensurability is described as conceptually distinct from, yet still a prerequisite for, comparability: Jansen, *supra* note 14, at 305; Ralf Michaels, Comparative Law by Numbers? Legal Origins Thesis, Doing Business Reports, and the Silence of Traditional Comparative Law 57 Am. J. Comp. L. 765 (2009).

[91] Bruce Chapman, Law, Incommensurability, and Conceptually Sequenced Argument, 146 U. Pa. L. Rev. 1487, 1487, 1492, n. 10 (1998); Bruce Chapman, Preference, Pluralism, and Proportionality, 60 U. Toronto L. J. 177, 191 (2010), (water barrels rather than dogs, to the same effect). For a recent discussion of Chapman's idea and example, see: Moshe Cohen-Eliya & Iddo Porat, American Balancing and German Proportionality: The Historical Origins, 8 Int'l J. Const. L. 263, 266 n. 23 (2010).

[92] "[W]hen ... we shift from everyday talk of pursuing various different ends to theoretical talk of maximizing a single quantity, 'utility,' this quantity should not be understood as an end of the same kind, only grander. There is simply no case for reducing these various ends to a single end in this sense. The most that can be said is that a person's ends are unified only in being his ends, things he values ... We mediate, but without such a mediating value." Griffin, *supra* note 89, at 32 (footnotes omitted).

[93] *Ibid.*, at 90.

[94] See *supra* Chapter 2, Part IV.

the aspiration to internal coherence,[95] which crucially includes theory-practice congruence[96] – what Lon Fuller regarded as the single most important feature of legality.[97] If all legal systems aspire to bridging the inevitable rift between their theory and their practice – their 'law in books' and 'law in action,'[98] their 'folklore' [99] or 'mythology'[100] and actual judicial practice, their 'towers' and 'trenches'[101] – that aspiration can presumably serve as a sound *tertium comparationis* with which to compare them. (Note that a functionalistic *tertium comparationis* is no longer available at this stage, as macro comparison would require the kind of 'substantive functionalism' ruled out above.[102]) That is to say that, although that *tertium comparationis* cannot but be external to the various systems being compared, it does not for that matter encroach on their integrity as distinct systems. For each one is then assessed as against *the peculiar set of collective commitments it has (internally) set for itself.*[103] The *tertium comparationis* inevitably is unitary and external, then, yet the standards for comparison can be plural and internal: "[the solution to the problem of comparability] has to be found in the context of a theory of prudential values … one that gets the mix between the personal and impersonal right."[104]

So a legal system in which rules X and Y are respectively put forward as 'principle' and 'exception' yet the legal actors in fact end up following rule Y far more often

[95] See *supra* Chapter 1, Part I, section iii.

[96] See *supra* Chapter 1, Part I, section vi.

[97] LON FULLER, *THE MORALITY OF LAW* 209–11 (1969).

[98] GEERTZ, *supra* note 51, at 10.

[99] Merryman, *supra* note 51.

[100] Pierre Legrand, European Legal Systems are not Converging, 45 *INT'L & COMP. L. Q.* 52, 61 (1996).

[101] See *supra* Part I, section ii.

[102] Part I, section iii. See likewise: Larouche, *supra* note 18, text accompanying note 28 ("it is … impossible to deliver on the promise of a comparison which would allow each system to 'express itself' and would separate significant divergence from functional equivalence.")

[103] See likewise: Giovanni Sartori, Comparing and Miscomparing, 3 *J. THEOR. POL.* 243, 252 (1991) ("'incommensurability' is currently brandished in a strong sense that implies that all our concepts are context-embedded to the point of being inescapably idiosyncratic. This is an overkill – if anything."); ALASDAIR MACINTYRE, *AFTER VIRTUE* xi (3rd ed. 2011) ("So it is possible for one such tradition to defeat another in respect of the adequacy of its claims to truth and to rational justification, even although there are no neutral standards available by appeal to which *any* rational agent whatsoever could determine which tradition is superior to which."); NIGEL SIMMONDS, *LAW AS MORAL IDEA* 54 (2007) "[The impetus behind the aspirational view] is not to protect established regimes from criticism but to indicate the availability of a form of immanent critique grounded in the regime's implicit claim to govern by law. Such a form of critique may, on occasion, be more powerful and pertinent than any criticisms which might be framed in terms of wholly independent values, precisely in so far as it draws upon values to which the regime is already making a tacit (albeit perhaps cynical) appeal."); Andrew Halpin, A Rejoinder to Glenn, 2 *J. COMP. L.* 88, 120 (2007) ("If commensurability holds good for a set of values or traditions, then there must be something within those values which allows them to be measured together in their own terms: one value must be capable of being assessed in terms of the other, or each value must inherently be capable of being reduced to an overarching value." Halpin however denies that such overarching value can be found).

[104] Griffin, *supra* note 89, at 119.

than they do rule X would, by its own standards, fare poorly in terms of theory-practice congruence: its self-representation as to the ordering of rules X and Y simply do not materialize in practice. Certainly, that system's individual score would be *lower* than that of a system wherein the actors' behaviour matches the official ordering. It has been observed, for example, that whereas French, English and German legal practice on the definition of contracts tend to converge in combining roughly equal parts of objective and subjective elements, it is self-consciously endorsed as such only in the German system.[105] In both the French and the English but not the German system, that is, the legal actors tend to represent that practice as different from what it actually is, namely, as overwhelmingly subjective in the French system, overwhelmingly objective in the English, and roughly equally objective and subjective in the German. It follows that an overall taxonomy of the three systems wherein the greater internal coherence of the German law (its ideal self-representation being better confirmed through its practice) lands it a category of its own would arguably be justified.[106]

In short, whereas the incommensurability of legal systems might prevent *direct* macro comparisons, it is no bar to *indirect* such comparisons wherein the systems are being compared in terms of proportional scores as against their distinct internal metrics of theory-practice congruence, to which they, as 'legal' systems, all aspire. As such macro comparisons do revolve around a feature shared by all legal systems, they in fact promote rather than undermine our ultimate objective of understanding each system on its own terms.

CONCLUSION

Not surprisingly, the hybrid ideal/material thread of law as collective commitment, and of the analytic framework developed in the last three chapters, runs through every step of the methodology just laid out. Once the comparatist has settled on a particular topic and target systems, she has no choice but to proceed to gather the relevant legal data by focusing on the material dimension of law, its problem-resolution function. She then will need to turn to its ideal dimension, however, so as to identify the part of that data that can be considered 'legally meaningful.' That will involve dialectically relating the functionalist (what legal actors *in fact do*) and expressivist (what they *say* they do) manifestations of the law in question. She will then move to the parallel reconstruction of these 'meaningful legal acts' into contrasting narratives respectively centred on the collective commitments peculiar to each system, which reconstruction act will entail, again, relating facts to ideals and vice versa, both within each system and as against those of the other system(s). Finally, she will be in a position to compare the overall narratives to one another without for

---

[105] Valcke, *supra* note 20.
[106] For a similar treatment of the French doctrine of '*l'acte clair*,' see: Vogenauer, *supra* note 56, at 889.

that matter encroaching upon the distinctness of each. She can achieve this through the proportional comparison of the extent to which each system has in fact lived up to its own, peculiar ideals.

I hope to have shown that such constant oscillation between facts and ideals ultimately serves to draw together functionalism and expressivism, similarity and difference, and micro and macro comparison. If so, comparative law as comparative collective commitments would indeed allow comparatists to embrace both sides of, and hence move beyond, the traditional dichotomies that have long divided them.

Epilogue

The Academic Discipline of Comparative Law

We seem to have landed in a very different place than that from which we took off. We departed from the 'malaise' of traditional comparative lawyers, their struggle to shake off the charges of purposelessness and general theoretical and methodological randomness relentlessly levelled at them over the last decades, their worry that they might indeed amount to little more than stamp collectors or baseball statistic hoarders ...

This book aimed to assuage that worry. It sought to demonstrate that it is possible to view legal family-, legal transplant-, common core-, and more standard micro (rule-to-rule)-comparatists as all collectively engaged in a highly valuable, and coherent, knowledge-building exercise about national legal systems. That knowledge being of the same kind as is produced through local legal practice, it is properly 'legal': it involves reconstructing the legal materials making up each system into the best possible *internal* understanding of that system, the best possible understanding of that system *on its own terms*. Yet that knowledge is *comparative*, insofar as it proceeds from the bouncing off of the various systems against one another, which results in its contributing a particular light to that reconstruction exercise. As such, traditional comparative law would very much qualify as a self-standing legal discipline, one distinct from legal history, legal philosophy, legal sociology and so on. It would constitute a legal discipline in its own right, bearing little resemblance if any to stamp collecting.

That demonstration involved developing an analytic framework and methodology that are consistent with extant traditional comparative law scholarship, and that accordingly can plausibly be regarded as already implicit in it. At the root of that framework lies a working conception of law that can accommodate 'meaningful legal comparison,' that is, comparisons contributing new knowledge about some or all of the legal entities involved. That working conception, which I call 'law as collective commitment,' was laid out in Chapter 1. While molded on the interpretive conceptions advanced by such contemporary legal theorists as Lon Fuller,

Ronald Dworkin, Neil MacCormick, Gerald Postema and Jeremy Waldron, law as collective commitment is thinner than these other conceptions – only as thick as is necessary to make law amenable to meaningful mutual comparison – as the analytic framework pursued here is one that should ideally accommodate the largest possible array of comparative projects. The key feature of law as collective commitment for our purposes is its hybrid ideal/material quality, for it is that quality that allows for law being inherently comparable, a preliminary requisite of its being ultimately *meaningfully* comparable.

Under that conception, the only self-contained entities that can be conceptualized as amenable to mutual comparison are legal systems, seeing that components of legal systems – rules, concepts, institutions – in contrast are devoid of meaning when taken on their own. Only legal systems, that is, appear as self-contained, meaningful entities standing *on a par* with one another, in the same way that, say, apples and oranges do within the 'fruit' category. Only legal systems, then, boast the simultaneous distinctness and commonality required for meaningful comparison, their distinctness indeed deriving from their material dimension, and their commonality, from their ideal dimension, as was argued in Chapter 2.

But comparing legal systems first requires overcoming the cognitive challenge posed by one's 'home bias,' the challenge involved in apprehending the epistemological framework (reasoning structures, cultural preconceptions, and so on) peculiar to any given legal system while already equipped with that of another. Chapter 3 critically reviewed the various ways in which traditional comparatists have handled that challenge and concluded that it indeed was not fatal to the comparative enterprise. It was suggested that one's outsider position does not bar the possibility of joining local legal actors in their collective reconstruction of their law and may in fact, if carefully managed, contribute enlightening new insights to that exercise – insights that the local actors would *themselves* recognize as enlightening. As outsiders inevitably move in and out of a number of legal systems at once, they are in a privileged position to seize on, highlight and ultimately boost the peculiarity of each.

Of course, bouncing off legal systems against one another entails being able to figure out where each one begins and ends, which is no easy task under law as collective commitment, as was seen in Chapter 4. As legal systems on that conception are interpretive communities, their edges are not determined from the outside, as can be done with geo-physical entities. Rather, they *self*-delineate, on the inside, through the very same kind of intellectual process as produces their contents. Like those contents, then, the contours of legal systems are fuzzy (a matter of degree) and fluid (constantly changing). Still, it was argued that the material dimension of law as collective commitment allows for these fuzzy and fluid communities to be ultimately anchored in something material, in particular, the rulings of their respective highest courts. These rulings are material in the sense of being immediately amenable to forcible enforcement, thus resulting in material consequences for the individuals involved. And inasmuch as they serve to frame and focus the community's discourse, they can be viewed as securing each such intellectual community with a material centre of gravity, in much the same way as queen bees do for their respective (fuzzy and fluid) bee swarms.

Standing back to observe how these material/intellectual communities interact on the global stage, we concluded that the traditional focus of comparative lawyers on national legal systems appears, at least under the current, Westphalian world structuring, fully defensible. In Part II of Chapter 4 we saw that none of the other entities branded as 'legal systems' under strong or even weak legal pluralism, in particular sub-legal systems (subsets of national systems) or supra-legal systems (mergers of national systems), can be conceptualized as self-contained entities amenable to meaningful mutual comparison. While some of these entities might arguably be understood as 'systems,' they would ultimately be systems of different kinds, thus barring the possibility of robust and balanced mutual comparison.

The methodological implications of the analytic framework developed in Chapters 1 to 4 were unpacked in Chapter 5. Whereas it is often thought that the large variety of extant comparative law studies necessarily translates into comparative law being methodologically plural, the possibility of bringing these studies together within a common framework, hopefully realized here, motions to at least some measure of methodological unity being correspondingly possible. To the extent that all comparative law projects would benefit from a deep understanding of each of their target legal systems on its own terms, the three-step methodology laid out in Chapter 5 would presumably be appropriate for all of them. However, it could nonetheless be dispensed with where pre-existing reliable such understandings are available, as there clearly is no need to reinvent the wheel in every comparative study. Even with respect to studies that would include reconstructing these understandings from scratch, moreover, one would expect said methodology to be supplemented with additional methodological guidelines, tailored to the specific purpose of each study. Harmonization or legal transplant initiatives, for example, clearly might benefit from supplementing any legal understanding of the rules involved with statistical and/or economic analysis of the practical effects of these rules in their respective jurisdictions. To that extent, the three-part methodology offered in Chapter 5 is both general and minimal, and even then, it would be minimally required only where pre-existing reliable internal understandings of the systems involved are unavailable.

As with the rest of the book, the hybrid ideal/material character of law as collective commitment seeps through every step of its proposed comparative method. The first stage of that method – data gathering – can be described as functionalistic insofar as it involves tracking the relevant legal materials in each system through investigating what legal materials would be used by the judges in that system for the purpose of resolving a same practical problem. The second stage – (gathered) data interpreting – consists of dialectically relating the functionalist (what legal actors *in fact do*) and expressivist (what they *say* they do) treatments of the various materials gathered, with a view to determining which among them can be considered 'legally meaningful,' and to gradually reconstructing these 'meaningful legal acts' into contrasting narratives respectively centred on the collective commitments peculiar to each system. That reconstruction act entails relating facts to ideals and vice versa, both within each system and as against those of the other system(s). The overall narratives are brought together in the third and final stage – (reconstructed) data comparing – which seeks to compare the extent to which the legal practice of each system matches up against its own, internal ideals. Through such *proportional* macro comparisons, it is possible, or so was it argued, to compare legal systems among themselves without, for that matter, encroaching upon the distinct identity of each.

Thus, the constant oscillation between facts and ideals here ultimately serves to bridge functionalism and expressivism, investigations of legal similarities and legal differences, resort to the law in books and the law in action, as well as micro and macro comparison, which make up the bulk of the comparative law literature produced to date. To that extent, comparative law as comparative collective commitments would indeed allow comparatists to embrace both sides of, and hence move beyond, the traditional dichotomies that have long divided them.

In their seminal work, *Designing Social Inquiry—Scientific Inference in Qualitative Research*, King, Verba and Keohane argued that all fields of research framed by a 'logic of inference' are 'scientific' and hence potentially qualify as 'academic disciplines' proper.[1] A logic of inference in their view captures the four features of (1) a goal of inference – "making descriptive or explanatory inferences on the basis of empirical information about the world";[2] (2) public procedures – "explicit, codified, and public methods to generate and analyze data whose reliability can therefore be assessed [by the entire scholarly community]";[3] (3) ultimately uncertain conclusions – acknowledging that certainty is ultimately unattainable and providing reasonable estimates of uncertainty;[4] and (4) content being the method – adherence to a validity-determining set of rules of inference.[5]

By those standards, comparative law as presently conceptualized qualifies as an 'academic discipline.' First, it aims to draw explanatory inferences about legal materials in any given legal system by reconnecting them among themselves and setting them off against such other inferences as may prove apt in other systems. Second, it evinces codified methods that, while perhaps long hidden from view, are increasingly coming to light and opening themselves up to public scrutiny, which process it was the very object of this book to contribute to accelerate. Third, such increased explicitness and publicness allow for the tentative understandings of legal systems or their components put forward by individual comparatists indeed to be potentially

---

[1]   Gary King et al., Designing Social Inquiry—Scientific Inference in Qualitative Research 3 (1994).
[2]   *Ibid.* at 7.
[3]   *Ibid.* at 8.
[4]   *Ibid.* at 8–9.
[5]   *Ibid.* at 9.

revisited by the whole community of peers, that potential being considerably magnified from the moment that said community is enlarged so as to encompass, as was here done, all ostensibly divergent streams of traditional comparative law scholars. Lastly, the present account offers clear criteria – 'meaningful legal comparison,' 'legal system,' 'reconstruction that local actors would find insightful,' – by which to assess the relevance and quality of comparative law scholarship. What is more, insofar as that account is presented as an implicit description of extant comparative law scholarship, any and all parts of it in turn are amenable to refutation as against that same body of scholarship. We accordingly may have moved from the malaise of comparative law to comparative law as a fully fledged legal discipline in its own right.

Finally, the argument of this book being successful would also bear on legal theory writ large. Insofar as legal theory has long made claims to universal validity, comparative law – the study of the *different kinds* of law encountered around the world – stands to supply it with an invaluable testing ground. That an interpretive conception of law such as law as collective commitment, here posited as just a working conception, tailored to the present enterprise, might make it possible to account for a whole field of legal literature hitherto escaping the purview of legal theory would serve, all else being equal, to validate that conception as against competing conceptions, in particular, natural law and positivism. It would open the way, that is, for interpretive theories of law to be regarded as offering, not just plausible working conceptions for the purpose of comparative law, but in fact superior conceptions *tout court*.

Index

aboriginal law, 36, 69, 82, 159
Adler, Emmanuel, 145
analogical reasoning, 124, 126
argumentation. *See* collective argumentation
    process; legal argumentation
Aristotle, 24
Austin, John, 47
authority
    persuasive *vs.* binding, 154–5

background rules of interpretation
    across legal systems, difference of, 113–14,
        115–17
    apprehension of, 117–21
    definition of, 113–14
    in foreign systems, 117, 118
    formal rules and, 114–15, 117–18
    internalization through conscious reflection,
        117–21
    local and common, 119–20, 127–8
    two levels of, 116

Canadian legal regimes, 82, 141
Cartesian method, 91
Cavell, Stanley, 104
circularity objection concerning mutual
    promises, 128
citizens
    as law-makers, 31, 32, 34
    vs. officials, 25, 26–7
    as self-governing agents, 28
civil law systems, 148, 154–5
cognitivism/constructivism debate, 91

coherence
    in assessment of legal arguments, 30
    as feature of law, 42
    in legal documents, 28
collective argumentation process, 25
collective enforcement, 38
Collingwood, R.G., 92
commensurability, 213
commitment, notion of, 23, 28, 32, 43, 52
common law systems, 148, 154–5
community, self-representation of, 39
comparative law. *See also* internal and external
        perspectives in comparative law
    as academic discipline, 1, 2, 3, 7, 219, 222–23
    bifurcation overload, 6, 7
    epistemological dilemma of, 11
    vs. global law, 212
    heterogeneity of, 131
    hybrid conception of, 10
    at international level, contribution of, 2
    legal theory and, 9, 12, 223
    limitations of research projects on, 110–11
    vs. local law, 130–1
    malaise of, 1, 6, 7
    as method, 6
    models for, 4–5
    reconstruction of, 11
    search for scientific value of, 6
    subjectivity issue, 131
    theoretical framework, 11
    theoretical randomness critique of, 5
    unification of domestic law as goal of, 1
    weeding of non-meaningful projects, 68